1994

Historical Linguistics

Historical Linguistics provides a comprehensive and clearly written introduction to historical linguistic theory and methods. Since its first publication in 1962 the book has established itself as core reading for students of linguistics. This edition has been thoroughly revised to include the latest linguistic and archaeological research. Recent decades have seen remarkable advances in the field of linguistic theory. The history and development of writing have been clarified. Typological advances have allowed a better understanding of the structure of early languages. Archaeologists and scientists dealing with prehistoric periods have supplemented knowledge of the speakers of early languages, broadening the view of their culture and society.

After introductory chapters sketching the field and drawing these developments into historical linguistic theory, *Historical Linguistics* presents basic research methods with illustrations of their application, taken largely from the Indo-European language family. Supplementary exercises utilize data from other language families.

The book will enable students to carry out independent work in historical studies on any language family, as well as up-to-date work in Indo-European.

Winfred P. Lehmann is Emeritus Professor in the Humanities and the Director of the Linguistics Research Center at the University of Texas at Austin.

An accompanying workbook for *Historical Linguistics* is published by the Summer Institute of Linguistics, 7500 Camp Wisdom Road, Dallas, TX 75236, USA.

Historical Linguistics: an introduction

Third edition

Winfred P. Lehmann

London and New York

First published 1992
by Routledge
11 New Fetter Lane, London EC4P 4EE

Simultaneously published in the USA and Canada
by Routledge
a division of Routledge, Chapman and Hall, Inc.
29 West 35th Street, New York, NY 10001

Typeset in 10/12 pt Times by Florencetype Ltd, Kewstoke, Avon
Printed in Great Britain by TJ Press (Padstow) Ltd, Padstow, Cornwall

British Library Cataloguing in Publication Data
applied for

Library of Congress Cataloging-in-Publication Data
Lehmann, Winfred Philipp,
    Historical Linguistics: an introduction/Winfred P.
    Lehmann. – 3rd ed.
    p   cm.
    Includes bibliographical references and index.
1. Historical Linguistics I. Title
P. 140.   L44   1992
417'.7–dc 20   92–45655

ISBN 0–415–07242–5
      0–415–07243–3 (pbk)

To
Ruth Preston Lehmann

Contents

Preface

Historical linguistics has made significant advances since the publication in 1973 of this book in its second edition. Among the most important, many linguists are now investigating the history of languages outside the Indo-European language family. Their investigations apply the methods that have been developed largely in historical study of the Indo-European languages. Accordingly, thorough grounding in the principles of historical linguistics may be best achieved by attention to the problems in these languages that were solved in applying and developing those methods.

Moreover, historical investigations have been greatly assisted by improved understanding of language, thanks to typological study. Soviet linguists have made special contributions in typology through their approach to language as a whole, supplementing in this way the earlier typological findings on phonology, morphology and syntax. Their contentive typology incorporates previous advances, notably those of syntactic typology during the last thirty years, and in this way provides a framework for evaluating hypotheses concerning all sections of grammar and the lexicon.

Typological contributions have also amplified the long-held position that language is a structure in which all the parts are interrelated – or, in Meillet's admired phrase, *où tout se tient*. For that reason, problems can best be understood by examining them in the context of a given language's structure. As a result, access to understanding the principles and methods of our field is best provided by examination of problems in the history of well-studied languages like English and other Indo-European languages. Their history is far better documented than is that of any other language family, as is clear from handbooks on languages of the world, such as that edited by Comrie (1987). Accordingly, problems in their history are especially useful for acquiring control of historical methods because applications and solutions are clarified when related to the structure of the language at the time and in earlier periods. For this reason the problems at the ends of chapters are taken chiefly from Indo-European languages; the workbook accompanying this work and published by the Summer Institute of Linguistics includes problems also from other language families.

Advances in the field have been refined through many conferences, and almost an overwhelming number of publications. Fortunately, some conferences are designed for syntheses of the insights resulting from the application of historical methodology to languages of diverse structures. And annual bibliographies, such as that of the Modern Language Association and the *Bibliographie Linguistique*, assist in access to the current state of affairs, especially now that the Modern Language Association bibliography has been computerized.

In spite of the expansion of historical study, this introduction maintains its aim of dealing concisely with the procedures and methods of the field, as well as with auxiliary fields such as the study of writing. Recommendations from readers have changed its format somewhat, as through the addition of a brief account of earlier historical study and a sketch of the increasingly important contributions of archaeology as they relate to those of linguistics. We may look forward to further such contributions, as palaeobiology and the other palaeosciences continue to expand our knowledge of early societies and the use of their languages.

The first three chapters may be regarded as preliminary: chapter 1 sketches the field; chapter 2 provides a brief history of it; chapter 3 discusses writing systems, a topic that has become increasingly important for understanding early periods, in view of Schmandt-Besserat's demonstration of the development from tokens to the first writing system.

These topics provide a basis for those of the second group of chapters used for classifying languages. Chapter 4 deals with the well-developed genealogical classification; 5 with typological classification; and 6 with areal classification.

The third group of chapters presents the methods: chapter 7, the comparative method; 8, the method of internal reconstruction; 9, glottochronology, which has turned out to be surprisingly useful in spite of adverse criticism.

With this information in hand, the fourth and major group of chapters treats linguistic change by levels: chapter 10, phonological change; 11, morphological change; 12, syntactic change, 13, semantic change. Chapter 14 concludes the fourth group of chapters with a brief statement of the impact of changes at one level on those of another.

Chapter 15 treats the interrelationships between findings of archaeology and linguistics, by which a fuller view of the societies maintaining languages is attained. The final chapter points out the necessity of dealing with language as a whole rather than by the levels sorted out in part for pedagogical purposes.

Recognition of the identified levels has been strengthened in linguistic discussion of the past two generations. The process has resulted from increasing attention to linguistic data, as in the concern for clitics during the last decade. The results have been well expressed by Sadock (1991: 5). Noting that "grammar consists of parallel organizational principles," he states that "this orientation resembles, in broad outlook, the sort of view that underlies descriptive grammars of the last century." The division of those grammars "into more or less independent sections [like] phonology, morphology, syntax, and semantics" is also found in historical grammars. One can only greet with satisfaction the recognition that our great predecessors maintained an accurate understanding of language.

Their aims, as indicated in greater detail in chapter 2, also accord with Sadock's for "a generative grammar . . . that is, a grammar that is explicit and formal and that makes clear and testable predictions." The early advances by Grimm and Bopp resulted from their explicit and formal presentation of solutions to grammatical problems, leading to the "testable predictions" of Verner, Saussure, Brugmann and many others. We may conclude that historical linguistics rests on a firm basis. We may also hope that the large-scale concern for the history of many languages continues, both for the improved understanding of these languages and for further refinement of historical linguistic theory.

As historians of sciences have come to recognize, sciences may be either historical or experimental. Chemistry and physics are experimental, whereas astronomy, biology and many others are historical, the subdivision to which linguistics clearly belongs. An accurate understanding of language, then, can only be achieved through mastery of historical linguistic methods and findings. I hope that this introduction will provide avenues to such understanding, and to further work on the many languages that need investigation.

W. P. Lehmann
Austin, Texas

Transcription and phonological symbols

An elementary textbook should provide an introduction to the standard handbooks in a field, including the transcriptions and transliterations they use. Unfortunately, these vary. The symbols proposed by the International Phonetic Association were based on compromises, and have not always been adopted. For example, those on pp. xi–xvi of the introduction to *Les Langues du monde*, do not always agree with the IPA symbols. Moreover, the IPA symbols have not necessarily been adopted in handbooks that have become standard, such as E. Prokosch's *Comparative Germanic Grammar* (1939). In addition, influential handbooks have proposed transcriptions of their own. Thus Bloomfield's *Language* (1933: 91) uses the symbol [e] for the vowel of *egg*, [ɛ] for the vowel of *add*. This value for *e* was maintained in the widely used Trager–Smith transcription, and is also used in this textbook for the vowel of *egg*. In view of the variation in use of symbols, patience and flexibility are necessary in the acquisition and interpretation of symbols. In general, the symbols used in this textbook are those found in the standard handbooks for a language or a field.

Consonant symbols: There are few problems in the interpretation of symbols for the stops: *p t k b d g*; *q* may be used to indicate a velar stop, or also for a labiovelar, as in Goth. *qius* "quick." The capitals *K G* are used for uvular stops.

The symbols for voiceless fricatives are relatively uniform in value: *f, s*; for the voiced counterparts, *v*, or *ƀβ* (bilabial) and *z* are used. For the voiceless interdentals *þ* or *θ* are used; for the voiced *đ* or *ð*. For voiceless velar fricatives the symbols *x* or *χ*, for voiced *g* or *[ɣ]*, though *χ* and *[ɣ]* may also be used for uvular fricatives. *h* is used for the aspirate.

The symbols *c* and *j* vary widely in use from language to language; they may be used for palatal stops. In Sanskrit they represent palatal affricates; commonly, a superposed inverted carat is used to specify such values, for example *č* as in church and *ǰ* as in *judge*. The symbol *j* is also used for the semivowel initial in *yes*, in part because of its value in German, as in *ja*.

Resonant symbols: The symbols *l r w y* are uniform in value, though *y* may also be used to indicate a high, front, rounded vowel. The standard use of *R* is for uvular resonants; in transliteration of runes, however, it indicates a voiced fricative, a resonant in the position of *z*.

For the nasals *m n* are standard, as is *ɲ* for the palatal and *ŋ* for the velar.

Consonantal diacritics: Of diacritics, . below a consonantal symbol indicates retracted articulation, as in Skt *ṭ ḍ* for retroflex stops. A dot, or a circle, is also used below symbols for semivowels to indicate vocalic articulation, as in the Sanskrit root *kṛ* or *kṛ̥* "do." A dot over or under *m* is a convention in Sanskrit to indicate nasalization of the preceding vowel.

To indicate a back *l*, a cross-bar through the symbol is used: *ł*.

Vowel symbols: For the vowels, *i e a o u* generally have the "continental values." Capitals, or reduced capitals: *ɪ ɛ ʊ* indicate lower or laxer variants of *i e u*. The compound symbols *æ* (*sat*) and *œ* (as in Germ. *Goethe*) indicate front vowels; *ə* and *ʌ* indicate central vowels; a barred *i*, *ɨ*, indicates a high central vowel.

For front rounded vowels *ü* and *ö* are commonly used, though *y* and *ø* are also found.

A tilde ~ over vowel symbols indicates nasalization, but when used in Greek it indicates circumflex accent.

A macron ‾ over vowel symbols indicates length, ˘ over them indicates shortness.

Accent symbols: The acute ´ generally indicates the chief accent; the circumflex ^ the next most prominent; the grave ` a lesser accent. In Sanskrit and in Greek forms, and in Japanese, the acute indicates high pitch. The circumflex indicates a compound accent (high–low) in Sanskrit and Greek; the grave indicates low pitch in Greek.

In Chinese superposed numerals indicate tones.

As a general principle one must bear in mind when interpreting symbols that language is based on relationships. In selecting symbols linguists attempt to denote essential contrasts in a given language. Symbols cannot therefore be exact equivalents in different languages. And scholarly traditions have often compounded the problems inherent in attempts to represent language with written symbols.

SYMBOLS USED IN FORMULAS AND RULES

- a hyphen, with other symbols indicates their relative position:

  t-   indicates a *t* in initial position;

  -t-   indicates a *t* in medial position;

  -t   indicates a *t* in final position.

> indicates "developed to, became"; for example PIE *t* > PGmc *þ*
< indicates "developed from"; for example PGmc *þ* < PIE *t*
= indicates "corresponds to"; for example PGmc *þ* = PItal. *t*

* indicates a nonattested, usually a reconstructed form, for example PIE **treys* "three"; placed after a form, for example Goth. *þreis**, it indi-

cates that the form is nonattested, but that we can be reasonably certain of it from similar forms or from other inflected forms of the same paradigm. Especially in synchronic statements, * is often used to indicate a nongrammatical sequence, for example * *a dog the.*

> OHG *drīe* > NHG *drei* "three"
> NHG *drei* < OHG *drīe* < PIE *treys*
> OHG *drīe* = Skt *trayas* = Goth. *þreis**

[ ] enclose material in phonetic transcription, for example Skt [trǝy]
/ / enclose material in phonemic transcription, for example Skt /tray/
" "enclose glosses, for example "three"; glosses are given for identification of cited forms, not necessarily to provide the central meaning.
Italics are used to indicate a citation.
Bold face is used to point up a term when it is defined in the surrounding text.

TECHNICAL TERMS

Technical terms are defined in the text and are better learned from such a context than from lists, but a few common terms are given here for convenience.

Dialect is used in historical linguistic texts for a subdivision of a language or a language family; for example English is an Indo-European dialect. The Midland dialect used across a central portion of the United States is readily understood by any speaker of the English language. In descriptive linguistic texts, on the other hand, the term dialect is used for a subdivision or variant that is mutually intelligible with other such variants. For example, German, though related to the Midland dialect and also an offshoot of Indo-European, is a separate language with its own dialects.

Etymon is the form from which another developed, for example PIE *treys* is the etymon of NHG *drei.*

Gloss is a word used to identify or define another word, for example Skt *tráyas* "three."

Reflex is a form that has developed from an earlier form, for example NHG *drei* is a reflex of PIE *treys.*

TERMS USED TO DESIGNATE DISTINCTIVE FEATURES

Only very brief characterizations are given here for those terms and abbreviations used in the text; for a longer discussion see Jakobson, Fant and Halle (1969).

Accent/act – greater energy
    á +act   a −act
Anterior/ant – obstruction in front of mouth

t +ant   š −ant

Back – body of tongue retracted

o, w +back   e, j −back

Consonant/cns – closed or nearly closed vocal tract

b + cns   i −cns

Continuant/cnt – uninterrupted air flow

f, m + cnt   p, b −cnt

Coronal/cor – blade or front of tongue raised

θ +cor   p, g −cor

High – body of tongue raised

u +high   æ −high

Low – body of tongue lowered

o +low   i −low

Nasal/nas – lowered velum

m, ẽ +nas   b, e −nas

Resonant/res – relatively open vocal tract; generally voiced

r +res   d −res

Round/rd – lips rounded

ū +rd   ē −rd

Strident/std – friction resulting from groove articulation

s, š +std   f, x −std

Tense – relatively great muscular tension, and duration; see also Jakobson, Fant and Halle (1969: 57–61)

aː +tense   a −tense

Vocalic/voc – open vocal tract and voicing

a +voc   k −voc

Voiced/vd – vocal cord vibration

d, m, o + vd   t, s −vd

Abbreviations

GRAMMATICAL TERMS

acc.	accusative
fem.	feminine
indic.	indicative
masc.	masculine
mid.	middle
nom.	nominative
nt.	neuter
pl.	plural
pres.	present
pret.	preterite
ptc.	participle; pret. ptc. – preterite participle
sg.	singular
suff.	suffix
voc.	vocative

LANGUAGES

Dating

M	Middle, e.g. ME Middle English
N	New, Modern, e.g. NE New English, Modern English
O	Old, e.g. OE Old English
P	Proto-, used only for reconstructed languages, e.g. PGmc Proto-Germanic. Any form labeled P could also be marked with *
Pre	a prior stage, e.g. Pre-OE Pre-Old English

Symbols used for geographical subdivisions

E	East, e.g. EGmc East Germanic
L	Low, e.g. LG Low German
N	North, e.g. NGmc North Germanic

S	South, e.g. SSlav. South Slavic
W	West, e.g. WSax. West Saxon
H	High, e.g. HAlem. High Alemannic

Languages

AE	American English
Akk.	Akkadian
Alb.	Albanian
Alem.	Alemannic
Arab.	Arabic
Arm.	Armenian
Att.	Attic
Ath.	Athapaskan
Aus. E	Australian English
Av.	Avestan
BE	British English
Chin.	Chinese
Crim.Goth.	Crimean Gothic
CS	Church Slavic
Dan.	Danish
Dor.	Doric
Du.	Dutch
E, Eng.	English
Egypt.	Egyptian
Fr.	French
Franc.	Franconian
Fris.	Frisian
G, Germ.	German
Gk	Greek
Gmc	Germanic
Goth.	Gothic
Heb.	Hebrew
HG	High German
Hitt.	Hittite
Icel.	Icelandic
IE	Indo-European
IIr.	Indo-Iranian
Ir.	Irish
Iran.	Iranian
Ital.	Italian
Itc	Italic
Jap.	Japanese
Lat.	Latin
Lett.	Lettish

LG	Low German
Lith.	Lithuanian
Luw.	Luwian
Myc. Gk	Mycenaean Greek
N	Norse
Pers.	Persian
Pol.	Polish
Port.	Portuguese
Pruss.	Prussian
Rum.	Rumanian
Russ.	Russian
Sax.	Saxon
Scand.	Scandinavian
Skt	Sanskrit
Slav.	Slavic
Span.	Spanish
Sum.	Sumerian
Toch.	Tocharian
Turk.	Turkish
Ukr.	Ukrainian

Map showing the principal language families of the world

ESKIMO-ALEUT
NA DENE
ESKIMO-ALEUT
ALGONKIN
WAKASHAN
FRENCH
PENUTIAN
AZTEC-TANOAN
SIOUAX
HOKAN
SPANISH
PORTUGUESE
QUECHUA
SPANISH
MALAYO-
POLYNESIAN
INDO-EUROPEAN
AFRO-ASIATIC
SINO-TIBETA

THE PRINCIPAL LANGUA

PALAEO-
ASIATIC

T U R K I C

CAU-
CASIAN

MONGOL

MANCHU-
TUNGUS

KOREAN

JAPANESE

PALAEO-
ASIATIC

M A L A Y O - P O L Y N E S I A N

CH'ARI-NILE

CONGO

ALTAIC	DRAVIDIAN	AUSTRO-ASIATIC	FINNO-UGRIC

AMILIES OF THE WORLD

1 Introduction

1.1 LANGUAGE IN CHANGE; MODIFICATIONS AT ALL LEVELS

Languages change constantly, a fact that becomes most noticeable when we read texts a few centuries old. For example, change at various levels of language is apparent in almost any passage of John Milton (1608–74), such as in these four lines from his Sonnet VII:

> How soon hath Time the suttle theef of youth
>> Stoln on his wing my three and twentith year!
>> My hasting dayes flie on with full career,
>> But my late spring no bud or blossom shew'th.

Writing this sonnet when he is about to finish his studies at the University of Cambridge, Milton expresses a concern that might trouble a student today. But the language would differ in many respects.

The differences in spelling may strike us first of all. Today the first adjective is spelled *subtle*; spelling reformers introduced this spelling by reference to Lat. *subtilis*. But Milton's spelling agrees with the pronunciation of his time and ours. He had strong views on spelling, as is clear from the double *e* rather than *ie* in *theef*, from the omission of *e* in *stoln* and so on. Because he followed specific rules that he devised in keeping with his metrical principles, his poetry today is presented as it was in his day; Shakespeare's works, by contrast, are usually modernized, since he did not involve himself in their publication. Milton even determined the arrangements of his lines, indenting lines two to four rather than line one, or none of the four, as many sonnet writers do. This principle of presentation may not be crucial for the understanding of the poem. But his format assists us in determining the meaning of his text, as formats do of texts in general. Historical linguists must therefore concern themselves with the written conventions of any text they study (see chapter 3).

When we read the sonnet today, lines 1 and 4 do not rhyme. We may assume that they did for Milton. Our assumption is confirmed by the spelling of *shew*. In Milton's day, *shew* had a variant form *show*, as did words of the same form, such as *shrew* and *chew*. For both of these words the alternative pronunciation has won out, though from the last two lines of his play *The Taming of the Shrew* it is clear that Shakespeare rhymes *shrew* with *so* (5.2.188–9). Since the time of Shakespeare and Milton one pronunciation and one spelling have been generalized, though the spelling may not indicate the pronunciation. *Shrew* and *chew* today rhyme with *new*; but *sew* rhymes with *so* and *show*.

Like rhymes, spellings, such as *(twen)tith* in the second line, give us clues about pronunciation in earlier periods; Shakespeare also used the form *twentith*, as we can determine from the rhythm of *Hamlet* 3.4.97: "A slave that is not twentieth part the tithe." Today we make similar inferences, often from nonstandard spellings; if someone writes *liddle* rather than *little*, we conclude that the writer voices the medial *t*, as do many speakers of American English. From such evidence we know that English sounds have been changing. This change is termed **sound change**, or **phonological change** (see chapter 10). In comparing earlier and later forms of any language, we find various types of phonological change.

The passage quoted from Milton also shows changes of form. In contemporary conversation, or even when writing poetry, we no longer use verb forms in *-th*. We recognize them from sayings, such as the one Samuel Morse sent as first message after inventing the telegraph: *What hath God wrought*; but we have generalized the *-s* ending in the third singular. Similarly, we have substituted *twenty-third* for *three and twentieth*. From earlier texts like those of Milton and Shakespeare we can determine the system of forms they used; we can also note the differences between them and the system of forms used in current English. Thereupon, by comparing the two systems, we determine changes in form. These are called **morphological changes** (see chapter 11). Material in other languages also gives data on morphological change and leads to the conclusion that all languages change in their system of forms as well as their system of sounds.

The selection from Milton's sonnet also illustrates alterations in syntax. Comparable, if prose, statements for the second and fourth line would have a different arrangement; for example, "the robber stole her money that night" and "my roses show/have no blossoms" or "my roses do not show/have blossoms." Besides changes in arrangement, also known as order, there may be changes in other syntactic devices, such as government (see chapter 12, **syntactic change**). Languages change more readily in sounds than in syntax, as we see when we study the history of most languages.

Besides changes in phonology, morphology and syntax, we must account for changes in meaning. Elements like *-th* have meaning, of course, for they indicate that the subject is in the third person. Such meaning is known as grammatical, in contrast to the lexical meaning of words. Change in lexical meaning is termed **semantic change** (see chapter 13). The phrase including the word *career* in Milton's sonnet corresponds to our "at full speed." And for Milton *subtle* meant "skillful, expert." Many words have changed in meaning since Milton's day. Others have been added to the language or adapted for special meanings. The large vocabulary of science is an example; in Milton's day *science* meant "knowledge in general."

In historical linguistics we study differences in languages between two or more points in time. As we investigate languages, we also find differences between two or more points in space. British English may still use the spelling *shew*, though with the same pronunciation as ours. It has also undergone sound changes that differentiate it from American English. From texts over several centuries, we know that in standard British English the syllable-final *r*, as in *year*, has been lost, with lengthening of the preceding vowel. In most sections of America, an *r* remains. Subdivisions of a language are referred to as **dialects**. The study of variations among dialects of a language is termed **dialect geography** (see chapter 6). Since dialect differences are closely linked with social groups, the study of dialect geography is included in the broader study known as **sociolinguistics**.

Study of variations in language from place to place is of great concern to historical linguistics, for changes may be introduced into languages as speakers of one language adopt elements of another. The process of introducing such elements is known as **borrowing**. The word *career*, for example, is French in origin; French *carrière* means "race-course"; in English it came to be used for humans rather than for horses. Since upper-class English speakers were bilingual in French and English, many words were borrowed by them from the French vocabulary.

On the other hand, the word *full* can be traced back to OE *full*, and to earlier stages preceding English, which are referred to as Proto-Germanic and Proto-Indo-European. These are the reconstructed ancestral languages of the various Germanic dialects, on the one hand, and of the various Indo-European dialects, on the other (see chapter 4). In Proto-Indo-European the initial consonant was *p*, as in Lat. *plēnus* and Fr. *plein* "full, fully." By tracing the history of words, and observing their phonological characteristics, we can determine two sets of words: **native words** and **borrowed words**. Native words are those like *full* that can be traced back to the earliest form of the language in question. Borrowed words, like *career*, are imported from another language.

The study of the history of individual words is known as **etymology** (see chapter 13). Etymological dictionaries may give the history of suffixes and phrases, but essentially they have entries for individual words. We call *full* a native word because we find **cognates**, that is, related forms of Eng. *full* in Germ. *voll*, OIcel. *fullr*, Goth. *fulls*, each of which we derive from Proto-Germanic, and thereupon from Proto-Indo-European. Moreover, these words are related to Eng. *fill*, Germ. *füllen*, OIcel. *fylla*, Goth. *fulljan* "cause to be full." When we relate words in other Indo-European languages, for example, Gr. *polús* "much," Lat. *complēre* "fill," *complētus* "full, complete," *plūs* "more," we find distinctive differences from the Germanic forms. Comparing these and many other forms, we determine their etymology. In this process we reconstruct the root, such as *pel-* "fill"; we also set out to reconstruct the words we may posit in Proto-Indo-European, the language from which the Germanic languages, Latin, Greek and many others developed (see chapter 4). We indicate reconstructed forms, such as the root *pel-* with an asterisk, *.

Since native words and borrowed words often exhibit different patterns, we must distinguish between them when we study the history of languages. Most native English verbs, for example, are monosyllables like *fill*. In contrast with borrowed words like *complete, deplete*, etc., which have incorporated affixes, English words are frequently used with prepositional adverbs, as in *fill up, fill out*. Borrowed words may accordingly exhibit different syntactic as well as different phonological patterns from those of native words.

We must also distinguish importations from dialects of a language, such as Northern English *kirk* in contrast with standard English *church*. Moreover, we attempt to determine the time of borrowings. NE *wine* and *vine* are both borrowed from Lat. *vīnum*; *wine* was introduced into the Germanic language about the beginning of our era, when Lat. *v* was still pronounced [w]; *vine* was introduced some centuries later when Lat. *v* was pronounced [v]. By maintaining the two forms, English provides information about change in Latin.

Words derived from the same source are called **doublets**. The study of doublets like *wine : vine, three : trio, five : penta(gon) : punch* (a drink made originally with five components) is illuminating in disclosing the history of languages. Investigations of the borrowings in languages, of the interplay between dialects and languages and of the effect of one language on another inform us about the history of individual languages. Many changes are brought about by the influence of one language or dialect on another.

Words like *wine* and *vine* also provide information about the cultural situation at the time these words were introduced. We know that Roman traders brought wine to northern Europe from around the beginning of our era. They traded wine for products of the area, such as furs and amber. As Roman civilization came to be adopted in northern Europe, grapevines were among the new plants introduced. In the meantime the pronunciation of the initial consonant in Latin had changed from [w] to [v]. By associating the forms of the word with the interrelationships between the Romans and the speakers of Germanic languages, we can infer the differences in the cultural situation. First only the product of the vine was brought north, but with advances in agriculture the plant itself was introduced.

Information provided by the words and forms of a language supplement other sources on early history; see chapter 15. Another early borrowing from Latin is the word for "write," Germ. *schreiben*, taken over from Lat. *scrībere*. The fact of borrowing this verb informs us that Germanic speakers at the time were nonliterate. They learned from the Romans how to write, and in German-speaking areas they borrowed the Latin verb for the process as well.

Information provided by language in this way may give us crucial data on early cultures. For example, the ancestor of our word *ore*, Lat. *aes*, Skt *áyas*, is PIE **ayas-* "metal." We cannot reconstruct words for specific metals in the proto-language, only for the general substance in contrast with stones. Accordingly, we conclude that the community speaking Proto-Indo-European was advancing from a neolithic culture. Words for specific metals, for example *copper, iron, silver,* were introduced only after individual dialects had developed as independent languages.

Investigating language for the information it carries about culture has been a major impetus for historical study during the past two centuries. The information can be relatively subtle. In addressing characters in his sonnets and plays, Shakespeare used the pronouns *thou, ye* and *you*; the first two are found only in intimate usage, as still maintained in German – for members of the family and close friends. As in the King James translation of the Bible, *thou* was also used in addressing God. From the occurrences of these pronouns we can determine relationships between Shakespeare's characters. When *thou* and accompanying verb forms are used, we know that the relationships are informal. The selection of pronouns, then, gives important clues for determining meaning. Moreover, the presence of pronouns in language to distinguish social relationships informs us of the degree of formality in a civilization. Since the Second World War Swedish speakers have given up a distinction comparable to that found in Shakespeare's day.

Advances in our knowledge of the history of languages and of the culture of their speakers has increased markedly over the past two centuries. It is useful to know the linguists who have provided the advances, as well as the advances, in part for understanding how progress has been made. Accordingly, information on the major linguists, their contributions and the important movements in historical linguistics will be sketched briefly in chapter 2.

1.2 INTERPRETATION OF WRITING SYSTEMS

Linguists commonly cite forms in a contemporary transliteration. They use symbols of the Latin alphabet with some elaboration, rather than native symbols – not the alphabets used for Gothic or Greek, nor the characters used for Sanskrit, nor those for Chinese and Japanese. Yet without knowledge of the writing system used for the language we study, we would have inadequate means for its interpretation. Greek θ, *theta*, for example, is regularly transliterated with <th>; but the consonant it represents was pronounced like the [t] in Eng. *taint* during the Classical Greek period, and later like our *th* in *think*.

Even if we can transliterate accurately, we may not know the pronunciation. We do not know, for example, the exact pronunciation of many Gothic words, such as *ains* "one," cf. Germ. *eins*. Gothic is transmitted in a writing system based on that of Greek of the fourth century AD At this time Gk *ai* was pronounced approximately like the vowel in Eng. *men*. We cannot be sure, however, that this was its only value in Gothic. Many linguists have held that the vowel of *ains* was actually a diphthong similar to the vowel of Eng. *mine* or Germ. *eins*. In deciding on the pronunciation, other information must be considered as well. Historical linguists must be able to deal with such information concerning written records when they concern themselves with Gothic or other languages attested in texts, or their conclusions may be naive. The problems involved in dealing with written records are discussed in chapter 3.

Transliterations for writing systems like the Greek or Russian alphabets are standard and readily interpreted. Transliterations like those for Chinese, however, often present problems of their own. The standard transliteration of the past, known by the name of its originators, Wade and Giles, used symbols that themselves need interpretation. The official system today is known as *pinyin*. Like the Wade–Giles system, it uses numerals to indicate tones: 1 = level tone, 2 = rising, 3 = falling–rising, 4 = falling. As for Turkish, some symbols of the Latin alphabet were adopted for Chinese sounds quite different from those we may associate with the letter on the basis of our practices. When such forms are cited, it is useful to indicate the values of those letters.

Writing systems, like languages, may be classified by general principles. If a writing system contains a small number of symbols representing vowels and consonants, approximately thirty or fewer, it is alphabetic. If it contains sixty to a hundred, it is syllabic; but some syllabic systems contain fewer symbols. And if like Chinese or Ancient Egyptian, it contains several hundred or more, it is logographic; the symbols stand for words. An understanding of the principles underlying writing systems is important in deciphering unknown writing systems. For details see chapter 3.

1.3 RELATED LANGUAGES; GENEALOGICAL CLASSIFICATION

The comparison of various languages led to the assumption that some languages are **related**, that they developed from a common source. This assumption came to be confirmed in large part through the linguistic situation in western Europe. For common words in French, Italian, Spanish, Portuguese and several other languages show consistent similarities and differences. Compare, for example, the words for "dear" and "field":

| "dear" | Fr. *cher* | Ital. *caro* | Span. *caro* | Port. *caro* |
| "field" | Fr. *champ* | Ital. *campo* | Span. *campo* | Port. *campo* |

The French [š] in these words, spelled *ch*, corresponds consistently with the [k], spelled *c*, in the words of Italian, Spanish and Portuguese.

From these consistent correspondences we assume that at least some French [š] developed from earlier [k] through phonological change. This assumption is supported by other examples, such as:

"candle"
Fr. *chandelle* Ital. *candela* Span. *candela* Port. *candeia* cf.
Lat. *candēla*

"house"
Fr. *chez* Ital. *casa* Span. *casa* Port. *casa* cf. Lat. *casa*

To assure ourselves that the change has indeed been in French we may look for French words in which the [k] has not changed. We find such words, as in

"school"
Fr. *école* Ital. *scuola* Span. *escuela* Port. *escola*, cf.
Lat. *schola*

Here the [k] was protected by the following [o].

After comparing these and other words we propose rules for phonological equivalents in related languages. If we express the parallel elements, the rules may be written: ("=" is read "corresponds to"):

Fr. [š] = Ital. [k] = Span. [k] = Port. [k]

We may also indicate relationships at different chronological periods and changes that have taken place. We then write rules such as:

Lat. [k] > Fr. [š], Ital. [k]   Fr. [š], Ital. [k] < Lat. [k]

(">" is read "became, developed to"; "<" is read "developed from".) We determine similar rules for morphological and syntactic patterns.

From correspondences like those presented here we also conclude that French, Italian, Spanish and Portuguese are members of one linguistic group or **language family**. The reason for their similarity is their common descent from one earlier language, Latin. Through such comparison we can relate other languages, assume that they developed from an earlier language and classify them as belonging to a specific language family. Determination of language families is known as **genealogical classification** (chapter 4).

Such relationships are assumed from observation of systematic differences as well as systematic similarities. Attention to the system is essential, for it is difficult to define what is similar, what different, until we analyse the system of any language. The French [š] is in some ways a more trustworthy indication of relationship than are the unchanged sounds of Italian, Spanish and Portuguese, for it can be systematically related to the [k] of these languages and of Latin. By examining other sequences in the systems of French and Latin, such as [sk], we note systematic similarities in specific environments. Moreover, often words that show no differences are borrowed, such as Germ. *Komputer* versus Eng. *computer*. For these reasons we insist on establishing relationships on the basis of systematic similarities and systematic differences.

We then look for recurrences among both similar and different segments of the subsystems of language. If we base relationships merely on similar words, our conclusions may be wrong, for we may find similar words in languages that are totally unrelated, such as Turk. *futbol* and Jap. *futobōru*, which are borrowed from Eng. *football*, or Pers. *bad* and Eng. *bad*, which are chance similarities. Historical linguistics advanced only after linguists abandoned the comparison of random words that looked alike from language to language and began instead to determine recurrent similarities and differences in the phonological, morphological and syntactic systems, as well as in the vocabularies of the languages they assumed to be related.

The languages that developed from Latin, commonly known as the **Romance languages**, are of great importance to historical linguists because they furnish both the materials for comparison and the earlier language from which the Romance languages developed. In the Romance languages problems of comparison and development are available for solution, and in Latin the solution can be verified. With such verification available to them, historical linguists can test their essential techniques and procedures, which were refined especially through work with the group of languages to which the Romance languages and Latin belong, the **Indo-European** family.

In 1786 Sir William Jones, an English jurist in India, observed that Sanskrit, the ancient learned language of India, was systematically similar to Greek and Latin, to his native language and to earlier forms of English. This observation had been made before, without widespread effect; after Jones's statement, however, scholars in Europe began systematic comparison of older forms of English and German with Latin, Greek, Sanskrit and other languages (see chapter 2). Their work in the nineteenth century led to the classification of these languages in the Indo-European family, and to the development of historical linguistics as a discipline. In the same way other language families were determined. The Hungarian linguist Sámuel Gyarmathi proposed the basis for the Finno-Ugric family in 1799.

1.4 TYPOLOGICAL CLASSIFICATION

In studying linguistic systems, linguists have observed that languages exhibit certain patterns corresponding to the type of language. The patterns may be phonological, morphological, syntactic, or they may extend over all subsystems, as we will see in chapter 5. Here we give brief phonological and syntactic examples.

Many languages have voiceless and voiced stops. When they do, the pairs $p : b$, $t : d$, $k : g$ are most likely, much more likely than postvelar pairs. Moreover, if more than one nasal is found in a language with such pairs, m and n are more likely than η. As a result, if we find η in a phonological system, we can predict that that system will also include m and n.

Languages like English, in which normal declarative sentences have verbs preceding their objects (**VO** languages) typically have relative-clause constructions following their antecedents. On the other hand, languages like Japanese, in which objects precede their verbs (**OV** languages), typically have relative-clause constructions preceding the nouns they modify. Moreover, English has prepositions, while Japanese has postpositions. Linguistic systems are in this way governed by general abstract principles. Such principles have come to be known as **universals**. Observation of systems by types permits us to understand patterns of change and to reconstruct earlier patterns on the basis of surviving residues (see chapter 5).

Typological and genealogical classification are quite independent of each other. Hindi and Armenian, for example, though related to English, are OV languages, while French and Modern Greek are VO like English. The contrasts give us important clues in dealing with the history of each of these languages, as we will observe below in greater detail. Such differences, as well as other characteristics, are important to know when examining languages of the present as well as the past.

Whether we analyse languages for their genealogical relationships or for their typological features, we need accurate descriptions and information on their use in the society of speakers. Such information about languages no longer spoken, like Hittite, or for earlier stages of languages still spoken, like Old English, is dependent on proper interpretation of the texts that have been transmitted to us. We also need to interpret the elements of the texts in their development; for this purpose specific methods are used.

1.5 METHODS USED IN HISTORICAL LINGUISTICS

1.5.1 The comparative method

For interpreting data in historical linguistics, two methods are especially important: the comparative method and the method of internal reconstruction. The comparative method (see chapter 7) may be illustrated by examining selected words from French, Italian, Spanish and Portuguese. If we examine the words for "eight":

Fr. *huit*   Ital. *otto*   Span. *ocho*   Port. *oito*

it would seem difficult to derive them from a common source. By assembling additional examples, we gather more information for deriving them, and for explaining the differing development in each of these languages. Compare:

| "milk" | Fr. *lait* | Ital. *latte* | Span. *leche* | Port. *leite* |
| "fact" | Fr. *fait* | Ital. *fatto* | Span. *hecho* | Port. *feito* |

Basing our conclusions on observation of changes in language, we reconstruct as the earlier forms of these words: **okto, *lakte, *faktu.*

These reconstructions by the comparative method can be corroborated by noting the Latin: *octō* "eight," *lactem* (accusative singular of "milk"), *factum* "fact"; moreover, we can account for the changes in these four languages and also see their essential regularity. In French and Portuguese the Latin [k] has been absorbed in the vowel; in Italian it has been assimilated to the following [t]; in Spanish it has been changed to the affricate [č] with loss of the following [t]. In four different geographical areas a sequence originally the same developed into four different sequences. Through comparison of such forms, knowledge of possible phonetic changes and of the earlier forms, we can determine the earlier shapes and those of most forms in French, Italian, Spanish and Portuguese.

Study of the relationships among English [f θ h b d g p t k] and corresponding consonants in the other Indo-European languages was important in developing the comparative method. In the earliest period of historical linguistics, Jacob Grimm (1785–1863) noted the systematic relationships among these consonants. Thereupon the Indo-European consonants from which they developed were reconstructed by means of the comparative method. We list these, with examples from Gothic and Sanskrit:

PIE p	PIE t	PIE k
Goth. *fadar*	Goth. *þrija*	Goth. *haurds* "(woven)
"father"	"three"	door, hurdle"
Skt *pitá* "father"	Skt *tráyas* "three"	Skt *kṛṇatti* "spins"

PIE bh	PIE dh	PIE gh
Goth. *broþar*	Goth. *doms* "fame,	OE *gūþ* "battle"
"brother"	(doom)"	
Skt *bhráta* "brother"	Skt *dháma* "glory"	Skt *ghnánti* "they strike"

PIE b	PIE d	PIE g
NE *pool*	Goth. *taihun* "ten"	Goth. *kuni* "race, kin"
Lith. *balà* "swamp"	Skt *dáśa* "ten"	Lat. *genus* "kin"

The systematic relationships between

Skt p t k	Gmc. f θ h/χ	as well as Gk p t k
Skt bh dh gh	Gmc. b d g	as well as Gk ph th kh
Skt b d g	Gmc. p t k	as well as Gk b d g

were stated by Grimm in rules that have subsequently become known as

Grimm's law. Because of the importance of Grimm's law in the development of historical linguistic theory, the data will be discussed more fully in later sections. Many desk dictionaries have entries on the law.

The comparative method can also be illustrated by comparison of other words, such as the numerals from "one" to "ten" in some of the Indo-European languages (see Table 1.1). The numerals in the unrelated languages, Chinese and Japanese, are given for contrast. Again we cite Gothic forms rather than Old English, in part because they are attested several centuries before Old English.

Although a complete account of the similarities and differences between the words of the first six columns of table 1.1 would require considerable space, we can readily note a few examples of consistent similarities and differences, such as the *t-* in columns 1 and 2 of the words for "two" and "ten" corresponding to *d-* in columns 3–6. By comparison, the Chinese and Japanese words do not permit us to assume correspondences with any of the columns. Jap. *tō* like NE *ten*, to be sure, has initial *t*, but the Japanese word corresponding to NE *two* has initial *f*; accordingly, we cannot find consistent similarities or differences between English and Japanese. The same holds true for English and Chinese.

We also note the systematic difference in vowel between Skt *a* and Lat. and Gk *e* in the first syllables of the words for "six," "seven," and "ten." Analysis of all the systematic similarities and differences between the Indo-European languages in accordance with the comparative method required the work of many linguists during the nineteenth and twentieth centuries, and it is still not complete. But even with as little material as the numerals from "one" to "ten," we can assume with confidence that English, Gothic, Latin, Greek, Old Church Slavic and Sanskrit belong to one language family, and that they developed from a common source.

1.5.2 The method of internal reconstruction

The comparative method, as just illustrated, is the most common procedure used in determining older patterns of a language. By examining the Japanese numerals cited in table 1.1, we can note another procedure, one especially valuable when we find no related languages. Without using forms other than those of Japanese listed above, we observe a pattern in these numerals: the double of the lower numerals begins with the same consonant as does its half, that is, *mi* "three" and *mu* "six," *yo* "four" and *ya* "eight." After determining this pattern, we might assume that the words for "one" *hi*(*to*) and "two" *fu*(*ta*) also had the same initial consonant at one time. By comparing words borrowed into Japanese from Old Chinese, we can support this assumption; the Old Japanese initial consonant is often written *F*.

This procedure is referred to as **internal reconstruction** (see chapter 8). As the example illustrates, older patterns are reconstructed by the use of

Table 1.1 Numerals in selected languages

English	Gothic	Latin	Greek	Old Church Slavic	Sanskrit	Chinese	Japanese
one	ains	ūnus	heîs	jedinŭ	ekas	i[1]	hitotsu
two	twai	duo	dúō	dŭva	dvā	erh[4]	futatsu
three	θrija (acc.)	trēs	treîs	trĭje	trayas	san[1]	mittsu
four	fidwor	quattuor	téttares	četyre	catvāras	ssu[4]	yottsu
five	fimf	quīnque	pénte	pęti	pañca	wu[3]	itsutsu
six	saihs	sex	héks	šestĭ	ṣaṭ	liu[4]	muttsu
seven	sibun	septem	heptá	sedmĭ	sapta	ch'i[1]	nanatsu
eight	ahtau	octō	oktố	osmĭ	aṣṭā	pa[1]	yattsu
nine	niun	novem	ennéa	devęti	nava	chiu[3]	kokonotsu
ten	taihun	decem	déka	desętĭ	daśa	shih[2]	tō

forms internal in a language; by contrast, the comparative method uses forms from three or more related languages for reconstruction. In Japanese we apply it of necessity, since languages assumed by some to be related to Japanese lack comparable numerals. We also must apply it if we wish to reconstruct earlier forms of languages that are themselves reconstructed. When we do so, we seek to determine typical or canonical forms that preserve the earlier patterning, as do the first two sets of numerals in Japanese cited above.

1.5.3 Application of these methods in Indo-European linguistics

The common source of the Indo-European languages was spoken before writing was in use in its geographical area, and we have no attested forms of it. With the methodology developed partly in the study of the Romance languages, linguists have reconstructed the "original" Indo-European language as far as our data permit. To indicate, however, that it is not attested, we label it with the prefix **Proto-** and refer to it as **Proto-Indo-European (PIE)**. As noted above, we place an asterisk (*) before a reconstructed or nonattested form. Since, however, a form identified as belonging to a proto-language is by definition unattested, when we place **P-** in a language abbreviation before a cited form, we may omit the asterisk.

If we use the method of internal reconstruction to posit forms earlier than Proto-Indo-European, we refer to them as **Pre-Indo-European**. We use the prefix **Pre-** similarly for other language material proposed as earlier than proto-forms. Whatever the period to which we ascribe the reconstructed forms, we attempt to deal with them as with attested forms. We may accordingly cite them in phonemic transcription, for example PIE /penk^{w}e/"five," or in phonetic transcription, for example PIE [peŋk^{w}e], though frequently the distinction is not made. Phonetic transcription is also important in representing PIE /s/; it has a voiced allophone before voiced stops, as in */nisdo-/ [nizdo-] "nest".

By comparing the words for "ten" in all the Indo-European languages we arrive at the reconstruction given in section 1.6. We can reconstruct other words as well, such as PIE /g^{w}ōws/ "cow" on the basis of OE *cū*, OIr. *bō*, Lat. *bōs, bovis*, Gk *boũs*, Lett. *guovs*, Skt *gáus*, and so on. We can also reconstruct morphological elements, such as the ending PIE [ti] from forms like that for "is" in Gk *esti*, Skt *asti*, and many other verbs. Similarly, we reconstruct syntactic patterns from those in the early languages; since early Sanskrit is verb-final, as are Proto-Germanic and Hittite, we reconstruct Proto-Indo-European as an OV language. When we reconstruct Proto-Indo-European, we are dealing with a language spoken before 3000 BC and we obviously do not have the kind of data that are available for Latin. But we can determine the essential elements of the Proto-Indo-European phonological, morphological and syntactic systems, and we reconstruct some of its vocabulary.

1.5.4 Glottochronology

While the method of internal reconstruction can be used in languages of
today to determine older stages, as well as relationships with other languages, many languages, as in the Americas or Australia, differ so greatly
that the comparative method cannot be applied, at least without a great
deal of preliminary study. In order to determine possible relationships,
Morris Swadesh in 1951 proposed a third method known as **glottochronology**. The method is based on the assumption that everyday segments of
the vocabulary are replaced at a definite rate. Further, that the words
maintained in related languages may be used for dating in much the same
way as radio-active decay has been used in dating biological materials. The
rate of decay was determined by examination of languages known for a
period of a thousand years or more, such as the Romance languages in
conjunction with Latin. It was then applied to other languages.

In the use of glottochronology (discussed in chapter 9), lists of one or
two hundred words are gathered from languages assumed to be related; the
proportion of related words is then determined, with no closer attention to
their similarities. Eng. *cow* and Germ. *Kuh* would be adequately similar,
but not *dog* and *Hund*. The method has been applied with success to the
languages of the Pacific and of Australia. But it has not lived up to the
hopes originally held for it, because varying conditions of the societies
using languages bring about varying rates of loss. None the less, specialists
in languages attested only today apply it to gain some information about
earlier relationships of the languages with which they are concerned.

1.6 SOUND CHANGE

The difference between PIE/dekm/ and NE/ten/ can be accounted for by
positing various types of change at the phonological level. PIE /d/, maintained in Lat. *decem*, became PGmc /t/; PIE /k/, also maintained in Lat.
decem, became PGmc /χ/, later /h/. Final *m* developed a preceding vowel,
and became *n*; *e* remained unchanged. In early Old English the /h/ from
PGmc /χ/ was lost between vowels, though /h/ was maintained in OSax.
tehan and OHG *zehan*. Having noted these changes, we can relate precisely PIE /dekm/ and NE /ten/.

Languages undergo changes of all similar sounds of a phoneme, such as
that from PIE /d/ to PGmc /t/. They also have changes that affect only some
words, and these in some of their occurrences; for example, the colloquial
pronunciation of NE *would you* is [wʊdžə]. Speakers may use either this
pronunciation, or the more formal [wúd yùw]. Because these changes are
not applied to every occurrence of [d] followed by [y], they are called
sporadic changes.

To understand changes like that of PIE d > PGmc *t* in the etymon of NE
ten or [dy] > [dž] in NE *would you*, we need to know articulatory

phonetics. Both changes involve only one feature of the sounds in question. PIE d became voiceless in Proto-Germanic. English [y] after [d] may become strident, as in the colloquial pronunciation cited here. Sound change generally takes place with the modification of one feature, whether the change affects all like sounds in a language or whether the change is sporadic.

Changes are stated in rules. In most historical grammars these are expressed as illustrated in the following rule:

PIE b d g > PGmc p t k

that is, Proto-Indo-European voiced stops became Proto-Germanic voiceless stops.

1.7 MORPHOLOGICAL AND SYNTACTIC CHANGE

When we compare the Modern English plural *ships* with the Old English counterpart *scipu*, we cannot account for the difference in ending through sound change. Rather, we must conclude that the plural ending was remodeled after that in such Old English nouns as *stānas* "stones" from sg. *stān*. That is to say, the change is not phonological but rather **morphological** (see chapter 11).

Study of even a small segment of language leads to the observation that forms similarly used may influence or modify one another. When, for example, we compare the Old Church Slavic word for "nine" with its cognates in the other Indo-European languages, we may assume that, like them, it should have begun with *n*. The simplest explanation for the initial *d* of OCS *devętĭ* is that it was taken over from OCS *desętĭ* "ten." Such influence is called **analogical**; we say that the Proto-Slavic word for "nine" was modified on the analogy of that for "ten". We also say that the *-s* marking the plural of *ship* was spread by analogy. Modification of this sort can be exemplified in sets of forms, such as the ordinal numerals in English. Modern English *fifth* has been modified from earlier *fift* on the analogy of *fourth*. Analogical modification may be based on semantic patterns, as in OCS *devętĭ*, or on syntactic patterns, as in the English *s*-plurals.

Change also takes place in syntax, as of the order of elements in clauses and sentences. In the Old English *Beowulf*, most sentences end in verbs; that is, the basic sentence pattern for early Old English has the object preceding its verb. At this stage the language is OV. The OV pattern, however, was undergoing change; in Middle English, objects consistently follow verbs, as they do in Modern English. As we will see in chapter 5, the change to a VO order was accompanied by other syntactic changes, as in comparative constructions.

Moreover, many inflectional endings were lost. For example, early Old English still contains examples of an instrumental case form. In late Old

English, the uses of the instrumental were taken over by the dative. Through changes in final vowels, the instrumental was no longer distinct, and was lost as a separate case form. In this way, syntactic changes may be brought about by sound changes. Later, as final endings were lost in English, the dative case itself was no longer distinct; most of its former functions are now expressed by prepositional phrases.

As we will note in greater detail in chapter 12, syntactic changes involve modifications in forms available for indicating syntactic categories. Many of the modifications are brought about by internal changes; others result from influences of other languages.

1.8 SEMANTIC CHANGE

Besides sound change and syntactic change, languages also undergo change of meaning. The meanings of single words may be modified. Goth. *haurds*, for example, meant "door," apparently because some doors were woven of reeds or withes; the underlying verb meant "spin, weave," as illustrated in the examples in section 1.5.1. NE *hurdle* is not used of doors, but rather for an obstruction in a sport. From this use it came to have an abstract meaning: "obstacle." The change of meaning was affected on the one hand by a change in culture, when doors were no longer woven; and subsequently the meaning was affected by internal change, when the word came to be used primarily in contexts referring to social and mental rather than physical activities.

Semantic change may also affect sets of words, or word fields. Examples may be found in kinship terms. In Old English, for example, a distinction was made between uncles on the father's side, OE *fædera*, and uncles on the mother's side, OE *ēam* (see *eme* in the *Oxford English Dictionary*). The distinction was subsequently lost, so that the English kinship system now has only one term, *uncle*. The semantic change in the set did not result from importation of the word *uncle* from OFr. *oncle*, but rather from a change of culture. In early Germanic times the maternal uncle occupied a special position in the family, a position that was later lost. As a result, there was no need to maintain two words for uncle. Moreover, we cannot say simply that a word was changed in meaning; rather, that a feature of meaning was modified in the kinship system. Thus, change in meaning may be comparable to change in phonological and morphological sets. As we will note in discussing semantic change (chapter 13), meaning has been studied primarily in relation to individual words, not in relation to semantic sets. Accordingly, our understanding of semantic change is poorer than our understanding of phonological, morphological and syntactic change.

1.9 EXPLANATIONS FOR CHANGE

Besides identifying change in language, linguists have attempted to account for it. Many modifications in language are superficial. For example, when the exploration of space became a major topic, new terms were introduced and the use of others was modified. These modifications, however, had little effect on the language. No new sound patterns or syntactic categories were introduced; and extended uses of words, as in *lunar landing* or *space shuttle* did not modify the semantic system of the languages that introduced such terminology. Further, the borrowed word *sputnik* applied by the Soviets for their spaceship, literally "fellow-traveler," brought no new sounds into the language, though it did introduce the morpheme *nik*. Attempts to account for modifications in linguistic structures cannot deal simply with such superficial innovations but must also treat change that affects the central structure of languages.

Three major explanations for change have been suggested: (1) The influence of one language on another, the results of which have been termed **borrowings**; (2) the imperfect learning of language by children; (3) the effects of the system or systems of individual languages.

1.9.1 Borrowing is readily observed in vocabulary

English has borrowed many words from French, Latin and Greek, and it readily takes over words from other languages as well. The extent to which borrowing affects syntax or phonology, however, is still inadequately known. Through bilingual speakers, French syntactic patterns such as phrases consisting of noun followed by adjective, for example *attorney general*, have been borrowed. Extensive bilingualism may bring about the importation of syntactic patterns more widely than in a few phrases. But when foreign patterns or sounds occur in borrowed words, they are generally modified in keeping with the patterns of the borrowing language, as in *menu, garage* and other recent borrowings from French into English. An extended period of influence may, however, lead to different results.

In dealing with borrowing, the attitudes of speakers must be taken into consideration. English has borrowed many words from French, but, except in specific periods, German has not. Sociolinguists have examined the attitudes of speakers regarding specific characteristics, such as the pronunciation of postvocalic *r* in words like *car* in New York City. The imitations of prestige patterns they found may lead to a better understanding of modifications in the past. If a neighboring language had great prestige, a borrowing language may have been modified in its sound system and syntactic system, as well as in its vocabulary.

1.9.2 Change has also been ascribed to the imperfect learning of language by children

Advocates of change resulting from language acquisition must demonstrate when and how such patterns are adopted. Everyone who has watched children learn languages has observed inadequacies in pronunciation, syntax and use of words. But these are gradually eliminated as the child grows up. Moreover, the imperfect patterns of one child often differ from those of another. It is accordingly difficult to establish that these patterns are taken over as innovations in a language. Specialists in language acquisition have begun to carry out the detailed studies that linguists like Jespersen and Meillet recommended. But as yet they have not provided general principles for possible changes resulting from imperfect language acquisition by children.

1.9.3 The structure of language as a system consisting of several subsystems may itself lead to change

From the early days of historical linguistics, languages have been assumed to be systems (see chapter 2). They also have subsystems which may bring about imbalance in one another. Moreover, these subsystems are never totally symmetrical; the lack of symmetry may be ascribed to a need for openness for expansion, or greater clarity in understanding, especially speech. If all possible slots, as of a sequence like *ba-*, were filled, there would be no redundancy in English. Other forces as well, such as dissimilation, have been proposed to account for the lack of some words; there are no English words *bab, baf, bav* in which a labial would conclude a syllable that begins with a voiced labial stop. But there is no overreaching reason for the absence of such a word; and if the situation arose for its inclusion, or it were devised for advertising purposes, any of these potential words could be introduced.

We may illustrate the lack of symmetry, and efforts to overcome it, by examining the English nasals. English has three nasals in final position, as in *bam, ban, bang*, but only two initially, as was true formerly in all positions. Such imbalances may be eliminated in the course of the history of languages, as the development of /ŋ/ to a separate phoneme indicates. Formerly, [ŋ] as in *strong*, was a variant of /n/ before *k* and *g*, as in *stronger*. Thereupon the final *g* was lost, and *ŋ* came to contrast with *n* and *m*, so that it became a separate phoneme. In this way English came to have three nasals in keeping with three voiceless and voiced stops:

```
p   t   k
b   d   g
m   n   ŋ
```

The symmetry is limited to medial and final position. There is no word beginning with ŋ contrasting with those beginning with *m* and *n*; the lexicon includes *Mab* and *nab*, but not **ngab*.

Moreover, the new pronunciation of *strong* as [strɔŋ] rather than [strɔŋg] brought about irregularity in the formation of comparatives; in contrast with such forms as *fine : finer, tame : tamer, strong* now "adds" a consonant – [g] – in the comparative [strɔŋgər]. In this way a regularization at one level may bring about an irregularity at another.

The effects of systematization are especially apparent in morphology, as in English verbs. Irregular verbs, like *hide, hid, hid*, have come to distinguish only between the present, on the one hand, and the past and past participle, on the other, like the regular verbs *like, liked, liked*. Few verbs remain that have three distinct forms, like *sing, sang, sung*; and only one verb has two different vowels in the past: *was : were*, in some varieties of English.

Moreover, we might conclude from examination of a single language that irregularities in the system of every language are constantly being eliminated. But Italian, with a system of nasals like those in Early Middle English, has not developed a separate phoneme ŋ. Moreover, the German irregular verbs are more complex than are those of English. Because of the varying effects of the system from language to language, we cannot ascribe change solely to simplification of irregularities in a language. It is obvious from complexities that seem very formidable to non-native speakers, such as the vowel harmony of Turkish or the broken noun plurals of Arabic, that children can acquire any language with no apparent difficulty. And having mastered the complexities, they may maintain them as the speakers of Turkish and Arabic have. Complexities in a system are apparently eliminated when adult speakers acquire another language. Examples may be found in pidgins; see section 13.8.3.

1.9.4 Implications of an improved understanding of change

The discussion above may well indicate that the causes of change in language are highly complex, as they are also in other social institutions. Detailed study of individual changes for which we have extensive information, like that of the pronunciation of American English *-t-* in *butter, bottle, bottom*, gives us a better understanding of how languages change phonologically. R-M. S. Heffner (1949: 129–30) listed the characteristics of *t* in words like those above, noting among other things that it was very short. Residual voicing was maintained during its duration; medial *-t-* then came to be voiced rather than voiceless. We need similar studies of specific morphological, lexical and syntactic changes.

Through information on change, we can explain the forms of language, especially those that are irregular. We can understand the vowel variations in *mouse : mice, goose : geese, man : men*, for example, by noting the Old and Pre-Old English forms of these words. And the vowel variation in *write* : *wrote* : *written, sing* : *sang* : *sung* we can understand by noting the related words in other Indo-European dialects and in Proto-Indo-European. Understanding the phonological, morphological, syntactic and semantic structure of any language through such comparison is an important aim of historical linguistics.

Moreover, by investigating languages for the changes they have undergone, we can determine their history and their interrelationships with other languages. Such knowledge is supplemented by archaeological findings; see chapter 15. After a century and a half of investigation the development of most of the languages in the Indo-European family is well known. The development of other language families has not been so fully determined, partly because data are lacking, especially from earlier historical periods. Furthermore, linguists have been primarily interested in determining the background of their own native languages, which with few exceptions have been Indo-European.

The success of historical linguistic study depends largely on the state of descriptive linguistics. Indo-European historical linguistics developed rapidly in the nineteenth century because thorough descriptions were available for Latin, Greek and Sanskrit; on the pattern of these descriptions, grammars were produced for other early Indo-European languages, such as Gothic, Old Church Slavic, Old Irish, and subsequently for the remaining Indo-European languages, such as Armenian and Albanian. Since equally detailed descriptions were not produced for many languages of other families, the historical grammar of these families is less advanced than is that of Indo-European.

Recent advances in many sub-branches of linguistics promise additional insights into the development of languages. Understanding of phonology has been increased through instrumental analysis of sounds, and through distinctive-feature analysis. Detailed syntactic and semantic studies have also been carried out. Moreover, typological investigation has deepened our knowledge of language systems and their components. As a result, data that remained unexplained may now be clarified.

More complete accounts of the development of specific languages and of language families will lead to improvement of historical linguistic theory and of the techniques employed in historical linguistics. In determining language families as well as in formulating principles for investigation of change, historical linguists have drawn in large measure from data in the Indo-European family. Accordingly, Indo-European linguistics occupies a preponderant role in the discipline, as it will in this textbook.

SELECTED FURTHER READINGS

For an introduction to the problems and methods of historical linguistics, see Pedersen (1931). The book provides a readable discussion of the principles of historical linguistics that were developed in the course of the nineteenth century, as viewed by a leading member of the neogrammarian tradition. Both editions are unfortunately out of print, so that students may have to resort to library use.

A concise but excellent statement on the development and principles of historical linguistics may be found in Meillet (1937: ch. 1 and Appendix I). A fuller statement may be found in Szemerényi (1989). Both works center on Indo-European.

Some of the important theoretical statements of nineteenth-century linguists have been made available in translation in Lehmann (1967), now, like Pedersen's book, out of print.

For studying the history of words, the Clarendon Press, Oxford, has published a number of dictionaries. Still useful is that of Skeat (1879–82), and in numerous subsequent versions. It was brought up to date by Onions (1966). For Indo-European etymologies see Buck (1949). Buck's dictionary is arranged like a thesaurus. For a dictionary with words arranged alphabetically under roots, see Watkins (1985).

PROBLEMS

1 Examination of earlier texts, such as those from the time of Shakespeare (1564–1616), is useful for understanding change in language, as we have seen from the four lines of Milton's sonnet. Here four lines of Shakespeare's Sonnet XI are given, followed by questions directing attention to later changes.

> As fast as thou shalt wane, so fast thou grow'st
> In one of thine, from that which thou departest;
> And that fresh blood which youngly thou bestow'st
> Thou mayst call thine when thou from youth convertest.

(a) Compare the spelling of the endings of the verbs at the conclusions of each of these lines, determining the pattern for the use of the apostrophe.

(b) Note the rhyme *departest* : *convertest*. Comparing the British pronunciation of *Derby*, and also the words *parson* and *Clark* besides *person* and *clerk*, indicate Shakespeare's pronunciation of the rhyme.

(c) Substituting today's pronoun of address, *you*, for *thou*, discuss the effects of the changed morphology of the verb on the four lines, rhythmically as well as in form.

(d) Note the syntactic use of *depart*, and put the clause into the current pattern.

(e) Contrast Shakespeare's meaning of *wane* and *convert* with that current today.

2 Doublets are highly instructive in reviewing the history of a language, its internal changes and the effects of its relationships with other languages. Look up in an etymological dictionary the members of any of the

following sets, and indicate their position in the English lexicon, as whether they are native words or borrowed words, and if borrowed, suggest why they were brought into the language.

two : dual : duet   due : debt
first : prime : primitive Gypsy : Egyptian
cow : bovine : beef   mint : money
task : tax   an : one

3 *The Dictionary of American Regional English*, Cassidy ed. (1985), gives two pronunciations for *chew*, [ču] with the variant [čiu] and [čɔ]. Recalling the discussion of *show* in regard to Milton's rhymes, account for the two variants in American dialects.
4 The ordinal numerals for "five" and "six" were formerly pronounced [fift] and [sikst], while those for "four," "seven," and "eight" were pronounced [fɔrθ], [sevənθ], [etθ]. Account for the current pronunciations of *fourth* and *fifth*.

Assuming that the suffix could have spread from [fift] and [sikst] to the three other numerals, what problems would you find in the ordinal for "eight"?
5 It is generally said that the irregular verbs of English are becoming regular, as in the widespread use of *dive, dived* rather than *dive, dove*. But through final-consonant simplification many speakers use for the past tense of *sleep* the form [slep] and for *keep* the form [kep]. How do you account for the production of such new irregular verbs?

Speakers who use the form [slep] also may make the past tense of *dream* with the form [dremt], though not without the final [t]. Account for its maintenance here in contrast with its loss in the past tense of *sleep* and *keep*.

2 The background of historical linguistic study

2.1 PRECURSORS OF HISTORICAL STUDY

For pedagogical reasons, we distinguish between historical linguistics and descriptive linguistics, as well as sub-branches with special emphases, such as sociolinguistics and psycholinguistics. But the distinctions are artificial, as a survey of the study of language demonstrates. Unless one limits oneself to an ideal form, all languages are changing. Linguistics, then, is properly a historical science, in much the same way as are geology, astronomy and other sciences that observe, describe and explain their object of study. They contrast in this way with chemistry and physics, where many conclusions are observed, described and explained through experimentation. While we are concerned in this chapter with highlights in historical study, we cannot disregard the intimate relationship between historical and descriptive study. In many ways historical study is built on descriptive study. Many of the basic problems in the history of language require detailed description for solution, as we see in the following.

In earlier periods the study of language was influenced and often directed by other than linguistic concerns. Initially, the concerns were religious. For the Greeks and Latins, on the other hand, attention to language was included in the fields of philosophy and rhetoric, although they produced grammars that were maintained through to the eighteenth century. During the Middle Ages the concerns were largely theological, with increasing production in the sixteenth and seventeenth centuries of grammars and treatises that often resulted from religious efforts. The information about many languages so assembled furnished a basis for the historical study that became prominent in the early decades of the nineteenth century. That study then developed its methodology and theory, as we observe in the following sections of this chapter.

Two questions that are still concerns of historical linguistics occupied early western thinkers about language: (1) What is its origin? (2) Why are there many languages rather than only one? Hebrew thinkers provided their answers to both questions. Regarding the first, they asserted that God named the major objects of creation: day, night, heaven, earth, seas

(Genesis 1.5–10); under God's guidance Adam subsequently named the animals and birds (Genesis 2.20). No source is given for other nouns, nor for verbs and other elements of speech; nor is the origin of language discussed further in the Old Testament.

The explanation for the diversity of language is also brief and simple. Originally "of one speech," the people offended God by setting out to build a tower that would reach into heaven and serve as their center. To scuttle the plan, God confounded their language. Unable to communicate with one another, they scattered, presumably by the social groups named after the descendants of Noah (Genesis 10 and 11).

2.1.1 Etymology

While the Hebrews did not elaborate on their answers in their sacred writings, western scholars in the Christian tradition took these answers as fundamental. Some concluded that language before Babel, given or prompted by God, involved a direct relationship between the word and the object or activity that it represented. The search for that early state consisted in etymology – "investigating the true meaning" – a topic that had already engaged Plato and his successors. Etymology in this sense continued to be a dominant concern through the Middle Ages.

The study of etymology built on work of the Greeks, especially the dialogue *Cratylus* of Plato (ca 427–347). The two proponents in the dialogue discuss whether words have their names by nature or by convention. The position of Cratylus, who held that names were given "by nature," came to be dominant. Since the Greeks were not interested in other languages, they could not provide etymologies on a historical basis. When names were not readily interpreted, for example words like *blackberry*, the Greeks and Romans resorted to etymologies that seem fanciful to us. For example, the Lat. *vulpēs* "fox" was explained as made from *volō* "I fly" and *pēs* "foot" because foxes run rapidly. Such etymologies have been ridiculed in handbooks. They are obviously incorrect historically; but we must remember the aim of the classical etymologists. Their etymologies were somewhat like modern interpretation of texts, though focussed on words.

It is also salutary to keep in mind that terms are shifted in meaning, or perspective, in linguistics, as in other sciences. The great American linguist, William Dwight Whitney (1827–94) proclaimed that "etymology, the historical study of individual words, is the foundation and substructure of all investigations of language" (1892: 55). Yet his widely used *Sanskrit Grammar* is purely descriptive. And Saussure's series of lectures, as indicated in 2.6, shifted the foundation to description.

2.1.2 The origin and essence of language

In seeking the origin or essence of language, scholars in the sixteenth century and many later assumed that the "one speech" of Genesis 11.1 was Hebrew. They then set out to derive all languages from Hebrew, though some selected another language, as Goropius Becanus did Dutch. The gradually expanding information about languages of the world, much of it assembled by Jesuit missionaries, led eventually to the rejection of Hebrew as first language in which all other languages had their origin. As a residue of the earlier assumption, the term Hamito-Semitic is still applied to a large group of languages.

While linguistic study in ancient India also was prompted by religious motives, the conclusions were far different from those in the west, largely because Indian thought is totally uninterested in history. The dominant motive for linguistic study in India centered on preservation of the exact text of the sacred hymns known as the Vedas. Consisting largely of hymns to gods, by the Indian view they had to be maintained without change in order to achieve their effect. Since Sanskrit, like all languages, was changing, efforts were made to decribe it punctiliously. As a result, the most complete grammar that has yet been produced for any language was compiled. It is ascribed to the grammarian, Panini; his dates are unknown, but he is assumed to have lived around 400 BC. Besides his work, Indian students of language produced many other treatises and also dictionaries. These remained totally unknown to western scholars until the end of the eighteenth century.

Other linguistic study also remained unknown, such as that of the Akkadians. From the end of the third millennium they produced dictionaries, as of Sumerian. But since their writing system was not deciphered until the middle of the nineteenth century, their work on language had no effect on the development of western linguistics. Nor did the work of medieval Arabic grammarians, which only now is attracting some attention.

Curiously, then, the contributions of earlier concerns with language were descriptions. From the time of the founding of the European universities, the first three liberal arts – the trivium – dealt entirely with language; the topics were grammar, rhetoric and logic. Latin was the language of instruction, and provided the pattern for grammars of modern languages. As a result, the historical linguists in the nineteenth century had complete control of Latin and also Greek; many mastered Sanskrit as well. The availability of descriptive handbooks in these important languages, as well as in the major Germanic languages, furnished means for the rapid advances that we will examine below.

150/19

2.2 THE SIXTEENTH TO EIGHTEENTH CENTURIES

The major concern with language during these centuries was descriptive; for New High German alone Jellinek required two volumes to deal with its treatment. Yet interest was growing in the classification and history of languages. We can mention only a few scholars. Konrad Gesner (1516–1565) set out to classify languages in his *Mithridates* of 1555; its subtitle indicates that Gesner attempted to deal with the differences between ancient as well as contemporary languages in the entire world. The title itself, used by later authors as well, is taken from the name of the king of Pontus (132?–63 BC), who reputedly spoke twenty-five languages.

Gesner's classification makes some use of historical relationships. He knew that the Romance languages are modern forms of Latin; but like other scholars of his time and later, he accepted the authority of the Old Testament, and assumed that Hebrew was the first and most ancient of languages.

The great polymath, Gottfried Wilhelm von Leibniz (1646–1714), rejected the Hebraic hypothesis. His primary interest in the historical and comparative study of language was to determine ethnic origins and relationships. He assumed an Ursprache that was divided into two subgroups: Japhetic and Aramaic. Japhetic in turn was divided into Scythian and Celtic; the subgroups of Scythian were Turkish, Slavic, Finnish and Greek; of Celtic, Germanic and Celtic. He also assumed mixtures, of which Latin was one. Aramaic in turn had two subgroups: Arabic, to which Hebrew belonged, and Egyptian.

While the classification of Leibniz has little value, his support for attention to collecting materials on many languages and describing them had great importance. It led ultimately to the large *Mithridates* of Adelung (1806–16). This work is descriptive and typological. It represents the culmination of three centuries of assembling material on as many languages as possible. Some of its data are faulty, yet many of its observations are valid. But they are little more than lists; and their purpose is not historical, as Adelung's arrangement of languages by the types of words, such as monosyllables, indicates.

While language description remained the primary interest of these three centuries, some individuals made a point of collecting material with which they began to classify languages in accordance with their genealogical relationship. The most remarkable of these may well have been Eugene Aram (1704–59), the only linguist to be romanticized in a ballad, and also in a novel by Bulwer-Lytton with his name as its title. His literary treatment resulted from a sensational murder that was long unsolved, but led to his hanging fourteen years after the crime was committed. His linguistic standing is due to his recognition that Celtic is related to the other Indo-European languages, and his belief that Latin is not derived from Greek. Both views differ from those of his great contemporary, Leibniz.

Other scholars proposed genealogical relationships, such as James Parsons in his *The Remains of Japhet* of 1767. While including some accurate classifications, Parsons, like earlier scholars, failed to provide the systematic proofs that inaugurated historical linguistics in the early nineteenth century. His work is of interest as an illustration of the groping towards the conclusions reached with the introduction of rigorous method. His title illustrates maintenance of the account in Genesis; even Sir William Jones, who is credited with providing the impetus for the new science, maintained its veracity. The required chronology, and the classification by the descendants of Noah, vitiated any possibility of accuracy. Historical linguistics takes its start from the work of Rasmus Rask, Franz Bopp and Jacob Grimm.

2.3 EARLY DEVELOPMENT OF HISTORICAL LINGUISTICS

The widely cited paragraph of Sir William Jones (1746–94) on the strong affinity of Sanskrit with Greek, Latin and other western languages had an impact long after its presentation in 1786. It took some time for Sanskrit texts to reach scholars, in view of the Napoleonic wars as well as slow transportation. Many texts were held up in Paris, where they attracted the brilliant young scholar, Franz Bopp (1791–1867). He continued his education in Paris, to work on Sanskrit manuscripts. Seminal works by him (1816) and Jacob Grimm (1822) then aroused massive interest in historical linguistics, shifting the study of language away from descriptive treatments.

Not all historical concern was directed at the Indo-European family. In 1799 the Hungarian Sámuel Gyarmathi (1751–1830) related Hungarian with Finnish, laying the basis for establishing the Finno-Ugric family.

The interest in historical linguistics was aided by the attention in the Romantic movement to earlier periods. Among the views of the movement it was held that contemporary social practices, whether in law, literature or language, could be best understood by knowledge of earlier stages. Thus the Grimm brothers assembled their immensely popular collection of fairy tales on the assumption that they were repositories of earlier literature. They also published a large work on early Germanic law. And when Jacob Grimm went on to write a grammar of the Germanic languages, its best-known section owed a great deal to two precursors, Friedrich Schlegel and Georges Cuvier.

Following a period of study in Paris, Friedrich Schlegel (1772–1829) published a book "on the language and wisdom of the Indians" (1808). Among its notable principles was the insistence on examining language for its innermost structure. That principle directed historical linguistic study from the start, not as often assumed only through the influence of Saussure or even later linguists. As a second dictum, Schlegel looked to comparative grammar for information on the genealogy of languages much as comparative anatomy clarified natural history.

Four years after Schlegel's publication, the distinguished anatomist Georges Cuvier (1769–1832), published a frequently reprinted treatise in which he asserted forcefully the close interrelationships of all parts of an organism. He had a tremendous impact on study in natural history, especially the treatment of fossils. According to Cuvier, "every organized individual forms an entire system of its own, all the parts of which mutually correspond and concur. . . . Hence none of the separate parts can change their forms without a corresponding change in other parts of the same animal." Adopting the well-explored organism as a model, linguists now used it as a guide for their conclusions much as linguists at the end of the century began to use mathematical models of language. Just as Cuvier viewed organisms as systems, with closely interrelated parts, so early linguists regarded language. They recognized that it underwent change, and they assumed that any change would affect other parts of the system. Moreover, in time they also adopted Cuvier's view that if one had only a remaining portion of a system, such as a fossil, the entire system might be reconstructed. The view had a decisive effect on Grimm's treatment of the Germanic obstruents.

Bopp's monograph on the Sanskrit system of conjugation in comparison with that of Greek, Persian and Germanic (1816) scarcely needed a further model, based as it was on the tightly knit system of Sanskrit, as well as on the presentation of that system by Indian grammarians. He followed it up with a comparative grammar (1833) that went through various editions, the last published after his death (1866–74). Standard throughout his lifetime, it reflects the prime interest of this early period in its concentration on morphology.

Three years after Bopp's monograph appeared, Jacob Grimm (1785–1863) published the first volume of his grammar, which consisted entirely of morphology. He then came to know a delayed publication (1818) of Rasmus Rask (1787–1832). In it Rask listed phonological relationships between Greek and Old Norse words, such as *patér* : *faðir*. But his presentation was centered on individual sounds, not on classes of sounds. After seeing the work, Grimm redid his first volume (1822) and in it formulated the rules that set the pattern for scientific historical phonology. Of a somewhat different pattern from our rules today, they demonstrate the same rigor.

Greek	*Gothic*	*OHG*	*Greek*	*Gothic*	*OHG*	*Greek*	*Gothic*	*OHG*
P	F	B(V)	T	TH	D	K	–	G
B	P	F	D	T	Z	G	K	CH
F	B	P	TH	D	T	CH	G	K

The rules are followed by long lists of examples, in a procedure that should be observed today for any use of the comparative method. Of equal importance, Grimm enumerated "instances, when the proposed comparisons fail," among them forms with Sanskrit voiced aspirates and the word "father" with its Gothic D in *fadar* rather than the expected TH. In this way Grimm sought to account for all examples, first through rules, then in notes on problematic forms.

Besides noting Grimm's rigorous examination of the data, it is instructive to observe its shortcomings and the subsequent improvements on his procedures. Grimm's phonological classes put together sounds that are later distinguished, such as the fricatives and aspirates under the term *Aspiratae*. Phonetics was poorly developed; the word "letter" was used for the sound as well as the written symbol, though when scholars wished to distinguish sounds from symbols, the sound was described as a letter with power (*potestas*). But in spite of such shortcomings, the rules demonstrated the phonological interrelationships of the Indo-European languages as Bopp's had done for the verbal systems. A firm foundation had therefore been laid for Indo-European studies, which were then pursued vigorously.

Grimm ended his highly productive career by publishing, with his brother Wilhelm, the first volume of the massive dictionary of the German language (1854). It was finally completed, under a succession of editors, in 1954, and is now under revision.

While Bopp and Grimm produced the fundamental works in grammar, August Pott (1802–87) undertook a large-scale work on Indo-European etymology (1833–6); a later edition was published in 1859–76 in ten volumes. Though soon superseded, Pott's work is especially notable because of his emphasis on phonology. In the first part of the nineteenth century great improvements were being achieved in phonetics, thanks largely to physicians who were dealing with speech problems. Ernst Brücke published a number of works in the field, such as his "Investigations into the formation of sounds and the natural system of speech sounds" (1849); "Concerning the aspirates of ancient Greek and Sanskrit" (1858); "On the pronunciation of aspirates in Hindustani" (1859), "Concerning a new method of phonetic transcription" (1863), "The physiological basis of New High German metrics" (1871). The titles indicate how investigations in phonetics not only informed linguists like Pott, but also prepared the way for some of the most notable publications in historical linguistics, such as the articles of Grassmann and Verner.

2.4 INCREASING RIGOR, AS ILLUSTRATED IN ATTENTION TO THE GERMANIC OBSTRUENTS

Grimm's rules relating the obstruents in Germanic with those in the other Indo-European dialects had such an impact that they were soon named Grimm's law. They are still cited in desk dictionaries. But the exceptions remained a problem to be pursued.

The first to be solved was the lack of the shift of *p t k* after Germanic fricatives, as in Goth. *sparwa*, Gk *sparásion* "sparrow," Goth. *stains*, Gk *s̓ia* "stone," Goth. *skaþis* "damage," Gk *a-skēthḗs* "undamaged," Goth.

nahts, Gk *nuktós* (gen.) "night." It became clear to a number of linguists in the 1830s that the shift did not take place in consonant clusters after Germanic fricatives. The observation not only solved one set of exceptions; it alerted linguists to examine sounds in context, not merely individual entities.

The second set of exceptions to be solved concerned the aspirates. Here Hermann Grassmann (1809–77) pointed out that the exception was in Sanskrit and Greek, not Germanic (1862). If the exception was in Germanic, Goth. *bindan* should have had as cognates Skt **bhandh-* and Gk **phenth-*; instead, we find Skt *badh-náti* "binds" and Gk *pentherós* "father-in-law." Grassmann's law, which states that the first of two aspirates in successive syllables, or at the beginning and end of a syllable, loses its aspiration in Sanskrit and Greek, clarified the second exception.

Grassmann's article also demonstrated that Sanskrit should not be taken as equivalent to Proto-Indo-European, but that it had undergone major changes like the other Indo-European dialects. Grassmann's observation had the further consequence that now linguists examined entire words, not merely individual sounds or those contiguous to them.

The third set of exceptions concerned words like Goth. *fadar* which had a voiced rather than a voiceless fricative corresponding to *t* in the other dialects, such as Gk *patér*. Grimm had listed the Greek word, but paid no attention to the accent. Karl Verner (1846–96) in 1875 published an article in which he demonstrated that if Indo-European voiceless stops in voiced surroundings were not preceded by the accent, they became voiced fricatives.

Verner's article had a tremendous effect, possibly greater than any other that has been published in the field. As probably its most significant effect, it gave linguists confidence that, if they took all data into consideration, they could solve all problems.

As another effect, it alerted linguists to the importance of examining accent and other suprasegmental phenomena. After 1875 many articles were published in which complex sound changes were explained as the result of accent.

As a further effect, it led scholars to examine the metrical principles of older verse. A huge number of works now appeared on Germanic verse form, and on metrical conventions in the various early dialects, as well as in other languages. The brilliant phonetician, Eduard Sievers (1850–1932), for example, also concerned himself with verse form in ancient Hebrew.

After a half century of assembling and describing the data, the stage was now set for explaining linguistic phenomena. A number of brilliant young linguists in Leipzig formed a group that set out to deal with language in accordance with specific principles. Taunted by their elders as neogrammarians, they adopted the name. Subsequent linguistic study was largely shaped by them.

2.5 THE NEOGRAMMARIANS

Filled with confidence after the impressive articles of Grassmann and Verner, linguists who had been attracted to Leipzig for study under the distinguished philologist, Georg Curtius (1820–85), formulated principles that provided the guidelines for clarifying the Indo-European family, and thereupon other language families. Karl Brugmann (1849–1919) wrote the essay that set their course. August Leskien (1840–1916) did notable work especially in Slavic, while insisting even more strongly than Brugmann on the principles. Berthold Delbrück (1842–1922) was the syntactician in the group. Hermann Osthoff (1847–1909) collaborated closely with Brugmann, producing many impressive monographs, such as his on the Indo-European perfect. We will deal largely with Brugmann's essay, often called the neogrammarian manifesto, since it is one of the few statements in our field that should be known to every linguist. But first we may recall briefly the situation of the time.

Bopp's huge grammar had been superseded by a shorter, but more principled handbook by August Schleicher (1821–68). In his *Compendium* (1871) Schleicher attempted to apply the procedures of the natural sciences. In this effort he was strongly influenced by the ideas on evolution. These may have led him to the innovation of reconstructing forms for Proto-Indo-European. Although he carried out important fieldwork on Lithuanian, Brugmann and his colleagues thought that too much attention was being given at the time to dead languages. In his words, "languages were indeed investigated most eagerly, but the human being who speaks, much too little" (Lehmann 1967: 198) Whether or not this statement was also directed against Schleicher, some linguists consider him a direct precursor of the neogrammarians.

In his essay Brugmann sees language as having a twofold basis, psychological and physical. He criticized his predecessors for having too little regard for the psychological basis of speech, because only through such knowledge could one understand sound change. A psycholinguistic view of language like his is often credited to later movements. But we will see that Trubetzkoy in his fundamental work published sixty years after the manifesto made the same point as did Brugmann.

Moreover, in Brugmann's view the living languages of today needed to be studied if one wished to deal with those of the past. As one of his important points he required the "comparative linguist" to emerge from "the hypotheses-beclouded atmosphere of the workshop . . . and to step into the clear air of tangible reality and of the present" (Lehmann 1967: 202), a recommendation that is not without pertinence for later times.

Holding such a position he stated the "two most important principles of the neogrammarian movement: first, every sound change takes place according to laws that admit no exception. Second, form association, that is, the creation of new forms by analogy, plays a very important role in the life of language" (Lehmann 1967: 204).

These principles have often been stated differently, as that sound change takes place without exception. But since Brugmann insisted on the psychological basis of change, the "laws" for him control the inner form of language. Morphological and syntactic interrelationships can modify their working. He illustrated the interplay between the two principles briefly, in the short essay, insisting especially that analogy operated in the ancient languages as it does in those of today. The principles have at times been exaggerated; as applied by Brugmann, they led to outstanding monographs that are still important to know, and to his fundamental Indo-European grammar.

The grammar was undertaken in collaboration with Delbrück, who prepared the syntax, while Brugmann did the phonology and morphology (1886–1900). Delbrück had previously published a number of monographs on Sanskrit and Greek syntax, showing that these languages and accordingly Proto-Indo-European were verb final. Besides stating that fact unambiguously, he pointed out other OV characteristics, such as the use of postpositions rather than prepositions. His presentation differs from that of today, but is none the less clear; even so, some current scholars fail to accept his conclusions on the OV structure of the proto-language that were based on thorough knowledge of the early texts, and later verified by Hittite. Delbrück's syntax, published in three volumes from 1893 to 1900, is still a fundamental handbook.

The two authors came to disagree on the distribution of materials between morphology and syntax, so that Brugmann alone published the second edition (1897–1916). It is highly important to know the views underlying the handbook. In his preface Brugmann calls his approach "systematic" rather than historical; he states that the time is not yet ready for a historical presentation of Proto-Indo-European. Later scholars have often failed to read his handbook in accordance with its approach. In a sense the work is descriptive; it includes copious lists of the forms that occur. Since Brugmann was meticulous with his facts, the work has not been superseded and will not be, even though later discoveries, as of the Anatolian languages, have expanded our information.

In accordance with his systematic presentation, a large number of sounds are reconstructed for Proto-Indo-European, rather than the phonemic system we posit. Further discussion of his procedures would be important for Indo-Europeanists. Yet what is essential for our purposes here is awareness of his systematic position, and attention to his important monographs which unfortunately have not been made available in English translation.

While the linguists in Leipzig were clarifying many problems in Indo-European linguistics, Hermann Paul (1846–1921) in Munich produced the theoretical handbook of the period. His "Principles of historical linguistics" went through five editions from 1880 to the last in 1920, which has been reissued. Paul also laid great stress on psychology. By erroneous interpretation of its title, his "Principles" have often been assumed to be directed solely to diachronic study; rather, the term "historical" sciences corresponds to our terms "humanities, social and behavioral" sciences as opposed to the "ahistorical physical sciences." We have noted that scientists today use similar terminology in classifying the physical and chemical sciences as experimental, but geology, evolutionary biology and astronomy as historical. Linguistics clearly belongs with them, since language is constantly changing. Yet, with its attention to older languages, Paul's book may have concentrated too heavily on change. When the erstwhile student at Leipzig, Leonard Bloomfield (1887–1949), set out to write his book on language, he considered it a supplement to Paul's, with greater attention to descriptive linguistics.

The neogrammarians were immensely productive. They founded journals. They produced handbooks, as on Old English by Eduard Sievers (1850–1932). These follow the pattern set by the handbook on Gothic by Wilhelm Braune (1850–1926); many of the handbooks have been re-edited, none as often as Braune's *Gothic Grammar*, now in its nineteenth edition prepared by Ernst A. Ebbinghaus. They solved many problems, including the bases of Germanic alliterative verse. And they summed up their findings in "Grundrisse," not only Brugmann's, but also Paul's for Germanic, Bühler's for Indic, Geiger and Kuhn's for Avestan, Brockelmann's large comparative grammar for Semitic. These provide encyclopedic treatments of many topics besides linguistics. They are still worth consulting, especially those that have been brought up to date. Whether they have or not, the Grundrisse and large comparative grammars remain highly valuable handbooks.

2.6 FERDINAND DE SAUSSURE

If anyone in linguistics merits a separate section in this chapter, it is Ferdinand de Saussure (1857–1913). Born in a distinguished Swiss family, which produced outstanding members in different fields through numerous generations, Ferdinand de Saussure in 1876 entered the University of Leipzig, which was then the center of linguistic studies. There he published a distinguished monograph: *Mémoire sur le système primitif des voyelles dans les langues indo-européennes*. It appeared in December 1878, with the date 1879, causing bibliographical problems ever since. In the *Mémoire* Saussure treated roots algebraically, positing as canonical form for Proto-Indo-European C*e*C. The roots that did not fit had by his hypothesis lost elements, for example *ag-* "lead," (*s*)*tā-* "stand", *dō-* "give." The lost elements he called *sonantes coefficients*. The *Mémoire* was recognized as brilliant, but its most brilliant conclusion was not accepted until Kurylowicz in 1927 equated sounds transcribed with *h* in Hittite with

Saussure's *sonantes coefficients*. Saussure's hypothesis is one of the most remarkable in our field, a stunning application of the method of internal reconstruction.

When the *Mémoire* was published, Saussure was studying in Berlin. He then returned to Leipzig to take his doctor's degree with a dissertation on the use of the genitive absolute in Sanskrit. During the final examination he was reputedly asked whether he was a relative of the famous Saussure.

After taking his degree, he accepted a position at the Ecole des Hautes Etudes in Paris, 1881, where he stayed until he accepted a professorship at Geneva in 1891. His stay in Paris led to its replacing Leipzig as center of linguistic studies, largely through his impressive student, Antoine Meillet (1866–1936).

Saussure published relatively little. In 1907–11 he gave three series of lectures on general linguistics. Wilhelm Streitberg expressed in his obituary the hope that they would be published. Ill health suspended the lectures in 1912, and on 22 February in 1913 he died.

The lectures were indeed published as the *Cours de linguistique générale* (1916), and should be mastered by every student of linguistics. The publication is not without problems, for his students, Charles Bally and Sechehaye, had to merge the lectures and provide some kind of continuity. Subsequently a variorum edition has been published, putting Saussure on some kind of plane with Shakespeare in critical study. Through the detailed scholarship given the *Cours* it has been found that the often-cited conclusion of the book is due to his editors.

As virtually every student knows, Saussure viewed the underlying structure of language as an abstract social system. Using three French words, he refers to language in general as *langage*, to the underlying structure as *langue* and to spoken language as *parole*. In this way of looking at language he shifted away from the psychological emphasis of the neogrammarians.

The section on historical linguistics may be the weakest in the book. Saussure sited it in *parole*. It is indeed true that when pronunciations change, as for American English *bitter*, activity takes place in the speech. But it is now generally held that the real change is in the system, that is in the *langue*.

The *Cours* is credited with implanting structuralism in linguistics. Actually, it simply reaffirmed the structural position established by Schlegel and Cuvier. Its effect also is broader, extending to literary criticism and other humanistic as well as scientific pursuits. Oddly, the *Cours* was sketchily reviewed in the United States, by Bloomfield (1923). In partial justification for the lacklustre reception, the book was not brought into the USA for some years, thanks to the stupid blockade of publications after the First World War. When the *Cours* became available, the basic ideas were already well known. Numerous subsequent commentaries have made up for the original reception; of these, works by Roy Harris are to be especially commended.

2.7 A SOCIOLINGUISTIC APPROACH IN HISTORICAL LINGUISTICS

While the neogrammarians were concentrating on clarifying the Indo-European family, a great deal of fieldwork was being carried out. American linguists were studying the native languages of their continent, German linguists the languages of Africa and Russian linguists the languages of the Caucasus. Their findings had a great impact on linguistic theory. Close analysis of the phonological systems of Slavic languages led Jan N. Baudouin de Courtenay (1845–1929) and his student Mikolaj H. Kruszewski (1851–87) to the modern conception of the phoneme as a systematic element of language in contrast with the phonetic entities of speech.

Sociology was also developing. The French scholar, Durkheim, was especially influential. His effect on Meillet is clear in the lectures that Meillet gave to the newly established Institute for Comparative Research in Culture at Oslo in 1924. The institute itself, with its focus on work in the Caucasus, provides further evidence of the concern with the social background of language.

Meillet's compact Oslo lectures are another work that every linguist should know. Their tenor may be illustrated by a sentence in the introduction: "a language cannot be understood if we do not have an idea of the conditions under which the people who use it live" (1925 (1967): 10). We may recall that Brugmann made a similar statement in his manifesto; but his emphasis was on the individual, in keeping with the concentration at the time on psychology. Meillet was very specific in his requirements that linguists deal with a language with reference to the society of its speakers. Although a student of Saussure's, he stated: "what interests the linguist is not the norms but the way in which the language is used" (*ibid.*: 133). After pointing out a few different situations, and noting that "the French of the grammars and dictionaries is known," he goes on to say that French "is only a set of rules. What is important for the linguist is to know how the people who speak French behave in relation to the rules" (*ibid.*:134). It would be difficult to repudiate more directly the concentration on the inner form of language to the exclusion of speech.

Meillet was a great synthesizer, and also a skillful organizer. He published handbooks on virtually all the Indo-European languages, as well as his authoritative *Introduction à l'étude comparative des langues indo-européennes*; the eighth edition was produced by his outstanding student, Emile Benveniste, in 1937, the year after his death. In using his works, one notes that he preferred to avoid reconstruction. During his well-attended lectures he is said never to have pronounced a reconstructed form. The lectures attracted scholars from various countries. All of the outstanding linguistic group at Oslo, Marstrander, Sommerfelt, Morgenstierne, Vogt, Borgstrøm, Stang and Bergsland went to Paris to study with him. When promising French students came to him, he reportedly directed individuals towards fields that were inadequately staffed. Benveniste was groomed as his successor, and was highly productive in spite of severe personal misfortunes. He and linguists like Renou for Sanskrit, Chantraine for Greek, Ernout for Latin, Vendryès for Celtic, Fourquet for Germanic, and others, made Paris without question the center of linguistic studies between the two world wars. Besides their teaching, each of them produced outstanding works in their fields.

It is useful to contrast the works, such as the etymological dictionaries, produced in the neogrammarian tradition with those in the French tradition. As one example, Alois Walde's etymological dictionary of Latin concentrates on form; that by Ernout and Meillet, on the other hand, concentrates on examination of words and their meanings. In their preface the two authors state that they are not aiming to replace Walde's dictionary. Their own aim is to "clarify the words as they have been used from Indo-European to Latin, and not to limit themselves to linguistic dissection" (1967: vii).

Linguistics profited in having the two traditions. Some students, like the noted Celticist, Myles Dillon, were fortunate to study under each. The rest of us must resort to consulting the handbooks in each.

The Second World War and its disastrous causes unfortunately interfered with both the French and the German tradition. In the meantime, a somewhat different approach was being developed in Prague, assisted by two brilliant Russian scholars, Nikolai S. Trubetzkoy (1890–1938) and Roman Jakobson (1896–1982). The war also directed their influence, in great part, towards the United States.

2.8 TRUBETZKOY AND THE SYNTHESIS OF THE PSYCHOLOGICAL AND SOCIOLOGICAL BASIS OF LANGUAGE

After the Second World War the innovative developments in historical linguistics were prompted largely by theoretical research and by archaeological discoveries. The theoretical research examined much more closely than had been done the relationships between elements in language, beginning with work in phonology. The archaeological discoveries provided unexpected new materials, but also greatly improved understanding of archaeological finds as a result of the application of precise scientific techniques in their analysis and explanation.

The phonological advances were presented in the third work that every linguist should know: *Grundzüge der Phonologie* by N.S. Trubetzkoy (1939), translated as *Principles of Phonology*. Like Roman Jakobson, he came to be associated with the notable linguists in Prague. Among previous contributions of the Prague linguists was the application of formal principles to discourse. In the earlier linguistic tradition, discourse had been treated under stylistics or rhetoric, somewhat apart from linguistics. Mathesius and others had abolished the separation, and formalized discourse, without gaining a large following until recently, when work with indigenous languages demonstrated the need to assume a higher level of linguistic structure than syntax.

As Trubetzkoy's presentation in his important work indicates, he made the signal contribution of combining Saussure's social view of the system of language with the psychological view of the neogrammarians.

To illustrate the view of language by which he treated phonology, we point out that Trubetzkoy followed Saussure in distinguishing carefully between the **act of speech** and the **system of language**. The act of speech is in his terms always unique; the system of language, by contrast, is general and constant, shared by all members of a speech community. This view of language would apply to reconstructed languages like Proto-Indo-European as it does to Classical Greek and to modern languages.

Also following Saussure, Trubetzkoy distinguished between the **signifier** and the **signified**. In the act of speech the signified is a concrete communication. But in the system the signified consists of abstract phonological, morphological, syntactic, discourse and lexical rules. Similarly, the signifier in the act of speech is a concrete sound flow, while in the system of language it consists of rules by which the sounds are ordered. To provide an example at the phonological level, with which Trubetzkoy was chiefly concerned, we distinguish in our analysis the sound flow, or the phonetic aspect, by putting the segments we determine in brackets, for example for *cat* [kʰǽt⁼]; the raised *h* indicates aspiration before the stressed vowel, while the equal sign indicates its absence. The rules or phonemic aspect, on the other hand, we enclose in slant lines, indicating only the elements that signal meaningful contrasts, /kǽt/. The rules embody values; in common terminology, they carry meaning.

Moreover, the system of language is made up of several partial systems; in these, for example, the grammatical categories form a grammatical system, the semantic categories form semantic systems. Language, then, is viewed much as in the major historical presentations. Historical handbooks may limit themselves to treatment of only a few systems, usually the phonological and the morphological. But major treatments, such as Schwyzer's grammar of Greek and Leumann's of Latin, encompass syntax as well, and also stylistics, that is discourse.

As a last point we may cite from Trubetzkoy's packed introduction his recollection that for the first international congress of linguists in 1928 three Russian scholars called for a holistic point of view in the study of language, and an extension of the principles to historical as well as descriptive linguistics.

Of the many important topics in the *Grundzüge* we will deal only with the notion of **marking**. Trubetzkoy, like earlier linguists, considered phonemic entities to be determined by oppositions. Through oppositions, sounds are distinctive, that is, they are phonemic. For example, the initial /k/ of *cat* differs from the initial /p/ of *pat*, so that they are distinctive elements in English. In addition, both have aspiration in this position before an accented vowel; but the aspiration is nondistinctive and accordingly not phonemic. Kenneth Pike shortened the terms for this fundamental observation about language to *emic*, for example /k/, and *etic*, for example [kʰ]. He and followers have extended the observation to many social activities, such as eating practices and games.

Similarly, *bat* and *gat* have distinctive initial consonants, and accordingly /b g/ are phonemes in English. German is very similar to English in this respect, distinguishing between initial /p b k g/ as in *platt* "flat," *Blatt* "leaf," *Klatt*, a proper name, *glatt* "smooth." But when *b d g* stand finally in words, they are not voiced, so that the past tense of *geben* is *gab* [gaːp], the third singular of *werden* "become" is *wird* [virt], the singular form of *Tage* "days" is *Tag* [taːk]. In such a pair of phonemes that contrast directly, like /t d/, the entity with the feature that is lost in certain positions was labeled by Trubetzkoy as the **marked** element; that is to say, voicing of obstruents in German consists of an additional **mark**. The concept of **marking** was widely extended, and is considered one of the important theoretical contributions of recent linguistics.

The concept of marking applies to grammatical and lexical elements as well. We may take as example the alternative principal parts of *dive*: *dove*, *diven* vs. *dived*, *dived*. The two earlier forms are marked in much the same way as are the voiced obstruents in German; they have a formation that is more complex, and they are themselves being replaced by the regular forms. Similarly, Eng. *brother* has two plurals, *brothers* and *brethren*. The second has specialized meaning, as in its use for members of a closed group; accordingly, it is the marked member of the pair. Marked elements in morphology, syntax, the lexicon and throughout language have a special value or meaning, are found in fewer positions, or are less commonly used, and are often on the point of being replaced.

Trubetzkoy's career was cut short by his untimely death in 1938, but Jakobson came to be established in Cambridge, Massachusetts. There his influence continued until his death.

Jakobson's ideas were especially influential on the generative movement. Besides the concept of marking, he introduced the use of distinctive features rather than entire phonemes. As we will see in chapter 10, statements of rules in distinctive features are much more precise than are the rules stated in phonemes. The term "generative" in the view of its chief exponent, Noam Chomsky, means explicit. Chomsky has also indicated that since a grammar should be totally explicit, the term generative grammar is a tautology. By identifying types of relationship in language, as through marking, and the specific components of sounds that are modified in change, the generative movement added greater precision to both the events and the processes in the life of language, reaffirming, as Trubetzkoy and Brugmann had done, the basic principles of the founders of historical linguistics.

2.9 TYPOLOGY AND HISTORICAL LINGUISTICS

In one of his last articles Trubetzkoy discussed the optimum phonological structure of an international auxiliary language, such as Esperanto. Examining languages like Chinese with no *r* in contrast with *l*, and Japanese with no *l* in contrast with *r*, he proposed among other suggestions that only one liquid be included in the phonological system of an auxiliary language. Among the numerous implications of the article we note only that in it Trubetzkoy applied typological findings to an area in which they had been disregarded. For Esperanto and other international languages simply took over the phonological systems of European languages, that is to say, the systems of speakers for whom such languages are needed far less than for speakers in Asia and Africa.

A second challenging article, "Thoughts about the Indo-European problem" (1939b), suggested that Proto-Indo-European was an amalgam of languages, not a language like Latin from which the various Romance languages developed, but rather one formed like a creole when distinct groups merged into a unified society. This article selected six typological characteristics of Proto-Indo-European, all of which are shared by neighboring languages. In short, it employed typological findings in grammar, using results of typological studies to solve a historical problem.

As we noted of the eighteenth and earlier centuries, typology has a long background in linguistics, but it was overwhelmed by the massive historical interest following Bopp and Grimm. Its disregard resulted in spite of the high standing of Wilhelm von Humboldt (1767–1835), one of its principal proponents. His most notable publication, "On the structural variety of human language and its influence on the intellectual development of mankind" (1836), sets out to examine the various types of languages in relation to their speakers. For Humboldt language "possesses only an ideal existence in the heads and spirits of men, never a material one" (in Lehmann 1967: 63) – that is, he is concerned with inner form.

His treatise proposes generalizations, such as the following:

No one can deny that Chinese of the old style carries an impressive dignity through the fact that only weighty concepts join one another directly, and in this way it attains a simple greatness by seeming to escape to pure thought through speech in discarding all unnecessary secondary relationships. The real Malay is not unjustly praised because of its ease and the great simplicity of its constructions. The Semitic languages preserve an admirable art of fine distinctions of meaning through many vowel gradations. Basque possesses in its word formation and in its constructions a special strength which proceeds from brevity and boldness of expression. Delaware and other American languages combine into a single word a number of concepts, for the expression of which we would need many.

(*ibid.*: 66)

While such characterizations may be admirable, they are not formal enough for application to historical developments. By contrast, some nineteenth-century linguists assumed a progression from analytic languages like Chinese to synthetic languages like Delaware in the course of language development. Since others proposed the reverse, the assumptions were not revealing. The prime concern of nineteenth-century typologists was understandably morphology, as we see in chapter 5; but it yielded little gain for historical study of language in view of the lack of inclusion of syntactic characteristics.

On the other hand, the systematization of phonology was highly useful in understanding change, as we note in chapter 10. Equally important has been the systematization of syntax. Greenberg in an important article of 1963 pointed out that verb-final languages also have postpositions, thus linking the two constructions and others through the role of government. Further, that they have preposed relative clauses, genitives and adjectives, linking the three constructions and others through the role of modification or agreement.

The series of observations in the article proved to be highly important for the historical study of syntax. Old English poems and other early material have postpositions and other residues of verb-final typology. These residues were gradually lost. We can conclude that English was developing from a verb-final language to a language in which verbs precede objects, that is, from OV to VO structure. When we find a similar situation in other Indo-European language groups like Indic, Greek, Italic and so on, we conclude that Proto-Indo-European was a verb-final language. Typology in this way assists us in explaining many constructions in the older stages of the language, and in reconstructing the syntax as well as the morphology and phonology of the language.

As we will see below, further insights from typology were provided through the increasing understanding of active–stative languages. Applied prominently in the large-scale grammar of Proto-Indo-European by Gamkrelidze and Ivanov (1984), the understanding clarifies many problems in the proto-language and permits more secure reconstruction of Pre-Indo-European.

2.10 HISTORICAL LINGUISTICS TODAY

As we noted above, archaeological investigations provided important new materials for historical linguists from about the beginning of this century. Excavations in Boğaz-köy (Boghazköy), a hundred miles east of Ankara,

Turkey, uncovered large amounts of cuneiform tablets, many of them in Hittite. In Chinese Turkestan Tocharian materials were discovered in caves. On Crete tablets were discovered that were long undeciphered; the two different writing systems were simply labeled Linear A and Linear B. Similar finds were made for other language families, such as the Semitic. The excavations at Ras Shamra and at Ebla have yielded many contributions to Semitic linguistics. Similarly, the prehistoric inscriptions found at Banpo as well as materials excavated at other sites in China have brought new excitement to early Chinese studies. Many of the finds cut across linguistic boundaries, such as the tokens that have illuminated the development of writing. In the course of time these discoveries have modified considerably our views of the early periods of these languages.

There have been so many recent advances that we can cite only some examples. The discovery of Hittite provided evidence that the coefficients that Saussure postulated in 1879 were actual sounds in the language. Labeled laryngeals, their identification by Kurylowicz in 1927 has greatly modified the phonological and also the morphological system that has been proposed for Proto-Indo-European.

The Linear B script was deciphered in the 1950s by Ventris, using code-breaking principles that he learned in the Second World War. The language concerned proved to be Greek. The tablets have made available Greek from 1450 BC, a date proposed for some Vedic poems, but otherwise no other Indo-European language material except for some Old Hittite texts. Our earliest previous Greek texts were the Homeric poems, established in their current form three-quarters of a millennium later. Although Mycenaean Greek is written in a syllabic script, poorly designed for an Indo-European language, the texts have been valuable for both historical Greek and Indo-European studies.

The discovery of Tocharian led to a revised view of the dialect divisions of Proto-Indo-European. Located far to the east, Tocharian maintained velars that had become sibilants in Baltic, Slavic, Albanian, Armenian and Indo-Iranian; earlier it had been assumed that there was an isogloss between western and eastern Indo-European. It now became clear that the change of velars to sibilants represented a sound change that extended over only a portion of the Indo-European sphere.

When we turn to other language families, we find the specialists applying the same principles as have the Indo-Europeanists. Some of the efforts may be examined in the collection of papers presented in 1987, and now published in *Linguistic Change and Reconstruction Methodology* (Baldi 1990). The papers deal with six groups: American Indian languages (pp. 17–129), Austronesian languages (pp. 133–267), Indo-European languages (pp. 271–390), Australian languages (pp. 391–472), Altaic languages (pp. 479–561), Afro-Asiatic languages (pp. 565–721). Students will have to consult the work in pursuit of their interests, because further review here would require too much space. The book provides an opportunity to see what specialists in these languages consider the current state of their field, its problems and possibilities for research, which are many. Yet many groups have not been included.

Important among these is Sino-Tibetan, the family that with Afro-Asiatic and Indo-European has written texts extending over more than three millennia. Selected statements may illustrate the state of research in each. Stephen J. Lieberman's summary report states that "reconstruction of the Afro-Asiatic phylum has been considerably more successful in finding cognate structure-words and syntactic usages and historical developments than it has been in producing an agreed list of reconstructible root morphemes" (Baldi 1990: 570). Jerry Norman, by contrast, states that

> a Chinese–Tibetan–Burmese affinity is unassailable, yet surprisingly little has been done in the field of Sino-Tibetan linguistic comparison. The phonological correspondences between Chinese and Tibeto-Burman have never been worked out in detail; and until this is done, comparative work cannot really get off the ground.
>
> (1988: 13)

These remarks may illustrate that for in-depth study of a language family, including a grammar of the proto-language with lexicon and information on the culture of its speakers, we have only the Indo-European family.

A large work, significantly entitled *Indo-European and the Indo-Europeans*, by Thomas Gamkrelidze and V. V. Ivanov (1984), has been available with such information for about a decade; the excellent translation into English by Johanna Nichols will make the work more widely accessible. The distribution of pages – 368 pages for the grammar and approximately 600 for the lexicon and data on culture – gives some idea of the attention to the authors' concern for Brugmann's recommendation to investigate "the human being who speaks" as well as the language.

That concern is also evident in a large number of works by archaeologists. These must seek to determine the earliest locations of the speakers – their so-called home or homeland. Varying views on the homeland of the Indo-Europeans have attracted a great deal of attention, also in the general media. In his book, *Archaeology and Language: The Puzzle of Indo-European Origins* (1987), Colin Renfrew associated the spread of the Indo-Europeans with the spread of agriculture, and accordingly placed their homeland in central Turkey. But the association is not necessary; Americanists have shown that the spread of corn-based agriculture from Mexico to the north did not involve the introduction of new languages.

By an alternative view, proposed by Schrader and others in the nineteenth century, the homeland was in south Russia. This view has been strongly advocated by Marija Gimbutas, who established the name *kurgan culture* for the way of life of early speakers of the Indo-European languages. J. P. Mallory supports the south Russian location in his book: *In search of the Indo-Europeans: Language, Archaeology and Myth* (1989).

Moreover, David W. Anthony has found the earliest evidence for the use of bridles for horses in south Russia; the horse was central for transportation in the Indo-European economy and also in its religious rites. Cultural evidence, as well as evidence for association with other language families, such as the Finno-Ugric, supports Schrader's position.

While such matters are proposed, much study remains in order to establish greater certainty. Archaeological investigations are yielding new information. Some of this has been interpreted, such as Denise Schmandt-Besserat's discovery of the origin of writing in the use of tokens. Tokens are first attested in strata dated around 8000 BC, at the time of the origin of agriculture. Following the increasing sophistication of their use to the first writing system in the Middle East is of great interest, with many implications that need to be investigated. Prominent among these is the question of single or multiple origin of writing in the ancient world, especially whether the Chinese hit on the idea of writing through information from the Middle East.

While specialists in the various language families are attempting to determine more precisely the grammar, lexicon and culture of proto-languages dated around 5000–3000 BC, other scholars are attempting to relate these language families, deriving the proto-languages from one at 10,000 BC or earlier. The major such attempt seeks to reconstruct *Nostratic*, the assumed mother tongue of Indo-European, Afro-Asiatic, Uralic and still other families. In their attempt, Nostraticists apply a weakened form of the comparative method. Unlike Grimm, they do not account for possible cognates in every language; nor do they list exceptions.

Joseph Greenberg has pursued a somewhat similar procedure in deriving virtually all the languages of America from *Amerind*. Yet his aim is classification, not reconstruction. None the less, his working procedures and conclusions have been vigorously criticized, as in papers of Baldi's edited collection (1990).

Whatever the efforts and conclusions of individual scholars, historical linguistics today is vigorous, favored with many problems and hopeful of solutions, especially when further information is discovered. For useful work and contributions, students must be thoroughly grounded in writing systems, methods of classification and principles of change throughout the systems of language. Having acquired such competence, they will find many opportunities to apply it and provide still further advances.

SELECTED FURTHER READINGS

Otto Jespersen's *Language* (1922: 19–99) includes a compact history of linguistic science. Important publications by the major linguists are available in English translation in Lehmann (1967). Like Pedersen's work, it is out of print, and must be consulted in libraries. Complete works by the major early historical linguists have been reprinted, with full introductions, in a series edited by Konrad Koerner. The first volume contains Friedrich Schlegel's *Über die Sprache und Weisheit der Indier* (1977). Sebeok (1966) provides a convenient avenue for information on the major figures through the reprinted obituaries published in it. While not devoted to historical linguistics, Harris and Taylor (1989) include brief informative essays on major figures and problems, such as "The Bible on the origin and classification of language" (pp. 35–45).

PROBLEMS

1 In the dialogue *Cratylus*, Socrates makes the following statement about the source (etymology) of the Greek word for "man."

> The name "human being" (*ánthrōpos*) indicates that the other animals do not examine, or consider, or look up at (*anathreî*) any of the things that they see, but the human being has no sooner seen – that is, *ópōpe* – than he looks at and considers that which he has seen. Therefore of all the animals the human being alone is rightly called human being (*ánthrōpos*), because he looks up at (*anathreî*) what he has seen (*ópōpe*).

Hjalmar Frisk in his Greek etymological dictionary states that no widely agreed etymology for *ánthrōpos* has been given, but he cites six suggestions, of which we note the following: 1) from **andr-ōp-os* "equipped with human sight" (cf. optical); 2) from **andr-hōpos* "with human appearance"; 3) from *anthr(o)-ōpos* "with bearded face."

Compare the procedures of Plato and Frisk, as well as the differing views of "etymology" represented by them.

2 Varro in *De lingua latina* gives etymologies, such as the following in V.99:

> Pecore ovillo quod agnatus, agnus. Catulus a sagaci sensu et acuto, ut Cato Catulus; hinc canis: nisi quod ut tuba ac cornu, aliquod signum cum dant, canere dicuntur, quod his item et noctulucus in custodia et in venando signum voce dat, canis dictus.

> "Because it is born to the flock of sheep, [it is called] *agnus* 'lamb.' A *catulus* 'puppy' [is so named] from its smart and acute sense, like [the names] *Cato, Catulus*; from it [is derived] *canis* 'dog'; unless, just as the tuba and horn, when they give some signal, are said to *canere* 'sing,' so it (*canis*) also gives a signal with its voice in guarding night and day, and in hunting, [and therefore] is named *canis* 'dog.'"

2.1 Discuss the procedures by which Varro determines etymologies, comparing them with the procedures used by Plato.

2.2 We derive agnus from PIE **ogʷhnos*, which has reflexes in Gk *amnós* "lamb" and OIr *ūan* "sheep"; a related verb is found in OE

ēanian, NE *yean* "to give birth to a lamb." Moreover, while the etymology of *catulus* "young animal" is not agreed on, the word is not from the base of *Cato*, i.e. *catus* "sharp";
A cognate is ON *haðna* "young goat." Similarly, *canis* is cognate with Greek *kúōn*, Sanskrit *śván-*, Old Irish *cū*, E. *hound*, and is not at all related to *canere* "sing." Discuss our advantage over Varro in having related languages to consult when providing etymologies.
What lesson may be drawn from Varro's failed procedures for mass comparison?

3 In his manifesto Brugmann discusses at some length views on analogy, saying among other things:

> Many believe that analogical formations arise principally in those stages of a language in which "feeling for the language" has "degenerated" or, as one also says, in which "the awareness of language has grown dim"; and thus they believe that one cannot expect analogical formations in the older periods of a language to the same extent as in the later. A strange way of looking at things!

(a) Examining some analogical formations in your language, for example Eng. *hardware*, *software*, *courseware*, comment on Brugmann's view as well as that of the linguists he is criticizing.

(b) In Brugmann's day some linguists still assumed that language was deteriorating, so that current forms in language were less natural than those of the past. Discuss such issues in relation to our views concerning language in change or in modification through analogy.

4 When dealing with sound change in the *Cours*, Saussure insisted that every word has only one reflex. Reviewing a possible exception, Lat. *collocāre* "to place" that is etymon of both French *coucher* "lay down" and *colloquer* "to collocate," he accepted *coucher* as the only reflex, accounting for *colloquer* as a learned borrowing.

(a) Discuss implications of this view for historical study. Which reflex of Lat. *vinum* in English would you identify as the reflex, *wine* or *vine*?

(b) In treating other examples, for example Lat. *cathedra* "chair" versus Fr. *chaire* "throne" and *chaise* "chair," he accounted for *chaise* as a dialect form. What are the implications of this procedure for reconstruction of a proto-language like Proto-Indo-European?

(c) As another example he sees Fr. *moi* "me" as the reflex of Lat. *mē*, treating Fr. *me* as a reflex of unstressed Latin *mē*. What effects would reconstruction of stressed and unstressed forms have for a proto-language?

3 The use of written records

3.1 THE IMPORTANCE OF UNDERSTANDING WRITING SYSTEMS AND THEIR TRANSLITERATION

Materials of concern in historical linguistics are available primarily through written records called **texts**. In order to interpret texts adequately, historical linguists must be equipped to deal with the writing systems used to record them, even though the texts are generally presented in transliteration. Transliterations, however, are often inadequate, occasionally even inaccurate; Gk φ, *phi*, θ, *theta*, χ, *khi*, as here, are transliterated with two symbols and, therefore, in transliteration lack parallelism with other Greek consonants, such as *p b t d k g*, even though they are quite parallel with them in Greek writing and phonology. Similarly, Skt *bh dh gh* are the traditional transliterations for writing symbols quite parallel to those for Skt *p t k*, etc. Yet for both Greek and Sanskrit the compound symbols are thoroughly installed and accordingly retained.

The transliteration for Sanskrit aspirated stops has introduced into historical linguistics the further inconvenience of two symbols for some single phonemes in Proto-Indo-European. Such troublesome transliterations can even become misleading to one who does not know their background. We cannot expect revisions that will remove such transliterational shortcomings, for the relatively few historical linguists are expected to have enough energy to master oddities in transliteration.

The glottalic theory has, however, introduced revised symbols for the Proto-Indo-European obstruents. These vary among proponents of the theory; some substitute d^h etc. for former *dh*, while using *d'* etc. to indicate the assumed glottalics. It will be interesting to observe the fate of the newly introduced symbols. In the past, historical linguists have persistently rejected most attempts to modify transliterations, on the grounds that such modifications would complicate the use of older handbooks. Thus, one of the first tasks in historical linguistics is to master the writing systems of languages under discussion, and also their standard transliterations.

In addition, historical linguists must understand the principles underlying writing systems. For, in spite of considerable investigation, the interpretation of some symbols, even in languages as thoroughly studied as Gothic, is still disputed. And new writing systems may be encountered, such as those discovered in Crete and now partially deciphered, or that discovered in Harappa, Mohenjo-Daro and other sites in the Indus Valley, for which decipherments have been proposed though not accepted. By following the development of the English writing system, we can observe the principles of development in writing generally, and some of the problems we face in dealing with texts.

Moreover, the discovery of the origin of writing in the last two decades has provided important new evidence on the development of civilization, and the increasing complexity of early society. Correlating this new evidence with early languages and the societies that maintained them provides some of the most interesting topics for research in historical linguistics. Many of these topics will require investigation for some time to come, as may be evident in the brief treatment that can be included here.

3.2 THE ORIGIN OF WRITING SYSTEMS

For some time archaeologists in the Middle East have been finding in their excavated sites small clay figures of various shapes: cones, cylinders, disks, spheres and so on. The purpose of the figures remained mysterious until Denise Schmandt-Besserat concluded on the basis of some similarities with the earliest Sumerian writing system that they represented materials, such as grains, oil and sheep (1992). That is to say, the figures were devised to record economic possessions. She labeled the figures "tokens," a name that has been generally adopted.

Through dating of the layers in which tokens are found, the earliest are placed at about 8000 BC, the period of transition between hunting–gathering and farming cultures. Villages in the Fertile Crescent (e.g. Syria, Iraq, Iran) of the period provide evidence of cereal cultivation and of trade, as of obsidian for cutting tools. As the economic situation of early societies developed, the tokens became more complex. We also have evidence of the increased complexities in social life of the time through the establishment of cities centered around temples. We learn about the life of the time through representations within the temples; among other scenes these picture citizens bringing goods to the temple, presumably as a kind of tax. The increasingly complex societies apparently required more precise accounting, which led to the production and use of a wide number of tokens.

The tokens were small, less than a half inch in extent. Apparently to avoid the problem that some might be lost for given transactions, spherical envelopes made of the ubiquitous clay were formed late in the fourth millennium to contain them. When baked or even dried in the sun, the envelopes, like the tokens, were virtually indestructible. Yet the envelopes provided a new problem by concealing the types of tokens contained in them. Thereupon the users hit on the idea of impressing the contained tokens on the outside of the envelopes before the moist clay hardened, so that the contents might be known without breaking the envelopes. In addition to such impressions, figures were drawn on the clay containers with a stylus.

Around 3200 BC a further innovation was introduced. It became clear that, rather than both tokens and inscribed envelopes, clay tablets alone might be inscribed. For example, the complex token of a sphere with a plus mark on it represented a sheep; rather than the token, or the impressed token, the symbol itself was inscribed on the tablet. Other shapes were less abstract, such as that for an arrow. The word for arrow in Sumerian was TI (transcription practice requires roman capital letters for Sumerian, italicized capital letters for Akkadian, and lower case for symbols representing Hittite and other languages making use of cuneiform, as well as for syllabic values). When the symbols were inscribed on tablets, the resultant documents consisted of signs standing for words rather than for the tokens. A logographic writing system had evolved.

Further developments followed in short order. Rather than simply arrays of symbols for nouns, devices were introduced to represent speech, that is, inflections and the like. As later in Japan, specific logograms were selected and used for their phonetic value. For example, the symbol for arrow was also used to represent the syllable *ti*. Sumerian is agglutinative. The syllabic values were used to write inflected syllables.

As a second development, the number of symbols was kept within limits. It is possible to have pictures for virtually all objects; the Chinese writing system is said to include almost 50,000 stylized pictures, generally referred to as characters. But an individual can memorize only a few thousand of them, and that with some effort; currently, steps are being taken to limit the number of characters used in Chinese and Japanese newspapers to fewer than 2,000. To retain more of them in memory even specialists have to write several thousand daily. In order to limit the number of such symbols, logographic systems, including the Chinese, make use of the rebus principle; a number of homophones may be represented by the same symbol. As an example, the word for "life" in Sumerian also was pronounced TI. The logogram for "arrow" was then used to represent "life" as well as "arrow." In this way, approximately 700 logograms were introduced to represent the Sumerian language.

Systems for the representation of speech were developed in this way and through these stages. Such systems were also taken over and adapted by societies speaking quite different languages. In the course of adaptation, systems were simplified. Symbols were reduced in complexity in order to speed up writing. Furthermore, specific symbols were devised for numerals. While it was cumbersome by our standards, the writing system devised for Sumerian represented an important advance in the development of civilization. Its usefulness cannot have escaped other societies. We have inadequate information to determine whether the invention of the Sumerians inspired those of the Egyptians and the Chinese, the two other early societies that developed writing systems. It is fairly certain that the Egyptians learned of the notion of writing in this way; Chinese scholars, on the other hand, favor independent origin for the Chinese system.

However early societies introduced writing, our knowledge of their languages must be attributed to the development of writing. The successive further stages in refinement of writing provides improved information on the languages concerned, as we indicate below. Adoption of specific writing systems also indicates language contacts. Accordingly, it is important for the historical study of language to be informed of the writing systems used for specific languages and of adaptations made to them.

In human history only three writing systems have been devised that have gone through a long series of development and adaptation for various languages: those of Egypt, Sumer and China. Each provides data on the interrelationship of writing and speech. The Egyptian system was developed most extensively and used most widely. Accordingly, we will present its history more fully than the others.

3.3 DEVELOPMENT OF THE EGYPTIAN WRITING SYSTEM

The earliest Egyptian texts we know, from the latter part of the fourth millennium BC, already show the features of an advanced writing system. This consists of approximately 500 symbols, known as **hieroglyphs** – sacred symbols, because the scribes were priests. Many of the symbols are pictorial representations of the object represented by the word they stand for; a representation of a head stands for *tp* "head"; a representation of a hand stands for *drt* "hand"; a representation of a lotus stands for *sšn* "lotus." (Vowels were left undesignated by the Egyptians whenever they used their semi-alphabetic system. Although Egyptologists have been able to determine the vowels of many words through comparative study, the transcriptions of hieroglyphs generally do not indicate them.)

Other hieroglyphs are less directly related to the words they stand for. A representation of a seated man with his hand at his mouth stands for *wnm* "eat"; a representation of a falcon may stand for *nsw* "king." Hieroglyphs may therefore represent words for actions or abstractions as well as for physical objects. Since they represent words rather than ideas, the term **logogram** is more appropriate than the formerly used terms **pictogram** or **ideogram**. The symbols themselves we describe as **logographic**.

A further characteristic use of hieroglyphs supports this designation. Some homophones came to be indicated by the same hieroglyph, on the rebus principle. The word for "ten thousand" *db'*, for example, was a homophone of the word for "finger" and was represented by the symbol for "finger."

In a further development, some hieroglyphs came to be used for just two

consonants, because one of the consonants of a word was lost by phonological change. Other words may always have consisted of two consonants.
For example, the word for "a swallow" (bird) was *wr*; this also came to be
used for *wr* "large" and as a partial representation of longer words such as
wrd "be weary." As a result of losses of further consonants, some hieroglyphs came to stand for words with only one consonant. The symbol for
"belt" represented *s*, that for "water" *n*, and so on. In this way twenty-four
such symbols came to represent one-consonant syllables. Their use illustrates the furthest development of the hieroglyphic system within Egypt.
To the time of its abandonment around the beginning of our era, the
Egyptian writing system maintained its full panoply of hieroglyphs, some
of which represented syllables, others words.

Although not directly pertinent in the study of the development of our
writing system, it is of interest to observe that a cursive script was developed early. When writing systems are used in everyday activities, writers
find it difficult to maintain elegance and clarity of representation. Widespread use and rapidity of writing as well as choice of writing materials are
responsible for many changes in the outward shapes of symbols.

Egyptians were no exception; very early they developed a cursive system
known as **hieratic**. It gave rise to another, more abbreviated system,
known as **demotic**. The symbols of both hieratic and demotic are quite
different from the handsome hieroglyphs usually depicted in handbooks
and often seen on Ancient Egyptian monuments.

3.4 THE GREEK DEVELOPMENT OF THE EGYPTIAN WRITING SYSTEM

It has long been suspected that our alphabet is an offshoot of the Egyptian
writing system. At the end of the first century AD, Tacitus stated this view
in his *Annals*, 11.14:

> The Egyptians first represented concepts by means of animal figures;
> these oldest monuments of human memory may still be seen engraved in
> stone. They claim to be the inventors of writing. From them the
> Phoenicians are said to have brought the script to Greece because they
> ruled the seas, and they received the credit for inventing what they only
> took over.

Tacitus in this statement maintained the position of earlier historians,
among them Herodotus; in Book 5, section 58 of his *History* he also says
that the Phoenicians brought "letters" to Greece.

Yet the link between the Western Semitic (Tacitus' Phoenician) and the
hieroglyphic system was unknown. In 1904–5 the archaeologist Flinders
Petrie found sixteen inscriptions in the copper and malachite mines of
Sinai, which Alan H. Gardiner later deciphered. These provided a link
between the hieroglyphs and the Phoenician system; they also showed how

the West Semitic twenty-two-syllable system, like the twenty-four-syllable system of the Egyptians, was based on hieroglyphs. Later West Semitic writing systems, like that maintained for Hebrew, modified the forms of symbols; but essentially the system remained syllabic, although symbols could be added to specify vowels. To understand some of the modifications, one must remember that the Semitic users of the symbols, and later the Greeks, were not consistent in placing the symbols. Some symbols were reversed, leading to a completely different appearance from those of the Egyptians.

Further modifications of shape were introduced when the Semitic system was borrowed by the Greeks, probably at the end of the ninth century or beginning of the eighth BC. At first, the Greeks wrote either from right to left, like the Semitic peoples, or from left to right, or both alternately (**boustrophedon** = like an ox in ploughing). Some symbols came to be reversed from their original form, for example, *B*. The ultimate shape of our alphabet was not fixed until the Latins took it over. Yet the essential modification of the Greeks was the conversion of the syllabic system of the Semites to an alphabetic system, and the introduction of symbols for vowels.

In naming the symbols, the Semites and Greeks used the **acrophonic** principle. The second symbol of the alphabet was called *beta* by the Greeks, after its Semitic name, see Hebrew *beth* "house"; the third *gamma*, see Hebrew *gimel* "corner"; and so on. The first symbol stood for ?, see Heb. ?*aleph* "ox," a consonant not found in Greek. When Greeks took over its name as *alpha*, it began with *a* rather than with a consonant phoneme. Accordingly, they used it to represent a vowel rather than a consonant. The symbols for *e* and *o* developed similarly from consonantal symbols in which the initial consonant was lost. A further symbol, *i*, which to the Semitic users represented a vowel as well as a consonant, was used solely as a vowel by the Greeks; the equivalent consonantal element had been lost in Greek. In this way the Greeks made the contribution of adding vowel symbols to the alphabet. This advance in writing systems has never been independently duplicated, nor have writing systems developed beyond it.

For a more complete representation of speech, symbols for stress, pitch and pauses are essential. Accent symbols were also developed and used by the Greeks in Alexandria. The use of accents did not, however, gain general currency; they were not adopted for the writing of Latin, nor for the writing systems devised for the various European languages. Only in modern times have linguists introduced them in systems of transcription, to bring about the remaining essential of an accurate writing system.

Other modifications introduced by the Greeks are of interest, though not of fundamental importance to understanding the structure of the alphabet. Among these are introduction of symbols for open *e* and *o* beside those for *epsilon* and *omikron* (close *e* and *o*). In Ionic Greek, *h* was not pronounced; the symbol for it, *H*, was taken over for *eta*, open *e*, comparing with the symbol *E* for close *e*. An open Ω for *omega* was introduced beside *O*. These modifications illustrate the Greek readiness to adapt the alphabet for representation of their language.

The Greeks introduced four additional characters to the Semitic set of symbols, those for *upsilon*, *phi*, *khi* and *psi*. We do not know the sources for these. *Upsilon* and *khi* may have been taken over from symbols in the syllabary of Cyprus. The discovery that Linear B was used to write Greek from as early as 1450 BC and our increasing knowledge of early Greek culture may help us to answer such problems in the development of the Greek alphabet.

3.5 OFFSHOOTS OF THE WEST SEMITIC AND GREEK WRITING SYSTEMS

There are other important offshoots of the West Semitic syllabary, each with various developments: Aramaic, with developments leading to Pehlevi; Syrian, with developments like Mongol and Manchu; and the Arabic writing system. All of these introduced vocalic writing only late. Another, the Indic **Brāhmī**, from which developed **Devanāgari** and many other south Asian scripts, remained syllabic, though the indication of specific vowels was obligatory.

Based directly on Greek were, among others, the Gothic system, developed in the fourth century, and the two Slavic systems, the **Cyrillic** and **Glagolitic**, both of the ninth century. Cyrillic was based on majuscules, capitals; Glagolitic probably on minuscules, small letters. Cyrillic is the system used for Russian. It has been adapted for a wide array of other Slavic languages, and also for non-Slavic languages in the former Soviet Union.

The Greek alphabet was most widely extended through the Latin. It was transmitted to the Romans by the Etruscans. In Etruscan the voiced : voiceless distinction between *g* : *k* was not made; accordingly, the third letter of the alphabet came to stand for [k], as it still does in English before *a o u*, as in *cat, cot, cut*. Modifications of the alphabet by the Romans were slight; the most important is the introduction of a modified *C* for the *G* sound.

Another modification is of interest in illustrating the dual function of the alphabet to represent numerals as well as sounds. In Greek the letters also stood for numerals, the first nine for the simple digits; the next nine, beginning with *i*, stood for "ten" to "ninety"; the last nine, beginning with *r*, for "hundred" to "nine hundred". This numerical function required maintenance of the same order when the system was adopted by others, such as the Goths. But the Latin speakers had a distinct set of signs that has been maintained as the set of Roman numerals.

Three symbols of the Roman numeral system, I V X, apparently had their origin in gesture-like signs; I represented a single finger, V one hand, X both hands. Other symbols maintained the Greek numerals, though the sounds associated with them were not needed; ↓ or ⊥ for "fifty" (Gk *khi*); ⊙, ⊂ for "hundred" (Gk *theta*);⊕ , M for "thousand" (Gk *phi*). The source of these eventually became unclear, and they were replaced by the letters *L C M*, which we use today when writing Roman numerals. A fourth of the higher Roman numerals, *D* for "five hundred," represents half of ⊕.

Maintenance of the symbols for their numerical use when not needed for sounds had a further result. When the Gothic alphabet was devised, the symbol for "six" did not correspond to a Gothic sound. Quite arbitrarily, the originator, presumably Wulfila, used it for the value [kw]. Accordingly, the numerical value of the symbol was primary; its value as a sound was determined by Wulfila.

Modifications of the alphabet after its use for Latin are superficial. With the breaking up of the Roman Empire, various "national hands" were developed in its political subdivisions. These differ slightly in form from region to region. A ready example survives today for Irish.

Cursives were also introduced. The study of these is the subject of **palaeography** and is not of direct concern to linguistics; palaeography, however, is essential to linguists dealing with medieval texts.

When scripts came to be too troublesome and unclear, reforms were introduced. The most important of these was the Carolingian, of about 800 AD. Its importance results from the prestige that the Carolingian script enjoyed at the time printing was introduced in Europe. The favored form of letters was the Carolingian minuscule; our printed fonts continue this form today. Other modifications, the selection of varying forms of *I* to stand for *I* and *J*, and *U* to stand for *U* and *V*, and the formation of *W*, introduced no new principles. Our alphabet today is not very different from the Latin.

Extensive modifications had been introduced in scripts for Germanic and Celtic languages, the bases of which are not wholly clear. The Germanic **runes**, based in part on a north Italian development of the alphabet, differ in order and purpose. The old runic alphabet contained twenty-four symbols, three series of eight, arranged probably according to a magical principle. The first six symbols of the first series are well known, through the name for the entire series, **futhark**. Runic symbols were used only for relatively short inscriptions, many of them on grave markers. The symbols we know from Latin were transparently adapted to simplify carving on wooden tablets, for example, ϝ for *F*, or, because the runes were read in any position, ∩ for *U*. Runic inscriptions are of interest to linguists because they provide our earliest Germanic texts, to philologists because they yield information about Germanic culture, covering especially the fifth to the tenth centuries, and to the general reader because of forgeries, a number of which have attracted attention. The most notable of these is the Kensington Stone, which purported to prove that Vikings had penetrated to Minnesota in the Middle Ages. Like other forgeries, it illustrates that linguists need to know the basis of their texts.

The **ogam** inscriptions, used for early Celtic, were made by putting notches or lines on the corners of posts. Series of one to five dots, or one to five lines extending to the right, to the left or in both directions of an edge, provided twenty symbols, five for vowels, fifteen for consonants. Although highly subject to weathering, the ogam inscriptions when legible are valuable in giving us our earliest Irish texts.

3.6 THE CUNEIFORM WRITING SYSTEM

As we noted above, the **cuneiform** or wedge-shaped script was developed by Sumerians around 3200 BC on the basis of the long tradition of tokens. It was taken over by Akkadians in the middle of the third millennium, and from them by various neighbors: by the Hittites and other groups in Asia Minor, who produced texts in the second millennium BC, by the Elamites, with texts in the three last millennia BC, and by various less-known groups. It passed out of use in the early part of our era, and subsequently became completely unknown, until cuneiform texts were deciphered in the nineteenth century. Through the cuneiform system we have our earliest Indo-European materials as well as our earliest Semitic.

Persian inscriptions provided the avenue to relearning cuneiform. By assuming that these inscriptions were to be attributed to the Persian kings, scholars supplied the names of these kings, compared readings of other words with Avestan and Sanskrit words, and eventually mastered the Old Persian texts, in this way deciphering the cuneiform system of writing.

The Old Persian texts themselves were relatively easy to decipher because only thirty-six syllabic characters, with five additional signs, were used to represent Old Persian. Mastery of Old Persian led to the reading of Akkadian, through the trilingual inscription of the Persian king Darius at Behistan, Iran. The proper names provided ready comparison. Thus values were determined for the cuneiform characters much as the values of the Egyptian hieroglyphs were determined from the Rosetta stone. Other Akkadian texts were then read, among them lists and grammars indicating the values of symbols in Akkadian. Still other texts were avenues to Sumerian. In this way the reading of cuneiform gave access to the history of the Middle East from the fourth millennium BC.

The earliest Sumerian texts indicate that the cuneiform system developed from pictures. An early form of the symbol for "star, god, heaven" is , for "vegetation" , for "enclosure" . When these symbols were inscribed with a stylus on clay tablets, they came to be stylized in wedge-shaped forms and shifted ninety degrees as are the two plants in the compound symbol for "garden" below. Apparently, the shift was made to keep the scribe from smudging copy. Ultimately,  "star" was written with three strokes . Compound symbols also were developed; that for "garden" was . Moreover, characters could be used merely for their phonetic value; 𒀭 was read as the syllable *an* as well as AN "god".

When cuneiform symbols were taken over by Akkadians, another complexity was introduced: symbols could be read either by their Sumerian or their Akkadian values. Since "god" in Akkadian is *ILU* and "heaven" ŠAMU, 𒀭 in Akkadian texts may have these readings as well as the Sumerian AN. When taken over by the Hittites the cuneiform system could be read with Sumerian, Akkadian or Hittite values, compounding the complexity further. Without parallel texts and dictionaries, interpretations of the Hittite texts would have been fantastically difficult.

The reading of cuneiform texts is aided somewhat by the presence of **determinatives**, symbols used with nouns to indicate morphological and semantic classes, such as plurals, gods, men, rivers, wooden articles and so on. Determinatives, used also by the Egyptians, are markers that have no phonetic value themselves, somewhat like capital letters for proper nouns and proper adjectives in English or for nouns in German. The symbols used for them may also be read as word symbols.

The cuneiform system therefore is a combination of a logographic and a syllabic system. Its offshoot used for Old Persian was virtually an alphabetic system.

3.7 THE CHINESE WRITING SYSTEM

A third system of writing, the Chinese has remained logographic. In Japan, however, a syllabic system, which is generally used in conjunction with logographs, has been developed from Chinese characters. In Korean an alphabetic system was designed in the fifteenth century. Like the Egyptian hieroglyphs and the Sumerian cuneiform symbols, Chinese characters developed from pictures. In early inscriptions the symbol for *mu*^{4} "tree" was , for *jih*^{4} "sun" ⊙, for *men*^{2} "gate" . When Chinese characters came to be inscribed on wood rather than on bone, the lines of characters were straightened, and the characters became stylized. Today *mu*^{4} is written 木, *jih*^{4} 日, *men*^{2} 門.

A small number of further characters resulted from combinations of simple characters. That for "east" is "the sun rising through a tree" 東. Another small group are symbolic pictures: *yen*^{2} "speak" is a mouth producing speech 言, earlier . The largest group was made up of components, one of which represents the meaning, the other the pronunciation; the second component is called the "phonetic." A homonym of *men*^{2} "gate" indicates plurality. The character developed for this consists of a form of "man" 亻 (to provide meaning) and the character for "gate" 門 as "phonetic" ; the composite character is 們. A similar process gave rise to 悶 *men*^{4} "mournful" (*men* plus "heart") and 捫 *men*^{2} "feel" (*men* plus "hand").

The large number of characters of this last kind provided the means for the most common arrangement of Chinese dictionaries. They are arranged by 214 characteristic elements, called radicals, and the number of additional strokes. The character *men* is made with eight strokes. The radical for man is ninth of the 214; to find 們 , one locates the set listed under the ninth radical, then the subset with eight additional strokes and finally the character 亻 . The radical for "hand" is 61, for "heart" is 64. Another system has been devised by which characters are arranged for shapes of their corners, but it has not replaced the long-standing dictionaries. Although, in writing rapidly, Chinese produce characters in cursive form, the stroke order and the number of strokes in conventional writing are still keys to their identification.

Until very recent times, the system of characters was the sole method of writing Chinese. Since Chinese morphs are monosyllabic and uninflected, the writing system is efficient, except for the need to memorize several thousand characters. In this century various attempts have been made to develop a simpler system of writing Chinese. None has succeeded in replacing the character system. The character system can be used for the various Chinese dialects, and accordingly throughout China. Any writing system that represented more directly the languages spoken would be useful only for each separate dialect.

Various systems of transliteration have also been developed. Since these use Roman letters, they are called Romanizations. That of Wade and Giles was long used most commonly for transliterating Chinese. Western spellings based on it have given rise to pronunciation of Chinese place names that are sometimes far from the original, such as Peking for [beyǰin], spelled *Beizin* by the current system, **pinyin**. This system was introduced by the communist government, and has replaced the former systems of transliteration in China.

When the Chinese system of characters was taken to Japan, means were devised to indicate inflectional syllables and particles. Certain characters were selected to indicate syllabic values, as for the particle *ka*. In the early period a great many such characters were so used, but in the course of time they came to be restricted in number and stylized. The character 加 "add to" was the one selected to indicate the syllable *ka*. Forty-eight such characters make up the Japanese **kana** syllabary. Of this there are two forms: the **hiragana**, used normally; the **katakana**, which compares in use to our italics. Hiragana symbols developed from rapidly written forms of characters; the hiragana for *ka* is か, in which 口 has become a simple stroke. The katakana symbols developed from abbreviated forms; the katakana for *ka* is カ in which the 口 has been entirely omitted.

Japanese is still written in a combination of Chinese characters with kana. In the word for "walk," for example, the Chinese character 歩 must be supplemented by the kana symbol for *ku* く to indicate the positive *aruku*; the negative *arukanai* is written 歩かない . This character has a totally different value when used in the compound for "infantry" 歩兵 *hohei* ("walking soldiers"), which represents a borrowing from Chinese. As a result of these different readings, the Japanese writing system is possibly the most complicated in use today. Although there are systems of romanization, as illustrated above, Japanese society much prefers the traditional system.

3.8 TYPES OF WRITING SYSTEMS, AS ALSO REFLECTED IN THE STAGES OF DEVELOPMENT OF KNOWN SYSTEMS

Writing systems, as suggested by the developments of the major systems discussed above, may be classified into three groups, with transitional types:

1 **logographic** – symbols represent words, for example early Egyptian
  1(a) **logo-syllabic** – symbols represent words or syllables, for example later Egyptian
2 **syllabic** – symbols represent syllables, for example Japanese kana
  2(a) **syllabic-alphabetic**, for example West Semitic, in which symbols represent consonants with varying vowels
3 **alphabetic**, for example Greek

It may be noted that the definitions of these terms vary among scholars. For example, Semitic scholars label the West Semitic writing system "alphabetic," even though they acknowledge that it did not represent vowels at the same level as consonants, like the Greek system. In the interests of accurate designations, the term "alphabetic" might well be maintained for systems in which symbols are included for vowels as well as consonants. Offshoots of the West Semitic system, such as those used for Arabic or Hebrew, are still largely syllabic; the preferred Hebrew text for worship even lacks the vowel points that were introduced in the Middle Ages.

In addition, the systems in use at any time are rarely pure representatives of one of these types. In contemporary English, numerals, such as 2, 2nd, ½, indicate words or morphemes, and are accordingly logographic, though the basic writing system is alphabetic.

Moreover, writing systems are rarely ideal. The alphabetic system used in English is uneconomical, for several entities may be used to indicate units otherwise represented by one entity, for example *ig* in *sign*, *i-e* in *sine*, *igh* in *sight*, *i* in *I*.

Worse still, English has the rare distinction of using the same combination of symbols to represent now two separate phonemes side by side, now a given single phoneme, now a given other phoneme; the *th* of *porthole*, *this*, and *thin* represent /th/, /ð/, /θ/, respectively. Possibly the restriction of /ð/ primarily to a small set of morphemes similar in use, and to initial position in these, has permitted this unusual situation to persist;

when found medially referring to /ð/, as in *father* and *neither*, *th* represents few minimally contrasting pairs, such as *either* : *ether*.

Writing systems may also represent morphological units, as do many spellings in English. The *-s* of *cats*, *dogs*, *horses*, for example, represents the plural morpheme rather than any phonological unit.

All such information must be taken into consideration when attempts are made to solve undeciphered writing systems. Like the three major systems, many of these started with pictures: the Aztec, Mayan, the Indus-Valley script, Proto-Elamite and Minoan. Such scripts are difficult to decipher. The Mayan system is in process of decipherment, with many syllabic signs identified; but these may also be logographic, so that inscriptions are difficult to interpret. Large-scale efforts have been expended to decipher the Indus-Valley or Harappan script; but these have not been successful.

Efforts to decipher syllabic systems have been more successful. Linear B, long obscure, was deciphered by means of lessons obtained from deciphering cryptographic messages; it is a syllabic system adapted to represent Greek, which it does poorly. Others, such as the Sinaitic, were deciphered by guess work. Syllabic systems are well suited to agglutinative languages, such as Japanese, and also to the inflectional Semitic languages with their simple syllabic structure. A syllabic system was devised by Sequoia in the last century for Cherokee.

Alphabetic systems are now produced when new writing systems are devised, as in many literacy projects for preliterate societies. The Latin alphabet is applied for most of them. Cyrillic has been installed in the former Soviet Union, and was introduced for the non-Chinese languages of China in the early days of the communist regime; but it was soon abandoned, and pinyin, like other efforts at Romanization, makes use of the Latin letters. Although the Greeks introduced symbols for pitch accent in the third century BC, writing systems do not indicate accents, because they are largely designed for native speakers. Only linguists of recent times have introduced symbols for all the phonemic entities in a language.

3.9 INTERPRETATION OF WRITING SYSTEMS, AND SUPPLEMENTARY EVIDENCE FOR LINGUISTIC PURPOSES

When any written material is analysed, the type of writing system must be determined, as well as its degree of correspondence with the language spoken at the time. Often, as in *sight* (see the German cognate *Sicht* [ziçt]) writing systems reflect an earlier stage of the language, as *gh* here reflects the former [ç] sound of English. Obsolete spellings are helpful for historical study, though possibly difficult to interpret. It requires some study to determine when postvocalic *gh* in English no longer represented a fricative. Our best evidence is derived from **inverse spellings** like Spenser's *whight* for *white*. This spelling would have been impossible when the fricative was still pronounced; from it, therefore, we receive information about the phonological development of English.

The most frequent imperfection in writing systems is failure to indicate some of the phonemes in a language. The writing system used for English is inadequate in failing to indicate pitch, stress and juncture. Punctuation marks, unsystematically introduced from about the beginning of our era, and capital letters are only approximate indications for pitch; the question mark, for example, serves to indicate high final pitch in sentences without interrogative markers, such as: *She left already?*, but it is also used when questions end with falling pitch, as in: *Who left?*. Some spelling conventions indicate stressed syllables, such as double *r* in *referred*, but in the British spelling *labelled* the double *l* does not. And spaces between words may be used to indicate junctures, as in *pot hole*, but in other words they do not, as in *have to*. Another feature poorly indicated is quantity. No provision was made for indicating long vowels in Latin; and when the Latin alphabet was adapted for Germanic languages, long and short vowels were not distinguished. Some conventions are applied in German to distinguish long vowels from short, as in *Staat* "state" as opposed to *Stadt* "city"; but *bat* "asked" is pronounced with a long vowel while *hat* "has" is short.

When writing systems provide insufficient information, we attempt to supplement it in various ways, most commonly by the analysis of poetry. Our surest means to determine Germanic quantities are based on the use of words in Germanic poetry. The following lines from *Beowulf* illustrate how analysis of poetic texts adds information not provided by the Old English writing system.

710   Ða com of more   under misthleoþum
       Grendel gongan,   Godes yrre bær;
       "Then from the moorland   under misty hills
       Grendel came gliding,   God's wrath he bore;"

Since the *Beowulf* manuscript does not use different symbols for short and long vowels, we cannot determine from it whether the *o*'s of *com*, *of*, *more*, *gongan*, *Godes* are short or long. But in Germanic poetry certain requirements were placed on the poet; each half-line was required to have two prominent syllables in which the vowels were long. Short vowels were permitted in the less prominent syllables, or in the prominent syllables if the lack of length was compensated for by a following consonant in the same syllable, as in *gongan*, or by an additional weakly stressed syllable, as in *Godes*. Since we know from the *m* alliteration of line 710 that *more* is metrically prominent, we must assume that its *o* is long; by converse reasoning we would assume the *o* of *of* to be short. Analysis of Old English poetry thus provides us with information about quantity and accentuation in Old English.

In this way, study of poetry may give us information beyond that provided by a writing system. Yet poetry manipulates phonemic patterns; it does not use them without modification. Therefore, it must be interpreted with the same care as are writing systems. Alliteration in Old English poetry permits us to assume that the *g*'s of *Grendel*, *gongan* and *Godes* were similarly pronounced. From alliteration we may also determine which other consonants were classed together by the Old English poets. But it tells us nothing about Old English vowels, for in Germanic verse all vowels alliterated with one another; further, when *g* became palatalized in Old English, as in *gieldan* "yield," it continued to alliterate with velar *g*. Poetic conventions, like writing conventions, must be understood before they can be utilized to provide linguistic information.

Writing systems may also be inadequate because of conventions maintained from the area in which they were formerly used. The writing system taken over for Old English presents other problems than the lack of marking for quantity. Old English contained some vowels that could not be represented by the simple symbols used for Latin, such as the *eo* of *misthleoþum*. We have no contemporary description of the sounds it represented; accordingly, its exact value is disputed. The compound symbol *eo* may reflect an Irish development. For in Old Irish manuscripts *e* may be used before *o*, especially in weakly stressed syllables, to indicate the pronunciation of the preceding consonant. In OE *menigeo* "multitude", we assume that *e* marked the preceding *g* as a palatal, with a pronunciation [menijo]. The Old English orthographic system is further complicated because it contains conventions of the Old Irish spelling system as well as the Latin.

Since writing systems are conventional and imperfect, we supplement in various ways the information we seek concerning the actual pronunciation. Mis-spellings help us to determine when conventional spellings do not reflect the spoken language. If humorists and bad spellers write *of* for *have* in Modern English, we may infer that *have* is commonly pronounced /əv/. Scribal errors are similarly informative for older materials.

Moreover, languages are rarely isolated. Words adopted from other languages inform us of the sound systems of both languages, as do borrowings out of a language. The biblical names found in the languages of Europe, from Old Church Slavic to Old English, give us information on them. From any name taken over into the European languages, even one as simple as *Mary*, reproduced as *Marija* in Old Church Slavic, as *Maria* in Old English, we can infer the value of the symbols because we know the Latin and Greek pronunciation. Conversely, we determine the pronunciation of names and words in Old Church Slavic, Old English and other languages from the manner in which they are represented when included in Latin and Greek materials.

This procedure has been used to determine the pronunciation of Old Chinese. Japanese borrowed many words from Chinese, first from the Shanghai area, later from the Peking area. As a result many characters have two pronunciations in Japanese; for example, the character for "man," Jap. *hito*, has the readings *jin* and *nin* as a result of the two stages of borrowings. To supplement the inferences based on the borrowings, which assist us in determining the initial parts of Old Chinese words, we make use of rhyming dictionaries. Chinese long preserved traditional requirements for poetry, including rhymes that were based on Old Chinese pronunciation. Poets had to look up the pronunciation of a word to determine if it would qualify as a rhyme. Since final elements underwent different changes from dialect to dialect, by consulting the rhyming dictionary, linguists could reconstruct the final parts of words.

Chinese, then, provides an example of drawing inferences from earlier forms of the language. The procedure has also been used with later forms, as in English; the OE *o* in *of* is pronounced differently in Middle English and current English from that of OE *mōd* "mood." We may also attempt to determine the pronunciation of Old English forms by comparing them with related forms in the other Germanic languages. But inferences based on related forms must be established with care. English *of* and *mood* have undergone various changes. We cannot insist that different vowels in current English reflect differences in Old English, although for these two words they do.

If, on the basis of their differing contemporary pronunciations, we assumed different pronunciations for the vowels in the Old English forms of *wood* and *mood*, our inference would be wrong. The vowels were alike in Old English; through subsequent changes they have become different. Because individual languages, and individual words, undergo various changes, etymological evidence must always be used cautiously in attempts to determine the pronunciation of related materials.

In recent attempts to interpret writing systems, increasing use has been made of structural evidence. Graphemic systems may be analysed for the internal relationship of their elements and for their relationship with the phonemic system of the linguistic material they represent. Writers with no linguistic training are more aware of the phonemes than of the allophones of their language. If, therefore, we find beside Old English:

i   u
e   o
æ   a

a *y*, as in *cyning* "king" and an *œ* as in *œxen* "oxen," we may conclude that these symbols represented phonemes in some stage of Old English. From the composite form of *œ* we assume it represented a front rounded vowel. The symbol *y* fits best into the Old English system of symbols if we assume that at one time it represented a somewhat higher front rounded vowel than *œ*. Although structural analysis may permit us to make inferences about the phonological system represented by the orthography, in its interpretation we must be aware of possible complications, such as conventions imported from previous writing systems and those developed in the language.

Because of the shortcomings of methods of interpretation, we welcome descriptions of the language or its writing system made in the past. Greek and Latin grammarians provide some indication of the values of the alphabetic symbols they used. A grammarian in medieval Iceland has given us similar information about Old Icelandic. Less explicit but equally valuable help comes from the rare writer, like Orm, who modified a traditional system in an attempt to give a better indication of his pronunciation. Various methods have been developed in attempts to determine the pronunciation and phonological systems underlying texts. By applying these methods we may be able to approximate the pronunciation of languages of the past, though subtle features may always be outside our grasp.

SELECTED FURTHER READINGS

Jensen (1970) provides an excellent survey of writing systems, with fine illustrations. A highly readable discussion of writing systems, their interpretation for linguistic purposes and their decipherment may be found in Pedersen (1931).

Senner (1989) includes twelve essays on writing systems by specialists in each, with excellent illustrations. Schmandt-Besserat (1992) treats the origin of writing in tokens to the development of the cuneiform script.

For a structure analysis of writing systems, see Gelb (1963), who presents a typology in accordance with which writing systems developed.

Translations of the *Beowulf* here and elsewhere are taken from *Beowulf*, Ruth P.M. Lehmann's translation (1988).

PROBLEMS

1 The Chinese writing system represents morphemes that vary in pronunciation from dialect to dialect, as between Mandarin, Cantonese, Shanghai (Wú) and other dialects.

(a) Discuss the advantages and disadvantages of such a writing system.

(b) If, instead of Chinese characters, publishers used pinyin, texts written in it would represent the spoken language. Because Putonghua (Mandarin) is the official language, official writings would be made available in it. Discuss the advantages and disadvantages of using pinyin in a country with many languages such as China.

(c) Since pinyin is a phonetic writing system, Putonghua written in it would be unintelligible for speakers of Cantonese, Wú and other dialects. Yet the aim of introducing pinyin is to enable Chinese citizens to read official documents and technical materials, like manuals for machinery, that are uniform throughout the country. Comparing the English system of spelling, which is equally intelligible to citizens of Australia, Britain, India and the United States, as well as to others, could you devise a pinyin system that might apply for all dialects of Chinese?

(d) To bring about a uniform form of spoken language throughout the country, the government has set out to teach Putonghua. Pinyin then would be intelligible throughout the country. What problems do you see in this effort?

(e) Learned texts, as on Buddhism, using only Chinese characters have been produced for use by Japanese as well as Chinese. Since Japanese is a verb-final language and Chinese is basically verb-medial, superposed numbers were placed beside characters to indicate the sequence in which they were to be read in Japanese. What qualifications would be required of anyone who used such texts? Could the system be applied for general purposes, such as newspapers?

2 Alphabetic systems are generally considered more advantageous than syllabic systems. Romanization systems have therefore been developed for the Japanese kana system.

(a) One method of Romanization in wide western use is known as the Hepburn system. In it letters were introduced that represent a compromise between Japanese and western sounds. As example we may cite Mount Fuji, the name of the fourth principal island, *Shikoku*, the name of the largest, *Honshu*, the name of Korea, *Chosen*.

By the New Official system of Romanization, letters are used to represent Japanese phonological structure. Japanese has a bilabial fricative, not a labiodental before *u* in the same series as *h* before *e a o*. Moreover, *-j-* is a variant of *z* before *i*. In the New Official system the mountain is represented as *Huzi*. Moreover, *Sikoku* is so represented because every *s* before *i* is pronounced [š]. Similarly, *Honsyuu* and *Tyōsen* are so represented because *sy* is pronounced [š] before [a o u] and *ty* as [č] before [a o u].

In view of these complexities, discuss the advantages and the disadvantages of Romanization. Which of the two Romanization systems identified here do you consider preferable, and preferable for whom?

(b) In the kana system 48 symbols are used. Since many words in Japanese consist of syllables made of up consonant plus vowel, for example *Yokohama*, the system is efficient for these. Words with long vowels, like *ōi* "many," may be spelled with two kana symbols representing *o*. But problems arise with clusters including *-y-*, such as the second syllable of *Tōkyō*. These problems are handled by using a kana symbol ending in *-i*, followed by one beginning with *y-*, for example *To-o-ki-yo-o*. When, however, a *t-* stands before *y-*, the cluster is pronounced [č], transcribed in Hepburn Romanization as *ch*, as in *Chosen* "Korea." Discuss problems such words may provide for native speakers of Japanese; and for non-native learners of the language.

3 After examining the problems with a logographic system like that of Chinese and a syllabic system like that of Japanese in comparison with the problems of an alphabetic system like that of English, discuss the advantages and disadvantages of the three types of representing a language.

(a) Discuss the fitness of the different types for languages of different structure. Chinese morphemes are monosyllabic. Japanese phonological structure is largely a sequence of syllables consisting of consonants followed by a vowel (the *-n* of many words, such as *Nippon* "Japan," is treated as a separate vocalic syllable, and transcribed with *ñ* in the New System). English, on the other hand, has many consonant clusters, as in *stretched*. To what extent are spelling systems developed that reflect the structure of the language for which they are used?

4 Efforts have been made to introduce a phonetic spelling system for English. George Bernard Shaw left much of his fortune for the effort; yet the effort failed. Discuss the following.

(a) For a phonetic system which pronunciation would be chosen as basic, British English, American English, in one of its varieties, the King's/ Queen's English? What effect would such a choice have on the speakers of other dialects? Compare the possible problems with those resulting from the introduction of pinyin for Chinese.

(b) Publishers and others, including many librarians, oppose such spelling reform. Why? What effect would it have on their books in print? What effect would it have on the use of printed materials of the last four centuries?

(c) For some decades the *Chicago Tribune* newspaper used simplified spelling for selected words, such as *tho* for *though*, *thru* for *through*. It then abandoned the effort. Why might the publisher have given up the idea? In discussing the abandonment, you may note the retention of *th* for the differing initial consonants of *though* and *through*, as well as for words like *pothole*. Moreover, you may compare the pronunciation of *o* in *some*, *sot*, etc.; similarly, of *u* in *put*, *putty*, etc. What, then, is the effect of selective reform?

(d) It is often said that mastery of the English spelling system requires three additional years of schooling in the countries with English as the language of education. What steps would you recommend to shorten the period?

4 Genealogical classification

4.1 GENEALOGICAL CLASSIFICATION OF LANGUAGES

In the first chapter we noted that many of the languages of Europe and Asia are interrelated. Evidence may be found in all components of these languages. Most apparent is the similarity of basic vocabulary: words for the lower numerals, kinship, domestic animals, everyday activities, the world around us. But even more convincing are the systematic similarities and differences that one finds in the sounds and forms.

From the phonological system we may cite initial *d-* in words of the same meaning in Sanskrit, Greek, Latin, Slavic, as in the words for "two" and "ten"; the reconstructed PIE **d* contrasts with **t* and **dh*, forming a subset of three members in the phonological system of Proto-Indo-European. As we have noted in chapter 1, such words systematically show **t* in Germanic where the other languages have **d*.

From inflection we may cite elements filling the same role in these languages, such as the ending in the third person singular indicative PIE [-ti], which contrasts with the first singular [-mi] and the second singular [-si]. From word formation we may cite similar constructions, such as compounds like English *Bluebeard*, meaning "a man who possesses a blue beard"; as we examine older forms of Indic and Greek, we find many such compounds.

In syntax, too, we find similar patterns, such as the distinct parts of speech: nouns versus verbs, both characterized by distinctive inflections. Such systematic similarities and differences cannot be due to chance. The only explanation for them is common origin of the languages in which the similarities are found. We say that languages having a common origin are related, and we classify them in a genealogical group commonly referred to as family. The term genetic classification is also used beside genealogical classification.

The Romance languages, which developed from Latin, provide proof for such an explanation. Since French, Italian, Portuguese, Spanish and the other Romance languages developed into independent languages only after the collapse of the Roman Empire, they furnish evidence in texts on how languages develop, on how we can establish relationships between languages that developed from a common source and on how we can group languages by degrees of relationship. The words listed in section 1.2 for "dear," "field," "candle," "house" are so similar that we can derive them without question from attested Latin words. Yet they also exhibit systematic changes from the Latin words, such as some losses of final elements and modifications of consonants and of vowels.

The systematic similarities and differences in many words of the Romance languages, as well as their systematic similarities and differences in morphology and syntax, give us evidence for assuming separate developments in the different areas in which Latin was once the common language. Subsequent study has provided evidence that all languages change by processes that have been identified in historical linguistic study. By examining languages that show systematic similarities and differences, we may determine earlier stages at which they were closer to one another, for example Old English and Old High German. Finally, we may reconstruct the language that was ancestor to the group, as was Proto-Germanic to Old English, Old High German and other languages discussed below.

In chapter 1 we also noted that evidence can be found for proposing that Latin in turn is related to Greek, Sanskrit and a number of other languages. Some of the evidence was apparent to linguists over two centuries ago. They examined the evidence in increasing detail, and proposed the large linguistic group known today as the **Indo-European family**.

Detailed study of the Indo-European family is important for understanding historical linguistic methods as well as for knowledge of the interrelationships of some of the world's most widely spoken languages. For the methods that have been found to apply in dealing with the Indo-European languages also apply to other language groups. Moreover, because of the political and economic role of the speakers using languages belonging to it, the Indo-European family is probably the most important, certainly the most widely used, today. For its distribution, and the location of other language families, see the map at the front of the book.

In attempting to set up any language family, the oldest known forms of a language are of great importance, as is identification of the period to which they belong. Accordingly, for any historical study we attempt to date the materials with which we are dealing. Approximate dates at which the oldest Indo-European materials are attested will therefore be given here.

An understanding of linguistic development also requires that we determine the interrelationships of language subgroups and languages within a family. The data involved in establishing such classifications are often complex. Details will generally be omitted here but can be found in grammars devoted to individual languages, such as Old English, or to individual subgroups, such as Germanic, the group to which Old English belongs. Moreover, successive stages of any language have been only approximately determined. Most proposed stages are based on nonlinguistic evidence. The division between Middle High German and New High German, for example, has often been dated at the time of the Reformation, in the early sixteenth century. Other criteria used have been the introduction of printing or political developments, as for the terminal date of Middle English, or simply the turn of a century. Although external forces on the language may have been important in spreading or giving prestige to one form of it, we should use only linguistic criteria for linguistic classifications. Since this has rarely been done, the dates given in handbooks for stages of a language must be checked for the criteria used in proposing them. Even when true linguistic dating is possible, students must note that languages never change abruptly; for the Germans or English of the fifteenth and sixteenth centuries, the period at which we demarcate Middle from New German or English, there were no more apparent differences between their speech and that of their children or parents than for speakers at seemingly serene linguistic times like the nineteenth century.

4.2 THE INDO-EUROPEAN LANGUAGE FAMILY

The discovery that the ancient and modern languages of much of India were related to the Germanic and to the classical languages of Greece and Rome provided the impetus for much of the historical linguistic study in the nineteenth century. When this discovery was made, scholars were greatly concerned with the origins and the early institutions of mankind. Availability of the Indic texts, which are even older than the Greek texts known in the nineteenth century, led the Grimm brothers, Rasmus Rask, Franz Bopp, and others to devote themselves to understanding the interrelationships between their own languages and those of Greece, Italy and India, in which materials had been preserved for several millennia.

The name given to the family by Thomas Young in 1813 is a compound composed of one unit representing the easternmost area, India, and one representing the westernmost area, Europe, in which the family is located. Such hyphenated compounds have subsequently been devised for many other language families: Afro-Asiatic, Sino-Tibetan, Malayo-Polynesian, and so on. Since the Germanic family is located farthest to the north and west, many scholars, especially in Germany, label the family Indo-Germanic by the designation proposed in 1810 by Conrad Malte-Brun. Others, using a term that the early Indic and Celtic authors applied to their own people, called the family Aryan; this name is now in disrepute because of a misuse of it for infamous political purposes. Other names have also been proposed, but the one used most widely today is Indo-European.

We will first examine, roughly in accordance with their distribution from east to west, the various subgroups of the Indo-European family of which representatives are spoken today.

4.2.1 The Indo-Iranian subgroup

Indo-Iranian is the name of the subgroup that was carried to the area of Iran and India in migrations more than three millennia ago. It consists of two subgroups, of which **Indic** is the more important, for **Iranian** texts date from a later period and are less abundant.

The earliest Indic text is the *Rigveda*, a collection of hymns as large as the *Iliad* and the *Odyssey* combined The oldest hymns are cosmological poems, composed somewhat before 1000 BC. The first two lines of the first hymn go as follows:

Agním īḷe puróhitaṃ yajñásya devám ṛtvíjam
Agni I-praise leader of-sacrifice divine ministrant
"I call on Agni as chief priest, divine performer of the sacrifice"

Many others of the more than one thousand hymns begin with a similar invocation to a god.

Materials used for transmitting texts disintegrate in the Indian climate, and accordingly we have no early records. But since the poems of the *Rigveda* and the other *Vedas*, that is, collections of hymns, were considered sacred, they were memorized and transmitted orally for many generations. We can vouch for the accuracy of the transmission, for most lines of the poems still conform to the metrical forms in which they were composed.

The veneration accorded the *Vedas*, which led to their careful preservation, yielded other results of importance to linguistics. As the language of the *Vedas* became obsolete and difficult to interpret, priests, or Brahmans, prepared commentaries. Among these were grammars, which informed later generations of priests how to interpret the hymns, even how to pronounce them – for a faulty pronunciation would scarcely achieve the intended aim of a hymn. The result of such linguistic analysis was a standardized language, so completely described and regulated, in the Indic term *saṃskṛta*, that it underwent few further changes. This *saṃskṛta* is known to us as **Sanskrit**, from the western pronunciation of the term. We date it from several centuries before 400 BC, the putative time of its greatest grammarian, Panini. A grammar attributed to him describes the language with such authority and completeness that ever after it has been learned by Indian scholars with no essential deviations. To this day Sanskrit is in daily use by a small number of Brahmans, and is thus comparable to Latin, Old Church Slavic and Classical Arabic as a language maintained for religious purposes.

Besides the *saṃskṛta* "regulated, cultivated, correct," there existed spoken languages called *prākṛta* "natural, popular (languages)," or **Prakrits**. We are much better informed on Sanskrit than on the Prakrits, for a great amount of learned material has been produced in India. Many of the learned texts are religious writings: the *Brahmanas* are interpretative tracts in Sanskrit; the *Upanishads* are devotional tracts. Moreover, the classical works of Indian literature were composed in Sanskrit, such as the *Mahabharata* and the *Ramayana*, epics much longer than any composed in Europe. Fortunately, Sanskrit dramas include female characters, for these were not permitted to speak the regulated language, and as a result we have in their lines, and those of characters of lower castes, examples of Prakrits. Examples also appear in other materials. Literary Prakrit is dated from about the beginning of our era. In the period before Christ, we accordingly have three stages of Indic: *Vedic Sanskrit* or *Vedic*, the language of approximately 1200–800 BC; Classical Sanskrit, following it and standardized at approximately 400 BC; and the Prakrits.

Vedic and Classical Sanskrit are often referred to as **Old Indic**, the Prakrits as **Middle Indic**, which we may date from about 400 BC to AD 1000. The Middle Indic dialect on which we have most information is **Pali**; it is the language in which the Buddhist canon is preserved. We may place it shortly before Christ, though Indic dates are highly uncertain because the Indians were quite unconcerned about history. Fortunately, contacts with the Greeks permit us to date a great Buddhist ruler, Asoka, around 250 BC. The many inscriptions he placed throughout India may be used to determine the state of the Indic dialects before the beginning of our era. At the end of the Middle Indic period, before AD 1000, we have materials in languages known as *Apabhraṃsas* "off-branchings." From the *Apabhraṃsas* developed the Modern Indic dialects. Most widely spoken of these is **Hindi**, official language of the Republic of India. Hindi was known formerly as Hindustani; its current form in Pakistan is **Urdu**. Hindi and Urdu differ especially in learned vocabulary, for Hindi bases learned terms on Sanskrit, Urdu on Arabic and Persian. Other Modern Indic languages are **Bengali**, **Gujerati**, **Marathi**, **Panjabi** and numerous less widely spoken languages, such as **Sinhalese** in Ceylon and **Romany**, the language of the Gypsies.

Iranian texts from before 300 BC are referred to as **Old Iranian** and are handed down to us in two dialects, **Avestan** and **Old Persian**. The *Avesta* is the sacred book of the Zoroastrian religion. Its oldest poems, the *Gathas*, are dated as early as 1000 BC and are as archaic in language as those of the *Rigveda*. The first line of Yasna 44 goes as follows:

tat θwā pərəsā   ərəš mōi vaocā ahurā
that you I-ask   truly me tell lord-of-life
"Of this I ask you; tell me truly, oh lord of life"

While this line is clear, the *Gathas* are very difficult to interpret because of numerous problems in transmission.

Old Persian is preserved primarily in the inscriptions of Darius (521–486 BC), and Xerxes (486–465 BC). The inscription of greatest importance is a long trilingual text in Old Persian, Akkadian and Elamite, which was chiseled on a stone cliff at Behistan, Iran. The Behistan inscription recounts the feats of Darius. Written in a cuneiform writing system, it not only preserved for us, until the discovery of Hittite texts, the oldest body of Indo-European texts surviving in their original form, but it also provided the avenue to the understanding of cuneiform. To illustrate the close relationship among Old Persian, Avestan and Sanskrit, we may cite words like that for "spear": OPers. and Av. *aršti-*, Skt *ṛṣṭi-* or OPers. *daiva-*, Av. *daēva-* "devil", Skt *deva-* "god".

We may date Middle Iranian from approximately 300 BC to AD 900. Various representatives of it are attested. **Pehlevi** or **Middle Persian** was the language of the Persian Empire. Farther east **Sogdian** and to the north **Saka** or **Scythian** were spoken and to this day are not completely described, partly because many of their texts were discovered only recently.

At present various Iranian languages are still in use: **Balochi**, of West Pakistan; **Pashtu** or **Afghan**, the official language of Afghanistan; **Persian** or **Farsi**, the language of Iran; **Kurdish**, spoken by various groups in western Iran, Iraq, Turkey and the former Soviet Union; **Ossetic**, in the northern Caucasus; and many others. Although still spoken by millions, the Iranian languages have been displaced in many areas by Turkic dialects and have a much smaller number of speakers than do the Indian languages. Since members of the two groups are spoken in much of southern Asia, Indo-Iranian has remained one of the most prominent subgroups in the Indo-European family.

4.2.2 The Armenian subgroup

Of **Armenian**, located in the southern Caucasus and western Turkey, we have no materials until the fifth century AD. We assume from Akkadian and Greek accounts that the Armenians migrated to Armenia some centuries before the beginning of our era. Yet the oldest materials we have were presumably composed in the fifth century AD and are almost exclusively translations of Christian writings. A considerable number of Armenian texts have survived; some Christian writers have had their materials preserved only in Armenian. The language of these texts is referred to as Old or Classical Armenian, which was maintained with few changes as the written language until the nineteenth century. Modern Armenian exists in two branches: the Eastern, spoken in the former Soviet Union and Iran; and the Western, spoken formerly in Turkey.

Armenian has been so heavily influenced by other languages, notably Iranian, that until late in the nineteenth century there was doubt whether it should not be classed as an Iranian dialect. Antoine Meillet (1926–8: I, 95) cited the Gypsy dialect of Armenian as an example of a language that may contain almost no native vocabulary but still maintains the native phonological and syntactic structure. The grammatical structure of Armenian, then, is Indo-European; exact correspondences can be set up for the basic vocabulary, such as *hayr* "father" = Lat. *pater*. Yet in spite of our certainty that Armenian is a language separate from Indo-Iranian, its precise relationship to the other Indo-European languages is not yet agreed on. Occasionally, it has been related to the poorly attested **Phrygian**.

4.2.3 The Albanian subgroup

The early history of Albanian is even more inadequately known than is that of Armenian. Our earliest records are from the fifteenth century AD. We have few further materials until 1685, when a Latin–Albanian dictionary was produced, followed by religious translations and collections of folktales in the nineteenth century. There are two dialects: **Geg** in the north and **Tosk** in the south, extending into Greece and Italy.

Albanian, like Armenian, has undergone many changes in its vocabulary, influenced successively by Latin, Greek, Slavic and Turkish. Its origins are difficult to determine. It has been considered by some scholars a modern representative of **Illyrian**, by others of **Thracian**. Both Illyrian and Thracian are poorly known Indo-European languages of the period before the beginning of our era. To determine the position of Albanian in the family, we must either have thorough reconstruction of its early stages, on the basis of descriptive work now being carried on, or we will need new early texts. Reconstruction is hampered by the small proportion of native material in the language; discovery of early texts is a matter of chance. Without one of these aids, however, Albanian of only the past few centuries can be described.

4.2.4 The Slavic subgroup

The **Baltic** and **Slavic** groups are attested only during the past millennium, yet languages in each contain relatively archaic characteristics. Among such characteristics are the large number of case forms in the noun declension of Lithuanian, which lacks only one of the cases found in Sanskrit, the ablative. Moreover, in its accentual system Lithuanian preserves for words a pitch accent that Classical Sanskrit had already given up. Yet our oldest extended Lithuanian texts date only from the sixteenth century AD. Our oldest Slavic texts date from the ninth century AD. The lateness of texts from both groups has made it difficult to determine precisely their interrelationship. Some scholars class both of them in one subgroup of Indo-European, **Balto-Slavic**; others maintain that the similarities between the Baltic and the Slavic languages are due to mutual influences exerted during a long period of contact. These scholars set up two independent subgroups of Indo-European, Baltic and Slavic. A choice between the two classifications depends on the interpretation of selected linguistic characteristics. Given only recent texts, we can scarcely state with assurance whether one subgroup or two are to be posited.

Speakers of Slavic dialects apparently were located in southeast Poland and western Russia at the time of the Romans. They spread out from this area and in the sixth and seventh centuries came into contact with the eastern Roman Empire in Bulgaria. The earliest Slavic documents we have date from the advent of Christianization. Shortly after 850 two missionaries, Cyril (Constantinus) and Methodius, carried Christianity to Slavic speakers and translated the Bible into their language. The language of the translation is known either as **Old Church Slavic** or **Old Bulgarian**. The Russian church has maintained it as its official language; accordingly, it occupies a position in eastern Europe similar to that of Latin in the Roman church.

The Slavic languages spoken today are classified in three groups: South, West and East Slavic. **South Slavic** comprises **Bulgarian, Serbo-Croatian** and **Slovenian**; **West Slavic** comprises **Czech, Slovak, Polish** and **Wendish**; **East Slavic** comprises **Great Russian, White Russian** or **Byelorussian** and **Ukrainian**. Through the political expansion of the Russian Empire, (Great) Russian was spread south into the Caucasus and east to Siberia; it has continued its expansion and today is one of the most widely spoken languages of the world.

Differences among the various Slavic languages are relatively slight, much smaller than those among the Germanic languages. One may assume, therefore, that there has been no long period of separation; this assumption is supported when we reconstruct Proto-Slavic, for we find it similar to Old Church Slavic.

4.2.5 The Baltic subgroup

The Baltic group consists of two languages still in use, and **Old Prussian**, which is known through translations from the sixteenth century and became extinct around AD 1700. Old Prussian is important for Indo-European studies because of its conservatism, especially in the vowel system. (Prussian was replaced partly by Lithuanian, partly by German; the name was then applied to German speakers of the area in which the Old Prussian language was spoken.)

Like Old Prussian, **Lithuanian** was first recorded in a translation of Luther's catechism, dating from 1547. As noted above, modern Lithuanian is remarkable for its conservative pitch accent, inflection and retention of formal distinctions, especially in the substantive. The word for "son" *sūnùs* is like that in Skt *sūnús* ; *eĩti* "he goes" has undergone fewer changes than has Lat. *it*. Lithuanian is accordingly one of the most important Indo-European languages for comparative study. The other surviving Baltic language, **Latvian** or **Lettish**, has undergone many more changes. It, too, is known from the sixteenth century; it no longer has a pitch accent, and many of its inflectional endings have been lost. A few dialects are attested for both Lithuanian and Latvian, but standard languages were established as Lithuania and Latvia became separate republics. Neither language has more than several million speakers today.

4.2.6 The satem–centum subdivision

In dealing with earlier stages of the Indo-European languages the groups we have so far discussed are often classed together as one of the two large subdivisions of Proto-Indo-European. The chief basis for this classification is a contrast of sibilants in these branches versus velars in the remaining branches. For example, in the word for "ten" we find:

	Skt *daśa*	Av. *dasa*	Arm. *tasn*	OCS *desętĭ*	Lith. *dẽšimt*
vs.	Gk. *déka*	Lat. *decem*	OIr. *deich*	Goth. *taihun*	

In the word for "hundred" we find:

	Skt *śatám*	Av. *satəm*	OCS *sŭto*	Lith. *šim̃tas*
vs.	Gk *hekatón*	Lat. *centum*	OIr. *cēt*	Goth. *hund*

The eastern languages are labeled **satem** after the Avestan form for "hundred"; the western are labeled **centum**. When this classification was first proposed, scholars assumed that the speakers of Proto-Indo-European had split into two groups and that in the eastern group a sound change took place that differentiated the eastern from the western dialects.

Questions have been raised concerning this division, largely as a result of observations about dialect classification. If there had been a fundamental split between eastern Indo-European and western Indo-European, we should expect it to be reflected in a number of differing characteristics for each group. Since we do not find such additional characteristics, we do not hold today that there was once a single predecessor of the satem languages. We interpret the distribution of velars in centum languages and sibilants in satem languages by assuming that by a sound change some velars were palatalized and became sibilants in the eastern section of the Indo-European speech community. Results of the change spread through Indo-Iranian, Armenian, dialects poorly known, Slavic, and into Baltic; but in Baltic not all palatalized velars were changed that show up as sibilants elsewhere. The satem situation is therefore typical in a speech community after a sound change has taken place and the effects have spread.

The change of palatovelar stops to sibilants did not affect the Anatolian languages or Tocharian, possibly because they had left the Indo-European speech community before the sound change took place, possibly because they were on its periphery (see sections 4.2.11–12). We may continue to speak of satem languages because the change of velars to sibilants provides one of the foremost Indo-European isoglosses, but we no longer assume that the Indo-European speech community early split into two parts.

4.2.7 The Greek subgroup

Although it has relatively few speakers today, **Greek** or **Hellenic** is important historically. Its spread into its current area, and its further expansion
and contraction, are also highly interesting for general historical linguistics.

We assume from Greek history, supported by deductions based on
linguistic evidence, that the present region of Greece was inhabited by
non-Indo-European speakers before 2000 BC. Place names like that of
Corinth, with an element consisting of *n* plus dental consonant, are found
also in Asia Minor; they are pre-Greek and were maintained by Greek
speakers, as were Indian place names in the Americas. Around 2000 BC
Greeks, or Hellenes, began to spread south and gradually became pre-
eminent in the present area of Greece, the islands and adjoining areas in
the Mediterranean and the west coast of Asia Minor. Greek historians tell
us about the last of the groups to emerge, the Doric speakers of around
1200 BC. From the introduction of Greek speech, we can suggest how
Indo-European languages may have been spread also in areas of which we
have less knowledge, such as India and Italy.

The gradual increase of our knowledge of early Greek is also of great
interest for historical linguistics. Until a short time ago the earliest datable
Greek material was from the seventh century BC. Vase inscriptions and
poetry – the *Iliad* and the *Odyssey* – were older but uncertain in date.
Although the fall of Troy is dated roughly at 1200 BC, there has been little
agreement on the date of the Homeric poems. The language of the
Homeric poems has been central in reconstructing Proto-Indo-European.
The first line of the *Iliad* reads:

Mēnin áeide, θeá, Pēlēiádeō Akhilēos
wrath sing! goddess of-P's-son of-Achilles
"Sing of the wrath of Achilles, the son of Peleus, goddess!"

Even in this one line there are archaisms, such as the genitive endings of
Achilles and the patronymic, son of Peleus. Proto-Indo-European as
reconstructed in the widely used handbooks is largely a construct based on
early Greek and Vedic Sanskrit.

Shortly after the beginning of this century, tablets were found in Crete
and the mainland, which for some time could not be deciphered; they were
classified by their scripts as **Linear A** and **Linear B**. A number of scholars
worked on Linear B after the Second World War, employing the methods
of cryptography towards its decipherment. In 1952 one of these, Michael
Ventris, published his conclusions, which demonstrated that the language
used in the Linear B tablets was Greek (see Ventris and Chadwick 1973).
This variety of Greek is usually referred to as **Mycenaean Greek**. The
tablets date from 1450 to 1200 BC. Accordingly, we now have very early
texts for Greek, similar in age to those of India. With the new material our
views of the dialect situation of Greek have been modified, as well as those
on the development of Greek from Proto-Indo-European.

Many problems in the interpretation of Mycenaean Greek result from the imperfect script in which it was written. Linear B is syllabic. Consonant groups are either broken up or simplified. Only the cumulative weight of evidence persuades us that Ventris's decipherment must be accepted. A Greek word for "king," *basileús*, is spelled in Mycenaean by syllabic symbols that we transliterate *qa-si-re-u*. These forms look quite different, but when we find "priest" *hiereús* represented as *i-je-re-u*, "fuller" *knapheús* as *ka-na-pe-u*, we accept the interpretation in spite of the inadequacy of the Linear B writing system for Greek.

In later Greek we have a diversity of dialects subdivided into two large groups: **West Greek** and **East Greek**. To East Greek belongs **Attic–Ionic**, the language of Attica and much of Asia Minor. Historically, the most important dialect is that of Athens, **Attic Greek**. Because of the intellectual domination of Athens, its dialect came to be that used throughout Greek-speaking areas and was called the common language, *koinē*, or Hellenistic Greek. This is the dialect spread by Alexander the Great (356–323 BC) throughout his empire and maintained as the general language far outside the Hellenic peninsula. It is the Greek used in the New Testament.

With the decline of Greek political power, the area over which the Greek language was used also shrank. Today it is largely confined to Greece, though there are still some speakers in other countries, notably Cyprus, Turkey and the United States. Except for **Tsaconian**, a dialect spoken in old Doric territory, the Peloponnese, modern dialects are descendants of the *koinē*.

4.2.8 The Italic subgroup

Italic was brought into the Italian peninsula during the second millennium BC, probably somewhat later than Greek was brought into the Hellenic peninsula. We know relatively little about the language situation in Italy before about 600 BC and can speak with assurance about it only from 250 BC. We divide the Italic languages attested into two groups, *Oscan–Umbrian* and *Latin–Faliscan*. The subsequent history of the Italic languages provides a dramatic example of language spread and displacement. Latin gradually displaced all the other Italic languages and was spread throughout the Roman Empire. Subsequently a number of dialects developed from it in the various sections of the empire and in Italy itself. From the time of the Renaissance the dialect of Florence was the basis for the standard language of Italy, but subsequently that of Rome has strongly influenced it.

Oscan has come down to us in approximately two hundred inscriptions, from the last two centuries BC. **Umbrian** is attested primarily through the Iguvine tablets, dated in the first century BC. Other related dialects are poorly attested. Oscan is important for Indo-European linguistics because it is conservative in vocalism. Formerly, it was assumed without question that Oscan–Umbrian belonged with Latin–Faliscan in the Italic subgroup. Recently, differences have been pointed out, largely in vocabulary, in which Oscan–Umbrian differs greatly from Latin–Faliscan. In grammatical structure, however, the two are sufficiently alike to suggest their retention in the Italic subgroup of the Indo-European family.

Only a few **Faliscan** materials have come down to us. Another Italic dialect surviving only in inscriptions is **Venetic**, spoken in northeast Italy before the beginning of our era. **Latin** is attested in an early inscription from Praeneste of approximately 600 BC, which is instructive because of its archaic language and its content:

MANIOS	MED	FHE	FHACED	NUMASIOI
Manius	mē		fēcit	Numeriō

"Manius made me for Numerius."

As the Classical Latin representation below the Praeneste forms may suggest, the language has changed considerably in a half millennium. Inscriptions of this sort, labeling maker and recipient, are found in artifacts in other Indo-European dialect areas and give us a great deal of information about changes in the language.

It may be noted that some scholars have suggested that this inscription is a nineteenth-century forgery; but it is unlikely that a supposed forger could have constructed the archaic forms. None the less, it must be remembered that the occasional individual takes great delight in attempting a forgery.

We have relatively few Latin texts from before 200 BC, but they are important, especially for their syntax. A law in Table 8 of the Twelve Tables reads:

Si membrum rupsit,		ni cum eo pacit,	talio	esto.
if limb	one-has-maimed	lest with him he-agrees	retaliation	let-be

"If someone has maimed another's limb, there should be retaliation unless he agrees on compensation."

The verb-final order, as in Vedic and much of Homeric Greek, maintains the syntax of Proto-Indo-European.

Subsequently, there are many literary texts, and also inscriptions giving us information on the spoken language. The spoken Latin, or **Vulgar Latin** (Latin of the people), was spread throughout the Roman Empire and was the basis from which the Romance languages developed. Since Vulgar Latin is not as completely attested as we might like, work has been devoted to reconstruction of Proto-Romance from modern dialects.

Classical Latin was long maintained as the written language throughout the Roman Empire. Accordingly, we have evidence for the emerging Romance languages only long after the collapse of the western Roman

Empire: **Italian** from the tenth century; **Provençal** from the eleventh; **French** from 842, in the Oaths of Strasburg; **Spanish**, **Catalan**, and **Portuguese** from the tenth and eleventh centuries; **Rumanian** from the sixteenth. Besides these seven important languages, three minor ones are attested from modern times: **Sardinian**; **Rhaeto-Romance**, **Romansch** or **Ladin**, spoken by approximately 100,000 speakers in Switzerland and Italy; **Dalmatian**, of which the last speaker died in 1898.

Through its spread to Central and South America, Spanish has become one of the most widely spoken languages; forms of it, differing from area to area, are used throughout this huge expanse except for Brazil, where Portuguese is the national language.

4.2.9 The Celtic subgroup

Celtic has many characteristics in common with Italic. Yet we cannot be certain of the relationship between the two subgroups, for no Celtic materials of any extent have been preserved from before our era. From place names, like Bohemia ("home of the Boii," a Celtic tribe), we assume that Celts early inhabited central Europe. We know that they expanded greatly in the second half of the first millennium BC. They established themselves in Spain, in northern Italy, and almost captured Rome. In Spain they left some inscriptions, which now provide us with our earliest materials in the subgroup. These are difficult to interpret, but they have given us important information, such as evidence that Celtic was also originally verb-final like Vedic and Hittite.

The Celts also penetrated into Asia Minor, as far as the present-day city of Ankara, and must have been distinct from other groups at the time of St Paul's missionary journeys, as we may note from his Letter to the Galatians. Moreover, St Jerome reported that they maintained their Celtic speech to his day, in the fourth century AD. During their expansion they became predominant in Gaul, Britain and Ireland. Since the beginning of our era, however, the Celtic languages have been steadily receding.

The Celtic languages are classified into two groups, one in which PIE /kʷ/ has become *p*, **p-Celtic** or **Brythonic**, the other in which it is a velar, **q-Celtic** or **Goidelic**.

Gaulish, attested in names and inscriptions from before our era, was a continental Brythonic dialect; it is no longer spoken. The remaining Brythonic dialects, **Welsh**, **Cornish** and **Breton**, are continuations of dialects spoken in Britain before the Roman invasion. Our earliest manuscript materials are glosses, words written in manuscripts to translate difficult words in the original, much as language students do today. We have glosses from around AD 800 for Welsh and Breton. Literary materials in Welsh survive in considerable quantity from the twelfth century. Today Welsh is the Celtic language with the greatest number of speakers. Breton, which was taken to the continent in the fifth and sixth centuries AD as a result of the Germanic invasion of England, is still maintained in Brittany. Cornish became extinct in the eighteenth century.

Of Goidelic, two languages are attested initially, **Irish** and **Manx**, of the Isle of Man, which is now extinct. We have Irish materials in ogam inscriptions (see section 3.3) from around the fifth century AD, followed by glosses written by Irish monks on the continent in the eighth century. From the eleventh century a large amount of literary material is attested. Irish was taken to Scotland from the fifth century; a third language is referred to as **Scots Gaelic**. In Ireland itself, several dialects developed, some of which have been completely supplanted by English. After the independence of Eire, an attempt was made to establish one of these, Munster, as the national language, but the attractiveness and usefulness of English have thwarted the government's efforts. Celtic, an important subgroup several millennia ago, has largely been replaced by other languages.

4.2.10 The Germanic subgroup

Much of the displacement of Celtic has been brought about by the **Germanic** languages. Speakers of Germanic languages began their migrations in the last centuries before our era, and continued them for more than a millennium, with penetration westward to Iceland, Greenland and America, eastward into former Baltic and Slavic territory, and southward as far as Africa. In a second expansion from the sixteenth century, Germanic languages were again carried westward to North America, southward to South Africa, India and Australia and to lesser land masses of the world. The expansion of the Germanic languages occasioned in the centuries around the beginning of our era by the *Völkerwanderung* "migration of peoples," may provide an example of how various less thoroughly documented languages were spread from the millennium before our era, such as the Semitic and Chinese. It should be noted, however, that such large-scale movements were not possible in earlier periods.

Our first information about the Germanic tribes comes from classical writers; Caesar and Tacitus have given us especially valuable reports. The Romans seem to have confused Germans and Celts. The name, German, may have been taken over from that of a small Celtic tribe; many attempts in the the past to explain its origin, such as taking the first element to mean "spear", are speculative – in Caesar's day that word still had an *s*, not an *r*. Apart from Germanic place and personal names, we have no data until the fourth century; our attempts to determine the early history of Germanic must therefore be based entirely on reconstruction. For this reason the classification of the Germanic dialects has until recently indicated their distribution several centuries after Christ rather than their earlier development. Handbooks generally speak of three subdivisions: **East**, **West**, and **North Germanic**. Linguistic indications suggest that we should rather speak of two: a *ggw* group, including the so-called East and North

Germanic dialects, in which *ggw* developed from *ww*, and *ddj* or *ggj* from *jj*; and a *ww* group, corresponding to the West Germanic dialects, in which *ww* and *jj* were maintained. In the past decades attempts have been made to distinguish subgroups in the *ww* group, often with greater reliance on cultural than linguistic data. We no longer believe that there was little intercommunication among Germanic subgroups in England, Scandinavia and northern Europe. Accordingly, late mutual influences may have effaced earlier relationships; such intercommunication is especially clear in the Scandinavian area.

Materials from the fourth century AD have come down to us in Norway and Denmark, in the runic inscriptions. These are composed in a formalized language in which vowels of unstressed syllables are maintained. Among the best known is that on one of the golden horns of Gallehus, Denmark:

Ek HlewagastiR HoltijaR   horna tawido
"I Hlewagastir of Holt made the horn."

Early runic inscriptions are attested from the various Scandinavian areas, especially Norway, before the eighth century, with little dialect differentiation, probably in part because the inscriptions were composed in a conservative language of priests. From the time of Scandinavian expansion, we speak of two groups: **East Norse**, consisting of **Swedish**, **Danish**, and **Gutnish**; and **West Norse**, consisting of **Norwegian**, **Faroese** and **Icelandic**. The language of texts composed in Norwegian and Icelandic before the thirteenth century is commonly referred to as **Old Norse**, though since most texts have been produced in Iceland, also as **Old Icelandic**.

Icelandic has a specially rich and interesting literature from the thirteenth century. Moreover, several grammatical treatises on medieval Icelandic have come down to us, thanks to which Icelandic is thoroughly known from the medieval period on.

Although the other Scandinavian languages are labeled as separate languages, they have continued to influence each other, so that to this day Norwegian and Swedish are mutually intelligible; Danes can readily understand Norwegian and Swedish, though their own speech may cause Norwegians and Swedes difficulties. Technically, such mutually intelligible forms of speech are known as **dialects**, and the term **language** is used for mutually unintelligible forms of speech. But for national forms of speech the term dialect is apparently undignified. The Scandinavian languages are therefore excellent examples of the nonlinguistic designation "language" for forms of speech used by a nation rather than for forms of speech unintelligible to native speakers of other languages. As we see below, the situation is reversed in China. Its various languages that are mutually unintelligible, such as Mandarin and Cantonese, are generally referred to as dialects.

The most extensive early Germanic materials are from a **Gothic** translation of the Bible. The translation, comprising the bulk of our Gothic texts, is ascribed to a Visigoth, Wulfila (311–83?). It has been transmitted to us by Ostrogoths, in manuscripts of the late fifth and early sixth centuries. Gothic is relatively archaic, and transparent in grammatical structure; accordingly, it is important for comparative Indo-European studies. The Visigoths in Spain and the Ostrogoths in Italy were absorbed by subsequent ethnic groups, and their languages became extinct. Between 1560 and 1562, however, Busbecq, a Flemish ambassador of Charles V to Turkey, took down in Istanbul about sixty words from two natives of the Crimea. Characteristics, such as the *d* in *ada* "egg" make it unmistakable that their speech was Gothic. It is referred to as **Crimean Gothic**. Before more material than Busbecq's was collected, it passed out of use.

The *ww* group comprises five dialects: **High German**, **Franconian**, **Low German**, **Frisian** and **English**. For all of them we speak of Old, Middle and Modern (New) periods. These designations are imprecise, and will remain so until historical linguists define language stages by linguistic criteria. For reference to existing handbooks, however, it is well to know that "Old" generally refers to Germanic languages before the twelfth century, "Middle" from the twelfth to the fifteenth century and "New" to the subsequent period.

High German is attested first in proper names from the end of the seventh century, in glosses from the eighth and primarily in religious texts of the ninth. From the earliest times there are distinct dialects. Alemannic in the southwest and Bavarian in the southeast are generally referred to as Upper German. Through the thirteenth century the cultural center of Germany was in the south; our medieval literary materials are thus chiefly in Upper German. During the fourteenth century the political center moved further to the north. The language spread by the increasingly powerful political units of Middle Germany was also used by the Reformers of the sixteenth century, the most important of whom was Martin Luther (1483–1546); it is the basis of modern standard German. Many dialects are still in everyday use. One of these, Yiddish, split off from the main body of German in the late medieval period. Lacking the speech of a long-established political center like Paris or Florence, the accepted standard for High German was fixed only at the end of the nineteenth century. The pronunciation was based on that of the stage (*Bühnenaussprache*).

Low Franconian, the dialect of Franconian that has developed into a national language, is known from a few documents in the old period. At present it is represented by **Dutch** and its dialect **Flemish**, which is attested copiously in the medieval period. **Afrikaans** is the form of Dutch that has been established in South Africa.

Before the eighth century there was close association between the dialects on the coasts of England and those of northern Germany. As a result these dialects share common innovations and are often given a special label, **Ingvaeonic**, or North Sea Germanic. From the eighth century, however, High German exerted a progressively stronger influence on the dialects of northern Germany, so that we note a break between the earliest materials handed down to us from the lowlands of Germany, labeled **Old Saxon** and the later **Low German**. Old Saxon is attested from approximately the same time as is Old High German. Middle Low German and Modern Low German have been constantly receding before High German, especially since the political centralization of Germany in the nineteenth century.

Frisian, spoken on the coast and islands off the Netherlands and western Germany, is attested from the thirteenth century. Not a national language, it is maintained in various dialects by comparatively few speakers.

English is attested first in names from the seventh century. Literary remains, such as *Cædmon's Hymn* and *Beowulf*, are generally dated somewhat before 750. The early literature was produced in the north, but virtually all materials have come down to us in West Saxon, the dominant dialect at the end of the ninth century. In Old English there were three distinct dialects, Kentish, West Saxon and Northern (or Anglian), which was further subdivided into Northumbrian and Mercian. To distinguish "English Saxon" from the Old Saxon maintained on the continent, Old English was formerly referred to as Anglo-Saxon, but this designation is passing out of use.

In Middle English the dialect situation is even more complicated, though we may follow a classification into four subgroups, Northern, West Midland, East Midland and Southern. The dialect of London, on the border between Southern and Midland, came to be the model for standard English. Like New High German, Modern English is therefore not a direct continuation of the prominent language of the older period; both languages have complex histories.

Since approximately 1600, English has expanded continually. It is now the language used most widely as a second language and as an auxiliary language for international communication; as a first language, however, Mandarin Chinese probably has more speakers.

4.2.11 The Tocharian subgroup

At the close of the nineteenth century, the above-mentioned languages were assumed to be the only members of the Indo-European family from which materials of any extent survived. Explorers then discovered, unexpectedly, in Chinese Turkestan Buddhist writings dating from the sixth to the eighth centuries that are clearly Indo-European. The language was given the name **Tocharian**, as the result of a mistaken identification.

There are two dialects, labeled A and B. Specialists who have been unhappy with these colorless classifications of a misapplied name have attempted with little success to introduce other labels: Agnean or East Tocharian for Tocharian A; Kuchean, or West Tocharian for Tocharian B.

One of the remarkable features of Tocharian is the preservation of palatals as *k* before back vowels; in other Indo-European languages of the east these palatals had become sibilants. This finding dealt a severe blow to the traditional classification of Indo-European into satem dialects in the east and centum in the west. We do not know how the speakers of Tocharian came to their location, nor how the languages died out.

4.2.12 The Anatolian subgroup

The second language of which abundant materials were discovered in this century has also been mislabeled with a name that has been fixed – **Hittite**. Excavations near the Turkish village of Boğaz-köy uncovered in 1905–7 large quantities of cuneiform texts that were produced during the time of the Hittite Empire, which flourished from approximately 1700–1200 BC. Many more texts are being found. Since they were written in cuneiform, they could be read at once; moreover, many contain Akkadian and Sumerian, so that the meaning of the texts, and of most Hittite words, can be determined. In 1915 Hittite was identified as Indo-European by Bedřic Hrozný.

Twelve years later Jerzy Kurylowicz identified sounds transcribed *ḥ* with reconstructions that Ferdinand de Saussure, solely on the basis of reasoning from internal evidence, had proposed in 1879. Saussure's prediction has been proved to be one of the most remarkable in linguistics; moreover, it gave great credence to the method of internal reconstruction. Kurylowicz's identification helped add to the great interest in Hittite and in the early history of the Indo-European languages. Some Indo-Europeanists, notably E. H. Sturtevant, also proposed a reclassification of the family because of the *ḥ*-sounds, other archaisms and the early time of the records. They suggested that Hittite was a sister language, rather than a daughter language, of Proto-Indo-European, and proposed the new label **Indo-Hittite** for the family.

The subsequently deciphered Greek texts written in Linear B have now given us Greek materials contemporary with Hittite. With arguments from linguistic evidence, the Linear B texts have led Indo-Europeanists of today to retain the old label. One may explain the archaic features of Hittite by assuming that Hittite speakers made up the first group to leave the Indo-European community. Assumption of a considerable period of separation would also help to account for the innovations in Hittite.

Among the Hittite texts are found materials in two other related languages: **Palaic**, which is close to Hittite; and **Luwian**, which forms a distinct group. Related texts in a different script dating from approximately 1400–500 BC have been given the name Hieroglyphic Luwian. The poorly attested languages **Lycian** and **Lydian** are also assumed to be related to

Hittite, as members of the Luwian group. The entire group is referred to as **Anatolian**, or **Hittito-Luwian**, and is considered a separate branch of the Indo-European family.

The discoveries in Asia Minor have broadened and deepened our knowledge of Indo-European. Hittite has preserved Indo-European palatals, possibly because the change of some of these to sibilants took place after the Hittites left the Indo-European community. Hittite also has a grammatical system much simpler than that of Indo-Iranian and Greek, which earlier were taken as patterns for reconstructing the Indo-European grammatical system. Adequate studies have not yet been completed to modify this view; some Indo-Europeanists, however, have suggested that the complex verb systems of Indo-Iranian and Greek represent later developments rather than a retention from the parent language, a view that is gaining further adherents.

4.2.13 Reconstructed Proto-Indo-European

With Hittite we are in a position to reconstruct Proto-Indo-European of a period before 3000 BC. Older attempts to relate Indo-European with other language groups, such as Semitic, are accordingly obsolete. We now construct forms of Proto-Indo-European different from those in the standard handbooks of the late nineteenth-century Indo-Europeanists. A century and a half of work has not solved all problems concerning Indo-European. On the other hand, it has contributed excellent information on the development of the languages used by at least half the people alive today. It has also provided the methods for determining and classifying other language families.

One of the most important tools in historical linguistics developed for genealogical classification is reconstruction of prior unattested forms, especially in the parent language. Yet reconstructions must not be misused. They are merely concise statements of our information on the earliest stage of a language family. We can reconstruct syntactic patterns as well as phonological and morphological items, as did August Schleicher, in writing a tale in Proto-Indo-European. All reconstructions must be open to modifications, however, as more information is assembled. In the 1930s Hermann Hirt rewrote Schleicher's tale in accordance with his views of Proto-Indo-European, and subsequently Ladislav Zgusta and I have rewritten that version. Discovery of early materials, like those in Hittite and Mycenaean Greek, has demonstrated the basic accuracy of our reconstructions; but details have been modified, also on the basis of further information from typology. This information has been especially useful in reconstructing even earlier forms of the parent language, which we refer to as Pre-Indo-European.

4.3 THE AFRO-ASIATIC LANGUAGE FAMILY, AND OTHER LANGUAGE FAMILIES OF AFRICA

Two other language families provide us with texts over a period as long as that for Indo-European: the Afro-Asiatic and the Sino-Tibetan. Neither family has been as thoroughly investigated as has the Indo-European. For example, each includes languages that have not yet been described. And proto-languages have not been set up for subgroups, as they have for subgroups of Proto-Indo-European such as Proto-Germanic. As a result, a proto-language has not been reconstructed. The two families cannot, then, be presented with the same authority as can the Indo-European family. Rather than providing models for historical reconstruction of poorly attested languages, both families need a great amount of work.

The **Afro-Asiatic** family, also known as the **Hamito-Semitic**, the **Afrasian** and by still other designations, comprises five branches: (1) **Egyptian**, one of the earliest languages attested, with records from the fourth millennium; (2) **Berber**; (3) **Cushitic**; (4) **Chadic**; (5) **Semitic**, attested from the early part of the third millennium. Although Egyptian and Semitic are known from virtually the same early date, the languages differ considerably, especially in their vocabulary. The difference is ascribed to strong influence of even earlier speakers, that is to say, substrata, on each in the sites where they came to be established. The time of the proto-language is placed as early as the sixth to the eighth millennium, with homeland in the region of the present-day Sahara.

The basis for relationship is in part typological. The languages typically have roots consisting for the most part of three consonants, such as KTB. Infixed vowel "schemes" characterize verb and noun forms; for example, in Hebrew KATAB means "he wrote," KITAB means "book." A series of verbal systems is characterized by affixes. The primary distinction in the verb is aspectual rather than temporal. Nouns had few cases, probably only three in the proto-language.

The Berber, Cushitic and Chadic languages are known only from recent times. They are spoken over a broad band across northern Africa. Of them, Hausa in West Africa of the Chadic subgroup, has the greatest number of speakers. Many languages of these three subgroups remain to be described.

While Egyptian is attested in a long series of texts to the beginning of our era, its descendant from about the fourth century AD, Coptic, survives today only as a religious language.

Semitic has four subgroups, each with several languages, of which only the most important are mentioned here: North Peripheral, in which **Akkadian** is the major representative; North Central, with Phoenician, Hebrew and Aramaic; South Central, with Arabic; South Peripheral, with southern Arabic and Ethiopic. **Phoenician** was carried to Carthage, and continued in use there as late as the sixth century AD, where it is known as

Punic; it is meagerly attested in inscriptions and in some lines of Plautus.

Hebrew is attested from about 1100 BC. It was carried to the south from Mesopotamia somewhat earlier by a small group of nomads under the leadership of Abraham, as we may note from Genesis. Although it remained an important religious and literary language, it was largely replaced from the sixth century BC by **Aramaic**, which is attested in numerous dialects. In one of these, utterances of Jesus are cited in the New Testament, for example, Mark 5.41, *Talitha cumi* "Maiden, arise!" Hebrew was revived as a spoken language around the beginning of this century.

Arabic was the last of the Semitic languages to be widely extended, with the spread of the Moslem religion. Its dialects are spoken today throughout much of the Middle East and North Africa. Like **Ethiopic**, of which several forms are spoken in Ethiopia, it is attested only after the beginning of our era.

The other languages of Africa are attested only from very recent times. As a result the major linguistic work on them has been directed at description. But steps have also been taken to classify them genealogically. A large family to the south of the Afro-Asiatic is the **Chari-Nile**, or Macro-Sudanic, including Dinka and Shilluk. Apart from small or poorly defined groups, most of the other languages of Africa, including the **Bantu**, are classed in the **Niger–Congo** family. One of these, **Swahili**, a trade language, is used for communication through much of eastern Africa by speakers of a great variety of languages. The **Khoisan** family, including Bushman and Hottentot, is located on the southern borders of the Niger–Congo family.

4.4 SINO-TIBETAN AND OTHER LANGUAGES OF THE FAR EAST

Historically the family is important because of its long series of texts, and culturally for its extensive influence, as well as for its large number of speakers. While speakers of the Afro-Asiatic family are fewer than 200 million, a billion and several hundred million speakers have a **Sino-Tibetan** language as their native tongue; **Mandarin Chinese**, now known also as **Putonghua**, probably has the largest number of native speakers of any language.

Although we have more than three millennia of Chinese texts, they provide many problems because they were written in a logographic script. Pronunciation, then, must be determined from rhymes and rhyming dictionaries, and from borrowings into other languages, such as Japanese. The borrowings inform us primarily about the beginnings of morphs; rhyming dictionaries about their ends.

While the Sinitic subgroup is well known and long studied, many languages of the Tibeto-Burman subgroup are still undescribed. Moreover, little comparative work has been carried out to determine interrelationships between the two subgroups. Formerly Thai was often classed with Sinitic; but now the parallelisms between Thai and Chinese are viewed as typological and resulting from borrowings, not genealogical.

Of the Tibeto-Burman subgroup, **Tibetan** has the longest series of texts, beginning from the seventh century AD. The large number of additional languages of the subgroup are classified into six further groups; the interrelationships among these remain to be determined.

The Sinitic subgroup includes a large number of mutually unintelligible varieties; these are classified under various headings, today generally seven. Traditionally called dialects, they differ considerably. Yet the use of one writing system throughout China created the impression of one language. The seven groups, then, are generally referred to as dialects. These are, roughly from north to south: **Mandarin**, **Wú** (spoken around Shanghai), **Xiāng**, **Gàn**, **Hakka**, **Mǐn** or **Amoy-Swatow**, **Cantonese** or **Yuè**. Since the Second World War the government has been trying to have all Chinese learn Mandarin, with the further aim of introducing a phonetic writing system to replace the characters when all Chinese came to know Mandarin. Both aims are long-range.

Chinese has been preserved in inscriptions on bone and bronzes from the second millennium BC; literary documents of some length, such as the works of Confucius and Lao-tzu, have come down to us from the first millennium BC. The materials before the sixth century AD are now generally referred to as **Old Chinese**. **Middle Chinese** extends to the thirteenth century, and **New Chinese** from then to the present.

Chinese has long exerted an influence on neighboring languages. As we have noted, the influence on languages to the south led formerly to the view that **Thai** may be related to Chinese. It is now generally associated with Laotian and Shan in a separate family, labeled **Kadai**.

While **Korean** and **Japanese** also took over many loanwords from Chinese, they differ typologically to such an extent, that they have never been related to Chinese. In contrast with noninflected Chinese, both have considerable inflection for verbs. But their own genealogical relationship has not been determined, even though some scholars relate the two, and assume a further relationship to the dubious Altaic family.

To illustrate the difficulties of demonstrating relationships of these languages, we may review that portion of the Japanese numerals remaining after the classifier has been removed. We then are left with:

1 hi(to)	4 yo	7 nana	10 tō
2 fu(ta)	5 i	8 ya	
3 mi	6 mu	9 koko	

It is scarcely remarkable that such short and simple forms would be difficult to relate further, especially since, as we noted above, *mi mu*, *yo ya*, *hi fu* may be analysed as of two morphemes each. Only the Luchuan dialects, spoken in the Ryukyu islands south of Japan, can be related confidently to Japanese. The complexity of syllabic structure exhibited by the Indo-European languages has greatly helped linguists to verify their interrelationships and to assemble the detailed information we have on their history today.

4.5 FINNO-UGRIC AND OTHER LANGUAGE FAMILIES OF ASIA; GENEALOGICAL CLASSIFICATION WITH RELIANCE ON TYPOLOGY

Finno-Ugric, with an island of **Hungarian** speakers in Europe and nomadic speakers of **Lappish** in Scandinavia, extends eastwards from Estonia through Russia far into Siberia, with **Mari** or Cheremis, **Mordvin** and other sub-branches. **Samoyedic**, spoken in far-eastern Siberia, is one of these; when Samoyedic is included with Finno-Ugric, the term **Uralic** is used for the family. The Finno-Ugric languages, with the exception of **Finnish** with 5 million, **Estonian** with somewhat over a million, and **Hungarian** or Magyar, with 14 million, are spoken by small numbers of speakers, and have been receding before other languages, notably Russian. None of the languages have texts before the thirteenth century; most texts are from the sixteenth century and later. With Indo-European and Hamito-Semitic, Finno-Ugric was one of the first families to be demonstrated through capable methodology.

The **Uralic** languages, like the Altaic, are verb-final in syntax, agglutinative in morphology and most exhibit sound harmony. Although sound harmony differs from language to language, it requires words to select sets of sounds, like front vowels or low vowels, throughout. For example, in Turkish the plural morpheme may be *ler* or *lar*; if the stem vowel is front, *ler* is used, as in *Türkler* "Turks"; if it is back, *lar* is used, as in *çocuklar* "children." Other language families of Asia have comparable typology, and on the basis of these some scholars have grouped them together in a large **Ural-Altaic** "family." Since Proto-Uralic is placed at 8000–5000 BC, only small segments of it have been reconstructed. Evidence for reconstructing Proto-Altaic is scanty. A recent panel of Altaic specialists even recommended giving up the label **Altaic** and the assumption of such a family (see Baldi 1990: 481).

Three language families have been classed together under the label Altaic: **Turkic**, **Mongolian** and **Manchu-Tungus**. The earliest records we have for any of them are the Turkic Orkhon inscriptions of the eighth century. The recency of the texts may suggest why it is difficult to reconstruct proto-languages for even these families, let alone Altaic or Ural-Altaic. None the less, some scholars relate Korean to Ural-Altaic, and others even include Japanese. Such proposed relationships, also for languages discussed below, are not based on evidence obtained through use of the comparative method, as has been done for the Indo-European languages.

The principal languages of the **Dravidian** family are spoken in south India. One of them, **Telugu**, has the second largest number of speakers in India. **Tamil**, with almost as many speakers, **Kannada**, and **Malayalam** are also important. Since the Dravidian language **Brahui** is still spoken in the north of India, it has been suggested that Dravidian was the most widely distributed indigenous language family in India when Indo-European speakers invaded it near the end of the second millennium BC. This suggestion has received support from the proposal that the Indus texts are Dravidian. The Dravidian languages are agglutinative, and have been related to the Altaic languages on the basis of their typological similarity.

4.6 THE LANGUAGES OF THE PACIFIC AREA, INCLUDING AUSTRALIA; GENEALOGICAL CLASSIFICATION RELYING ON GLOTTOCHRONOLOGY

A very large number of languages in southeast Asia and the Pacific have been classed together in the **Austric** family, and further in **Austro-Tai**, though the evidence for reconstructing even the proto-languages of its assumed subgroups is small.

The three subgroups are: (1) **Austro-Asiatic**, extending from eastern India to Vietnam, and consisting of the **Munda** and **Mon-Khmer** subgroups; of the many languages, **Vietnamese** has most speakers, approximately 20 million. (2) **Tai-Kadai**, of Burma, southern China and Thailand. (3) **Austronesian**, extending from Madagascar to Easter Island, and from Hawaii to New Zealand.

Various classifications have been proposed for Austronesian. In order to sort out the subgroups of the 500 languages, the method of glottochronology was applied. On the basis of the results, the former classification into the four geographical groups, Indonesian, Melanesian, Micronesian and Polynesian, has now been abandoned, but two different subgroupings have been proposed. The language with the greatest number of speakers is **Bahasa Indonesia**, selected as national language of Indonesia and often known simply as Indonesian; it is based on **Malay**, a language of Malaya that came to be used as a trade language in Indonesia.

Glottochronology was also applied to determine the subgroups of the 200 Australian languages. The results identified a **Pama-Nyungan** family extending through much of the continent, and 29 other families in the northwest; it has also been proposed that these belong together under a group labeled Northern. The two are further combined under **Proto-Australian**. Like the languages of New Guinea, those of Australia are being described, so that eventually there may be more a secure basis for genealogical classification.

4.7 THE LANGUAGES OF THE AMERICAS; MASS COMPARISON

On the basis of study in the nineteenth as well as this century, many specialists in American Indian languages have set out to classify these languages in accordance with the methods used for the Indo-European languages. As a result, 54 families were proposed for North America, 23 for Mexico and Central America and around 75 families for South America. In 1929 Edward Sapir introduced a different approach for classification. Employing bolder methods of determining relationships, he proposed linguistic **stocks**, on the basis of broad structural similarity. His classification resulted in six stocks for North America extending into Mexico: **Eskimo-Aleut**, **Na-Déné**, **Algonkin-Wakashan**, **Hokan-Siouan**, **Penutian**, **Aztec-Tanoan**. While respecting Sapir for his brilliance, many American Indian specialists continued in their attempt at genealogical classification.

Recently, Joseph Greenberg proposed only three families for the Americas on the basis of mass comparison: Eskimo-Aleut, Nadéné, and **Amerind** comprising all the rest. This procedure relies on identification of lexical and morphological items. If an item can be found in any one member of a family that is comparable to an item in another, it is assumed to be an inherited trait. The comparable items then are taken as evidence of original relationship between the families in which such an item is found. The classification has given rise to considerable controversy, with Greenberg insisting that well-established families like the Indo-European were initially determined in this way and many specialists in American Indian languages requiring more specific evidence, as through sound laws. The controversy will only be resolved if further detailed comparison is carried out that will determine the subgroups, propose their proto-languages and reconstruct Proto-Amerind on the basis of them.

In contrast with the reliance on typological features for the Altaic classification, mass comparison is based on identified characteristics; the American Indian languages vary considerably in typology. When one considers the huge number of languages in the Americas or in Africa or in the Pacific in contrast with those in the Indo-European family, and when one compares the huge amount of attention to the Indo-European languages over more than two centuries, it is clear that a great deal of study must be devoted to these languages before genealogical classification will be as secure as that for the Indo-European languages.

4.8 MACRO FAMILIES; NOSTRATIC

At the end of his survey of nineteenth-century historical linguistics, Holger Pedersen suggested that a number of language families – Indo-European, Hamito-Semitic, Finno-Ugric, Turkic, the Caucasian languages and possibly others – may well be related. He proposed as the name for the macro-family Nostratian (based on Lat. *nostrās* "our countrymen"), now replaced by **Nostratic**. The suggestion was subsequently pursued, especially by Soviet linguists.

Two approaches have been followed in the efforts to support the suggestion. By one, items in the proto-languages of the posited families are compared and older items hypothesized on the basis of them. Credibility of the results therefore relies on the accuracy of the proto-forms in these families. We have seen that proto-forms are essentially nonexistent for Proto-Afro-Asiatic. Moreover, as noted above, specialists in Altaic have denied the validity of even assuming such a family. Widely accepted proto-forms are available only for Proto-Indo-European and then not without disagreement. It is not surprising, therefore, that Nostraticists arrive at different conclusions when they reconstruct Nostratic. None the less, some scholars remain devoted to the aim. And the notion of positing early languages has great appeal for the media, as well as for prehistoric anthropologists and biologists.

By another approach, selected lists of elements that are assumed to belong to the universal equipment of any language and express the "stablest meanings" are sorted out and compared. For example, rather than 200 or 100 words as used in glottochronology, Dolgopolsky selected fifteen. These are as follows: first-person marker, two, second-person marker, who/what, tongue, name, eye, heart, tooth, verbal negative, finger/toe nail, louse, tear (noun), water, dead.

While words for the meanings may be found in any language, a given form may not be maintained. For example, the Latin word for "tongue" is *lingua*, which is assumed to be related to the English word, if with unclear phonology as are also Lith. *ilgas* and OIr. *tenge*; the Greek word is *glôssa*. The variation has been explained as resulting from taboo. Social groups commonly substitute words for objects or activities that must not be mentioned except under specific circumstances, so that in time the word itself may be lost. Speakers of Proto-Indo-European applied taboo to names for dangerous animals like the bear, and to those for important parts of the body, such as the hand and the tongue. For western cultures, taboo has been applied to terms for the divinity, sexual relations and excretion. Recently, the area has been shifted to sex and race; the word *negro* has become very rare or been totally lost. In much the same way the original word for "tongue" was lost in Greek and another term was substituted, to remain as the taboo was superseded.

In view of forces like taboo affecting language, even a severely limited set of terms encounters problems. Establishment of macro-families then faces numerous hazards.

4.9 THE LIMITS OF GENEALOGICAL CLASSIFICATION

It may be apparent that the constant change of language eventually leads to stages that can no longer be readily related to stages thousands of years earlier. Few languages families are as well documented as the Indo-European; one of its members, Greek, provides us with texts extending over 3,500 years. Such a sequence of texts, also in the Indic sub-branch and somewhat less extensive in the Italic, made possible the current state of Indo-European studies. When, on the other hand, we attempt to reconstruct Proto-Indo-European from language data of the present, we encounter numerous problems. Even a fairly transparent set of cognates, cited in support of the possibility of reconstruction from material available only today, such as Eng. *tooth*, Germ. *Zahn*, Fr. *dent* and so on, fails to provide data for reconstructing PIE *(e)dont- "eater." Moreover, it would require a great deal of courage to reconstruct an r/n noun declension for the proto-language on the basis of words like English *water* and Norwegian *vatn*, or to propose that Proto-Indo-European was verb-final in syntax on the basis of the languages attested today. In short, the constant loss of elements results in limits to our reconstructions.

Moreover, languages themselves may be totally lost in favor of neighboring languages, as were Cornish in the eighteenth century, Dalmatian in the nineteenth, and many others known from history, such as Oscan and Umbrian in Italy. As with Oscan and Umbrian, we may be fortunate in having texts, as we also do for Akkadian, Hittite, Tocharian and others. But many languages named in historical sources have vanished without leaving texts. When such languages were lost, related languages may have survived. Some may be the only member of a family or stock to do so, such as Sumerian, Burushaski and Basque. Genealogical classification for such languages, then, is totally impossible. In short, the degree of success in genealogical classification depends in great part on available information. We have also noted that such success depends on the extent of attention given a language family. The Hamito-Semitic family, for example, did not receive nearly as much attention as did the Indo-European in the nineteenth century, and accordingly its classification is far less complete.

Of language groups, the Romance languages have been most thoroughly studied. As an example of the advanced state of their study, we may note that effects of phonosymbolism, as well as sound change, have been demonstrated in their development. In the Indo-European family, certainly for older stages, our primary goal is recognition of sound correspondences in phonology, and similar results at the other levels of language. Achievement of this goal has made possible a credible reconstruction of much of the proto-language from the fourth millennium before our era. We would, however, be highly cautious about proposing to account for specific forms on the basis of phonosymbolism.

Even though we cannot account for the Indo-European languages to the extent of the Romance, the extent of reconstruction achieved for Proto-Indo-European is available for no other family, as we have noted. We have also indicated problems that remain to be solved for comparable understanding of the Hamito-Semitic, Sino-Tibetan and Finno-Ugric families, and thereupon for other families.

Some aims of genealogical classification have been achieved for these families, as we may illustrate for Hamito-Semitic. There is some agreement on the phonological, morphological and syntactic system for Proto-Semitic, as well as identification of many lexical items. But because we cannot reconstruct Proto-Hamitic, Proto-Berber, Proto-Chadic or Proto-Cushitic, we are unable to reconstruct the parent language.

We may note a further difference between our control of the Indo-European family and many others. In the Indo-European languages we set out to explain every form and every item. We may account for them as native or as borrowed. When we do, we determine the relationship between the native form and the form in the proto-language, or we seek the source of the borrowed form and determine the relationship between the forms in the two languages. For example, we can trace the English word *ore* to its Proto-Indo-European etymon, and we can relate the English word *copper* to its source in the name of the island *Cyprus*. It is clear from the preceding paragraph that we cannot achieve comparable explanation for any other language family.

Yet such explanation is the goal of historical linguistics. In the second section of this chapter we have sketched the basis for such an achievement in Indo-European linguistics. A similar achievement is the aim of genealogical classification and of historical linguistic study for other language families as well. In the absence of such classification, we may resort to typological classification, by procedures noted in the following chapter.

SELECTED FURTHER READINGS

A compact compilation on language families that includes samples of annotated texts is *Les Langues du monde*, prepared in a second edition (1952) by a group of linguists under the direction of Marcel Cohen, though the names Antoine Meillet and M. Cohen have been maintained from the first edition. A more recent survey, lacking samples of texts, is Voegelin and Voegelin (1977). A more select treatment is Comrie (1987); it may be noted that 531 pages are allotted to Indo-European languages and 448 to all others. Baldi (1990) includes sets of essays on American Indian, Austronesian, Indo-European, Australian, Altaic and Afro-Asiatic languages. Moreover, competent summaries may be found in encyclopedias, such as the *Britannica*; these are especially useful for their maps.

PROBLEMS

1 In determining subgroups of the Indo-European family, various characteristics have been applied. One we have noted is the contrast between sibilants in Indo-Iranian, Armenian, Slavic, Baltic and Albanian and tectal stops in Tocharian, Anatolian, Greek, Italic, Germanic, Celtic. Other characteristics show different distributions. Among these are the following.

(a) When a dental comes to stand before *t* in word formation, the cluster becomes Indic *tt*, Iranian, Greek, Baltic and Slavic *st*, Italic, Germanic and Celtic *ss*. (The results in other dialects, for example Armenian and Albanian, are unclear.) As a solution to the developments, it has been proposed that the initial result was *-tst-*. This cluster was then reduced as stated above. Account for the distribution of *tt st ss*. What information does the distribution give us about the relationship between the subgroups, for example Greek with reference to Indo-Iranian and Italic? How do you account for the difference between Indic and Iranian?

2 Germanic and Armenian have been distinguished from the other subgroups through large-scale shifts of the obstruents, as described for Germanic in Grimm's law. These shifts have been treated as independent developments in the two subgroups. Moreover, it has been assumed that these two dialects disrupted the obstruent system of the protolanguage.

(a) When we examine the Germanic situation in conjunction with phonemic theory, we note little disruption of the system. The threefold contrast of the obstruents ⋅that may be represented by *t dh d* is maintained in Germanic by *þ ð t*. Except for the effects of Verner's law, disruption is found only when *s* preceded *t*, so that PIE *t* in this environment fell together with the reflex of PIE *d*. Other dialects, however, collapsed original contrasts; for example, in Iranian, Slavic and Baltic *dh* fell together with *d*. Viewed phonemically the disruption in these dialects is greater than that of the Germanic shift. Discuss the interpretation of phonological developments in accordance with the theories one holds.

What conclusions about earlier relationships between Slavic, Baltic and Iranian can we draw from their treatment of the *dh* sounds?

(b) By the glottalic theory the Proto-Indo-European obstruent system consisted of .three elements we may represent as *t d t'*, the last glottalized; both *t* and *d* have aspirated allophones, for example [t tʰ d dʰ]. By the theory the allophone [tʰ] became the most frequent one in Germanic, yielding *þ*; similarly *dh* to *ð*. And *t'* became lenis, yielding *d*. In other dialects, for example Sanskrit, the unaspirated allophone of /t/ became most prominent. In Iranian, Slavic and Baltic the unaspirated allophone of *d* became most prominent, falling together with the reflex of *t'*. Discuss in accordance with the glottalic theory the shift in Germanic by contrast with those in other dialects. Which approach, the phonemic or the glottalic, allows the simplest explanation of the relationships between the proto-language obstruent system and those of the daughter languages?

3 When dialects split away, it is generally assumed that a bifurcation occurs; for example, when American English *-t-* became *-d-*, there was a contrast between the *-d-* speakers and all others.

In subgrouping languages this observation is often neglected. For example, Proto-Germanic is generally assumed to have yielded three subgroups: East, North and West. As we have seen, there is a strong argument in favor of a classification into North (including East) and South (rather than West) on the basis of the change of *-jj-* to *-dd/ggj-* and of *-ww-* to *-ggw-* in North (and East) Germanic. Moreover, in North Germanic the second singular preterite ends in *-t*, as opposed to *-i* in the south; cf. Goth. *banst*, ON *bazt*, OE *bunde*, OHG *bunti* "thou didst bind."

Yet there are also agreements between East and West Germanic, as in the use of Goth. *is*, OHG *er* as anaphoric pronoun "he" as opposed to ON *hann*. Moreover, Goth. *haban*, OHG *habēn* "have" contrast with ON *eiga* "have."

Agreements between North and West Germanic are found primarily in (1) the loss of the reduplicated preterite, as in ON *heldom*, OE *heldon* "held" in contrast with Goth. *haihaldum*; (2) the loss of the mediopassive; and (3) in umlaut, for example Goth. *gasts*, cf. runic *-gastiR*, ON *gestr*, OE *giest* "guest."

Using these criteria, comment on the classification of early dialects. How useful is reliance on loss in such classification? Reliance on lexical items?

Tendencies in a language, known as drift, may direct parallel developments after languages have split into dialects. Which of the changes above may be the result of drift? And if it is, how useful is it for subclassification?

Gothic is attested primarily from Wulfila's Bible translation of about 375 AD. After that only short sequences have been preserved for us, such as names. By contrast, we have no Old English, nor Old High German material of any extent until the eighth century, and North Germanic material even later. How might the time of our materials affect our view of the classification? In view of the different dates for our materials, which of them would be most useful: phonological, morphological or lexical?

4 Examine the classification of any of the following language families in a handbook or an encyclopedia, preferably contrasting the presentation in several: Finno-Ugric, Afro-Asiatic (Hamito-Semitic), Altaic, Austronesian, Dravidian.

(a) Determine the basis of the subclassification, whether lexical, phonological or other, such as typological.
(b) State uncertainties of the authors of the classification, including reasons for them. Is there likelihood that the uncertainties can be resolved by acquisition and analysis of new data?

5 Typological classification

5.1 AIMS OF TYPOLOGICAL CLASSIFICATION

Languages may be classified on a totally different basis from that used to determine genealogical relationship, that is, by attention to their type. In typological classification, selected features may be used to sort out languages, or for that matter any items of human culture, such as tools or social systems, for example, those employed in kinship systems. Linguistic classification by types has the advantage that a language of any period may be sorted into a specific group; languages attested only today can be so treated, as well as languages attested several millennia ago. Moreover, it has become clear that determination of types provides understanding of the structure of a given language. It is also obvious that such understanding is in accordance with the bases selected for typological classification. Over the past three and more centuries different bases have been selected, and different procedures have been employed, with gradual improvement in methods and results.

Identification of selected characteristics grew out of the attention to languages of the nonwestern world during the seventeenth and eighteenth centuries. As noted above, these reached their culmination in Adelung's *Mithridates* (1806–16). When we examine its classification, we note that it sorts languages into two types: monosyllabic and polysyllabic. Chinese is the first of the monosyllabic languages to be presented by Adelung; of the many polysyllabic languages we may compare his treatment of Turkish.

For each, Adelung includes statements on phonology, as that Chinese has no final consonants other than nasals and that it has tones, while Turkish has many phonological elements and generally places the accent on the last syllable of words. Further, that Chinese is uninflected, while Turkish has six cases. Moreover, patterns of syntax are given, such as the Chinese comparative construction with modifier before the simple adjective (corresponding to Eng. *more* (*accurate*)) followed by the standard, and the Turkish construction with the ablative form of nouns before the simple adjective. However accurate many of these observations may be, Adelung's *Mithridates* today is chiefly of interest in illustrating the great amount of information concerning languages that was compiled in times of cumbersome travel.

Adelung's classification was determined before linguistics was influenced by Cuvier's pronouncement on the need to base research into human pursuits on structures in which all parts are interrelated. With its simple lists of characteristics, *Mithridates* was generally disregarded in the nineteenth century. The new emphasis on morphology now directed typological study.

In 1818 August Schlegel proposed the typological classification that was widely followed and elaborated through the nineteenth century. It still has popular currency. According to this classification, languages may be **analytic (isolating** or **root** – with no inflection) like Chinese or Vietnamese; or they may be **synthetic (inflectional)** like Latin and Greek. The agglutinative languages, like Turkish and Japanese, were further assumed to make up a transitional class.

Agglutinative languages are differentiated from inflectional languages because they maintain bases distinct from endings and they show little morphophonemic change at morpheme boundaries; moreover, they have few suppletive forms like those in *good, better, best*. Contrast the Turkish inflections of *yol* "way" and *kuş* "bird" with those of Lat. *via* and *avis*:

Nominative	yol	via	kuş	avis
Genitive	yolun	viae	kuşun	avis
Dative	yola	viae	kuşa	avī
Accusative	yolu	viam	kuşu	avem
Ablative	yoldan	viā	kuştan	avī

The Turkish endings can be neatly separated from the stem and are the same for both examples, though with modifications by phonological harmony; by contrast, in Latin the endings have merged with the vowel of the base and can only be determined by historical methods. By means of such methods, we can propose that the stems of "way" and "bird" are **via-* and **avi-*, and that the endings on these two nouns are parallel to one another; but, as in other inflected languages, we cannot sort out the endings as readily as we can those of agglutinative languages.

When we examine Proto-Indo-European, we can separate the endings almost as if they were affixed as in Turkish. This transparency was interpreted by early nineteenth-century scholars as indicating that inflectional languages developed from agglutinative. Although this nineteenth-century view was based solely on morphological phenomena, the intent behind it illustrates the importance of typological classification for historical linguistics. If we can determine specific frameworks to classify the components of various types of languages, we will be able to use them in studying language change.

A framework of sounds has been used for some time in studying phonological systems. During the past generation, a framework for syntactic systems has been produced; with its help we can relate selected syntactic characteristics with specific sentence patterns. As a result, we can now deal with syntactic change in much the same way historical linguists of the past have dealt with phonological change. For just as phonological systems are never completely in balance, so syntactic systems are not completely consistent within a standard framework. Inconsistencies within a syntactic framework may be accounted for as the results of historical change.

A framework for semantic systems would permit us to deal as rigorously with semantic change as we have with phonological change. Until now only partial semantic frameworks have been produced, among them a framework for kinship systems; it will be examined in the chapter on semantic change. In a major important advance, Soviet linguists have extended typological systems to include the lexical as well as the grammatical system, labeling the approach "contentive typology." We will examine the procedures that have been proposed to deal with languages in accordance with the devices selected for establishing typologies.

5.2 PHONOLOGICAL TYPOLOGY

The primary elements that have been used in phonological classification are phonemes and their arrangements. Among the arrangements studied are configurations of vowel phonemes arranged in accordance with their place and manner of articulation. Some languages have a triangular system of vowels, such as that of the short vowels of some Arabic dialects:

$$i \qquad u$$
$$a$$

or the system of five short vowels in Classical Latin:

$$i \qquad\qquad\qquad u$$
$$e \qquad o$$
$$a$$

or the system of seven short vowels of contemporary Italian:

$$i \qquad\qquad\qquad\qquad\qquad u$$
$$e \qquad\qquad\qquad o$$
$$\epsilon \qquad\quad \mathrm{\inverted c}$$
$$a$$

Other languages have rectangular systems, such as Tonkawa:

$$i \qquad o$$
$$e \qquad a$$

or Turkish, with its eight-vowel system:

i	ü	ı	u
e	ö	a	o

or English, with the nine-vowel system proposed by some linguists:

i	ı	u
e	ə	o
æ	a	ɔ

Such configurations assist us in understanding rearrangements resulting from sound changes. For example, the Latin system was expanded in Italian, but the basic configuration was maintained. The New High German system, which developed from a short vowel system in Old High German similar to that of Latin, introduced front rounded vowels, *ü* and *ö*, modifying the system in a different way from Italian:

i	ü		u
e	ö	o	
		a	

Yet in both Italian and German the development that led to the new system can readily be understood on the basis of the earlier configuration. Specialists have determined the specific changes in each language that led to the changed systems.

Configurations like those given above are based on only a few distinctive features: height, backness and rounding. Two degrees of height are evident in Arabic, Tonkawa and Turkish; three in Classical Latin, English and German; four in Italian. Two degrees of frontness or backness are evident in Tonkawa and three in English. The apparent four of Turkish are found in a system with three characteristic features: height, backness and rounding; accordingly, there are only two degrees of backness (front and back), each further distinguished by rounded and unrounded elements. For a precise account of the changes in languages it is advantageous to determine the distinctive features on which the configuration is based.

Consonant systems too may be classified for configurations of phonemes. English has a relatively large number of fricatives and relatively few stops; moreover, all these obstruents have voiceless and voiced pairs.

p			t		č	k
b			d		ǰ	g
	f	θ		s	š	
	v	ð		z	ž	
m			n			ŋ
w		r	l	y		h

Sanskrit, on the other hand, has a large number of stops, few fricatives and a symmetrical arrangement of aspirated and nonaspirated stops.

p	t	ṭ	c	k
ph	th	ṭh	ch	kh
b	d	ḍ	j	g
bh	dh	ḍh	jh	gh
m	n	[ṇ	ɲ	ŋ]
	v l r		y	
	s	ṣ	ś		h

If we compare with the current English consonant system that of Old English, we find that the voiced members of the fricative and affricate series developed in late Old English times or subsequently. After they developed, the opposition of voicing came to apply to all English obstruents.

In early Sanskrit, voiceless aspirates were introduced, contrasting with the voiced aspirates, as in the dental position:

$$
\begin{array}{ll}
t & th \\
d & dh
\end{array}
$$

As with vowel systems, the configurations of consonants assist us in understanding changes that have occurred.

In addition to comparing configurations of phonemes, we may compare the use of distinctive features throughout phonological systems. Distinctive features have been proposed for various articulatory and acoustic characteristics. If classified for the distinctive features proposed by Roman Jakobson, the stop systems of Czech and French pattern like the vowel systems of Wichita and Arabic:

	Czech		French		Wichita		Arabic	
Diffuse	t	p	t	p	i	u	i	u
Compact	c	k		k	æ	a		a
	Acute	Grave	Acute	Grave	Acute	Grave	Acute	Grave

We would expect the systems illustrated here to be subject to different modifications, in accordance with their use of distinctive features.

With a distinctive-feature analysis, we can point precisely to the changes introduced in systems, though the specific distinctive features characterizing phonemes in earlier periods may be uncertain. Yet some are clear, such as the extension of continuant articulation in Proto-Germanic in contrast with Proto-Indo-European; compare PGmc *f θ χ* with PIE *p t k*. For improved understanding of specific phonological changes, we attempt to determine the distinctive features of a system as well as its phonemes.

5.3 MORPHOLOGICAL TYPOLOGY

Besides August Wilhelm Schlegel (1767–1845) a succession of brilliant linguists concerned themselves with typology in the nineteenth century, all centering on morphology: Wilhelm von Humboldt (1767–1835), Heyman Steinthal (1823–99) and Franz N. Finck (1867–1910). Finck extended the list of types from the three: analytic, agglutinative and synthetic, to eight. His set is based on three possible segments of words: roots, stems, inflections, and on the relationships between these segments in a given language. The root is the meaning-bearing element, for example Lat. *fer* "carry!" The stem is made up of a root and an element placed before the inflectional element, as in Lat. *fer-i-mus* "we carry." From the type that he analysed as consisting solely of roots to the type that in effect combined all elements of a sentence into a synthetic whole, he saw a gradual progression.

The eight types are as follows, with characteristic languages for each:

Isolating	Chinese	root-isolating
	Samoan	stem-isolating
Inflected	Arabic	root-inflected
	Greek	stem-inflected
	Georgian	group-inflected
Elements not combined with base	Subiya (Bantu)	juxtaposing
	Turkish	agglutinative
	Eskimo	polysynthetic or incorporating

Finck did not assume that languages would correspond exactly with any one of these types; but the set provided a framework in which to place any language. His classification was never expanded. Nor did he relate his morphological types with possible syntactic or semantic types. Edward Sapir (1884–1939) in his book *Language* (1921: 150–1) proposed a comparable classification that involved semantic analysis. But his framework was not adopted for historical study.

We may note still that Finck also characterized languages by the relationship between a situation and the expression of it in the language. To illustrate that characterization of his, we may choose as a situation a man approaching. This situation would be analysed into two components: an actor and an action. In expressing the situation, a Chinese speaker reports it by matching each component with a word: $t'a^1$ "he" lai^2 "come." A Turkish speaker would use only one word, *geliyor*, combining the two situational elements. An English speaker would use three, *he is coming*, introducing more words than there are components in the situation.

By this criterion the languages would be arrayed as follows:

Eskimo	(one word includes several elements of the situation)
Turkish	
Georgian	(intermediate between Eskimo and Chinese)
Arabic	
Chinese	(one word corresponds to one element of the situation)

Greek   ⎫
Samoan ⎬   (intermediate between Chinese and Subiya)
Subiya   (one word corresponds to less than one element of
                the situation)

Some nineteenth-century linguists assumed that languages evolved, as
did human beings. Either the most complex type, for example Eskimo, was
taken to be oldest, or the root-isolating type, for example Chinese. For
such scholars, arrays like those of Finck would be important in providing a
basis for determining the stage of development in a language or language
family. The dominant linguist in the Soviet Union, whose influence pre-
vailed until the early fifties, Nikolaj Marr (1864–1934), held such views,
taking the root-isolating as the most primitive. The position was abruptly
rebuffed by Stalin, when China and the Soviet Union came to be closely
aligned. While fascination concerning the relationship of language and
thought, and their possible evolution, is still prominent for some scholars,
most historical linguists consider such problems outside the sphere on
which they have information.

Moreover, morphological typology has not provided insights into development of other segments of language. As a result, it is largely of interest
for interpreting linguistic statements of the past.

5.4 SYNTACTIC TYPOLOGY

In an important essay in *Universals of Language* (1963), Joseph Greenberg
(1915–) pointed out that the normal position of verbs with regard to their
objects in a language is correlated with the position of elements in other
syntactic patterns, such as comparative constructions. Moreover, if verbs
normally precede their objects, relative constructions follow the nouns
they modify, as do adjectives and possessives. Further, languages with
V(erb–)O(bject) order have prepositions rather than postpositions. If, on
the other hand, objects precede their verbs (**OV** languages), the order in
these constructions is reversed.

The parallel constructions in consistent languages result from two syntactic processes: government and modification. Prepositions and postpositions, referred to under the cover term **adpositions**, are comparable to
verbs in governing objects; comparatives have a similar relationship with
the standard in the comparison. Accordingly, in the constructions illustrated below, 1, 5 and 6, have a comparable pattern. On the other hand,
adjectives and possessives, like relative clauses, modify nouns; their pattern, then, is parallel in a consistent language, as in 2, 3 and 4.

To indicate the patterning in consistent languages, we illustrate the
selected constructions with the VO language Portuguese and the OV
language Japanese. Spanish and French could also serve as consistent VO
languages; Turkish and Quechua as consistent OV ones. The patterns are:

1 (a) Normal word order in declarative sentences: *John saw the dog;*
(b) *Mary saw the cat.*
2 Relative construction: *John saw the dog that ate the meat.*
3 Descriptive adjective: *John saw the big dog.*
4 Possessive construction: *John saw the dog of his neighbor.*
5 Adposition: *John saw the dog from the window.*
6 Comparative construction: *The dog is bigger than the cat.*

	VO	OV
1 (a)	João viu o cachorro.	Tarō ga inu o mita.
	John saw the dog	Taro dog saw
(b)	Maria viu o gato.	Jirō ga neko o mita.
	Mary saw the cat	Jiro cat saw
2	João viu o cachorro que comen a carne.	Tarō ga niku o tabeta inu o mita.
	John saw the dog that ate the meat	Taro meat ate dog saw
3	João viu o cachorro grande.	Tarō ga takai inu o mita.
	John saw the dog big	Taro big dog saw
4	João viu o cachorro do siu vizinho.	Tarō ga kinjo no hito no inu o mita.
	John saw the dog of his neighbour	Taro neighbourhood's man's dog saw
5	João viu da janela o cachorro.	Tarō ga mado yori inu o mita.
	John saw from-the window the dog	Taro window from dog saw
6	O cachorro é maior que o gato.	Inu ga neko yori takai.
	The dog is larger than the cat	Dog cat from large

In applying such frameworks, several cautions are important. The patterns given here are the normal ones. But normal or unmarked patterns are often modified for emphasis; they are then said to be marked. For example, in Portuguese the verb may also be initial in the sentence *Viu João o cachorro*; this order is used to single out the verb and its meaning. In view of the possibility of reordering sentence elements in marked constructions, it may be difficult to determine the normal order of sentences when we are dealing with languages of the past. The difficulty is compounded by the kinds of texts that have survived; these are often literary, which make great use of marked constructions. Therefore it is advisable to locate constructions that have normal, unmarked word order.

The most secure of these is the comparative; it is never changed for literary effect. English poets would never say "He you from is better," even though they might use postposed adjectives, as did Longfellow in "This is the forest primeval."

Another syntactic construction that is relatively secure is found when two sentences with one of the same elements are co-ordinated; for example, "John saw the dog (and) Mary saw the cat." When such sentences are co-ordinated, the repeated verb may be omitted in a pattern labeled gapping; for example, "John saw the dog and Mary the cat." When gapping involves verbs with objects, as in this example, the verb is maintained in the first sentence of consistent VO languages. In consistent OV languages, on the other hand, it is maintained in the last. Compare the gapping constructions of Portuguese and Japanese for the sentence: "John saw the dog and Mary the cat." *João viu o cachorro e Maria o gato. Tarō ga inu o to Jirō ga neko o mita.* Again we may note the unlikelihood of the OV pattern in English; we do not expect the sentence **John the dog and Mary saw the cat.*

If we can find examples of the comparative construction and of gapping in texts, we may determine the underlying order of sentences, and accordingly the basic type of the language in which the texts are written.

As we will note in further detail below, identification of these and other characteristic patterns in different stages of a language provides information on syntactic change and its direction. For example, Homeric Greek has many comparative constructions like that illustrated for Japanese, while in later periods the comparative constructions are like those in English. From these and other patterns in the two stages of Greek we can determine that the language was developing from OV to VO structure.

As another example, we may note that English has maintained the OV pattern for descriptive adjectives. By examining such syntactic irregularities we can gain insights into the earlier structure of languages. Adjectives are conservative in maintenance of earlier structures. For example, although the unmarked order for adjectives in French is in accordance with the VO pattern, a small group of the most frequent, like *bon* "good," *jeune* "young," *haut* "high," has maintained the OV order. Such conservative patterns in syntax are comparable to maintained morphological patterns in words of the everyday language, for example *man : men, woman : women, mouse : mice, go : went : gone, sing : sang : sung.* Residues like these are of great importance for historical linguists in providing clues to explore for determining the patterns in earlier stages of a language.

5.5 TYPOLOGY BASED ON A SINGLE PARAMETER

The syntactic conclusions presented in section 5.4 are based on linguistic processes, that is, government and modification or agreement. In contrast with such an approach, some linguists have attempted to provide a model based on one construction or process.

As first we may mention Pater Wilhelm Schmidt (1868–1954), who concerned himself with the language families of the world and with their typological classification (1926). In his treatment of syntax he considered the position of the genitive crucial. Moreover, he related other characteristics to it, in this way proposing implicational features. Among such characteristics are position of the accusative (object) and use of pronouns.

But in addition he aligned the position of the genitive with the cultural stage of a society. Preposed position he saw as the primitive structure.

Thereupon, with the introduction of agriculture, women came to occupy a much more prominent role. Their control of wealth through produce and other attendant customs led to matriarchy. It also led to a more rational view of life. Because postposed position of the genitive and accompanying characteristics were for Schmidt in keeping with more rational societies, the genitive came to be placed after nouns, resulting in other syntactic changes.

In view of our observations in section 4, Pater Schmidt's association of syntactic positions is highly interesting, though his data, as he admits, are often poor. But his further association of language with culture seems to us rash. He formed his views at the conclusion of a period in which linguistics and psychology were closely aligned. While later linguists have made grand claims about the relationship of language and mind, those claims too have remained unverified. Later scholars have also made statements about OV order as primeval, as well as about early matriarchal cultures. But as the current status of Pater Schmidt's views may indicate, such statements have little scientific basis, however appealing they may be to generalists and to the media.

In his attempt to propose one process, Vennemann (1975) adopted a logical point of view. For him the basic process involves relating an operator and an operand. That is to say, the process is comparable to government; such elements as verbs and adpositions are taken as operators controlling nouns and other operands. Modifying constructions are similar, with relative clauses, genitives and adjectives as operators and nouns and other elements modified as operands. The assumption of a single principle may be commendable, but in language the treatment of modifiers differs considerably from that of governing elements; for example, modifying elements like adjectives and relative pronouns are often inflected to indicate relationships with nouns they modify, whereas governing elements like verbs and prepositions remain fixed with regard to objects that themselves often have inflected forms to indicate the relationship.

Adopting a different relationship as central, Nichols (1986) finds it to be that between head and dependent. That relationship is comparable for all basic syntactic constructions that consist of two such elements. Nichols identifies as heads, possessed nouns with reference to a possessor, nouns with reference to a modifying adjective, adpositions and verbs with regard to their objects, auxiliary verbs with regard to main verbs, and main-clause predicates with regard to subordinate clauses. While principally concerned with setting up a typology, Nichols also proposes genealogical preferences for either head-marking or dependent-marking. The Indo-European languages, for example, are dependent-marking, with objects indicated by inflections, as in accusative case forms; yet the morphological marking has been reduced over the course of time, as in English. None the less, Nichols proposes that through painstaking analysis of relationships and processes, historical developments can be clarified. The approach may yield results when applied rigorously to those linguistic families that have not been securely established, as in the Americas, Africa, Asia, the Pacific and Australia, as Nichols suggests. The proposed typology then remains to be exploited by specialists in these fields.

These three approaches may serve to illustrate the statement above that typologies may rest on various bases. The success of any such base depends on its recognition of underlying principles in language. Like other sciences, linguistics relies on theories; when upheld through applications, the theory in question gains in credibility.

5.6 CONTENTIVE TYPOLOGY

For some time Soviet linguists have been developing a typological approach that includes consideration of the lexicon. The approach is named after its wide scope, that is, attention to content as well as to syntax and morphology.

Contentive typology posits two large classes of language. In one, government is the basic process, as in English, where verbs govern objects, as treated above. In the other class, the basic process is agreement among sets, as of animate nouns and active verbs, or of inanimate nouns and stative verbs. This class was first distinguished in 1917 by Edward Sapir, though in recent years its characteristics have been more fully determined by Soviet scholars.

5.6.1 Government-based languages

Languages in which government is the basic process for the production of sentences may be either **accusative** or **ergative**. Since accusative languages are like English, or the major languages of the western world, their characteristics do not need to be spelled out at this point.

Ergative languages differ from accusative languages in their expression for subjects of intransitive verbs. These select the same form as do objects of transitive verbs, as the following Georgian sentences illustrate.

mama-mokla irem-i   daeca irem-i
the father killed the deer fell the deer
                           "The deer fell."

The case that is used to indicate the subject of transitive verbs is known as the ergative; the case used to indicate the subject of intransitive verbs and the object of transitive verbs is known as the absolutive.

While the method of indicating subjects and objects differs in accusative and ergative languages, both are comparable in distinguishing subjects and objects when pertinent, that is, with transitive verbs. This distinction may be viewed as essential in communicating. Languages use various devices to express this distinction, as does English with nominative and accusative forms in sentences like *He saw her*. The subject of intransitive verbs does not require a special form since it does not need to be distinguished from an object. Accordingly, ergative languages make such sentences with the same form as that used for objects, as if we used the expression **Her went*. Such use of the objective case for the subject of intransitive verbs would be as unambiguous as is use of the nominative in *She went*.

As for all large classes proposed in linguistic study, there are various subclasses of ergative languages as well as of accusative languages. These do not concern us here; their characteristics may be pursued when such subtypes are encountered. Here it is especially important to observe that the lexical structure of accusative and ergative languages is comparable in permitting inanimate as well as animate nouns to function as subjects and objects of appropriate verbs. As in the sonnet of Milton of chapter 1, the subject of *steal* as of many other verbs may be an inanimate item like *time*, or an animate being.

5.6.2 Active–stative and class languages

This group of languages, as noted above, characterizes sentences by aligning active or animate nouns with active verbs, and inactive or inanimate nouns with stative or inactive verbs. Nouns and verbs fall either into an active or an inactive class. Equivalents for words like *chair, house, rest, be small* would be stative; equivalents for words like *man, horse, run, grow* would be active. As one point of interest, active languages may have two words for concepts that may be viewed as active or inactive, for example, *fire* (blazing or quiescent), *water* (flowing or still), *sit* (seat oneself or be sitting), *lie* (lay oneself down or be lying).

In active languages, for example Na-Déné, Sioux, and Tupi-Guaraní, a sentence is typically constructed of nouns and verbs belonging to one class. Different inflections for stative as opposed to active verbs, however, permit active nouns to be aligned with stative verbs. In this way a stative verb like *rest* may be used with man, as well as in sentences like *The chair rests on the floor*.

Active languages, as they are generally known, have many further characteristics. They include few or no adjectives; as in the illustrations above, which include "be small," stative verbs take the place that adjectives occupy in accusative and ergative languages.

Moreover, they have little inflection for nouns, often lacking plural forms. Verbs, on the other hand, have copious inflections, especially those in the active class; stative verbs have fewer distinctive forms, as in the plural.

Further, because transitivity is not a central force, there is no place for a passive. Verb systems, on the other hand, have inflections for centripetal and centrifugal force. Centripetal force implies that the meaning of the verb has an effect on the subject, as in the Middle Voice of early Greek and Sanskrit; a centripetal inflection may indicate reflexivization, like the middle in Odyssey 1.15: *lilaioménē pósin eînai* "desiring [middle] husband to-be" = "desiring him to be her husband." The phrase refers to Calypso, who desires Odysseus to be *her* husband; the reflexive meaning is given by the Middle form of the verb. Centrifugal force, on the other hand, implies that the meaning has an effect on other persons or objects.

In addition, active languages lack a verb for "have." They may express the meaning through use of a locative, comparable to the use of the dative in Latin, as in *mihi est liber* "to me is a book" = "I have a book." Similarly, nouns may not be inflected for genitive or possessive case; juxtaposition of animate and inanimate nouns may indicate the relationship.

As a final characteristic listed here, active languages make great use of particles. Rather than modal forms, they include particles that indicate modal force like that of the subjunctive.

In the following sections we will indicate briefly how the recognition of active languages has clarified some residues in the early Indo-European languages.

We may note briefly still that class languages make up a distinct group as opposed to active languages characterized above. In class languages, nouns and verbs are marked by specific prefixes or suffixes for semantic classes, as in the following Swahili example: *wa-le wa-toto wa-zuri we-me-kudja, ni-me-wa-ona* "the children beautiful two have come, I have seen them" = "the two beautiful children have come; I have seen them." The classes resemble gender classes, though they are more specific. Class languages, like Bantu, also include many more than the three gender classes of Indo-European.

Klimov (1977) has proposed that class languages are an early form of active languages. Yet since they have not been demonstrated to have a genealogical relationship with the major families examined here, we will not discuss their characteristics further.

5.7 USES OF TYPOLOGICAL FRAMEWORKS TO ACCOUNT FOR PATTERNS OF IMBALANCE IN A LANGUAGE

Because languages are constantly changing, their systems and subsystems are never in complete balance, as we noted for the English stops, fricatives and nasals above. We also observed that unbalanced patterns provide clues for assuming earlier structures, as well as leads for possible changes. For example, the unbalanced distribution of English /ŋ/ today may lead us to propose the two-member system of nasals that we find in Old English.

Evidence is also provided for earlier structures through residues. These are commonly found among words in the everyday vocabulary. We account for them by noting that children acquiring language learn such forms separately; only later do they relate irregular adjectives like *good* :

better : *best* to regular sets like *fine* : *finer* : *finest*. They may or may not attempt to regularize them; and their social group may or may not permit them to do so, as English speakers so far refuse regularization of *good* : **gooder* : **goodest*. Those not regularized are important for reconstructing earlier stages of a language.

In carrying out such reconstructions we assume a framework. The framework may be a simple subset of phonemes, like the nasals, or a morphological subset, like the adjectival pattern of comparison. The framework may also be a syntactic or contentive pattern as sketched above. Such a framework is not viewed as an ideal pattern; it simply represents the results of our observations on language. Languages have not been found, for example, in which ŋ is the only nasal, or *n* and ŋ the only two nasals. Similarly, the other frameworks mentioned have been formulated on the basis of our observations of morphological, syntactic and contentive patterning.

We may illustrate briefly the use of the active-language framework in accounting for problems in Proto-Indo-European. As one of the long-observed features of its noun inflection, Vedic Sanskrit attests few examples of plural forms for the oblique cases like the instrumental, dative and ablative. Moreover, these forms are treated differently from the singular forms in syllabification; the endings are regarded as distinct words, not as affixes. Further, the endings in these three cases of the plural are made with a -*bh*- marker, in contrast with more differentiated endings in the singular. When Hittite was discovered, its plural was found to be even more defective. Other Indo-European languages also provide problems in plural forms; for example, Baltic and Germanic have an -*m*- suffix in the dative while Latin, like Sanskrit, has a labial stop, -*b*-.

Until recently, no successful explanation of these irregularities was given. Then, when active structure came to be known, it was proposed that the imbalance between the forms in the singular and the plural of nouns reflected an earlier period when Pre-Indo-European was an active language. As noted above, active languages often have few inflected forms in the plural. We will see further evidence below in favor of the assumption that Pre-Indo-European was active. At this point we are merely concerned to point out that information on typological structures permits us to provide explanations for features in language that have seemed to be problematic.

5.8 RESIDUES IN ENGLISH FROM EARLIER OV SYNTACTIC STRUCTURE

Typological investigations have demonstrated that SVO languages like English have prepositions rather than postpositions. We have no constructions like Lat. *mēcum* "me with" = "with me." With nouns as well as with pronouns we place adpositions before the entities that they govern.

English, however, has maintained forms like *herein, therein, thereupon, whereupon*, especially in legal language. Although the first element is an adverb in English rather than a pronoun, as in Lat. *tēcum* "with you" etc., these English compounds are similar to other Latin expressions in which *cum* follows, such as the adverb *quōcumque* "wherever, anywhere," or adverbs that are parallel in formation, such as *quo-ad* "as far as, to the degree that."

When we examine Old English texts, we find that "prepositions" are placed after the adverbs *her, ðær* and *hwær*. Moreover, when used with such adverbs, they are treated as separate words; other words may even stand between the adverb and the preposition, as in *þæt þær ma monna inne ne wære* "that there were no more men therein." Furthermore, the pattern is widely used with personal pronouns as well, as in the sentence: *Da cwæd se Hælend him to* "Then the Savior said to him." The pattern is also found after nouns in early texts; the most widely cited pattern may be *Beowulf* 19: *Scedelandum in* "in Scandinavia."

Indo-European languages that are attested earlier, like Greek and Sanskrit, have many such patterns; grammars inform us that "Sanskrit prepositions should rather be styled postpositions, as they are generally put behind nouns." Hittite only has postpositions.

We may therefore consider the current English forms, *herein* etc., residues of the former OV syntactic structure. Typological classification has provided means to recognize such residues in a language; thereupon we take steps to account for them.

5.9 USES OF TYPOLOGICAL FINDINGS FOR HISTORICAL PURPOSES

Through positing frameworks like those briefly sketched for OV and VO languages on the basis of typological study we may explain the presence of unusual patterns in a language.

It is useful to note patterns to examine for information on earlier structures. As we have seen, adverbs may maintain older syntactic patterns; they are often said to be frozen forms, that is, fixed forms, as of noun inflections that have been maintained in adverbial use. They may then provide leads for proposing the earlier syntactic structure of a language. Moreover, pronominal forms are often conservative, as we may note from the English personal pronouns that are inflected for nominative, genitive and accusative. Irregularities in morphology may give us information on earlier phonological patterning, as in pairs like *hit* [hit] vs. *hitter* [hidər], *strong* [stroŋ] vs. *stronger* [stroŋgər].

Findings of contentive typology have given us means to account for situations in the early Indo-European dialects that were unsolved by our predecessors. An example is the presence of two words for "fire" in the several dialects. Greek has the same word as do we, *pūr*, as does Hittite with *pahhur*; but the Latin word is totally different, *ignis*, with a direct cognate in Skt *Agnis*, the god of fire. Meillet recognized that the first was inanimate, the second animate, and he ascribed the inclusion of two words in the vocabulary to different views of Proto-Indo-European speakers from the views of modern peoples (1937:339–40). His proposed explanation called on cultural reasons. But we seek linguistic explanations for linguistic facts. When information on active languages became available, the linguistic explanation was provided. Of the two words for "fire" in the pre- or proto-language, one (maintained in Lat. *ignis*) was for fire as an active element, the other (maintained in Eng. *fire*) for it as a state. When the language became accusative in structure, only one was necessary in each dialect; the selection made in each was the result of forces we cannot reconstruct.

Typological classification has given us information to deal with languages as structures, in keeping with Cuvier's conclusion of 1812. The structures are based on patterns of relationships. To some extent the patterns are symmetrical. But in view of the constant change of language, there are asymmetries in language. These provide some of the redundancy that makes for easier understanding in the presence of noise. The typological approach has accordingly been very helpful in accounting for regular patterns as well as aberrancies in historical linguistics. It has acquired a much greater usefulness than was assumed by its early proponents. The typological classes that we determine provide evidence on structural similarities and differences that has clarified many patterns in languages.

SELECTED FURTHER READINGS

Finck (1909) provides a concise summary of the morphological typology practiced in the nineteenth century. For the typology of phonological systems, a fundamental work is Trubetzkoy (1939). For typological principles of syntax, illustrated with languages of different structures, see Lehmann (1978). Klimov has presented contentive typology and the typology of active languages in two important monographs: *Tipologija Jazykov Aktivnogo Stroja* (1977) and *Principy Kontensivnoj Tipologii* (1983). Nichols (1986) is the basic treatment of typology based on marking of heads and dependents.

PROBLEMS

1 Turkish is an agglutinative language with vowel harmony. As illustrated in section 5.2, it has an eight-vowel system with unrounded and rounded front and back vowels, and two levels: high and low.
   (a) Examining the following noun inflections, determine the patterns of vowel harmony for front and back vowels. Then determine the pattern for high and low vowels.

	hand	village	woman	end
		Singular		
Nominative	el	köy	kadın	son
Accusative	eli	köyü	kadını	sonu
Genitive	elin	köyün	kadının	sonun
Dative	ele	köye	kadına	sona
Locative	elde	köyde	kadında	sonda
Ablative	elden	köyden	kadından	sondan
		Plural		
Nominative	eller	köyler	kadınlar	sonlar
Accusative	elleri	köyleri	kadınları	sonları
Genitive	ellerin	köylerin	kadınların	sonların
Dative	ellere	köylere	kadınlara	sonlara
Locative	ellerde	köylerde	kadınlarda	sonlarda
Ablative	ellerden	köylerden	kadınlardan	sonlardan

(b) Determine the two allomorphs of the plural marker and state their distribution.

(c) Determine the case endings and state the distribution of their allomorphs.

(d) Tocharian has developed a similar nominal inflection, as illustrated by the singular and plural forms of the word for "house." (Unattested forms are marked with the asterisk; the perlative case has the meaning "through," as well as other uses.)

Nominative	waṣt	waṣtu
Accusative	waṣt	waṣtu
Genitive	waṣtis	cmolwis
Instrumental	*waṣtyo	*wastuyo
Comitative	*waṣtaśśäl	*waṣtwaśśäl
Perlative	waṣtā	*cmolwā
Dative	waṣtac	*waṣtwac
Ablative	waṣtäs	waṣtwäṣ
Locative	waṣtaṃ	waṣtwaṃ

Determine the two allophones of the plural marker and state their distribution.

(e) Determine the case endings.

(f) The Tocharian inflection clearly resembles that of Turkish. When we compare inflected forms in other Indo-European dialects, we find them attached to the root, often undergoing changes in the process. For example, the genitive of the word for "foot" is as follows: Skt *padás*, Gk *podós*, Lat. *pedis*, Goth. *fotaus*. From other evidence, such as borrowings, we conclude that Tocharian was in long contact with Turkic languages. Compare the means of declension in the two languages, indicating similarities and differences.

2 The following is a paragraph from the Anglo-Saxon Chronicle for the
  year 894.

þa   se cyning hine þa   west wende mid þære fierde
then the king   him   there west turned with the   (English) army
wið   Exan cestres, swa ic ær   sæde, & se hære
against Exeter (gen.) as   I earlier said and the (Danish) army
þa burg be seten hæfde; þa   he þær to gefæren wæs, þa   eodon
the city be-set   had; when he there to fared   was then went
hie to hiora scipum
they to their ships

"Then the king (Alfred) turned west with the army against Exeter, as
I said earlier, and the (Danish) army had besieged the city; when he
had arrived there, they went to their ships."

  (a) Determine differences in word order from that of Modern English.
  (b) Determine differences in morphology.
  (c) Point out arrangements in the sentence that are characteristic of OV
     order.
3 Indo-Europeanists have long been puzzled by similarities between the
  perfect and the middle. Both express state. For example, Skt *veda*, Gk
  oĩda, Goth. *wait* (English (God) *wot*) are from the root **weid-* "see," yet
  they mean "know" < "I have seen and accordingly I know." And the
  middle forms, Skt *śete*, Gk *keĩmai* mean "am lying down." Moreover,
  each of these categories has distinctive endings largely in the singular.
  The present indicative, on the other hand, has a full set of endings;
  endings that were lacking in the other two categories were taken over
  from it.
  (a) Gamkrelidze and Ivanov (1984) as well as other Indo-Europeanists
     have now proposed that both categories are reflexes from a Pre-Indo-
     European stative inflection. Sketch the process of such a
     development.
  (b) Noting that active languages distinguish aspect, that is, incompleted
     versus completed action, rather than tense, suggest how forms of the
     stative conjugation may have developed into the perfect and forms of
     the active conjugation into the present indicative.
  (c) We have noted how in the process of a shift from completed state to
     past tense the root **weid-* shifted in lexical rather than grammatical
     meaning. Another example is the root **gen-* "know," which in
     Germanic developed the meaning "can, be able." Account for such
     shifts in meaning.

6 Linguistic communities

6.1 COMPLEXITY OF LANGUAGE

In discussing languages, we generally refer to them with a generic name, such as English, or Sanskrit, or Old Chinese, or Proto-Semitic. These references may seem to imply that languages consist of a single unified grammar and vocabulary. But dialect studies have demonstrated that, though a language has common structural features and vocabulary, it also shows variations from one group of speakers to another. In any language there are subsets of dialects of various types: geographical, social, functional and occupational. All of these must be studied and described for each language to account for changes it has undergone.

Geographical differences in a language are determined by the extent of its use, by the cultural interrelationships of its speakers, by the duration of settlement of its speakers and so on. A language like Chinese that is spoken over a vast expanse has many dialects. Moreover, since the speakers forming social units in China had little contact with one another, the dialects differ considerably. The differences have been amplified because the dialects have been in use for several millennia. Even languages like British English and German, which became separated from other Germanic dialects less than two millennia ago, have many dialects. Maintenance of dialects, as well as loss of distinction among them, results from social, cultural and political conditions of the speakers.

Social differences are determined almost completely by cultural interrelationships. In general we may expect even in nonliterate groups at least three forms of speech: a cultivated, a common or standard, and a nonstandard – in modern societies, an uneducated. The cultivated form of speech is used in literary, religious, prophetic or even political utterances and writings. Nonstandard forms may be found among antisocial groups, such as criminals, or a rebellious younger generation, or among rustics. The standard forms are taught in schools, used in general social interchange, and in literate societies are considered to be "correct."

Functional differences also reflect cultural interrelationships. Although their variety differs from language to language, we may speak of at least two styles, formal versus informal, though in many languages there are more. Until recently Japanese included, besides a formal and an informal, an epistolary style for use in formal letters; further, there was a style used to and by dignitaries. And as a unique phenomenon in languages, at least today, only the Japanese emperor may use *chin* "I." A reflection of the dignified style was applied with humorous effect in Gilbert and Sullivan's operetta, the *Mikado*; the word means "honorable gate" and was used to refer to the emperor in somewhat the same way as the *Sublime Porte* was used for the former Turkish government. The American media and government officials have a comparable way of reference, as by using *Washington* in reference to the government.

Such geographical, social and functional varieties of language are imposed on each other. It is well known that President Kennedy made his political statements with a New England accent, modified by eastern schooling. Among British statesmen, like Churchill, on the other hand, the social force was greatest, with little or no geographical overlay. There may be, then, geographical as well as formal and informal varieties of nonstandard, standard and cultivated speech. Somewhat different are occupational subsets. Specialists of various kinds: engineers, politicians, jockeys, linguists, have developed their own jargons, which consist largely of special vocabularies. These may be applied in any of the subsets sketched above.

These statements apply to language as a complex set of conventions used by a group of speakers. Subsets are also found within an **idiolect**, the language of a single speaker. Speakers may change their place of living, their social status, their relations to their associates, their occupations, and by these changes virtually be forced to introduce changes in their language. If we constructed a model for a language or a language family, we would have to include in it such multistratal units for each dialect, and by implication for each idiolect.

These subsets of a language provide the possibility of additions, changes, losses. For example, as technological features are introduced, modified or retired, language referring to them also changes; since automobile transportation has replaced horse-drawn vehicles, terms like "livery stable" are rarely encountered. When the Greeks established themselves in the Hellenic peninsula, they transferred reference of the word for "beech" to oaks. As the Roman emperors came to insist increasingly on their dignity, they were referred to in the plural with the equivalent of "your majesties," for which the third person plural pronoun could be substituted. As a result, the equivalent of "they" was used in addressing them, leaving reflexes to this day in German, where the third person plural *Sie* "you" < "they" and third person plural verb forms are still used in formal address to individuals and groups. In this way variety in language provides built-in mechanisms for change. Some linguists ascribe change in language primarily to the interplay of dialects and languages.

Besides taking account of individual use as opposed to social use in sketching the complexity of language, we must also note use by different generations of speakers. As children acquire their language, further possibilities are provided for the introduction of change. Some linguists assume that language acquisition is the basic cause of change in language.

Since change in language is the prime concern of historical linguistics, we must view the modifications of the various components of language in the dimension of time. We may arbitrarily select any two points of time for such study. Our results are more useful, however, if we compare the varying language of two or more periods that have been differentiated by considerable changes in structure (see chapter 10).

Such changes may be introduced in the interplay of geographical dialects. They may also be introduced from without, from other languages. Upon introduction, they may be adopted from speaker to speaker, along lines of communication. If so, we may find wedge-shaped lines of differences, so-called isoglosses, along basic routes of travel, such as the Rhine river. Changes may, on the other hand, be transmitted from center to center. Hans Kurath (1939) pointed out that all the chief colonial centers in America except Philadelphia lost preconsonantal *r*; apparently Philadelphia – the second largest city in the British Empire in the eighteenth century – alone withstood spread of this change from across the Atlantic.

Any group of speakers with distinct patterns of usage, such as students, linguists or specialists in space research may introduce new forms and usages. If such groups are influential, these innovations may affect the language of others.

Among studies of social dialects on a language is Friedrich Kluge's investigation of the German student language, published in 1895. In this study he indicated especially the sources of various German words. One example is the word *flott* "excellent, beautiful," which students borrowed from nautical language, where it meant "afloat, swimming," and the like. Studies of the social dialects of other languages have disclosed similar innovations.

Other such studies have been concerned with the spread of changes. In an admirable study, nicely summarized in Bloomfield's *Language* (1933: 328–31), G. G. Kloeke illustrated successive changes of the words for "house" and "mouse" in Dutch. The words obviously are used in different social contexts. A change of the Germanic vowel [uː] to [yː] that originated in a prestige area was extended more widely for "house" than for "mouse," reflecting the greater use of the word for "house" in communication outside family groups. Investigations by William Labov have demonstrated how speakers in New York City may favor specific pronunciations in certain social situations (1972: 43–69). For example, speakers who do not normally use *r* in words like *third* are very careful to use it when they find themselves in an elevated social situation.

Accordingly, the recognition that language is composed of geographical, social, functional and occupational dialects, and of dialects varying with the age of speakers, illuminates the ways in which languages have changed and changes have been extended.

6.2 DIALECT GEOGRAPHY

The growing convictions about the regularity of sound change after 1870 led to great interest in the study of different dialects, first of all geographical dialects. In spite of the clarifications produced by Grassmann and Verner for the first Germanic consonant shift, and by other linguists for such problems elsewhere, some elements in the standard languages still showed irregularities. It was then tentatively assumed that standard languages, such as literary English, contained irregularities because they were mixed. To find pure languages, one would have to collect the speech of the everyday people. Study of their speech to deepen the information about change in language was supported by interest aroused by the Romantic movement.

Following Jean Jacques Rousseau (1712–78), scholars and literary figures from the end of the eighteenth century came to concern themselves with folkways. Using more than the occasional phrases of "rustic dialect" found in the poetry of William Wordsworth (1770–1850), writers like Robert Burns (1759–96) and Johann Peter Hebel (1760–1826) preferred their native speech to the more general literary languages. In an attempt to show that dialects as well as literary languages had respectable pedigrees, some linguists devoted their attention to dialects. In 1821 Johannes A. Schmeller (1785–1852) published the first grammar of a dialect, Bavarian. Although other scholars followed Schmeller's example, dialect study before 1875 was more concerned with social and historical than with linguistic problems, as scholars attempted to relate contemporary dialects with ancient tribal groups. In nomenclature and popular conceptions, their work has had a lasting effect. Old English is still often referred to as Anglo-Saxon. With this label the suggestion is made that Angles carried to Britain the Anglian dialect, and Saxons the Saxon dialect, where they subsequently merged to form English. Similarly, in Germany the labels for dialects continue old tribal names that are still used as area names, such as Bavarian and Franconian. In subsequent dialect study, less colorful, and also less misleading, labels are used, such as Northern, Midland and Southern in the United States.

Under superficial examination the early dialect study seemed to support the neogrammarian hypothesis that "sound change takes place according to laws that admit no exception." In standard English, for example, initial *v* and *f* both represent OE *f*, apparently without pattern, as in *vat*, *vixen* versus *father*, *folk*. Yet in the Somerset dialect spoken by Sophie Western's father in Henry Fielding's novel *Tom Jones* (1749), every OE *f-* is a *v-*. Squire Western says *vather* and *volk* as well as *vat* and *vixen*. Although

Georg Wenker set out to collect similar material in German dialects, hoping to find similar consistencies there, his work led virtually to the converse of his original aim; it has contributed greatly to our understanding of complexity in language.

Wenker's dialect work has the further importance that with the project of his counterpart in France, Jules Gilliéron (1854–1926), it furnished the patterns for later dialect investigations and interpretation of the results. Subsequent studies and conclusions have been largely based on the activities of these two men.

After preliminary investigation in the Rhineland, Wenker began to collect material from every section of Germany. His procedure was to prepare forty sentences and send them out to schoolteachers in 40,736 localities, later expanded to 49,363. The sentences, which dealt with everyday matters, were chosen carefully to give data on dialect differences. Sentence 1 reads: *Im Winter fliegen die trocknen Blätter durch die Luft herum.* "In winter the dry leaves fly around through the air." (See Mitzka 1952: 13–14, for the entire set.) Teachers were asked to transcribe the sentences in accordance with the characteristic speech in their districts. Sets were then returned to Marburg for analysis. Each of the sources for material was eventually to be put on a map, and the characteristic features of dialects were to be plotted by the location of their occurrences. Publication of the maps did not get under way until 1927 and is not yet complete. The plotting of dialect distribution on maps, however, led to the terminology used in detailed study of the language data.

The study of the varying forms of speech in one language is known as **dialect geography**, or dialectology. In plotting their findings on maps, dialect geographers compile **dialect atlases** containing maps of the features investigated. Terminology for dialect spread was fashioned after that used in map-making. On the pattern of isobar and isotherm, **isogloss** is a term used for a line drawn from location to location along the outer limits of characteristic features. The interpretation and linguistic significance of varying patterns of isoglosses was developed as the German and French dialect materials were analysed and described. Moreover, procedures of collecting dialect materials were improved as subsequent dialect geographers profited by the experience of their predecessors.

The advantage of the German collection is its broad coverage. For a relatively small area like that of Germany, close to 50,000 recordings provide great breadth of information. Yet Wenker's dialect project also had shortcomings; for one thing, it has not been completely published. To this day scholars who wish to use the German materials must go to the archives in Marburg. More serious shortcomings lie in the transcriptions, which were made by untrained observers. Everyone has idiosyncrasies in recording; with untrained workers there can be no attempt to correct these, or even to determine them. These shortcomings are especially serious in phonological study, for which the German project was best suited. The forty sentences provide little material on morphological variation, less on lexical differences. When these shortcomings became apparent, efforts were made to repair them.

To provide material collected by trained observers, young scholars undertook the collection and description of speech in various localities. Numerous monographs were published, supplementing the inadequate materials of the atlas. Bach (1950: 214–26) gives a densely printed selection of them. To provide the deficient lexical material, Walter Mitzka in 1938 sent out a second set of materials, questions designed to secure names of everyday items, such as plants and animals. His results are being published in a German word-atlas, and in monographs dealing with individual items. To provide contemporary records of pronunciation, Eberhard Zwirner undertook in the 1950s to collect tape recordings of German dialects from more than 1,200 localities. His recordings, though brief, preserve speech for subsequent interpretation. Tape recordings have the further advantage that copies may readily be provided to other investigators. With these supplements, ample materials are available for German dialect study, and provision has been made to remedy the deficiencies of Wenker's initial undertaking.

Gilliéron, editor of the French atlas, planned from the start to avoid the pitfalls encountered by his German predecessor. He selected and trained one worker, Edmond Edmont, to collect all material for the French atlas. Edmont, who had an excellent ear, provided accurate, reliable and consistent records. Cycling from point to point, where he established himself in congenial surroundings, he collected material by direct questions rather than through a highly restricted set of sentences. In the years of collecting, 1896–1900, Edmont gathered material from 639 locations, providing less coverage than had the German project. Under its superb organization, however, the French atlas was completely published by 1910. Gilliéron must therefore be credited with providing the pattern according to which the materials of many subsequent projects were published.

6.3 MODELS AND TECHNIQUES FOR COMPREHENDING LINGUISTIC COMMUNITIES

In addition to examining language as a structure, historical linguists proposed models for comprehending the languages maintained by linguistic communities in relation to one another. The first model widely used for depicting linguistic relationships was the family. After Sir William Jones called attention to the connections between Sanskrit, Greek, Latin and Germanic, linguists set out to determine and represent the relationships between these languages. They did so by likening related languages to members of a family, and in this way created terminology that we may deplore in its literal sense but that we in great part maintain.

We speak of the Indo-European group and other such groups as a

language family. Greek and Latin, and other Indo-European languages, may be called **sister languages**. And we may speak of the **parent language**, Proto-Indo-European; formerly the term primitive Indo-European was used, but the connotations of the adjective led to its disuse. We also say that Greek is **descended** from Proto-Indo-European. The languages in a family we call **related**; words or other linguistic entities that we can trace to a common source we call **cognates**. The type of classification is known as *genealogical*, or often **genetic**, in spite of the biological connotation of genetic.

The family model was useful in working out the interrelationships of languages. The Germanic languages had obviously undergone changes different from those of Greek or Latin; we indicate the subsequent independence by labeling them **sister languages**. After some thought, however, shortcomings of the family model are obvious, for modern Germanic languages like English and German are related to Modern Greek not as sisters, but rather as distant cousins. When viewed over a great expanse of time, a language family behaves differently from a natural family, for its members may grow old without dying, and may develop new interrelationships that are hard to label with relationship terms which are not cumbersome. Shortly after the middle of the nineteenth century, a new model was proposed that solved some of these problems, continued others, and raised still others – the **family tree**.

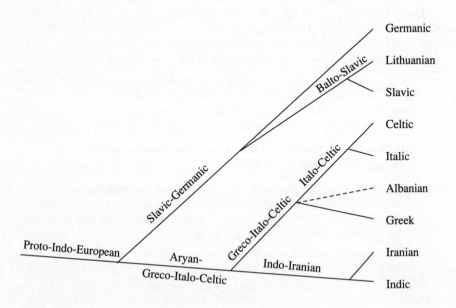

Figure 6.1 Schleicher's Indo-European family tree.

The suggestion that the relationship between subgroups of a language is similar to that between branches of a tree was propounded by August Schleicher, who was strongly influenced by views on evolution. His model is more sophisticated than that of the family, permitting a clear view of languages and also their various further developments – from original branches through smaller and smaller sub-branches, which show relationships in both time and space.

As with the family model, we use terminology today that is based on the view of a language group as a tree. We say that English **branched off** from Germanic, which in turn is a branch of Indo-European and so on. But, very early, dangers in this model became apparent.

One shortcoming the family-tree model shares with the family model is its depiction of a language as a biological organism. Languages, unlike animals or trees, do not have an independent existence. They are sets of conventions, like conventions of fashion, games and other human behavior. Changes are introduced in them by their speakers, not spontaneously by the language itself.

The shortcoming that caused replacement of the family-tree model, however, is the view of language change it requires. If English is really a distinct branch of the Indo-European tree, it should permit no modification by another branch or sub-branch that separated from the stem earlier, such as Latin or Sanskrit. Yet we know that many Latin words, and also Sanskrit words, have been borrowed into English. Even more troublesome, we find common changes taking place in neighboring languages that long before had separately branched off from the parent language.

Yet because of its simplicity and partial appositeness, the family-tree model still influences views and provides terminology. Virtually all genealogical relationships have been based on it. But a troublesome misconception results from names of successive stages of a language, like Old English, Middle English, New English. These terms suggest that we view New English as a direct descendant of Old English. We know, however, that modern standard English developed from the London dialect, a Midland form of speech, while our chief Old English materials have come down to us in a West Saxon form. To try to trace modern standard English directly to the language of *Beowulf* or of Alfred's works causes difficulties. Similarly, New High German is not a direct descendant of the Middle High German found in important medieval literature. New High German is essentially a central German dialect, while Middle High German was a southern German dialect. In using the family-tree model, these important facts of linguistic history are concealed. Equally troublesome, archaeologists and other nonlinguists seem to assume that linguists account for languages through a succession of sound laws rather than as conventions maintained by linguistic communities that have undergone various influences. The variety of influences became clear as dialect studies were increasingly pursued.

Primarily because of the inadequacy of the family-tree theory in accounting for linguistic changes, the **wave theory** was proposed as dialect studies
disclosed how changes were spread in language. In accordance with the
theory, changes may be introduced at some point in space of a language or
languages spoken over a given area. These then may spread like waves on a
pond that are caused by an object hitting the surface of the water. With this
theory, proposed in 1872 by Johannes Schmidt, the Indo-European languages may be depicted as follows.

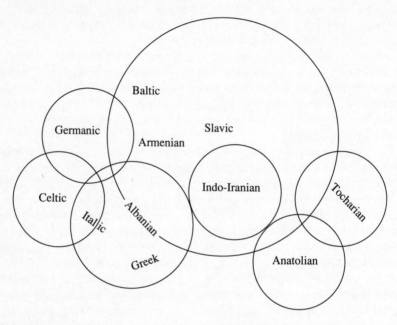

Figure 6.2 A revised form of Schmidt's representation of the distribution of the
Indo-European languages.

In permitting us to show flexibly interrelationships between languages,
and changes affecting them, the wave theory is preferable to the family-
tree theory. Both, however, view language far too simply.

If languages were relatively homogeneous, either theory would be
acceptable. For "sound change could take place according to laws that
admit no exception" either along the branches of a tree or over an expanse
in which languages or dialects exist side by side. When, however, studies
carried out by dialect geographers showed that a language is subdivided by
area into dialects – and by different social and occupational groupings –
any bidimensional model, even when supplemented by the third dimension of time, was seen to be inadequate. We now view language as a set of
social conventions so complex that a simple biological or geometrical

model is totally inadequate. Yet the problems encountered in the use of such models, as well as in the early dialect projects, have provided guidelines for later dialect investigations. We may illustrate the resultant methods by noting the planning for the American project.

After consultation with linguists who had directed earlier dialect studies, the project was designed to avoid shortcomings that had been disclosed by these. (See the report of Hans Kurath in Kurath *et al.* 1939.) Under the direction of its carefully chosen editor, Kurath, great attention was given to:

1 Selection and training of field workers.
2 Selection of informants and locations to investigate.
3 Preparation of a questionnaire.

The fieldworkers, already highly trained linguists, were given further training in the summer of 1931 under two eminent dialect geographers, Jud and Scheuermeier. To cover an area as large as New England, having a number of fieldworkers is essential in spite of the resultant diversity of recordings. Yet the anticipated diversity among the fieldworkers was not unduly great. Moreover, the training by Jud and Scheuermeier provided a check on possible idiosyncrasies of individual workers that was missing in Edmont's excellent work.

Just as the selection and training of fieldworkers illustrates the increase in precision of dialect geography since 1876, the care in selection of informants indicates the increasing awareness of the complexity of language. Speakers were chosen from each age group. Since this was the first large-scale dialect study in the United States, special care was taken to include speakers more than seventy years old. Moreover, speakers from three selected social groups were included: those with little formal education and restricted social contacts; those with some formal education; and those with advanced education. All information about speakers and other pertinent data about speech communities was carefully noted, and is available to analysts.

For the preparation of worksheets comprising the questionnaire, samplings were made to determine points of variation among speakers, which in turn suggested items to investigate. Worksheets were thereupon designed to elicit specific forms but also to allow flexibility. Moreover, fieldworkers were to note if a speaker indicated that a form was rarely used, old-fashioned, amusing, or whether it elicited other attitudes or responses. Adequate information was collected and made available so that linguistic facts could be understood not only by linguists but also by historians, geographers, sociologists and others interested in the social and cultural history of New England (Kurath *et al.* 1939: ix). Simultaneous tape-recordings are now possible, with which other linguists may check transcriptions. In this way dialect geographers collect material of any breadth and precision that scholarly resources, finances and time permit.

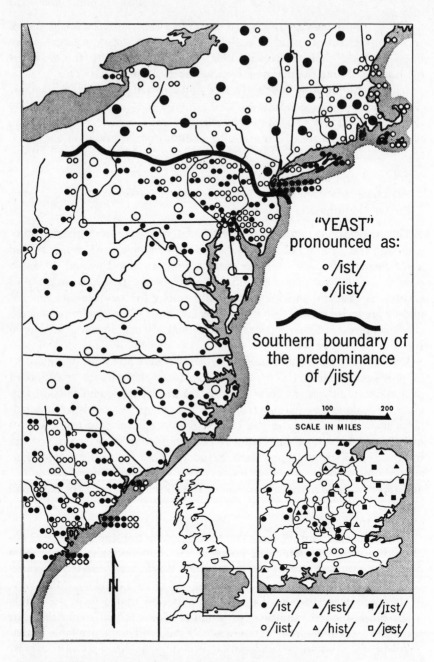

Within the image:

"YEAST"
pronounced as:

o /ist/

• /jist/

Southern boundary of
the predominance
of /jist/

0   100   200
SCALE IN MILES

• /ist/   ▲ /jest/   ■ /jɪst/
o /iist/   △ /hist/   □ /jest/

Map 6.1 The pronunciation of *yeast* in the Atlantic States.
Note the precision used in providing the information, and the insert map giving
the distribution of pronunciation in southern England, by which the sources of
American dialect forms can be explored. Taken from Kurath and McDavid
(1961). Included with the permission of Hans Kurath.

The American project covered New England, with subsequent publication of an atlas (1939–43). Further collecting in America has been carried out, also by regions (see map 6.1). The efforts involved in covering a territory the size of the United States are so huge that such smaller projects are called for. In other countries as well, the arranging of dialect collections, rather than preparation of national atlases, now forms the general pattern. For unless a language area is small and homogeneous, the results of dialect collection are so extensive that they are not readily accessible. In France, for example, numerous studies covering only a section of the country have been undertaken in attempts to provide fuller and more up-to-date information than that in Gilliéron's atlas.

One massive project that has been inaugurated aims to provide a dialect atlas of Europe, including the European part of the former Soviet Union. Information on the questionnaire has been made available; one can only hope that the project will be pursued until its aims are met. Unfortunately it has now been stopped. Some of these may be achieved through technological advances. Instead of maps prepared by workers, they are to be produced by computer. When the procedures have been achieved, detailed data on language will be much more readily accessible.

Computerized procedures have also been applied in the production of the *Dictionary of American Regional English*, prepared at the University of Wisconsin under the direction of Frederic Cassidy. Two volumes, covering words from A–C and D–H, have been published. The well-planned project will no doubt continue publication as rapidly as such a complex undertaking permits. The vast amounts of data must now be interpreted for their contributions to our understanding of linguistic development.

6.4 FINDINGS ON THE EFFECTS OF LANGUAGE CHANGE AND THE SPREAD OF INNOVATIONS

The availability of data from the German and French dialect projects resulted in various contributions to our understanding of language and change in language, as we indicate in this and later sections.

It soon was apparent that the boundaries between languages and those between dialects could not be precisely defined. Isoglosses differ from item to item. Since the division between High German and Low German was among the most highly investigated among language interrelationships, many of the procedures of dialect geography were worked out in solving problems concerning it.

The chief items differentiating High German from Low German are the reflexes of Proto-Germanic *p t k*. These remained in Low German, as in English, but have become fricatives and affricates in High German.

The changes in initial, medial, and in final positions may be summarized as follows:

1 Late PGmc *p- t- k- -pp- -tt- -kk-* > OHG *pf ts k(x)* (we may use the unchanged English items to indicate the original, Proto-Germanic sounds).

Eng. *pool* : Germ. *Pfuhl*   Eng. *shape* : Germ. *schöpfen*
Eng. *tongue* : Germ. *Zunge*   Eng. *sit* : Germ. *sitzen*
Eng. *cow* : Germ. *Kuh*, but   Eng. *wake* : Germ. *wecken*, but
Swiss *kxū*   Swiss *wekxen*

2 Late PGmc *-p- -t- -k- -p -t -k* > OHG *-f(f) -s(s) -x(x)*

Eng. *hope* : Germ. *hoffen*   Eng. *up* : Germ. *auf*
Eng. *water* : Germ. *Wasser*   Eng. *it* : Germ. *es*
Eng. *cake* : Germ. *Kuchen*   Eng. *book* : Germ. *Buch*

According to the principles of sound change formulated by the neogrammarians, we should expect to find that all late PGmc *-k- -k* became *x* (*ch*) over the entire High German territory. Sounds in the same environment were assumed to change consistently, without exception, throughout a dialect area. When, however, the data assembled by Wenker's questionnaire were examined, different isoglosses were found for words similar in structure, such as German *machen* "make," *ich* "I" (see map 6.2).

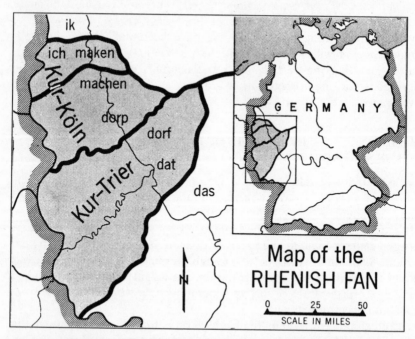

Map 6.2 One of the classical areas of investigation in dialect study shows the extent of spread of the change *k* > *x* in Germany, and the enclave in which PGmc *t* is unshifted in *dat, wat, it, allet*. Shadings indicate the Rhenish Fan and the enclave.

Although the isoglosses for these two words are virtually identical from the eastern extent of German speech to the neighborhood of the Rhine, at that point they separate. The isogloss for *machen* crosses the Rhine near Benrath, somewhat south of Ürdingen, the point at which that for *ich* crosses the river. The two isoglosses are labeled after the villages, the **Benrath line** and the **Ürdingen line**. Their divergence near the Rhine plus that of other isoglosses, which fan out at this point, led to the label the **Rhenish fan** and require an explanation.

The explanation can be furnished from cultural history. The Benrath line corresponds to the extent of Cologne's influence from the thirteenth century; the Ürdingen line, to its influence from the fourteenth to the sixteenth centuries (see Bach 1950: 133–4). The forms for "make" were fixed at the early time; those for "I" later. One can account for the different isoglosses by assuming that a sound change $k > x$, had taken place in southern German-speaking territory and that its effects were gradually extended northward. The extent of spread of innovation in any word is determined by the cultural prestige of speakers who use it. Findings like those for Germ. *machen* and *ich*, repeated many times over in various dialect studies, as of Chinese as well, led to a more accurate understanding of language change and its spread. They also led to greater concern with social and cultural patterns of communities in which a given language is spoken.

As indicated above, the three voiceless stops *p t k* of Upper German were shifted. The results of the change were extended northward and adopted in varying degrees in accordance with the extent of prestige of the southern German dialects; the absolute limits of adoption may be indicated by a line extending across German-speaking territory from approximately Cologne eastward, just south of Berlin. Subsequently, German dialects have been differentiated largely by the extent to which they employed this rule for each of the three stops in the stated environments. In Low Franconian and Low German the rule was not introduced at all, leading to a differentiation of the continental West Germanic area into two major subgroups, as chart 6.1 indicates.

The importance of identifying cultural areas for their impact on language may be illustrated by the developments in Berlin. When the Benrath line approaches the city, it makes a bend upward and then falls back to the line that would be relatively straight across the German-speaking area. The bend reflects the late choice of Berlin as capital. Earlier, the dominant political forces had been in the south. The political shift brought use of High German into the city. The isoglosses reflect the social as well as the linguistic situation.

Somewhat comparably, initial *p t k* (and intervocalic *pp tt kk*, which apparently were similarly articulated) became the affricates *pf ts kx*. This shift was not extended as far to the north as was that of medial and final stops, leading to subdivisions of the High German territory (see chart 6.1). The dialects in which this rule was adopted are known as Upper German, in contrast with the Middle German dialects in which the change of medial

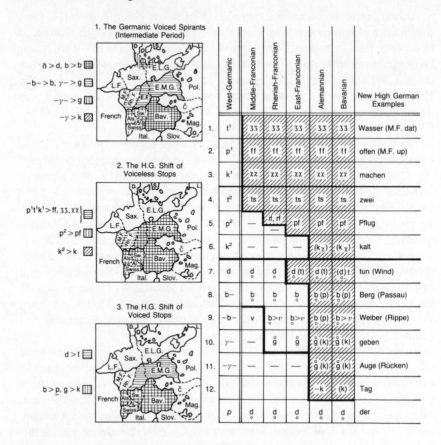

Chart 6.1 The High German Consonant Shift.

Chart 6.1 is taken from Eduard Prokosch, *The Sounds and History of the German Language* (New York: Holt, 1916, p. 130).

and final stops was adopted, and Low German, in which neither change was adopted.

The distinction between Upper German and Middle German was reinforced by the devoicing of *b d g* in Upper German. The effect of these changes in the continental Germanic languages may illustrate the bases for the differentiation of dialects. A comprehensive series of changes, adopted in part by contiguous areas, leads to subdivisions of a given linguistic area in accordance with the extent of the social groupings.

Even in such large-scale shifts, the changes may not be carried out in all words, as we may illustrate by the unshifted *t* in *dat, it, wat*, the German forms for *that, it, what* in the Mosel Franconian area. Here *-t* shows up as *-s* in words like *great*, Germ. *gross*, but not in the words cited or the *-et* ending of the adjective, for example, *allet* rather than standard German *alles*, (nom. sg. nt.) "all." Although various explanations have been given for these unshifted forms, they may be ascribed to difference in syntactic environment. We may assume that the unshifted *dat, it, wat, allet* were adopted from weakly stressed sentence positions, in which the change of $t > s$ was not carried through. We may conclude that syntactic as well as morphological environments may affect the extent of a sound shift.

6.5 CLASSIFICATION OF DIALECTS

Such problems encountered in dialect geography studies led to a questioning of former views concerning (1) the regularity of sound change and (2) the usefulness of setting up dialects. Extreme rebellion against the tidy view of language ascribed to the neogrammarians may be illustrated by Gilliéron's slogan, "Every word has its own history," and by Gaston Paris's statement on the virtually imperceptible gradations from dialect to dialect in French, even into Italian.

No one can deny that every word, like every social convention or every artifact, has its own history. But the statement is as misleading as is the slogan: "Sound change takes place according to laws that admit no exceptions." A word is a composite of morphemes and phonemes. Since the allophones of the phonemes vary with their environment, every word will have undergone changes different from all other words. To conclude that one should describe every word separately indicates a poor understanding of the social functioning of language. Even worse are the linguistic studies that deal with the history of individual sounds from proto-languages to the present. Studies based on such methods resemble lists rather than descriptions. Neither phonemes nor morphemes are independent entities in language; rather, they pattern with other sets and subsets of phonemes and morphemes. Fortunately, dialect geographers, like historical linguists who learned much from the neogrammarians, have come to understand the disadvantage of basing methodology on slogans.

The usefulness of positing dialects was graphically questioned by Gaston Paris in his story of the travelers who proceed slowly from Paris to Italy. Traveling a few miles at a stretch, and adapting their speech constantly to each local dialect, they would scarcely notice differences in speech in the French area; they might not even notice when they crossed the supposedly greater boundary from France to Italy. For even here they would not find an abrupt speech cleavage such as they would encounter if they crossed into Germanic territory.

In spite of the absence of sharp dialect, or language, boundaries, dialect geographers have not abandoned subclassification of languages. When classifying dialects, they have progressed from a reliance on isoglosses for important linguistic features, such as the *machen* isogloss, through **bundles of isoglosses** to correlation methods. Contemporary investigators seek to learn whether a list of features is present at given points. They then correlate their results and connect points having similar correlation coefficients with lines known as **isopleths** or **isogradients**. These may represent not only various isoglosses but also folk customs, such as tales, superstitions and agricultural practices. Such compound isoglosses may reflect earlier political boundaries, which in turn were probably determined to some extent by geographical features. Isopleths, accordingly, indicate areas of culture that may have exerted an effect on language. In this way the study of dialects has come to be closely associated with the study of other social phenomena, and has been extended to the branch of language investigation that is known as sociolinguistics.

6.6 CHARACTERISTICS OF DIALECT AREAS

Although given a common label, speech within a language or dialect is not uniform. Languages as well as dialects generally have a center that is touched by relatively few isoglosses. Such centers, which speakers regard as areas of prestige, are known as **focal areas**. Innovations transmitted from them are accepted by surrounding areas as far as the prestige of the focal area extends. As an example we may cite the distribution of *tonic* (a soft drink) in New England. Its general use around Boston indicates the extent of influence exerted by the speakers in the Boston area. Outside the area, *tonic* has not succeeded in replacing older forms.

At the limits of well-defined speech areas, we find **transition areas**. These may show characteristics of two neighboring focal areas, as do western New Hampshire, central Massachusetts and Rhode Island in their terms for the drink referred to around Boston as a tonic.

Further characteristic types of area, known as **relic areas**, lie beyond the extent of expanding isoglosses. Relic areas are generally found in locations that are difficult of access for cultural, political or geographic reasons. They may be discontinuous, as are the relic areas on Map 6.3, in which final *r* is preserved.

The status of preconsonantal and final *r* in New England, as in *hard*, *far*, may illustrate the various types of area. Around Boston there is little evidence for this *r*; isoglosses would be remote from the city. We conclude as from the word *tonic* that Boston is a focal area. In western Massachusetts and elsewhere along the Connecticut River, usage is divided, with some speakers pronouncing, others dropping, *r*. This is a transition area between the *r*-speech of the Hudson Valley and the *r*-less speech of Boston. In addition, we find the *r* of this environment maintained on Martha's Vineyard, Marblehead and Cape Ann, which are relic areas.

Since the time of the German and French dialect projects, which established much of the methodology of dialect geography, many studies have been made of speech communities and their subdivisions. We have noted above Kloeke's investigation of the Dutch words for "house" and "mouse." The investigation disclosed that successive innovations for both words spread from the cities of Antwerp and, later, Amsterdam, which were focal areas, leaving relic areas on the periphery of the country. Moreover, on the borders between Low German and Dutch speech, the spread of the innovations was checked in a transition area. The proposal of these three types of areas has accordingly been supported by further dialect study.

6.7 FINDINGS THAT CLARIFY DISTRIBUTION OF LINGUISTIC FEATURES

The studies of dialect distribution within languages have led to better understanding of speech communities and of the distribution of linguistic features. From the findings of dialect geography in contemporary speech communities, attempts have been made to explain the linguistic situation of past periods, as in the Proto-Indo-European community.

Among the Indo-European languages, verb endings with a characteristic *r* to mark the middle voice are limited to Celtic, Italic, Hittite and Tocharian. Celtic and Italic were at the western periphery of the European area; the two other subgroups were probably located elsewhere on its periphery. We may therefore account for the *r*-middles as relic forms that survived in the peripheral areas of the Indo-European community. Germanic, Greek, Baltic, Slavic, Albanian, Armenian and Indo-Iranian make up the central dialects. Innovations in the middle voice, patterned on endings for the active voice, were spread through this central area but did not eliminate the *r*-endings on the periphery.

Another innovation that spread through a part of the central area is the change of some *k*'s to sibilants, as in the word for "hundred." The languages with the innovation are Indo-Iranian, Armenian, Albanian and, imperfectly, Slavic and Baltic. Applying the findings of contemporary dialect geography in this way to ancient speech areas has given us a much more flexible, and realistic, view of their interrelationships.

Linguistic study may also lead to an understanding of earlier cultural relationships. For example, if we had only linguistic information about prior settlement patterns in Louisiana and Texas, we could still determine from the distribution of words for "small bonus" the predominant influence of French and of Spanish settlers.

After millennia have elapsed, such distribution may become clouded, and its interpretation may require intricate analysis. Nevertheless, interpretations of this sort have been attempted for areas of the Romance languages, with the aim of determining prior language communities. But, since no data survive from these, the conclusions must be viewed with reserve.

The history of individual words has also been clarified by dialect geographers, especially by Gilliéron. He was greatly interested in the relationships of homophones to each other, assuming that in the course of time one of them would be eliminated. This process is referred to as **loss by collision**. In the French collections he found good material in support of his thesis. The word *viande* "food," from Lat. *vīvenda*, the neuter plural of the quasigerundive

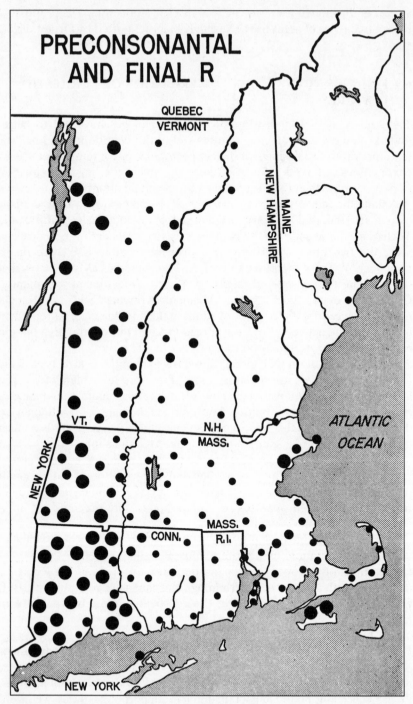

Map 6.3 Distribution of preconsonantal and final *r*.

of *vīvere* "live," replaced *char* < *carne* "food, meat" in the focal area of Paris, where *char* came to be homophonous with the Old French form of *chère* "dear" < Lat. *cara*. In this way he provided one explanation for some losses in language, although his successors suggest that he exaggerated the extent of loss by collision. Yet the examples they provide are from different subsystems of the language, such as the noun *bear* and the verb *bear*, or *two*, *too* and *to*. When sound changes lead to homonymity for items used in similar environments such as *gat*, for "cat" and "rooster" in southwestern France, the likelihood of substitutes for one of the homonyms is great. In one of his classical studies, Gilliéron demonstrated how the words for "pheasant" and "vicar" were substituted for the old word for "rooster" in precisely the area where it coincided with the word for "cat."

Another phenomenon accounted for by dialect geography studies is the occurrence of **blends**. These are likely in compounds. In western Germany two words for "potato," *Erdapfel* and *Grundbirne*, gave rise to *Erdbirne*. In the western Taunus area two words for "brake," the native *Hemme* and *Meckenick*, from Fr. *mécanique*, have given rise to *Hemmenick* (see Bach 1950: 158ff. for these and others). Such blends are found especially in transition areas. By noting such effects of dialects in their interrelationships we can account for developments in language, as illustrated here, to extend our understanding of individual words as well as grammatical features in the history of languages.

6.8 MIXED LANGUAGES, PIDGINS, CREOLES

Historical linguists have long held that languages as well as dialects may influence one another, leading to linguistic changes. The kinds of influence and of changes reflect the social situation in which the interaction takes place.

If linguistic communities that speak different languages interact on an everyday basis, as in multilingual communities like those of India, many elements from one language may be incorporated in the other, and a **mixed**

Opposite: The map shows the distribution of preconsonantal and final *r*, illustrating the influence of the focal area Boston, transitions to other dialect areas, and relic areas.

An *r* preceding a vowel, as in *road*, *borrow*, *far out*, is pronounced in all parts of New England. But before consonants and finally, as in *hard*, *how far?*, usage is regional: in western New England and in New Brunswick the *r* is dropped, while the Connecticut Valley is mixed and unstable in practice.

Martha's Vineyard, Marblehead, and Cape Ann, all secluded communities, appear as "*r* islands" in eastern New England, where this *r* is still losing ground. On the other hand, the *r* is gaining ground in the Connecticut Valley.

The largest circles indicate regular use of this *r*; the smallest ones, sporadic use; and the remainder, rather evenly divided usage.

Taken from Kurath *et al.*, 1939. Copyright, 1939, by The American Council of Learned Societies. Included with the permission of Hans Kurath.

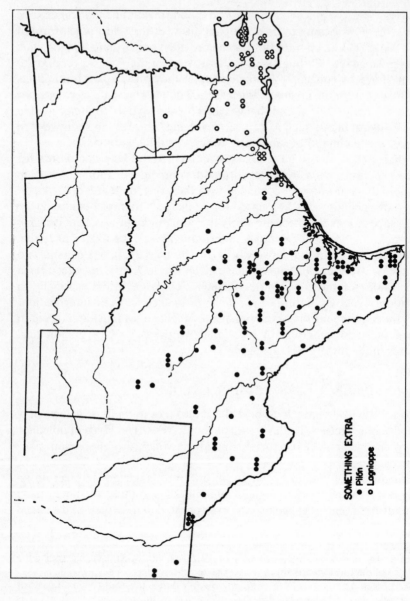

Map 6.4 Indicates the distribution of words for 'a small bonus', *lagniappe* and *pilón*, in the Texas area. The extent of French influence is clearly demarcated from that of Spanish. Taken by permission from Atwood (1962).

SOMETHING EXTRA
● Pilón
○ Lagniappe

language may result. The designation is a relative term and has been long disputed. Some linguists of the 19th century were severely critical of the concept; others define it by their own criteria. The designation, then, may be used in a weak and in a strong sense.

If groups of speakers with different native languages interact only for certain purposes, as for business carried out between sailors and indigenous peoples, a composite language known as a **pidgin** may result. A pidgin may develop where a number of different indigenous languages are spoken, as in New Guinea. The term is generally used by linguists when referring to a second language that is used in limited interactions. Jespersen and Hall characterize pidgins as minimal languages. In the course of time, members of communities with only a pidgin in common may intermarry. If enough such marriages take place, the pidgin may in time become the basic language of a given community. When it is the native language of such communities, it is known among linguists as a **creole**. An example is Haitian Creole. In Papua, on the other hand, the former trade language has been recognized as an official language, and is referred to as New Guinea Pidgin. Fuller details on pidgins and creoles are given in section 13.7. Here we are concerned with the types of communities in which mixed languages as well as pidgins and creoles develop, and with attempts to account in this way for phenomena of languages of the past.

When we examine English, we find that the vocabulary consists of two segments: native words and borrowed words. The native words generally belong to the everyday language; the borrowed words belong to the language used for learned purposes, for church, government, military, science. Further examination indicates the source of the borrowings, and also the time of their adoption. The English-speaking community was Christianized by Latin-speaking missionaries from the late seventh century. Rome remained the dominant influence in ecclesiastical matters until the time of Henry VIII. During this period the ecclesiastical vocabulary of English was established on the basis of Latin. In referring to matters concerning the church and theology a language that consisted of everyday words making up the grammatical structure was mixed with Latin and Greek ecclesiastical terms. In this register of English, a mixed language developed.

In much the same way, after the French-speaking Normans conquered the Saxons in 1066, the political and military terms were based on French. And when science became prominent in the 17th and later centuries, technical terms were based on Latin and Greek components. In this way the vocabulary of English is that of a mixed language.

But in these interchanges the systems of sounds and forms were largely unaffected. The phoneme /ž/ was introduced in part through French words like *beige* and *rouge*, but also through combinations of [zy] in such words as *vision*. Moreover, we have noted above how its development brought parallelism in the system of fricatives. The phoneme /ž/ is therefore in part also a result of systematic forces. In the system of forms, the third plural pronoun was taken over through a different set of contacts from the Scandinavian settlers in English in *they, their, them*; these replaced native forms like [əm], which, however, is still used in unaccented positions. Moreover, the progressive forms of the verb, *is walking* beside *walks* etc., are attributed to influence from Celtic; they are found in no other Germanic language, and a comparable verb form exists in Celtic. Because English has been modified in phonology and morphology as well as in its lexicon, English may be regarded as a mixed language, though some linguists object to such a classification.

The Indo-Aryan languages are far more modified by influences from the indigenous languages of India, chiefly Dravidian. An entire set of consonants, retroflex *ṭ ṭh ḍ ḍh ṇ ṣ*, was introduced. Moreover, many elements of morphology and syntax were incorporated, as well as lexical items. Where an Indo-Aryan and a Dravidian language are spoken in the same community, the same syntax is used for both. Comparable situations existed elsewhere, as in Africa. Arabic has been a language of prestige in much of the continent for more than a millennium. It has brought about modifications in the indigenous languages, and also in many languages of Asia, much as Latin and French did in English. The extent of any such influences may be determined from descriptions of individual languages.

Linguists have attempted to account for linguistic characteristics of earlier languages through mixture in this way. As we will see in greater detail below, it has been assumed that languages like French owe something of their difference from Spanish, Italian and other Romance languages to the influence of Celtic speakers on the Latin spoken in Gaul. The two languages existed side by side for at least five centuries. Among other items attributed to the influence of Celtic is the fronting of *u* and *o* in such words as *lune* < Lat. *lūna* "moon" and *sœur* < Lat. *soror* "sister." Similarly, the High German consonant shift, illustrated in section 6.4, has been attributed by some linguists to the influence of earlier indigenous peoples. Unfortunately, we have no way of testing the validity of such claims. As we will see later, such proposed explanations for the changes have aroused considerable controversy.

Attempts have also been made to account for some early languages as pidgins. When tribal groups came into contact with one another, as in general hunts, speakers of different languages must have had some means to intercommunicate. Such attempts are attested in recent periods, as among the Indian tribes in Oregon. A large number of languages had evolved in the separate valleys. When groups from different tribes met, they made use of a pidgin that has been well documented.

The most widely discussed suggestion of a pidgin-like origin for a proto-language is that of Trubetzkoy (1939). Observing that Proto-Indo-European included characteristics that were found in neighboring languages, he suggested that instead of ascribing these to one language in the course of its development, they indicated a pidgin origin for Proto-Indo-European. In view of Trubetzkoy's prestige, the suggestion continues to be cited, even though there is even less evidence for it than for the suggestions of Celtic influence on French and English.

Among the Afro-Asiatic languages Akkadian has clearly been strongly influenced by Sumerian, but scarcely to the extent of pidginization. Strong modifications in Egyptian of the fourth millennium have also been ascribed to mixture with earlier languages. The extent of influence may in time be determined by careful examination of native structures and external modifications, as has been done for English.

6.9 AREAL LINGUISTICS

A specific kind of social contact among speakers of different languages has been studied in areal linguistics. The pace-setting work is that of Sandfeld (1930). He examined shared characteristics among the languages of the Balkans. These consist not only of Indo-European languages of various subgroups, for example Slavic, Italic, Greek, Albanian, but also of the non-Indo-European language, Turkish. In spite of the considerable differences between these languages, Sandfeld assembled a set of characteristics found to some extent in each of them. The principal shared features are a postposed article, a comparable periphrastic future tense and replacement of the infinitive with an element comparable to a verbal noun. Sandfeld ascribed the common features to widespread bilingualism. As we have noted above, multilingual speakers tend to use the same syntax in each of their languages. A long period of bilingualism would then lead to adoption of selected features in an area with multiple interlingual contacts.

Another such area that has been identified is western Europe. Benjamin Lee Whorf (1956) ascribed a set of common features such as articles and periphrastic verb forms, to bilingual speakers; in this instance the bilinguals had Latin as one of their languages. Whorf found the common set of features so characteristic that he proposed the term SAE (Standard Average European) for what he considered one language in contrast with vastly different languages such as the Amerindian, with which he was chiefly concerned.

A third area so identified is the Asian subcontinent, with its many Indo-Aryan and Dravidian languages, as well as Munda and languages of other families. We have already noted the introduction of retroflex consonants into the Indo-Aryan languages. Murray Emeneau (1956) ascribed the use of different stems in singular and plural of nouns, and numeral classifiers to areal influence.

Many further examples of linguistic areas could be cited. The use of numeral classifiers, and also tones, in many east Asian languages is considered an areal characteristic. Common features are also found in languages of Central America, of Australia, and sections of Africa. Wherever bilingualism is frequent, characteristics may be adopted among languages.

It is difficult to suggest just what features will be taken over. Some of them seem to be features that are useful to indicate precision in simple communication, such as numeral classifiers. Others seem preferred for their clarity of representation, such as periphrastic constructions as opposed to those with morphological markers on words. Yet there are so many variables to take into consideration that it is difficult to generalize concerning features that will be adopted.

Features would scarcely be adopted if a language already had means to express them. For example, we would not expect the spread of articles to languages with numeral classifiers; articles are used to express definiteness, a function that is also indicated by numeral classifiers. On the other hand, languages have patterns that are incomplete; we have noted the lack of parallelism in the voicing of fricatives in Old English. Borrowings from French may have contributed to achievement of parallelism. Besides the structure of a language, the kind of contact is also significant. As Meillet indicated at some length (1925 (1967): 77–89, 133–8), "the variety of situations with reference to speakers is infinite" (*ibid.*: 133). It is clear that the kind of language community and of the cultural conditions in that community affect the course of development and change of a language. On the basis of studies that have been carried out we can cite some observations and propose some generalizations, like those given above. It is also obvious that any linguist dealing with a dialect, language or language family must be informed of the community maintaining it, as well as of its background and its typological characteristics.

SELECTED FURTHER READINGS

A large number of studies have been carried out in dialect geography, as well as considerable publication. For access to them one may consult Pop (1950), and after 1950 the bibliographies in linguistics. In addition, handbooks for the various areas are available. Kurath *et al.* (1939) discuss general principles as well as providing information on the work carried out in New England. For England one may consult Harold Orton and Eugen Dieth (1962–8); for Germany, consult Bach (1950); for French, Dauzat (1922).

Individual studies that illustrate the application of the principles of dialect geography to restricted fields are Atwood (1953) and Kurath and McDavid (1961). For a study of social dialects in their interrelationships with one another see Labov (1966). A theoretical statement relating the findings of dialect geography with change is Weinreich, Labov and Herzog (1968: 95–195).

For application of the family-tree and wave models to the Indo-European languages, see Pedersen (1931): 311–18.

Thomason and Kaufmann (1988) give a recent survey on the forces involved in language contact, and the effects, with copious examples and large bibliography.

PROBLEMS

1 (a) In volume I of Orton and Dieth (1962–8), covering the northern counties of England, numerous words are given in answer to the question "What do you call the place where you keep pigs? *creeve, creevy, mucklagh, pig-cote/crow/hole/house/hull, (pig) cree/sty, pig-gery.*" Yet in answer to the question; "What do you call the man who looks after those animals that give us wool?" only three words were elicited: *(shep-)herd, shep.* Account for the difference in the number of items for the two concepts.

   (b) The initial question to elicit terms for "pigsty" was replaced by the following: "What do you call the place where you keep the animals that go (i. grunting)?" Why was the change made?

   (c) Similarly, the initial question: "What do you call the place where you keep hens?" was replaced by "What do you call the place where you keep the birds that lay eggs for you?" Answers to this question were: *chicken/hen coop, hen-cot(e)/cree/crow/hole/house/hull/hut/loft/pen/place/roost, poultry house, shade.* How many of these terms do you know? When one consults the *Dictionary of American Regional English* for words that have been listed (A–C), terms like *creeve* and *(hen)cree* are not included. Why might they not be in use in this country?

2 Besides the shift of *p t k* in Old High German, *b* and *g* shifted to *p* and *k*, as in OHG *kepan*, NHG *geben* "give." Few words that underwent the shift have been maintained in Modern German; one is *Pracht* "splendor," cf. English *bright*.

   (a) Suggest why the shift of *p t k* was maintained, but not that of *b g*. (In framing your answer you may recall that the center of political power shifted to Middle-German speaking areas in the Middle Ages.)

   (b) Compare the results of the two shifts: *p t k* to *pf/f, ts/s,χ, b g* to *p k* with the results of the Proto-Germanic consonant shift.

   By the glottalic theory the Proto-Germanic shift was from glottalic stops to voiceless stops. Does the Old High German shift provide support for the assumption of glottalics in Pre-Germanic?

   (c) PGmc *þ* shifted to *d* throughout Low and High German, cf. Germ. *Dank*, Eng. *thank*; Germ. *Erde*, Eng. *earth*. How does this shift relate to that of the other Old High German obstruents? To that in Proto-Germanic?

   Noting that German did not have a parallel voiced dental fricative, such as *ð* vs. *þ* in English, discuss the motivation for the shift to *d*.

3 (a) It is often stated that speakers in neighboring areas seek to use similar forms and pronunciation for ready understanding. But Alf

Sommerfelt cites a Norwegian dialect in which the speakers introduced a change of *ei* to *ai* to provide a greater contrast with a neighboring dialect (1962: 222). What might be the motivation for such a development?

(b) Biologists have been studying animal communication. In observing two dialects of sparrows in Argentina that are associated with the territory in which the birds nest, Nottebohm concluded that the dialects play a part in the mating systems of the two groups of sparrows (1970: 950–6). He makes the further inference that the dialects in this way "encourage the emergence of locally adaptive traits." Discuss such possible forces in the development of different human languages, as of the many that developed in the Americas.

4 In chapter 3 of his monograph of 1808 Friedrich Schlegel considered the relationships between Sanskrit and other Indo-European dialects, asking first whether Sanskrit was the oldest of the related languages and possibly their source. Then he adds: "Can't it just as well have arisen through mixture of the others, or by these means have preserved the similarity?"

We have noted that Trubetzkoy proposed a similar origin for Proto-Indo-European by merger of neighboring languages.

In an article, "Random cases with directed effects, the Indo-European language spread and the stochastic loss of lineages" (1991: 287–91), Robb proposes "as a theoretical hypothesis [that] the pattern of Indo-European can simply arise from a kind of social Brownian motion, in which a large pattern invents itself out of countless little perturbations between adjacent language communities."

Discuss the persistent attempts to account for Proto-Indo-European in this way. Could a similar explanation be provided for other proto-languages?

By contrast, American Indian specialists, including Greenberg, go to great pains to propose one or more ancestral languages. Why the different approach?

Recalling Latin and its numerous daughter languages, discuss the attractiveness of the suggestions by Schlegel, Trubetzkoy and Robb as opposed to the view of an ancestral language comparable to a spoken language today that subdivided into a number of daughter languages.

7 The comparative method

7.1 THE COMPARATIVE METHOD: A TRIANGULATION PROCEDURE FOR RECONSTRUCTING EARLIER FORMS

The three preceding chapters have presented spheres in which linguists deal with language. In genealogical classification the dimension delimiting the sphere is time; languages are examined for relationships with their earlier stages, and these in turn for their sub-branches. In this way, English is examined for its similarities and differences with regard to Middle English, Old English and Proto-Germanic, from which other sub-branches, such as the Scandinavian languages developed. Proto-Germanic in turn is examined for similarities and differences with regard to Proto-Italic, Proto-Indo-Iranian, etc. and also with Proto-Indo-European. The procedure is comparison for the purpose of determining earlier stages of a language and other languages to which it is related.

In typological classification, the dimension of time is disregarded. Turkish today may be compared with Sumerian of 3000 BC, Berber today with Old Irish. All available languages are compared for characteristics that are widespread, in the search for those that are universal. As Meillet pointed out, these "two types of comparison, equally legitimate, differ absolutely. . . . The agreements which are established result from the general unity of the human mind, and the differences from the variety of types and degrees of civilization" (1925 (1967): 13). While comparing languages to determine "universal laws," in Meillet's expression, typological study is also concerned to learn "about the general characteristics of humanity" (*ibid.*). That aim may be the principal goal of typological study, but the results also serve as guidelines for reconstruction carried out by use of the comparative method. For example, on the basis of our knowledge from typological investigations, we would not reconstruct a language consisting solely of vowels, nor one consisting of lists of nouns rather than sentences. As we have illustrated above, we seek much more specific universals, also the interrelationships among them. The two types of classification in this way supplement each other.

In the third type of comparison, the sphere may be limited in various ways: by geographical extent, by social interrelationships, by occupations. Subclasses of a language are determined by cultural relationships, and these in turn are determined by the extent of contacts among speakers. Determination of such subgroups is important for historical study because subgroups of speakers maintain different elements of language. A capital city, such as Oslo, may have closer contacts than do outlying districts of Norway with other countries, as Olso did with Denmark, and may then develop a subclass of Norwegian that differs from that in those dialects lacking such contacts. Similarly, a social class like the Brahmins of India, may maintain a literary and religious language, Sanskrit, with an effect on the colloquial.

While speakers of subclasses of a language, that is dialects, can understand one another, characteristics differing from dialect to dialect may lead to shifts, with effects on subsequent stages of a language. Comparison for dialects, then, may be viewed as a delimitation of the extent of the sphere examined in genealogical comparison. It would be pointless, for example, to include the Arabic borrowings into Urdu when setting out to reconstruct the Old Indic dialects of the northwest part of the Asian subcontinent. Nor do we use the Latin and Romance elements of English when we relate it to the other Germanic dialects. For such classification we use the native elements of the language.

The three types of classification in this way differ, but they complement one another. When Akkadian is found to be verb final, for example, the results of typological comparison are examined with reference to those achieved from genealogical classification. The verb-final characteristics, then, are interpreted as borrowings from Sumerian, because the Semitic languages are verb initial, as reflected in many other characteristics of Akkadian. Similarly, when *k*'s are found in dialects of northern England, as in *kirk* as opposed to *church*, the characteristic is traced to the dialect of English influenced by Scandinavian settlers in the area. In short, the data of language may be compared in various ways, with differing results, all of which illuminate a language in some way, often providing explanations for its features.

When linguists speak of the **comparative method (CM)**, however, they refer to a procedure for determining earlier forms, generally of unattested languages. In using the method, we contrast forms of two or more related languages to determine the precise relationships between these forms. We indicate this relationship most simply by reconstructing the forms from which they developed.

As an example of a problem (for which we know the solution), we may cite the contrast between the medial consonants used by some speakers of American English (AE) in words like *atom*, *bitter*, *little*, and those used in other English dialects, such as British English. In some AE dialects the -*t*- in these words is voiced, so that *atom* and *Adam*, *bitter* and *bidder* are pronounced alike. If these pronunciations are maintained, future historical linguists will find in related languages the forms:

AE /ǽdəm/   :   BE /ǽtəm/ for *atom*
AE /bídər/   :   BE /bítə/ for *bitter*
AE /lídəl/   :   BE /lítəl/ for *little*

They would also find pronunciations like those of British English in Australian and other dialects of English. Setting such forms side by side, they would posit an earlier form, that is, an **etymon**, in the following manner:

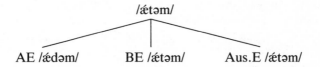

/ǽtəm/

AE /ǽdəm/   BE /ǽtəm/   Aus.E /ǽtəm/

Using the "triangulation" symbolized here, they would propose that the etymon for these three forms was like the British and Australian English **reflexes**. The American English reflex, on the other hand underwent a change by which the medial /t/ was voiced.

This illustration represents a first step. One would assemble all words with medial /t/ in British and Australian English to examine their American English counterparts.

As a further step, one would examine other words made from the same base, especially in American English. For example, the word /hitter/, pronounced [hídər], is an agent noun related to the verb /hít/. The unvoiced /t/ in the verb supports the assumption that /t/, rather than /d/ is the earlier sound, and accordingly that American English has undergone the change. We may note that the decisive evidence for reconstructing the /t/ is not the most frequent reflex; rather, that evidence is found in American English forms which did not change.

A further contrasting pair is the simple form of adjectives, for example *fat*, and the comparative, *fatter*, pronounced [fǽdər]. Such voicing does not occur in the comparative of similar adjectives, for example *quick* : *quicker*, *fast* : *faster*. From these pairs we assume that after the accented vowel the forms with [ər] should have the same consonant as those without it. To account for forms like [fǽdər] as well as [hídər], we conclude that in a restricted set of words, that is, those with medial [t], a sound change has taken place regardless of the morphological status of the word. For *hitter* is an agent noun based on /hit/ plus /ər/, and *quicker* belongs to a totally different category, in being derived from the adjective /kwik/ plus the comparative suffix /ər/.

Because in taking these steps we have found that some medial /t/ do not change, as in *faster*, we go on to examine /t/ in all environments. In one of the intervocalic environments the change did not take place, that is, when the following syllable is /ən/, as in *button*, *kitten* and so on. AE *button* is pronounced very much like BE *button*. The equivalence provides further evidence that it is American English in which the change of /t/ in *atom*, *bitter*, *little* took place.

In investigating the situation further, we would go on to examine the role of accent, and look for forms with medial /t/ but with differing accentuation, such as *atomic*. We conclude that if the accent falls on the second syllable, the t is not voiced. We find similar lack of voice in words like AE *attire*. In this way we would seek to examine all environments in which medial /t/ occurs.

We may have cited enough examples to demonstrate that use of the comparative method requires examination of all the instances of a sound under consideration; other environments are cited in the exercises after this chapter. Yet the evidence presented here may illustrate why the comparative method is effective.

Through our examination using the comparative method we have concluded that in some American English dialects medial /t/ has changed to /d/ when it follows a stressed vowel and stands before /ə/ plus /l/ or /m/ or /r/, or before /ɪ/ and other weakly stressed syllables. Such sound changes are generally restricted to certain dialects and to certain environments, as we will see in chapter 10. If other dialects can be found in which the change in question has not taken place, we can compare the contrasting forms and thereupon posit the etymon, finally verifying our conclusion by determining residues in the dialect that has undergone change. The comparative method has been tested on so many such examples that we are very confident of its effectiveness. As we have seen, the intricacies of language change generally provide enough evidence to support conclusions based on use of the comparative method.

To provide another illustration we may cite Romance language forms given in chapter 1: Fr. *champ*, Ital. *campo*, Span. *campo*, Port. *campo*. In reconstructing the earlier initial consonant we would posit [k]. We could verify this assumption by noting Lat. *campus* "field," and also by observing the consistent changes of such initial [k] in French and their maintenance in Italian, Spanish and Portuguese. Because Latin is available for checking reconstructions made from the Romance languages, the comparative method has gained credence by examination of such forms. It may be observed, however, that the Romance languages developed from spoken Latin rather than from the literary Latin of our classical texts. Accordingly, the fit between the reconstructed forms and the attested literary forms is not perfect. We have evidence of spoken Latin, as in the plays of Plautus and in graffiti on the walls of catacombs and Pompeii; but we find it useful to apply the comparative method to determine that language as well as to test results against literary Latin.

In a similar way we may determine the forms in a reconstructed language. As an example we may take the third singular present of the verb "be" in Proto-Indo-European. We would compare forms such as Skt *ásti*,

Lith. *ēsti*, Gk *ésti*, and others by the triangulation procedure illustrated above for *atom*:

PIE *ésti*

Skt *ásti*   Lith. *ēsti*   Gk *ésti*

In these forms, our chief problem is the Sanskrit *a*; we would propose provisionally that Skt *a* developed from PIE *e*. We would then look for evidence within Sanskrit for this assumption. That evidence is less obvious than the evidence cited above for the Romance languages, but it is still decisive. It was not apparent to the early historical linguists until the 1870s.

The evidence is found in reduplicated forms. In the Sanskrit perfect, the canonical reduplication is made with the initial consonant plus *a*, as in *tatána* from the root *tan* "stretch." The perfect of the root *kṛ* "make," however, is *cakára*. That is to say, the *k* is prefixed, but also palatalized. In the 1870s a number of linguists almost simultaneously recognized that the palatalization resulted from a following front vowel, that is *e*, as attested in Greek. Evidence, although long unrecognized, then, is found in Sanskrit to support the conclusions based on the comparative method for positing PIE /e/. The finding illustrates the power of the method, as well as the importance of examining all possible forms in a language when making historical statements.

We would also seek to reconstruct morphological paradigms by using the method. Having determined the third singular present indicative of the verb "be," we would deal with other forms, such as the first person. Here we find:

Skt *ásmi*   Lith. *ēsmi*   Gk *eimí*

After the evidence found in reduplication, we no longer have a problem with the initial vowel **e*; now Greek provides a difficulty with the sequence *ei* indicating a long close *ē*. We account for the lengthened *ē* through loss of the *s* with compensation in quantity of the preceding short *e* vowel. Support for such compensatory lengthening is found in many languages as in French, for example *état* as compared with English *estate*; we will cite further examples in chapter 10. We will also deal at greater length below with the use of the comparative method for reconstruction in morphology and syntax.

Before examining further examples we may indicate briefly shortcomings of the method. Of chief importance is its limitation by the amount of information. The method offers no means of reconstructing elements that are completely lost in subsequent stages of the language. Today we reconstruct the root of "be" as **ʔes*, but through use of the method of internal reconstruction (see chapter 8). With the comparative method we could not determine that the Proto-Indo-European forms began with a glottal stop, because this is not attested in forms that have come down to us. After positing the glottal stop by internal reconstruction, we find evidence, however, comparable to that of the palatalization of velars in Sanskrit reduplication.

We also support our results by comparing sets: the set of vowels in two or more languages, of stops, and so on. To support our reconstructions of Proto-Indo-European forms, as of the verb "be," we determine the entire Proto-Indo-European phonological system, as we illustrate with the obstruents.

7.2 THE COMPARATIVE METHOD APPLIED TO INDO-EUROPEAN OBSTRUENTS

We may illustrate the application of the comparative method to sets of phonological entities by examining forms containing Greek and Latin obstruents shown in table 7.1. For the first three rows of the first two columns – the voiceless and voiced **orders** of the labial, dental and velar **series** – the results of our comparison would permit little dispute for the entities with which we are concerned. In both Greek and Latin we find oppositions between voiceless and voiced stops, among labials, dentals and velars; we therefore assume the same phonemes for Proto-Indo-European.

Table 7.1 Obstruents of Greek and Latin

		1	2	3	4
I	Gk	patḗr "father"	beltíōn "better"	phrā́tēr "clansman"	
	Lat.	pater "father"	dē-bilis "weak"	frāter "brother"	
II	Gk	treîs "three"	déka "ten"	aná-thēma "offering"	heptá "seven"
	Lat.	trēs "three"	decem "ten"	fēci "did"	septem "seven"
III	Gk	he-katón "hundred"	génos "kin"	khamaí "(on the) earth"	
	Lat.	centum "hundred"	genus "tribe"	humus "ground"	
IV	Gk	(a) poû "where" (b) tís "who"	baíno "come"	(a) phónos "murder" (b) theíno "strike"	
	Lat.	(a) quō "whither" (b) quis "who"	veniō "come"	dē-fendō "ward off"	

Accordingly, we would posit table 7.2 for the system from which the obstruent systems of Greek and Latin developed. For the last two columns and the last row, however, we would find it difficult to posit earlier forms on the basis of the material provided here. We can suggest such forms with greater assurance if we add material from other Indo-European languages.

The comparative method was sharpened largely by its application to the obstruent system of Germanic. In Germanic the obstruents had undergone various changes that were not determined before the studies of Rask and Grimm. By careful comparison these two founders of historical linguistics

Table 7.2 The development of obstruent systems in Greek and Latin from Proto-Indo-European

	Greek		*Latin*		*Proto-Indo-European*			
	1	2	1	2	1	2	3	4
I	p	b	p	b	p	b	–	
II	t	d	t	d	t	d	–	–
III	k	g	k	g	k	g	–	
IV					–	–	–	

demonstrated the changes that had taken place in Germanic. Their work, and that of their successors, led to the development of the comparative method. This work also indicated the need for precise analysis of all the forms in related languages. Adding to our Greek and Latin examples cognate words from Germanic and Indic illustrates how these cognates enable us to fill out our reconstruction of the Proto-Indo-European obstruents. (In table 7.3, unless otherwise labeled, the Germanic examples are from Gothic. Examples in a wide variety of dialects to support the reconstruction of PIE *b* do not exist. We therefore cite a cognate from Baltic, and admit the possibility that the phoneme as well as the words listed here are dialectal, not Indo-European.)

Table 7.3 Proto-Indo-European obstruents

		1		*2*		*3*	
I	Gmc	fadar "father"	Eng.	pool		broþar "brother"	
	Skt	pitá "father"	Lith.	balà "swamp"		bhrā́tā "brother"	
II	Gmc	þrija "3"		taihun "10"		doms "fame"	sibun "7"
	Skt	tráyas "3"		dáśa "10"		dhāma "glory"	saptá "7"
III	Gmc	hunda "100"		kuni "race"		guma "man"	
	Skt	śatám "100"		jánas "race"		kṣás "earth"	
IV	OIcel.	hvat "what"	OHG	queman "come"	OE	gūþ "battle"	
	Skt	kás "who"		gámanti "they go"		ghnánti "they strike"	

The examples cited here support the inferences drawn from comparison of Greek and Latin; they also supplement them, especially for row IV. The obstruent system reconstructed for Proto-Indo-European was based largely on these four dialects, as shown in table 7.4.

Table 7.4 The dialectual base for a reconstruction of the Proto-Indo-European obstruents

	1	*2*	*3*	*4*
I	p	b	bh	
II	t	d	dh	s
III	k	g	gh	
IV	k^w	g^w	g^wh	

Additional material must be supplied to support convincingly the reconstructions in row IV. The conclusions given here are based largely on Latin and Germanic evidence, as in the forms Lat. *quis* and OHG *queman*. The entities posited in column 3 are based primarily on Skt *bh dh gh* but also on Gk *ph th kh*. We will return to these conclusions below.

7.3 THE COMPARATIVE METHOD APPLIED TO THE GERMANIC OBSTRUENTS

A review of the study of the Germanic phenomena during the nineteenth century contributes to understanding the development of the comparative method and other methods of historical linguistics. Rask pointed out in 1818 the relationships between the Germanic obstruents and those of the other Indo-European dialects. In 1822 Grimm made the important contribution of indicating the system underlying the relationships. Proto-Indo-European voiceless stops of all four series are represented by voiceless fricatives in Germanic; Proto-Indo-European voiced stops, by Germanic voiceless stops; Proto-Indo-European voiced aspirates, by Proto-Germanic voiced fricatives that later in most Germanic languages became voiced stops. The consistency of correspondences in other positions, such asmedially in the examples of table 7.5, indicates its value in historical linguistics.

Table 7.5 Proto-Indo-European obstruents, with examples

		1	2	3	4
	PIE	p	b	bh	
	Gk	*anepsiós* "cousin"	–	*nephélē* "fog"	
I	Lat.	*nepōs* "grandson"	Lith. *trobà* "building"	*nebula* "mist"	
	Skt	*nápāt* "descendant"	OWelsh *treb* "house"	*nábhas* "mist"	
	Gmc	OE *nefa* "nephew"	Go. *þaurp* "village"	Germ. *Nebel* "fog"	
	PIE	t	d	dh	s
	Gk	*phrā́tēr* "clansman"	*édomai* "I shall eat"	*eruthrós* "red"	*hestía* "hearth"
	Lat.	*frāter* "brother"	*edō* "I eat"	*ruber* "red"	Vesta
II	Skt	*bhrā́tā* "brother"	*ád-mi* "I eat"	*rudhirás* "bloody"	*vásati* "lives"
	Gmc	*broþar* "brother"	OE *etan* "eat"	OE *rēad* "red"	*wisan* "be"
	OCS	*bratrŭ* "brother"	*jadętŭ* "they eat"	*rŭdrŭ* "red"	
	PIE	k	g	gh	
	Gk	*déka* "ten"	*agrós* "field"	*steíkhō* "climb"	
III	Lat.	*decem* "ten"	*ager* "field"	*vestīgium* "trace"	
	Skt	*dásá* "ten"	*ájras* "plain"	*stighnoti* "climbs"	
	Gmc	*taihun* "ten"	OE *æcer* "field"	*steigan* "climb"	
	PIE	kʷ	gʷ	gʷh	
	Gk	*lúkos* "wolf"	*érebos* "underworld"	*nípha* "snow"	
IV	Lat.	*lupus* "wolf	–	*nix, nivis* "snow"	
	Skt	*vṛkas* "wolf"	*rajas* "cloud"	Av. *snāĕžaiti* "it snows"	
	Gmc,OIcel	.ylgr "she wolf"	*riqis* "darkness"	OE *snāw* "snow"	

By means of these and other examples, we may verify the obstruents just posited for Proto-Indo-European. We can most simply state the development of the Proto-Indo-European obstruents into Germanic by using the following formulas. We read ">" as "became" or "developed into."

Proto-Indo-European obstruents into Proto-Germanic

PIE p t k kʷ	>	PGmc f θ χ χʷ
PIE b d g gʷ	>	PGmc p t k kʷ
PIE bh dh gh gʷh	>	PGmc ƀ ð ǥ (ǥʷ)
PIE s	>	PGmc s

We could state similarly with appropriate formulas the development of the Proto-Indo-European obstruents in the other Indo-European dialects.

If we wish to indicate the relationship of the obstruents from dialect to dialect, we use the sign "=" in our formulas, reading it "corresponding to," for example:

Skt	t d dh	=	PGmc	þ t ð
Gk	t d th	=	OCS	t d d

We can also state our previous formulas in reverse order, for example:

PGmc ƀ ð ǥ (ǥʷ) < PIE bh dh ǥh ǥʷh

reading "<" as "developed from."

7.4 RELATIONSHIPS EXAMINED WITH THE HELP OF THE COMPARATIVE METHOD

As we have noted in section 7.1, when we study the relationships between two or more languages, we must make comparisons for all environments, not merely for the initial and some intervocalic environments as we have done here.

In such comparison we find a variety of interrelationships.

1 The sounds concerned may have been maintained in both languages; Lat. *p* in *pater* and Gk *p* in *patér* are examples.

2 The sounds concerned may have been maintained in one language and may have undergone change in the other; Lat. *p* in *pater* and Gmc. *f*, as in Goth. *fadar*, are examples.

  When only two languages are attested, it may be difficult to determine which maintains the original form. One may find in either language unchanged sounds in specific environments to use as guides, as we did above in AE *set* beside [sédər]. The occurrence of *p* after *s* provides important evidence in reconstructing PIE *p* from Latin and Germanic, for after *s* Germanic has maintained PIE *p*, as in Goth. *speiwan*, see Lat. *spuō* "spit." Since Latin has generally maintained PIE *p*, we conclude that Lat. *p* more closely represents the Proto-Indo-European sound than does the Gmc *f*; and we find further support for this conclusion in other Indo-European dialects.

3 The sounds concerned may have undergone change in both languages; the *b* in Lat. *nebula* and the *b* in Germ. *Nebel* both come from PIE *bh*. Reconstructing the etymon of such forms may be very difficult. After a century and a half of attention, the etymon of Gk *ph*, Lat. *b* or *f*, Skt *bh*, Gmc *b* has not been determined to everyone's satisfaction. If unchanged items cannot be found in certain environments, as in Goth. *speiwan*, one must rely on knowledge of the various kinds of sound changes. Such information is presented in chapter 10. When the sounds have changed in both languages, we may find a variety of developments.

(a) The sounds concerned may merge completely, as did PIE *d* and *dh* in OCS *jadɛtŭ* "they eat" and *rŭdrŭ* "red." Such complete mergers cause great difficulties for reconstruction. We cannot determine whether a voiced stop in the Slavic languages developed from a Proto-Indo-European voiced stop or a voiced aspirate except in some forms through the type of intonation.

(b) The sounds may merge in part, as did medial *dh* and *bh* in Lat. *ruber* "red" with *b* from PIE *dh*, and *nebula* "fog" with *b* from PIE *bh*. By comparing sounds in other orders, for example, the Latin voiceless stops in *frāter* "brother," with the medial dental maintained, and *nepōs* "grandson," with the medial labial maintained, partial mergers may be cleared up, especially if we find cognates in related languages. The lack of parallelism in the Latin reflexes of PIE *bh dh gh* leads us to suspect changes in this order between Proto-Indo-European and Latin.

(c) Moreover, the mergers may be complex, as in the following Greek examples: (i) *poũ* "where" (where Gk *p* = Lat. *qu* as in *quod*) : *patếr* (where Gk *p* = Lat. *p*); (ii) *tís* "who" (where Gk *t* = Lat. *qu* as in *quis*) : *treîs* (where Gk *t* = Lat. *t*); (iii) *kúklos* "circle" (where Gk *k* = Lat *qu*, Gmc. *hw* as in OE *hwēol* "wheel") : *he-katón* (where Gk *k* = Lat. [k] as in *centum* "hundred"). Again, one must sort out the situation in the language concerned. Analysis of standard Greek indicates that the reflexes of PIE k^w, g^w, g^wh show up as labials before *a o*, as dentals before *e i* and as velars before *u*. The complex set of mergers is the result of a development within Greek. To the extent we can judge from our Linear B materials, labiovelars were still maintained in Greek until approximately 1000 BC, and even later in some Greek dialects; because of borrowings from dialects, the rules given above do not apply to all words in standard Greek.

These examples of mergers in individual languages illustrate that the comparative method can be used to determine earlier forms, even after a number of changes. By noting carefully the environment in which each change occurred, we can generally reconstruct the earlier situation, unless there has been a complete merger.

7.5 ADVANTAGES AND SHORTCOMINGS OF THE COMPARATIVE METHOD

The comparative method has been highly successful in permitting us to reconstruct earlier forms than those attested. For example, the evidence for the labiovelar order is not clear in the widely known dialects of Indo-European, as illustrated above; yet labiovelars were reconstructed for the proto-language. When Hittite texts were discovered, evidence was found for velar and labial articulation, supporting the reconstruction of the labiovelars in Proto-Indo-European. The Hittite form corresponding to Gk *tís* is written *ku-iš*.

Another reconstruction by the comparative method that was later verified is Bloomfield's Proto-Algonquian cluster *çk*, which he proposed on the basis of Fox and Ojibwa *šk*, Cree and Menomini *hk* and related clusters. Later, in Swampy Cree, he found a distinct reflex of this cluster, *htk*, and other evidence to support his reconstruction (1929: 99–100). Since use of the comparative method has in this way been demonstrated to be successful, careful application of it is highly trustworthy.

The comparative method, however, has various shortcomings. Reconstructions achieved by use of the method are less precise phonetically than is the information on which they are based. On the basis of Gk *ph*, Gmc *b*, Slav. *b*, Lat. *b*, Skt *bh* and Arm. *bh*, we may posit PIE *bh*, but we cannot determine precisely its pronunciation. As we see further below, the results of the comparative method have now been restated on the basis of typological findings. We also cannot state whether the Proto-Indo-European labiovelars were articulated as velars followed by labial rounding, as velars with simultaneous labial closure, or as still other sounds.

We lose information also in the complexity of the language we reconstruct. In normal use of the comparative method we proceed backward by triangulation and eventually posit for each subgroup a dialect-free phoneme. In reconstructing the Proto-Indo-European voiceless velar stop *k*, for example, we proceed from comparison of Gk *k*, as in *he-katón*, with Itc *k*, as in Lat. *centum*, to comparison with Gmc *χ*, as in Goth. *hunda*, with Indo-Iranian *ś* as in Skt *śatám*, and so on. It is likely, however, that the dialects of Indo-European were not uniform; further, that they reflect a nonuniform situation in the parent language. Some forms, for example, which are expected to contain a sibilant in Baltic and Slavic, have a velar; for example: Lith. *akmuõ*, OCS *kamy* versus Skt *aśmān*, Av. *asman-* "stone," Gk *ákmōn* "anvil." If Proto-Indo-European had been completely regular and dialect-free, all of these forms except Greek should have a sibilant rather than a velar. Although the comparative method ideally requires us to reconstruct a dialect-free Proto-Indo-European, such irregularities suggest that the parent language already had dialects. With care we may apply the comparative method in all rigor and, from forms like those for "stone," assume dialects within the parent language. Much as the results of typological study have permitted us to extend our conclusions based on the comparative method, the findings from research on linguistic communities have provided means to interpret those conclusions. Yet the method itself is not designed to yield anything other than a dialect-free corpus.

7.6 REFINEMENT OF THE COMPARATIVE METHOD BY STUDY OF THE GERMANIC OBSTRUENTS

The comparative method was being refined throughout the nineteenth century. We may illustrate its development by observing the increasing precision applied to the description of the obstruent system of Germanic in its relation to that of Proto-Indo-European and those of the other dialects.

In 1822 Jacob Grimm published general statements on the relations between Germanic obstruents and those in the other languages. Labeling *p t k* **Tenues**, *bh dh gh* (and *f θ χ*, etc.) **Aspiratae**, *ƀ ð g* and *b d g* **Mediae**, he stated that Indo-European **T** > Germanic **A**, Indo-European **A** > Germanic **M**, Indo-European **M** > Germanic **T** producing a circular scheme:

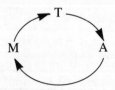

On the basis of subsequent changes in the High German area, where *t* became *ts*, as in Germ. *zu* pronounced [tsu] versus Eng. *to*, he assumed that this change repeated itself in the Germanic languages. The shifts, then, were taken to be the results of a law. Thereupon the formulation has been called **Grimm's law**; as such it is widely known, included even in desk dictionaries. Although other linguists have gained a somewhat restricted renown through the discovery of a "law" that states a minute change in some language, the term law is overblown for a statement of correspondences. Today we may retain the label for established "laws," like Grimm's, but otherwise we avoid the term in this sense.

As one of the excellences of Grimm's account in 1822, the words that did not comply with the rules were listed. The lack of correspondences came to be known as "exceptions" to Grimm's law. Subsequent accounting for them contributed greatly to the development of historical method in the nineteenth century.

7.6.1 Solution of the first set of exceptions to Grimm's law

The first exception to be solved concerned the maintenance of Proto-Indo-European voiceless stops after Germanic fricatives, as in the following examples:

PIE	*pt*	Goth.	*hafts* "married"	=	Lat.	*captus* "captured"
	sp		*speiwan* "spew"	=	Lat.	*spuō* "spit"
	st		*ist* "is"	=	Lat.	*est* "is"
	sk		*skadus* "shadow"	=	Gk	*skótos* "darkness"
	kt		*nahts* "night"	=	Lat.	*nox, noctis* "night"

In these and other examples the stop after the Germanic fricative did not change. The lack of change was ascribed to the environment. Within decades after Grimm had published his rules, linguists accounted for the first exception by stating that voiceless stops remained unchanged when they followed Germanic voiceless fricatives.

This solution indicated the importance in historical linguistics of examining immediate environments and observing phonetic characteristics. Although Grimm himself showed little interest in phonetics, his successors studied the production of sounds thoroughly. As a result, articulatory phonetics was greatly developed in the nineteenth century, reaching a high level in the works of Maurice Grammont, Otto Jespersen, Eduard Sievers and Henry Sweet.

7.6.2 Solution of the second set of exceptions to Grimm's law

Explanation of the second group of exceptions gave rise to a further advance in method. Involved here were Germanic voiced fricatives and stops that seemed to correspond irregularly to Indo-European voiced stops rather than to voiced aspirated stops, as in:

PIE	*bh . . . dh-*	Goth.	*-biudan* "offer"	=	Skt	*bódhāmi* "notice"
	dh . . . gh-		*dauhtar* "daughter"	=		*duhitá* "daughter"
	gh . . . gh-		*gagg* "street"	=		*jánghá* "leg"

If the correspondences had been in accordance with Grimm's rules, the cognates in Sanskrit should have had initial aspirates.

As we have observed in chapter 2, Hermann Grassmann accounted for the lack of correspondence by pointing out that all such forms contained Proto-Indo-European aspirates in two successive syllables; further, that in Indic and Greek one of the two successive aspirates had been dissimilated to an unaspirated stop. The irregularity was then not to be ascribed to Germanic, but rather to the supposedly more archaic Sanskrit and Greek.

We will examine the Sanskrit and Greek dissimilation of aspirates at great length in the next chapter. Here we are chiefly concerned with the further refinement of the comparative method based on Grassmann's findings. Observing that his explanation was based on examination of the elements in successive syllables, linguists now learned that they could not deal only with entities and their immediate environments, for sounds might be affected by other noncontiguous sounds. Grassmann's observation led them to examine entire syllables and words, as well as individual sounds.

7.6.3 Solution of the third set of exceptions to Grimm's law

Accounting for the third set of exceptions led to another refinement. These exceptions comprise forms in which a Proto-Indo-European voiceless stop had become a voiced fricative in Germanic rather than a voiceless fricative. Voiced fricatives can be assumed from OSax. *sibun*, OIcel. *faðer*, OE *sweʒer*; as the other dialects indicate, these often became stops later. Examples are:

PIE *p'* > PGmc. *ƀ*:   Goth. *sibun*, OE *seofun*, OSax. *sibun*,
                            OHG *sibun*; Skt *saptá*, Gk *heptá* "seven"

PIE *t'* > PGmc. *ð*:   Goth. *fadar*, OIcel. *faðer*, OE *fæder*,
                            OHG *fater*; Skt *pitā́*, Gk *patḗr* "father"

PIE *k'* > PGmc. *ɡ*:   OE *sweʒer*, OHG *swigur*; Skt *śvaśrū́ṣ*,
                            Gk *hekurá* "mother-in-law"

The Danish linguist, Karl Verner, observed that the accent in Sanskrit and Greek never preceded the obstruents that corresponded in Germanic to voiced fricatives. He formulated a law to account for these developments, including PGmc. *z* < PIE *ś* (this *z* became *r* in all Germanic dialects but Gothic):

PIE *ś* > PGmc. *z*: OIcel. *snør*, OE/*snoru*, OHG *snura*;
Skt *snuṣā́*, Gk *nuós* < **snusós* "daughter-in-law"

We may restate Verner's law as follows: Proto-Indo-European voiceless stops became Proto-Germanic voiceless fricatives; in voiced surroundings these voiceless fricatives, plus the already existing voiceless fricative *s*, became voiced when not immediately preceded by the accent.

Verner's article probably had a greater effect on historical linguistics than has any other single publication. As one result, linguists recognized that they could no longer limit their attention to consonants and vowels but that they had to consider accent as well. The suprasegmentals now were taken into account. In the last decades of the nineteenth century many articles in the linguistic journals deal with the suprasegmental patterns manipulated in verse. Many other articles attempted to explain sound changes by recourse to suprasegmentals. Although some of these were overly enthusiastic, after 1876 linguists paid attention to the pitch and stress patterns of language, as fourteen years earlier they had learned to take into account entire words, and several decades earlier, immediate environments. Accordingly, after Verner, linguists dealt with all the phonological entitites of an utterance.

7.7 THE NEOGRAMMARIAN HYPOTHESIS, A CONCLUSION BASED ON SUCCESSFUL USE OF THE COMPARATIVE METHOD

Verner's explanation of the last large group of exceptions to Grimm's law had the further effect of giving linguists complete confidence in their rules and laws. Observing that greater attention to the matter of language permitted them to account for residues and for diverse developments, a group of linguists after 1876 proclaimed that "sound change takes place according to laws that admit no exception." These linguists, referred to as neogrammarians by somewhat scornful elders, proclaimed that if one assembled all the facts, and analysed them accurately and thoroughly, one could state exceptionless principles or laws for the development of language.

This assumption is known as the **neogrammarian hypothesis**. The principles of the neogrammarians are stated in an article written by Karl Brugmann (1878) that is often referred to as the neogrammarian manifesto. It should still be read by every linguist. Among Brugmann's criticisms of linguists is their concentration on abstract patterns with lack of attention to living languages. In keeping with his stress on language as it is used, he and the other neogrammarians did not assume that sound changes operated without exception in all lexical sets. For example, they excluded nursery words such as Goth. *atta* "father" and onomatopoetic words such as NHG *kikeriki* as well as its equivalent *cock-a-doodle-do*. The extent of such sets has been one of the hotly argued problems of historical linguistics.

The new movement centered around Leipzig. Its leading young scholars, Brugmann, Delbrück, Osthoff, Leskien and others adopted the label neogrammarian for themselves. Encouraged by their new scientific method, they proceeded to deal with many problems and to publish handbooks that have been in use since their day. Braune's *Gotische Grammatik*, subsequently revised (Braune and Ebbinghaus 1981), provided the pattern for most historical grammars of the past century and is still the standard handbook for the language after many editions.

For decades the neogrammarians also attracted to Leipzig brilliant young students, such as Leonard Bloomfield. Through their students and their publications, the neogrammarian school exerted a great effect on linguistics. The principle that sound laws operate without exception encouraged linguists to uncover all the facts involved in language change, for it assured them that thorough study would yield results. In spite of occasional excesses, the neogrammarians applied the comparative method with great skill to various problems in language. They also produced major handbooks that have not been superseded to this day, such as Karl Brugmann's *Grundriss der vergleichenden Grammatik der indogermanischen Sprachen* (1897–1916).

7.8 USE AND AMPLIFICATION OF THE COMPARATIVE METHOD

In the course of historical linguistics, observations and statements have become increasingly precise. We noted above that Grimm's formulation consisted of three major rules, and that the entities of the rules, T A M, represented general classes. Grimm's classes, especially A and M, do not correspond to sets of similarly articulated sounds. Improved statements of Grimm's law in the half-century after its formulation added greater precision by indicating in each of its rules the actual sounds involved.

These improved statements represent the sounds with phonetic symbols. Thus the rule PIE *p t k k^w* > PGmc. *f þ χ χ^w* refers to the subclass of the Indo-European voiceless stops that was found in all environments except after PIE *s* and PGmc *fþ χ* from Proto-Indo-European voiceless stops. The other rules refer to other subclasses of phonemes occurring in specific environments, that is, to allophones. On the basis of other examples cited in this chapter, we assume that sound change takes place by such subclasses, which make up sets in individual languages. Thus the labiovelars must have developed three sets of allophones in early standard Greek. The allophones before *a o* were characterized by labial articulation. The allophones before *i e* were characterized by fronted articulation. As these allophones developed the assumed characteristics further, they merged with *p t k*, *b d g*, *φ θ χ*. In Germanic, on the other hand, the labiovelars developed different allophones, as the Germanic reflexes given above indicate.

In standard grammars the Greek changes of the earlier labiovelars are represented by rules like the following:

PIE *k^w g^w g^w h*	>	Gk *p b φ*	before *a o*
PIE *k^w g^w g^w h*	>	Gk *t d θ*	before *i e*
PIE *k^w g^w g^w h*	>	Gk *k g χ*	before *u*

Such rules represent the change accurately, if at some length.

Although sound changes take place by allophones, only one feature of the allophone is generally modified. Thus the stop [t] became a continuant [þ] in Proto-Germanic. And the labial feature of early Greek *k* was lost in Greek before *u*. To indicate the specific modifications, rules may be stated in distinctive features.

Such rules have the advantage of representing the general structural principles of the language. For example, when we state a rule for the development of Proto-Indo-European voiced stops to Proto-Germanic voiceless stops, such as PIE *d* to PGmc *t*, the rule indicates that not only PIE *d* but also every stop is voiceless in Germanic. That is, the rule is valid for Gmc *t* from PIE *t* as well as for Gmc *t* from PIE *d*, as well as for PGmc *p k kʷ*. This rule might then be stated as follows:

[−resonant]

→   [−voiced]

[−continuant]

Because the other Proto-Germanic obstruents, *f þ s χ χʷ ƀ ð g gʷ* were [+continuant], when this rule applied, it indicates a general feature of articulation in the language as well as a sound change.

The chief problem with the precise rules given by means of distinctive features results from our ignorance of the details concerning earlier languages. We know that the three sets – (1) *p t k kʷ*, (2) *bh dh gh gʷh*, (3) *b d g gʷ* – contrasted in pre-Germanic. We can even be reasonably sure that set 1 consisted of voiceless stops, set 2 of voiced aspirated stops and set 3 of voiced stops (now assumed with glottalic offglide). But when we propose distinctive features for the members of each set, we have little evidence for these proposed features. Some linguists assume that pre-Germanic *p t k kʷ* were lenis stops, as in some contemporary dialects of German; others assume that they were fortis. Assumptions for the distinctive features of *bh dh gh gʷh* are even less certain. On the other hand, when detailed analysis will permit us to determine the features of earlier sound systems ,with greater precision, the stating of rules in distinctive features will add to our understanding of earlier languages.

Such additional understanding has now been attempted by inferences based on typological investigations. These inferences are centered on the infrequency of /b/ in Proto-Indo-European, which Jacob Grimm already pointed out in 1822. We discuss it in greater detail below. Here we mention briefly that two similar proposals have been made suggesting that the phoneme was rare because it was glottalic. In glottalic series, the labial is often missing, but that is true when the series is voiceless. Using this information to account for the rare "b," Gamkrelidze and Ivanov (1973) and Hopper (1973) proposed that the series assumed to be voiced stops in Proto-Indo-European, that is (*b*) *d g gʷ*, was actually glottalic and unvoiced. Their "glottalic theory" obviously modifies the long-standing view of the Indo-European obstruents. It has therefore elicited considerable argument, and also opposition. We cite it at this point to illustrate how typological findings have provided means to extend the results of the comparative method.

7.9 USE OF THE COMPARATIVE METHOD FOR MORPHOLOGICAL AND SYNTACTIC PHENOMENA

When the comparative method is discussed, applications are generally cited for the phonological sphere. Yet the first major monograph in Indo-European studies is Bopp's of 1816, which dealt with the morphological system. While Bopp did not reconstruct nominal and verbal paradigms in Proto-Indo-European, he equated different surface forms in Sanskrit, Greek and other dialects, assuming them to be comparable with one another. For example, the third singular form of the root for "bear" is *bhárati* in Sanskrit, *phérei* in Greek. Treating each of these forms as members of a parallel paradigm, Bopp had no problem assuming a third singular present indicative active verb form for Proto-Indo-European. In the same way, many other verbal and nominal forms were assumed, to yield a comprehensive grammar of the proto-language. That is to say, the comparative method was applied to morphology from the early part of the nineteenth century.

Application to syntax and to semantics is more recent. We will discuss it in the chapters on these spheres, but here illustrate how it is applied to syntactic as well as to phonological and morphological categories and elements. As we have observed, the method is applied to abstract sets. Until we have a framework, we cannot determine sets. We noted in chapter 4 that such a framework is now available in syntactic study. Here we discuss only one set, the comparative construction. We have seen that two distinct comparative constructions may be proposed in languages. The construction like the English "higher than a mountain" has the structure: adjective–pivot–standard, and is characteristic of VO languages. The Japanese construction, *yama yori takai* "mountain from high," has the reverse construction, standard–pivot–adjective, and is characteristic of OV languages. A morphological marker, like *-er* may or may not be used in comparatives; Japanese has none.

Examining the early Germanic languages for comparative constructions we find sequences like the following:

ON *Voluspá* 64 sólo fegra
"sun (than) fairer"
OE *Beowulf* 1850 þæt þē Sæ-Gēatas sēlran næbben
            that you (than) the Sea-Geats a better do not have
            "The Geats have no one better than you."
OHG Otfrid 5.18.9 ist in allen oboro
            is them all (than) higher
            "is higher than all of them"
Gothic Skeireins
ni þe haldis
not (than) that more likely
not more likely than that"

All of these comparatives have the structure: standard–pivot–adjective (SPA). The pivot is generally indicated by the dative case endings. Applying the comparative method to these syntactic constructions in the Northern, Western and East Germanic dialects, we reconstruct an OV type comparative construction SPA for Proto-Germanic, much as we reconstructed the earlier form of /t/ in recent English.

In this way the comparative method can be applied to any syntactic construction that can be identified as a representative of a given framework. Through its use for syntactic and semantic patterns, as well as for morphological and phonological, future historical grammars will be far more complete than are current grammars in the presentation of the language. For the comparative method can be applied to all components of language in much the way we have illustrated with patterns in the phonological component.

SELECTED FURTHER READINGS

Meillet (1925) provides an excellent introduction to the comparative method; it is also available in English (1967). Good accounts are given in competent handbooks, such as Bloomfield (1933: ch. 18), Anttila (1989: ch. 11), Bynon (1977: part I. 7), Hock (1986: ch. 18). A rigorous as well as comprehensive treatment may be found in chapter 12 of Hoenigswald (1960).

Notable articles in the development of historical linguistics, such as those of Grassmann, Verner and Brugmann, have been assembled and translated in Lehmann (1967).

PROBLEMS

1 The following sets of related words may be used to reconstruct the Proto-Indo-European etyma of the indicated sounds by the comparative method.

(a) The Sanskrit sibilants:

ś	Skt *śvá-*	Gk *kúōn*	Lat. *canis* "dog"
	Skt *śru-*	Gk. *klúō*	Lat. *clueō* "hear"
ṣ	Skt *naṣṭa-* "lost", past participle of *naś*		
	Skt *aṣṭā*	Gk *oktṓ*	Lat. *octō* "eight"
s	Skt *saptá*	Gk *heptá*	Lat. *septem* "seven"
	Skt *asti*	Gk *esti*	Lat. *est* "is"

Noting the environment, especially of Skt *s*, determine any internal changes in Sanskrit and reconstruct the Indo-European sibilant.

(b) Sanskrit *a*

Skt *bhar-*	Gk *phérō*	Lat. *ferō* "carry, bring"
Skt *nabhas-*	Gk *néphos*	Lat. *nebula* "cloud, sky"
Skt *aṣṭā*	Gk *oktố*	Lat. *octō* "eight"
Skt *patis*	Gk *pósis*	Lat. *potis* "lord"
Skt *ajāmi*	Gk *ágō*	Lat. *agō* "drive"
Skt *ájras*	Gk *agrós*	Lat. *ager* "field"

Determine the Proto-Indo-European system of low short vowels. In some Sanskrit words, velars before PIE *e* are palatalized, for example *jani-tắ*, Gk *genétōr*, Lat. *geni-tōr* "begetter." What information do such words give us regarding the vowel in Pre-Sanskrit?

2 When using the comparative method to reconstruct morphological paradigms one must note the modifications resulting from analogy. The following are forms of the verb "be":

		Sanskrit	Greek	Latin	Gothic
Singular	1	ásmi	eimí	sum,	im
	2	ási	eĩ, essí	es	is
	3	ásti	estí	est	ist
Plural	1	smás	eimés	sumus	sijum
	2	sthá	esté	estis	sijuþ
	3	sánti	eisí	sunt	sind

(a) Determine the Proto-Indo-European root, and its variant after dealing with the following questions. In determining the root in the plural, note the position of the accent and its effect on the vowel of the root. Note also the losses of final vowel in Latin and Gothic with their stress accent.

(b) Indicate forms in which the root of the singular has been introduced into the plural.

(c) Account for the form of the root in the plural.

(d) Account for the Latin first-person form *sum*.

(e) The Proto-Indo-European plural endings are reconstructed as **mes*, **te*, **e/onti*. Account for the forms in the dialects.

3 Examine the forms of medial -*t*- in various environments of current English, comparing it with the following:

(a) Often voiced in the prepositional phrase *át it*, but not in *atáll* (*at all*).

(b) Often voiced in the sequence *it isn't*, but not in the phrase *it wasn't*.

(c) Not voiced in the phrase: *Get out of here* [get áwtǝ hir] but in the question *Get it?*

If your own pronunciation differs from that suggested here, state as much, and attempt to determine the pattern of speech.

4 In his analysis of the syntax of the *Śatapathabrāhmaṇa* Delbrück found that adpositions in early Sanskrit are postpositions, e.g.:

índra sahá "with Indra"
svargáṃ lókam ábhi "heaven to" = "to heaven"

The same position is found in Homeric Greek, though less frequently, for example *nées pára* "ships near" = "near the ships." We have noticed that they are placed after nouns occasionally also in Germanic and in Latin, for example Lat. *mēcum* "with me." Besides reconstructing the Proto-Indo-European adpositional pattern, discuss the increasingly frequent position of the adpositions before nouns.

8 The method of internal reconstruction

8.1 INTERNAL RECONSTRUCTION AS ILLUSTRATED BY GRASSMANN'S LAW

The method of internal reconstruction is designed for reconstructing earlier forms from data within one language, often itself a reconstructed language. The method is based on recognition of the multilevel structure of language. Change may take place in any one level, for example the phonological, leaving irregular patterns in another, for example the morphological. By examining the irregularities in contrast with the regular patterns, we reconstruct earlier forms. Before examining its use for reconstructed languages, we provide illustrations that can be verified; for example, the phenomena treated by Grassmann's law.

When we examine the forms of the perfect tense in Sanskrit and Greek, we find many of them with reduplication. That reduplication generally involves prefixing of the initial consonant of the base, followed by a vowel; for example, Skt *da-daú*, Gk *dé-dō-ka*, cf. also Lat. *de-dī* of the present *dō* "give." If, however, in Sanskrit and Greek, roots with an aspirate are reduplicated, the prefixed consonant does not maintain aspiration; for example, in perfect forms based on PIE **bhū-* "become": Skt *ba-bhú-va* "he has become," Gk. *pé-phú-ka* of *phúō* "develop." Using the comparative method to reconstruct the initial consonant here, we find ourselves with a problem; reduplicated consonants are generally prefixed without change, as in the Sanskrit forms based on the root **dō-*.

If we assume that the canonical pattern of reduplication is that found with unaspirated roots, we propose that the same pattern was found originally also for aspirated roots. We then reconstruct the earlier reduplicated forms of **bhū-* as follows: Skt **bha-bhú-va*, Gk. **phé-phū-ka*. When we reconstruct forms in this way, without taking another language into account, we are using the method of internal reconstruction (IR). The differing initial consonant in Sanskrit and Greek indicates that we have dealt with each language separately. Having done so, we may apply here the comparative method, as Grassmann did, and reconstruct Proto-Indo-

European **bhe-bhū-.* . ., knowing that the initial consonant was devoiced in Greek.

As Grassmann pointed out, we do not find the perfect forms with aspirated initial consonant in Sanskrit and Greek because in each language one of two aspirates of successive syllables was dissimilated. The changes may be described in Grassmann's formulation: the first of two aspirates beginning successive syllables or a syllable that also ended with an aspirate lost its aspiration.

The examples cited from the Sanskrit and Greek perfect illustrate one morphological complication resulting from the loss of aspiration. Another is found in inflected forms, when aspirates are modified by contiguous elements. The nominative of "hair" in Greek, for example, is *thríks*, the genitive *trikhós*. This paradigm seems to select arbitrarily from the two possible aspirates. Yet each form is readily explained. In the nominative the aspiration was lost when the nominative marker *s* was placed after *kh*, as in *ónuks*, *ónukhos* "claw"; accordingly, there was no aspirate with which the initial *th* of *thríks* might be dissimilated. In the genitive, on the other hand, the medial *kh* was maintained, and the initial consonant was dissimilated, yielding *trikhós*. As we did above in dealing with aspiration, we compare similar inflections like *kḗruks*, gen. *kḗrūkos* "herald," in which the consonants remain unchanged. We conclude that "hair" should have aspirated consonants in both positions, and reconstruct pre-Greek **dhrigh-*.

8.2 WHY THE METHOD OF INTERNAL RECONSTRUCTION DISCLOSES EARLIER FORMS

The method of internal reconstruction as applied to the phonological level is made possible because sound change takes place without regard to morphological sets. Allophones change, regardless of their position in morphological elements. A sound may then undergo change in some morphs of a morpheme in which it occurs in specific phonological surroundings, but remain unchanged in other morphs of the same morpheme. Moreover, in parallel morphemes with different sounds, the change may not take place, as we may illustrate with the example of AE *-t-*.

As stated above, AE *-t-* has become *-d-* in specific environments, such as those in the forms given in bold type below:

tick	sin	bid	hit
ticker	sinner	bidder	**hitter**
ticking	sinning	bidding	**hitting**
ticks	sins	bids	hits
red	black	fast	fat
redder	blacker	faster	**fatter**

We have noted above specific environments in which the change occurred;

further, that the change did not take place in other consonants, such as the [k], [n], [b] of the words above. Consequently, we conclude that the change was not produced by addition of the morphological suffixes, *-er*, *-ing* and the comparative suffix *-er*. Moreover, because the *-t-* is unchanged in nonmedial environments, we assume that [t] was the former pronunciation throughout, and reconstruct it also for the forms that now have -[d]-.

In sum, the method of internal reconstruction is applicable because sound change does not take place in specific morphological categories, such as agent nouns in *-er*, gerunds in *-ing* or comparatives in *-er*. Rather, it takes place in phonological sets. If these can be identified, we can posit the earlier situation.

As with the dissimilated aspirates of Sanskrit and Greek, the new phones generally merge with those of other phonemes. For many speakers of American English, *bitter* is pronounced like *bidder*. Similarly, Sanskrit b resulting from the dissimilation of *bh* in *ba-bhū-va* merged with the existing /b/. We may be able to determine such merged phones by their characteristic phonological environment in order to apply internal reconstruction. In Sanskrit, for example, we suspect any /b/ that is initial in its syllable and precedes an aspirate of being a reflex of earlier /bh/. Future students of English will also suspect any /d/ found after a stressed vowel and before an unstressed vowel, especially if it maintains an interchange with /t/.

8.3 INTERNAL RECONSTRUCTION APPLIED TO RECONSTRUCT PROTO-GERMANIC FRICATIVES

In examining the Proto-Germanic fricatives we may observe how linguists came to identify the environment in which they underwent change. We may also note the gradual loss of evidence for applying the method.

The fricatives show a voiceless form in the present and the preterite singular, a voiced in the preterite plural and participle, as in the verbs for "choose" and "freeze":

	Preterite	Preterite	Preterite
Infinitive	*3 sg.*	*3 pl.*	*ptc.*
*kiusan	*kaus	*kuzun	*kuzan-
*friusan	*fraus	*fruzun	*fruzan-

On the basis of these forms we may conclude that the voiced variant *z* is found intervocalically after *u*. Yet in other verb forms, such as PGmc. *nesan* "be saved" : *nazjan* "save" we conclude that the distribution is not related to specific vowels. The actual environment may have been difficult to determine from Germanic alone.

As we have seen above, Verner determined the characteristic environment by comparing Sanskrit and Greek forms. In these languages he noted that the position of the accent differed in the perfect singular and plural, which correspond to the preterite singular and plural in Germanic. For example, the cognate of **kius-* in Sanskrit is *juṣ* "taste, attempt" (Skt *j* indicates a palatalized *g*, and is pronounced like the *j* in Eng. *just*; *ṣ* indicates a retroflex *s*). The perfect third person singular, corresponding to PGmc **kaus-*, though with reduplicated *ju-*, is *jujóṣa*; the third plural is *jujuṣús*. We posit a comparable change in the plural of the Germanic accent, on the basis of which we propose the reason for the difference in voicing. The difficulty of determining the environment may be indicated by the length of time it took linguists to solve it; Verner's article appeared more than a half-century after Grimm published his rules.

By the time of the individual Germanic dialects, the original distribution was even more obscured, for in Old Icelandic, Old English, Old Saxon, Old High German and less well-attested dialects, the reflexes of PGmc *z* had fallen together with those of PGmc *r*. Of "choose" we find the following forms in these dialects:

OIcel.	kiōsa	kaus	køron	kørenn
OE	cēosan	cēas	curon	coren
OSax.	keosan	kōs	kuran	gikoran
OHG	kiosan	kōs	kurun	gikoran

Detailed study of the interrelationships between *r* and *s* in such forms led to reconstruction of the Proto-Germanic situation, and from this of the Proto-Indo-European.

For the solution of such problems, study of the distribution of similar phonemes is useful in a sub-set like the fricatives. Parallel with the PGmc *s* : *z* contrast, we find that of *θ* > *ð*, OHG *d*; PGmc *ð* > OE *d*, OHG *t*, as in:

OE	sēoðan	sēað	sudon	soden	"seethe, boil"
OHG	siodan	sōd	sutun	gisotan	

Similarly, we find a contrast between the reflexes of PGmc *χ* and *g*:

OE	tēon	tēah	tugon	togen	"pull" (cf. *tee*)
OHG	ziohan	zōh	zugun	gizogan	

As illustrated in the Old English infinitive for "pull," later changes may completely obscure the original pattern.

We may, however, find evidence of the earlier pattern in archaic texts, especially poetic texts like *Beowulf*; line 1036b reads *on flet tēon* "lead into the hall." This verse must have at least four syllables; accordingly, we interpret the *-ēo-* as a late written form for earlier **tēhan*, rather than as a vocalic unit.

Eventually the evidence is completely lost. If we had only Modern English·and no Old English materials, the only verb paradigm showing the original Proto-Germanic distribution of voiceless versus voiced fricatives would be *was* : *were*. The distribution is maintained also outside of inflectional paradigms, as in *lose* : *forlorn*, and in the increasingly rare *seethe* : *sodden*; the last is now used only as an adjective. Change may not take place as quickly for all phenomena; but this section illustrates that in a period of 2,000 years virtually all evidence for internal reconstruction may be lost.

8.4 INTERNAL RECONSTRUCTION APPLIED TO GERMANIC STRONG VERBS

The verb forms cited in 8.3 and below illustrate that internal reconstruction of phonology may be applied with greatest assurance in inflectional paradigms. We find excellent examples in the strong verbs of the Germanic languages. Forms are given here in Gothic and Old English, though Gothic alone would be adequate for our reconstructions. The class numbers 1–5 are traditional for the verbs in question.

1	Goth.	beitan	bait	bitun	bitans	"bite"
	OE	bītan	bāt	biton	biten	
2	Goth.	kiusan	kaus	kusun	kusans	"choose"
	OE	cēosan	cēas	curon	coren	
3	Goth.	-bindan	-band	-bundun	-bundans	"bind"
	OE	bindan	band	bundun	bunden	

Sound changes have obscured some of the relationships: for example, except before *r* and *h*, PGmc *e* > Goth. *i*, as in *kiusan* and *bindan*. And in Old English, the diphthongs of the first two forms underwent considerable change. Yet we have enough evidence to posit the second elements of the vocalic segment of the roots, Goth. **beit-**, **kius-**, and **bind-** as reflexes of the resonants PGmc *y w n*. Assuming **e* before these in the first form, we posit for Proto-Germanic the roots **beyt-*, **kews-*, **bend-*.

If we label the *b t k s d* of the roots Consonants and the *y w n* Resonants, we can derive these three classes of verbs from roots with a pattern of variation for Proto-Germanic:

   C*e*RC-   C*a*RC-   CRC-   CRC-

(PGmc *y > i*, *w > u*, *n > un* when between consonants, as in the CRC forms.) In view of their parallelism, the three different strong-verb classes of the Germanic languages were originally one class.

From analysis of the Gothic materials, we can readily posit the Proto-Germanic variation. From the later Old English materials, in which various sound changes had taken place, for example PGmc *eu* > OE *ēo*, PGmc *au* > OE *ēa*, internal reconstruction would be somewhat more difficult.

Examining further Germanic verbs, we find the same variation between PGmc *e* and *a* in the first two forms of classes 4 and 5, which have a Proto-Germanic structure C*e*C- (the preterite plural and preterite participle are different in pattern and will not be accounted for here).

4	Goth.	stilan	stal	stēlun	stulans	"steal"
	OE	stelan	stæl	stǣlon	stolen	
5	Goth.	wisan	was	wēsun	*wisans	"be"
	OE	wesan	wæs	wǣron	*wesen	

A highly structured set of forms, like those of the strong verb in Germanic, assists us greatly in reconstruction of prior stages of a language from internal evidence alone. We are also fortunate in having cognate forms in Indo-Iranian, Greek and other dialects that support our reconstruction of these Germanic verb classes into one original class. Substituting PIE *o* for PGmc *a*, we posit the Proto-Indo-European patterns underlying the four forms:

$$Ce(R)C- \qquad Co(R)C- \qquad C(R)C- \qquad C(R)C-$$

These formulas may be illustrated by the Greek verb forms: *leípō* "I leave" with *e*-vowel; *lé-loipa* "I have left" with *o*-vowel; *élipon* "I left" with only the reflex of the resonant, as in OE *biten*. Such forms verify our reconstruction from the Germanic data.

8.5 INTERNAL RECONSTRUCTION APPLIED TO INDO-EUROPEAN ROOTS

If morphological patterns are adequately structured, even phonemes that have disappeared may be reconstructed by internal evidence. Most Indo-European roots have a structure CeC-, for example **bher-* "bear," **gʷem-* "come," **sed-* "sit." (**Root** is a term that has become established for Proto-Indo-European base morphemes, as opposed to derivational and inflectional morphemes. Forms of a specific shape in language, such as roots consisting of two consonants, PIE **bher-* plus a vowel, or in the Semitic languages of three, for example Heb. *k t b* "write," are known as **canonical forms**.) A small number of widely attested Indo-European roots, however, have only one consonant, for example **ag-* "lead," **dhē-* "place,"**es-* "be." Saussure suggested in 1879 that at an earlier stage of Indo-European, these were parallel with roots of the structure CeC-; the missing consonants had subsequently been lost, leaving the aberrant roots. Saussure also reconstructed two lost consonants, calling them *coefficients sonantiques*.

Saussure's reconstructed bases and consonants were not widely accepted. When Kurylowicz dealt with Hittite, however, he identified reflexes for some of the lost consonants, which subsequently had been called laryngeals. Today, therefore, we reconstruct these roots with two consonants, PIE **heg-* instead of **ag-*, PIE **dheʔ-* instead of ** dhē-*, PIE **ʔes-* instead of **es-*. The confirmation of Saussure's brilliant hypothesis through Hittite has added considerably to our confidence in the method of internal reconstruction.

The varying forms of Proto-Indo-European roots presented in section 8.4 represent morphs restricted in distribution. We therefore make the further assumption that at an earlier stage the three different vocalisms are to be reconstructed as one. In examining the bases of classes 1 to 3, which are extended roots, we posit the original form as Ce(R)C-, assuming that with accentual variation this became C(R)C-, as in *dr̥ṣtás* "seen" beside Gk *dérkomai* "I see." We also derive Co(R)C-, as in Gk *dédorka* "I have seen" from Ce(R)C-; Indo-Europeanists differ in accounting for the change of *e* to *o*, but, as in G *dédorka*, *e*-vowels that lost the chief accent when Proto-Indo-European had a pitch accent may have shifted to *o*.

These vowel variations in Proto-Indo-European roots, which have reflexes in the various Indo-European languages, such as NE *bite, bit, bitten*: *choose, chose, chosen* : *bind, bound, bound* : *steal, stole, stolen* : *was, were*, are the result of **ablaut**, or **apophony**. They have been accounted for through principles of internal reconstruction developed in the study of historically observable sound changes. The effort that has been devoted to arrive at an understanding of ablaut, and the obscurities still remaining, may indicate the complexities that are involved in the reconstruction of languages for which we do not have texts going back one or more thousand years. But the reconstructions achieved for Proto-Indo-European may also indicate hope of some success for use of the method in other language families, if an adequate number of forms with morphological variation is maintained through subsequent periods of sound changes.

If the sound changes that take place yield a complete merger, the method of internal reconstruction can be used only in situations like the Proto-Indo-European root, where we have clearly definable morphemes. For that reason we can reconstruct an earlier form for the verb **es-* "be" but not for the first-singular pronoun **eg-ō*, which has no other forms beside it. As we have seen in section 8.3, the interchanging forms of Proto-Indo-European roots permit us to reconstruct earlier forms.

When, however, we find complete merger in morphemes of varying shapes, we cannot apply the method. In Iranian, for example, *bh* and the other aspirates fell together with unaspirated stops, and we have no evidence for Grassmann's law. Similarly, if two Pre-Indo-European morphemes fell together and had the same phonological shape in Proto-Indo-European, we could not distinguish them for the earlier stage of the language.

If, on the other hand, sound changes result only in a partial merger, as of the dissimilated Sanskrit aspirated voiced stops with unaspirated voiced stops, we can apply the method of internal reconstruction, unless the resulting morphophonemic variation has been obscured by subsequent sound changes, or by analogical changes (see chapters 10 and 11).

Generally, isolated forms like *forlorn* or *sodden* preserve longest the evidence we can use in internal reconstruction. Yet from isolated forms it is very difficult to apply a technique using morphophonemic variations.

Alternating morphemes from the most frequent layers of the vocabulary, such as *was* : *were*, are also likely to preserve means for applying the method of internal reconstruction; because they retain the original morphological variation, as well as the phonological, they are more useful than are isolated forms.

The constant changes and losses in language eventually obscure entirely the morphophonemic variation resulting from earlier sound change. Ultimately, they eliminate the morphophonemic contrasts that may be used in internal reconstruction. In the Romance languages, for example, we find very little evidence for the ablaut of Proto-Indo-European.

8.6 INTERNAL RECONSTRUCTION APPLIED TO MORPHOLOGY AND SYNTAX

Just as phonological reconstruction can be carried out when we examine aberrant sound patterns within morphological frameworks, so morphological reconstruction is possible when we examine aberrant syntactic patterns within language frameworks. We have seen in section 5.6.2 that active (–stative) languages have been identified, and that their essential characteristics have been determined. These characteristics can now be used in reconstructing morphological and syntactic patterns, as in Pre-Indo-European.

Here we restrict ourselves to the verbal system, which in active languages consists of two conjugations: one includes verbs with active meaning, and includes a large number of forms; the other includes verbs with stative meaning, and includes fewer forms. When we examine the reconstructed morphological system of Proto-Indo-European with this structure in mind, we note evidence in both meaning and form for a contrast.

Proto-Indo-European has many indicative forms that indicate activity, such as "come," "go," "eat," "drink." These contrast with middle forms, which often indicate a state, and with perfect forms, which indicate a state resulting from previous action, as in Gk *oîda* "I know." Moreover, the indicative conjugation has a set of endings for all persons. By contrast the perfect has characteristic forms only for the first, second and third person singular and the third plural. Other forms of the perfect paradigm in the dialects are based on the active indicative forms.

The middle acquired a full paradigm in much the same way. These characteristics of the Proto-Indo-European verb system, then, are comparable to those of the verb system of active languages both in meaning and in number of forms.

When we consider these two features – the stative meaning of the perfect and many middle forms, and the relatively poor set of forms in these two paradigms – we account for them by assuming that at an earlier stage Proto-Indo-European was an active language.

We support this conclusion by determining other characteristics of

Proto-Indo-European, such as the small number of case forms in nouns, especially in the plural and dual. But we will not pursue these, because our chief interest at this point is not the reconstruction of Pre-Indo-European but rather an illustration of how we may apply the method of internal reconstruction to morphology.

We may now use similar procedures in syntax. Noting that the VO framework implies prepositions and comparative constructions with the sequence adjective–pivot–standard, if we find predominance of these constructions in a language, we conclude that it is VO. We may reconstruct its patterns according to that framework. Accordingly we would expect to find relative clauses placed after nouns, as well as genitives, and with less assurance adjectives after nouns as well. Conversely, if we find postpositions and comparative constructions of the sequence standard–pivot–adjective, we reconstruct an OV language, with the expected relative constructions for the framework.

If, however, we find a mix of prepositions and postpositions, and of the two comparative constructions, as well as the other primary characteristics, we conclude that the language is in the process of large-scale syntactic change. Our conclusions about reconstruction may then be based on residues.

As in any science, the evidence must be carefully assembled and evaluated. We may have too little evidence to propose an earlier stage. If so, we list the assembled data and leave it for later linguists to interpret, who may in the meantime have assembled more data, so that the evidence may be properly evaluated.

8.7 INTERNAL RECONSTRUCTION APPLIED TO RECONSTRUCTION OF CATEGORIES

Continuing our examination of residual characteristics in Proto-Indo-European, we may examine the means for indicating possession. Because the means in the nominal system would require lengthy exposition, we will only review the expressions for "have" in the dialects.

These vary remarkably. In Greek, the verb for "have" is *ékhein*, in Latin *habēre*, in Lithuanian *turèti*, in Old Church Slavonic *imĕti*. The Germanic verb is that in English, cf. Goth. *haban*; it resembles the Latin verb, but cannot be related to it because of the *b* in each of the two forms. Other dialects, such as Celtic and Indo-Iranian, have expressions like the Latin *mihi est* "to me is" = "I have," which Buck considers the Indo-European means for expressing "have" (1949: 740).

When we account for this situation, we recall that stative languages do not include the category of transitivity. Instead, sentences are constructed by matching active nouns with active verbs, stative and inanimate nouns with stative verbs. Active languages express possession verbally through sequences using a locative or dative construction for the possessor, for example "near me, to me" plus the verb BE, as in the Latin *mihi est* construction. This characteristic gives us further evidence for considering Pre-Indo-European to be a stative language.

We explain the diversity of expressions for "have" in the dialects by assuming that when they became accusative in structure, they required a transitive verb for "have." Accordingly, speakers in each of the dialects selected one or more suitable verbs; one of these typically came to be used for "have." Residues survived for some time in the dialects, such as Gk *moí esti*, Lett. *būt* "be" with the dative, and so on. Such residues, as indicated above, provide further support for reconstructing the earlier expression as we have done.

8.8 INTERNAL RECONSTRUCTION APPLIED TO THE LEXICON AND THE SEMANTIC SYSTEM

Residues may also provide means for reconstructing earlier lexical and semantic structures. Active languages, as we have noted, distinguish between active/animate and stative/inanimate/inactive nouns and verbs. There are, however, items that may be interpreted as active or as inactive, such as "fire," "water," "to lie," "to sit" (in repose, or down). Water, for example, may be regarded as flowing or as a stable item; similarly, fire may be regarded as active, or as a state. Active languages often have two words for such items.

As a long-noted lexical feature, Proto-Indo-European includes two words for common items and activities, such as "fire," "water," "to lie," "to stand," etc. Citing only the words for "fire" we note that our word in English is also found in Gk *pūr* and in Hitt. *pahhur*. The other word is found in Lat. *ignis*, Skt *ágni-*, Lith. *ugnis*, OCS *ognǐ*. Buck cites Meillet's suggestion that "the first group, regularly neuter, denoted fire as a lifeless element, while the second group, regularly masculine, denoted the active personified fire of religious cult" (1949: 71). While this is an interpretation, it does not explain the situation.

In accounting for the twofold set for "fire" and other Proto-Indo-European items, we propose that they reflect the Pre-Indo-European active system in which there were two words, one active, the other inactive. The active word is that in Latin and Sanskrit, as Meillet indicated; the inactive was selected in Germanic, Hittite and Greek. Much as the speakers had to select a means for expressing "have" when the language changed from active to accusative structure, so they selected one or the other lexical item for "fire," "water" and the other concepts that had two designations in the active stage of the language. The selection would have been determined by social conditions that are beyond our knowledge. But the linguistic facts are clear.

It is important to point out still that distinguished linguists like Meillet proposed to account for twofold sets of words, as for "fire," by ascribing such a feature to the primitive mentality of the speakers in that early period. As we have learned more about language, we reject explanations for linguistic data relying on such notions. Instead, we provide linguistic explanations for linguistic data, including problems like that discussed here. Our explanations are given on the basis of our knowledge of language, and on the assumption, as stated by Meillet, of "the universal similarity of the human mind."

8.9 INTERNAL RECONSTRUCTION IN USE TODAY

As linguists deal with more and more languages attested only today, the method of internal reconstruction assumes increasing importance for reconstructing earlier stages, and for securely determining genealogical relationships. The principles that need to be applied in that use are clear. When a language has been described, irregularities are determined, such as *was* : *were*, or two words for "fire." These may be residues from earlier periods. Interpreting them, we may then reconstruct previous entities or categories or structures.

The proposed reconstructions must be evaluated by their agreement with structures at different levels, often referred to as higher levels, as illustrated above with the American English pronunciation of *setter*, etc. The reconstructions may also be evaluated by abstract patterns, such as those in syntax for OV as opposed to VO languages, and as those in the lexical and semantic spheres for accusative or ergative as opposed to active languages, as for equivalents of "have."

In applying the method we must remember that language is a social convention open to various influences. Elements with aberrant characteristics may be borrowed, such as titles like *attorney general*, in which the position of the adjective is maintained from French. To avoid unwarranted inferences based on such elements, the method of internal reconstruction must be employed with the discretion required in all human and social sciences. If applied appropriately, the method yields the securest evidence for determining earlier genealogical relationships of proto-languages.

SELECTED FURTHER READINGS

Chapters 7 and 10 of Hoenigswald (1960) deal generally with the method. For an application to an American Indian language see Chafe (1959: 477–95). For a series of extensive applications, see Kurylowicz (1964); see also Anttila (1989: ch. 12), Bynon (1977: part I.2.2), Hock (1986: ch. 17).

PROBLEMS

1 In the Japanese verb system the past of many verbs is formed with -*ta*, as in the following given above the indicative form:

motta	totta	katta	kaita	dasita
motsu "hold"	toru "take"	kau "buy"	kaku "write"	dasu "put out"

(a) Determine the form of the root.
(b) On the basis of the general patterning, the stem of *kau* may be assumed to end in a consonant. Propose a likely consonant. (The negative of the first three verbs is *motanai, toranai, kawanai*. Do these forms support your assumption?)
(c) The past of other verbs is formed with -*da*.

isoida	tonda	sunda	shinda
isogu "hurry"	tobu "fly"	sumu "live"	shinu "die"

Determine the form of the roots.
(d) What general process is involved when the past suffix is added to these roots?
(e) If you were applying the method of internal reconstruction, what evidence could you use from the contrast between *kaita* and *isoida* to reconstruct the root?
(f) By internal reconstruction, what do you posit as the underlying form of the past suffix?

2 Approximately seventy years after Sievers proposed a rule for the variation of resonants, Franklin Edgerton published a major study on it (1943: 83–124). While Sievers dealt with *i/y* and *u/w*, Edgerton treated the six resonants in the various environments. For brevity we cite examples of all six resonants in only one environment, inasmuch as they are parallel in their variation. The forms are reconstructed Proto-Indo-European.

Between vowels: **áyos* "metal," **bhewō* "I am," **bherō* "I bear," **sélos* "marsh," **somós* "same," **ménos* "mind."
Initially before vowels: **yéwo-* "spelt," **wésenti* "lives," **régʷos* "darkness."
Between consonants: **diktó-* "showed," **bhr̥tó-* "borne," **gʷm̥tó-* "come."
Initially before consonants: **íd* ptc, **úd* ptc, **r̥kp̥o-* "bear."
Finally after consonants: **ésti* "is," **médhu* "honey," **yékʷr* "liver."
Finally after vowels: **-tay* 3 sg. mid., **sūnow* "son" (voc. sg.)

(a) Determine the allophones by environment.
(b) From examples in the *Rigveda*, Edgerton proposed a third allophone, for example *iy, r̥r*, etc. This allophone is found after two consonants (C), or after a long vowel and consonant, as in the following forms:

-C **siyēm* "may I be," -C **duwō* 'two'

Reflexes of this allophone in Germanic led Sievers to propose his rule, for example Goth. *nasjis, sōkeiþ*, 2 sg. pres. of -*j-an* verbs followed by the ending PIE *-esi*. Reconstruct the Pre-Germanic second-singular forms of these two verbs.

(c) Edgerton called his "most important new discovery" the "converse of Sievers' law." By the converse, sequences of vocalic and consonantal resonant show up as the consonantal allophone after short syllables, as in Skt *cakre* from Pre-Indic *cakṛre* "were made." Noting the Japanese treatment of English *system* as *shisutemo*, *theory* as *seori*, comment on the credibility of the converse rule. To what extent does it support Edgerton's statement of the allophonic variation of the resonants?

3 In Greek and Sanskrit, some perfect forms vary in vocalism between the singular and the plural, as in oĩda "I know," *ísmen* "we know," *pépoitha* "I believed," *pépithmen* "we believed." Compare Skt *véda* "I know," *vidmén* "we know."

(a) If you were setting out to determine by internal reconstruction the cause of the vowel variation from these forms, which would you use? What difficulties would you encounter?

(b) Another example of the variation is found in Skt *bubódha* "I knew," *bubudhimá* "we knew." To what extent could you use these forms to supplement your conclusions? Suggest the Proto-Indo-European vowel of the root in the singular.

(c) Compare the forms of Sanskrit root *kṛ*: *cakára* "I did," *cakṛmá* "we did." Suggest the Proto-Indo-European vowels of the singular and plural.

(d) The Gothic forms corresponding to Gk oĩda : *ídmen* are *wait* : *witum*. To what extent could you reconstruct the Proto-Indo-European vowel variation from them?

(e) To what extent could you propose a reason for the variation between the vowels of the stem in the singular and the plural on the basis of these forms? The method of internal reconstruction is supposedly useful for reconstruction on the basis of one language or one dialect. Comment on strict application to any one of the three dialects exemplified here for determining the Proto-Indo-European vowel alternation in the perfect paradigm.

9 Glottochronology

9.1 GLOTTOCHRONOLOGY

The comparative method and the method of internal reconstruction are difficult to apply for languages attested only today. For example, if we selected the word *horse* for its cognates in Indo-European languages today, we would find Germ. *Pferd*, Dan. *hest*, Fr. *cheval*, Gk *álogo*, all of which are unrelated. If we had no older materials from these and other Indo-European languages, we would be unable to use such a common word and item in the cultures of their speakers to relate the languages.

Aware of these problems, Morris Swadesh in 1949 proposed a totally different method. It is based on the assumption that the common words of a language are maintained at a definite rate. While the word for "horse" may have been lost, those for "cow," "fish," "goat," "goose," "louse" have not been. In Swadesh's view, if one identified the words of the **basic core vocabulary**, and also the rate of loss, one could determine the time when two related languages became independent. He named the method lexico-statistic **glottochronology**.

We may illustrate the method with five words from his list: *animal, four, head, I, sun*. In standard German the corresponding words are *Tier, vier, Kopf, ich, Sonne*. Since the first and third are not related, we find 60 percent agreement between the two languages. Our next step would be comparing this percentage with the expected rate of loss.

The rate of loss was arrived at by testing the method against lexical loss in languages with a long series of texts, like Latin and the Romance languages. Such tests yielded a figure of 80–85 per cent of loss over a thousand years. That is to say, taking the lower figure for ease in computation, we would find that Modern English has preserved 80 per cent of the basic core vocabulary of the language in the year AD 991 and 64 per cent of it at the beginning of our era. The figure for three millennia ago would be 51 per cent, for four millennia ago 40 per cent, and so on. If we date late Proto-Indo-European at 3000 BC, we would expect Modern English to have maintained about 30 per cent of its basic core vocabulary.

If we went on to apply the method to determine the time of separation of

English and German, we would expect that each language would have maintained 80 per cent of the basic core vocabulary, but not necessarily the same 80 per cent. Accordingly, by the method we would expect the two languages to have a common basic core vocabulary of 64 per cent after a thousand years, if 80 per cent were the rate of maintenance. The figure of 85 per cent is more realistic, though the computation for the illustration here would have been more tedious.

To permit ready determination of the time of separation, or **time depth**, of two related languages, Robert Lees (1953: 113–27) devised a formula. By the formula the time depth, **t**, is equal to the logarithm of the percentage of cognates, **c**, divided by twice the logarithm of the assumed percentage of cognates retained after a millennium of separation, **r**:

$$t = \frac{\log c}{2 \log r}$$

Using our five items from English and German we determine t as follows:

$$t = \frac{\log 60\%}{2 \log 85\%} = \frac{-0.511}{2 \times -0.163} = 1.561$$

By the formula, English and German separated approximately 1.561 × 1,000 years ago, that is around the year AD 430. Since the date of the invasion of England by the Angles and Saxons is given as AD 440, the result corresponds to our historical information.

In such a short list, the range of error may be great. To reduce the chance of error, one would prefer a long, carefully designed list. Swadesh devised several. In most investigations either of two lists, one of 100, another of 200 words has been used. (The lists are reproduced at the end of the chapter.) Even with such lists, the range of error must be computed; see Lees (1953: 124) or Gudschinsky (1956: 204–5). Typical conclusions are given in length of separation, plus or minus a number of years, determined from the range of possible error. Gudschinsky, for example, concludes that 'Ixcatec and Mazatec were a single homogeneous language, 2,200±200 years ago' (*ibid.*: 205).

9.2 CRITICISMS OF GLOTTOCHRONOLOGY

While the method was warmly greeted by many linguists working with indigenous American languages, others published criticisms. As one proposed shortcoming, the existence of a basic core vocabulary from culture to culture has been disputed. Sjoberg and Sjoberg (1956: 296–300), for example, have shown that in the cultures of south Asia some items referring to natural objects like the sun should not be included among the basic core; for they belong to the widely borrowed religious vocabulary. Such criticism led to review of the basic core vocabulary.

As another problem, considerable duplication has been found within languages for elements posited in the basic core vocabulary. In applying

Swadesh's lists to Athapaskan languages, Hoijer (1956: 49–60) noted that over half the items fail to meet Swadesh's criteria. In Navaho, for example, "this, that" corresponds to five items, no one of which can be clearly matched to the items on the English list; similarly, nouns like "tree," "seed," "grease" and verbs like "eat," "kill," "know." That is to say, the basic core vocabulary may correspond to the English set of words, but other languages may be differently segmented conceptually. The words elicited in such languages may then be difficult to compare rigorously.

It has also been demonstrated that the rate of retention is not constant from language to language. Meillet long ago pointed to a Gypsy dialect of Armenian that contains few Armenian lexical items, while showing the central structure of the language. Clearly, the rate of loss in English, Lithuanian and Greek is much lower than that for this Armenian dialect. On the other hand, the rate of retention in Icelandic is remarkably high; the society was long isolated, and maintained old cultural practices, including attention to Old Icelandic literature. These examples may illustrate that social conditions must be taken into account when evaluating results. Yet if different rates of retention must be proposed from language to language because of social differences, the generality of glottochronology is eliminated, and its usefulness is greatly diminished. Moreover, we are not always informed of the social conditions of indigenous peoples in earlier periods, as we are of the Icelanders'.

For these reasons glottochronology has been dismissed by many linguists who question whether it is a useful procedure. For languages may undergo differing developments in their semantic structure as well as in their grammatical structure. No universal list may then be possible. But, as we see below, ever smaller lists, from Swadesh's original list of somewhat more than 200 words, have been constructed to meet the problems cited above.

When the aims of glottochronology are carefully directed, and if the method is used within a language group and a culture area for the goals of determining relative dates of separation or establishing groups of languages, the problems discussed above may be minimized. Precisely for these purposes, it has been applied by specialists in the languages of the Pacific area, with results that we may briefly summarize.

9.3 GLOTTOCHRONOLOGY APPLIED TO THE AUSTRONESIAN AND AUSTRALIAN LANGUAGES

A workshop at the 1987 Linguistic Institute reviewed the status of research on six language groups, among them the Austronesian and the Australian; papers by the participants were subsequently published (Baldi 1990). Investigations into both of these groups of languages have made interesting uses of the methods of lexicostatistic glottochronology. Blust in his summary points out that 959 Austronesian languages have been documented, as opposed to only 144 Indo-European, and that the data for Austronesian are quite recent. Moreover, much of the older data consists of borrowings. And the number of specialists who have dealt with Austronesian is small so that the large number of grammars and handbooks produced for the Indo-European language family is lacking. As a result of the many problems and the small number of specialists, the comparative method and the method of internal reconstruction have scarcely been applied.

By contrast glottochronological findings have been adapted. Among these is "the explicit marking of time-depth for every etymon" (Blust, in Baldi 1990: 142). By this procedure the relationships among the numerous languages can be more precisely determined. Moreover, many borrowings that have been identified as cognates have been recognized as late innovations.

In a more traditional use of glottochronology Isidore Dyen in 1965 published a classification based on "a matrix of computer-generated pairwise lexicostatistical percentages for some 245 Austronesian languages" with results that were, however, disputed (in Baldi 1990: 147). While Dyen defends his methods in the same volume, they are now being further examined with the help of the time-honored methods. Through use of glottochronology, then, Dyen contributed a classification that could subsequently be refined, as is now being done.

Glottochronology was similarly applied to group the Australian languages. The application resulted in identification of 29 "phylic families"; of these families Pama-Nyungan includes about 90 per cent of the estimated 200–250 distinct languages on the continent when it was settled by Europeans in 1788 (Dixon, in Baldi 1990: 393–401). Subsequent attempts have been made to determine more precisely the Pama-Nyungan relationships. Further, to reduce the number of the remaining 28 "phylic families" with relatively few languages. In short, the methods that Swadesh instituted have been applied to gain some control over large groups of languages attested only in recent times. Further investigations can go on to refine the classification and reconstruction. Swadesh's method has accordingly demonstrated its usefulness.

9.4 LEXICOSTATISTICS APPLIED TO DETERMINE THE 'OLDEST RELATIONSHIPS' AMONG LANGUAGE FAMILIES

In 1903 the noted Danish linguist Holger Pedersen proposed that the Indo-European, Hamito-Semitic, Uralic, Altaic and possibly other families were related. He provided a name for the putative earlier group that now is generally given as **Nostratic**. In spite of intense interest, also in general circles, in the assumption of such an early ancestor of these many languages many linguists see little evidence for Nostratic and reject the hypothesis.

In an attempt to provide a "mathematically rigorous procedure" to investigate the hypothesis, Aaron Dolgopolsky determined a list of fifteen items (1986: 34–5). These, presumably, are essential in every language, including that of a community of speakers ten or more millennia ago when Proto-Nostratic would have been spoken. The list is of interest for various reasons. The fifteen items are as follows: first-person marker, "two," second-person marker, "who/what," "tongue," "name," "eye," "heart," "tooth," verbal negative, "finger/toe-nail," "tear" (noun), "water," "dead." We will not pursue Dolgopolsky's procedures after the item has been identifed .

But we may point out difficulties even with this highly selected list. The item "water" may have two designations in an active language; if such a language becomes accusative, or ergative, a crucial item among the fifteen may be reduced in value. Moreover, some of the items may be subject to loss of modification by taboo; the word for "tongue" in the Indo-European languages exhibits various forms, from Lat. *lingua* to Skt *jihvā*; moreover, Greek has a totally different word in *glōtta*. In addition, first- and second-person markers may not be stable, nor even found in a language, such as Japanese and Chinese. Further, the verbal negative may be replaced, as in Fr. *pas*, which originally meant "step." In short, even such a reduced list involves problems. And when we recall the rate of retention in languages, after six millennia the number of maintained cognates is comparable to items similar by chance. In conclusion, the efforts to provide firm evidence for positing a language grouping like the Nostratic on the basis of lexicostatistics may yield only tentative hypotheses.

Similar procedures are being used to support the Nostratic hypothesis through scrutiny of morphological elements. These procedures may supplement the conclusions derived from lexical analysis. As for the Australian languages, which may have an even greater time depth than the proposed Nostratic, a lexicostatistical approach may yield general conclusions, which then can be pursued with the help of the two other methods.

9.5 GLOTTOCHRONOLOGY TODAY

In a posthumously published book, *The Origin and Diversification of Language*, Swadesh reappraises the usefulness of glottochronology (1971: 271–84). Maintaining its validity, he compares the fates of words in his hundred-word list with that of electrons. He states that "physicists can calculate the average time for the loss of an electron, but cannot predict when an electron will be lost from any particular atom" (*ibid.*: 283). The comparison may illustrate the basis of Swadesh's confidence. Fluctuation that obeys certain rules has been found in large masses of entities. If the entities of language are comparable with these, we may agree with Swadesh that one of the hundred words "will be replaced by another root within approximately seventy years," while others will be maintained.

Further attention to the results of studies in fluctuation carried out under chaos theory may illuminate loss or change in language, including change of phonological and other elements. Until now, glottochronology has made more modest contributions, as indicated above with reference to the Austronesian and Australian languages.

SELECTED FURTHER READINGS

Swadesh's views may best be examined in his posthumous book (1971); it includes a complete bibliography of Swadesh's publications. A clear statement describing the use of glottochronology is Gudschinsky (1956), which contains a bibliography of the early work. For a vigorous critique, see Bergsland and Vogt (1962: 115–53). Troike (1969: 183–91) found through use of the 100-word list "close correspondence of . . . data to known historical developments," and concluded that his study "adds another test case to the slowly accumulated body of data confirming the validity of the glottochronological method." The statements on results of glottochronological use in languages of the Pacific are found in Baldi (1990). Dolgopolsky's article is translated in *Typology Relationship and Time* (1986: 27–50). The book also contains articles on Nostratic.

The following list of 200 words is taken from Gudschinsky's article; the list of 100 words used by John A. Rea is set in italic, with his additional words, numbered 94–100 appended. In eliciting one must not search for cognates. Exact cognates exist for the words used in 9.1, for example *Haupt* for *head* and *cup* for *Kopf*, yet the normal response of a German speaker asked to give the equivalent of *head* is *Kopf*. Equivalents in usage rather than etymological cognates must be used as the basis for glottochronology.

Lists for glottochronology

1 *all*	51 float	101 narrow	151 *stand*
2 and	52 flow	102 near	152 *star*
3 animal	53 flower	103 *neck*	153 stick
4 *ashes*	54 *fly*	104 *new*	154 *stone*
5 at	55 fog	105 *night*	155 straight
6 back	56 *foot*	106 *nose*	156 suck
7 bad	57 four	107 *not*	157 *sun*
8 *bark*	58 freeze	108 old	158 swell
9 because	59 fruit	109 *one*	159 *swim*
10 *belly*	60 *give*	110 other	160 *tail*
11 *big*	61 *good*	111 *person*	161 *that*
12 *bird*	62 grass	112 play	162 there
13 *bite*	63 *green*	113 pull	163 they
14 *black*	64 guts	114 push	164 thick
15 *blood*	65 *hair*	115 *rain*	165 thin
16 blow	66 *hand*	116 red	166 think
17 *bone*	67 he	117 right – correct	167 *this*

18 breathe	68 *head*	118 rightside	168 *thou*
19 *burn*	69 *hear*	119 river	169 three
20 child	70 *heart*	120 *road*	170 throw
21 *cloud*	71 heavy	121 *root*	171 tie
22 *cold*	72 here	122 rope	172 *tongue*
23 *come*	73 hit	123 rotten	173 *tooth*
24 count	74 hold – take	124 rub	174 *tree*
25 cut	75 how	125 salt	175 turn
26 day	76 hunt	126 *sand*	176 *two*
27 *die*	77 husband	127 *say*	177 vomit
28 dig	78 *I*	128 scratch	178 *walk*
29 dirty	79 ice	129 sea	179 *warm*
30 *dog*	80 if	130 *see*	180 wash
31 *drink*	81 in	131 *seed*	181 *water*
32 *dry*	82 *kill*	132 sew	182 *we*
33 dull	83 *know*	133 sharp	183 wet
34 dust	84 lake	134 short	184 *what*
35 *ear*	85 laugh	135 sing	185 when
36 *earth*	86 *leaf*	136 *sit*	186 where
37 *eat*	87 leftside	137 *skin*	187 *white*
38 *egg*	88 leg	138 sky	188 *who*
39 *eye*	89 *lie*	139 *sleep*	189 wide
40 fall	90 live	140 *small*	190 wife
41 far	91 *liver*	141 smell	191 wind
42 *fat* – grease	92 *long*	142 *smoke*	192 wing
43 father	93 *louse*	143 smooth	193 wipe
44 fear	94 *man – male*	144 snake	194 with
45 *feather*	95 *many*	145 snow	195 *woman*
46 few	96 *meat – flesh*	146 some	196 woods
47 fight	97 mother	147 spit	197 worm
48 *fire*	98 *mountain*	148 split	198 ye
49 *fish*	99 *mouth*	149 squeeze	199 year
50 five	100 *name*	150 stab – pierce	200 *yellow*

94 *breast*   95 *claw*   96 *full*   97 *horn*   98 *knee*   99 *moon*   100 *round*

PROBLEMS

1 (a) The following are items found in Swadesh's list. One such word – usually the first matching word – was selected from each of the first ten chapters in Buck's dictionary. The equivalents are given here. Superposed numbers in each row indicate cognates. Select any five pairs of languages, such as Sanskrit with each of the other dialects, and determine the number of retained cognates. Then use Lees's formula to determine the time depth for such a pair.

	Sanskrit	Greek	Latin	Lithuanian	OCS	Gothic
"earth"	kṣam-[1]	khthṓn[1]	terra	žěmė[1]	zemlja[1]	airþa
"man"	manu-[1]	ánthropos	homṓ[2]	žmogùs[2]	člověkŭ	manna[1]
"animal"	paśu-	thḗr[1]	animal	žverĩs[1]	zvěrĩ[1]	dius

"skin"	tvac-	dermá	cutis	oda	koka	-fill
"eat"	ad-[1]	edō[1]	edere[1]	válgyti	jastĭ[1]	itan[1]
"sew"	sīv-[1]	hráptō	suere[1]	siũti[1]	šiti[1]	siujan[1]
"live"	jiv-[1]	zōō[1]	vīvere[1]	gýti[1]	žiti[1]	liban
"cut"	kṛt-	témnō	secāre	piauti	rězati	maitan
"turn"	vṛt-[1]	trépō	vertere[1]	versti[1]	obratiti	wandjan

(b) Note the difference between the distribution of some of these words, for example "skin" and "cut" as opposed to "eat" and "sew." What explanation might be given for the retention of one base throughout a set, for multiple innovations in another set?

(c) Use the words here, or the fifteen in Dolgopolsky's list, on cognates in any language family of your interest to determine the time depths of the languages you select.

10 Sound change – change in phonological systems

10.1 MODIFICATION AND CHANGE

What do we mean by sound change? When languages are compared at various periods, we find correspondences between their elements. In comparing Middle English with Modern or New English, for example, we observe obvious correspondences between ME *set*, NE *set*, somewhat less obvious correspondences between ME *wīf*, NE *wife*; ME *hūs*, NE *house*. We conclude that NE *set*, *wife*, *house* are the contemporary forms of ME *set*, *wīf*, *hūs*, and we label these New English forms **replacements** for the Middle English. The replacements [wayf] for ME [wi:f] and [haws] for ME [hu:s] have resulted from modifications in the language. Modifications that lead to the introduction of new phonological elements in a language, to loss or to realignments of old elements, we refer to as a **sound change**. This term is used only for events that result in disruption of the phonological system.

The investigation of sound change is one of the chief concerns of historical linguistics. Through knowledge derived from observation of the sound changes that have been documented in many languages we are able to explain modifications that take place in any further language. For the processes are much the same, though they must be scrutinized within the structure of the language being investigated. Moreover, that knowledge assists us in reconstructing languages of the past. Again, we have observed that change in past periods has taken place in ways that have been documented in well-known languages, such as the Romance. In view of the importance of understanding change within a given structure, our examples of change will be taken from English as much as possible, since its stages have been well described.

In the next four chapters we will examine change at various levels, the phonological, morphological, syntactic and semantic. In each chapter we examine correspondences between elements at two or more stages of a language, and then we discuss the processes, patterns and spread of such change within given systems. Finally, we examine proposed explanations for modifications and change.

Between the English of Chaucer (d.1400) and that spoken today, probably all elements in the phonological system have been modified. Some of the modifications were very minor; Chaucer's pronunciation of ME *set* would probably be understood by us today, though in details it might seem peculiar. Other pronunciations of his, we might not understand at all, such as his ME *see* /se:/ versus our NE *see* /siy/, ME *tōth* /to:θ/ versus our *tooth* /tuwθ/. Historical grammars concern themselves largely with such striking changes. Yet to understand the process of change in language, we will first examine briefly replacements that do not disrupt the system and that therefore seem minor or not worth notice in general historical surveys of a language, but that may eventually lead to changes.

One feature of Chaucer's pronunciation of *set* that may have differed only slightly from ours is his articulation of /t/; it would probably remind us of the *t* used by a Spanish speaker. Since we have no descriptions of Chaucer's pronunciation, we cannot be sure of this conclusion, but we can assume that at one time English /t d n/ were dentals. Over the past centuries their articulation has been progressively retracted, so that they are now alveolars. As this retraction took place, it did not bring about changes in the morphological, syntactic or semantic systems of the language. Nor was the system of phonemic contrasts affected; NE /t/ contrasts with NE /p k/ etc., just as did ME /t/ with ME /p k/ etc. This modification of /t/ has accordingly not led to a sound change.

Another modification that must have been introduced in the course of the history of English is the aspiration of voiceless stops before stressed vowels when not preceded by /s/, as in *pool* [pʰuwl] versus *spool* [sp⁼uwl], *tool* [tʰuwl] and *cool* [kʰuwl]. We assume that Germanic /p t k/ in such words were unaspirated because they developed from /b d g/, or from glottalics in accordance with glottalic theory. At some time between the changes described in Grimm's law and the present, aspiration must have been added in words like *pool*, *tool*, *cool*. But like the alveolar pronunciation of NE /t d n/, this modification has had no effect on the phonological system of English. For the aspirates are automatic variants, or allophones of /p t k/ in specific environments.

In time, such modification may lead to disruptions of the phonological system, that is, to sound change. Most linguists assume, for example, that PIE /p t k/ first became aspirates [pʰ tʰ kʰ] before they were changed to fricatives in the Proto-Germanic etyma of words like NE *five*, *three*, *hundred*. But since the phonological system of contemporary English has not been changed by the introduction of [ph th kh], the altered pronunciations are simply modifications, not sound changes.

While such modifications are apparently going on constantly in language, we have little information about them in languages of the past. Speakers, including scribes, take account only of changes in phonological systems, not of modifications. Scribes may introduce new spellings after sound changes take place, or they may betray changes by inconsistencies or errors in spelling. With a long series of texts, we can therefore document changes that have taken place in individual languages.

Historical English linguists are fortunate in having many texts by means of which they can study change. As illustration we will examine the beginning of Chaucer's Prologue to the *Canterbury Tales*. The lines are given first in conventional Middle English spelling, accompanied by a literal translation, then in phonemic transcription, accompanied by a Modern English phonemic transcription. Middle English patterns of morphology and syntax have been maintained so that the phonological changes would be better illustrated.

Middle English
1 Whan that Aprille with his schoures swoote
2 the drought of March hath perced to the roote
3 and bathed evry veyn in swich licour,
4 of which vertu engendred is the flour;
5 whan Zephirus eek with his swete breeth
6 inspired hath in evry holt and heeth
7 the tendre croppes, and the younge sonne
8 hath in the Ram his halve cours yronne,
9 and smale fowles maken melodye,
10 that slepen al the nyght with open ye –
11 so priketh hem nature in her corages –
12 than longen folk to goon on pilgrimages.

Translation
1 When (that) April with its sweet showers,
2 has pierced the drought of March to the root,
3 and bathed every vein in such moisture (liquor),
4 from whose effects (virtue) flowers are produced;
5 When Zephirus also with his sweet breath,
6 has inspired in every wood and heath,
7 the tender crops, and (when) the young sun
8 has run half of his course through Aries,
9 and (when) the small birds (fowls) make (their) melodies,
10 which sleep all the night with open eyes –
11 thus nature inspires them in their spirits –
12 at that time people want to go on pilgrimages.

Middle English phonemic representation
1 hwan θat aːpril wiθ his šuːres swoːte
2 θe druχt of marč haθ peːrsed toː θe roːte
3 and baːðed evri vein in swič likuːr
4 of hwič verteu enǰendred is θe fluːr
5 hwan zefirus eːk wiθ his sweːte breːθ
6 inspiːred haθ in evri holt and hɛːθ

```
 7  θe tendre kroppes and θe yunge sunne
 8  haθ in θe ram his halve kuːrs irunne
 9  and smales fuːles maːken melodiːe
10  θat sleːpen al θe niχt wiθ ɔːpen iːe
11  sɔː prikeθ hem nateur in her kuraːjes
12  θan longen folk tō gɔːn on pilgrimaːjes
```

New English phonemic representation

```
 1  hwen (ðæt) eypril wið hiz šawərz swiyt
 2  ðə drawt əv marč hæz pirst tuw ðə ruwt
 3  ænd beyðd evriy veyn in səč likər
 4  əv hwič vərčuw enǰendərd iz ðə flawr
 5  hwen zefərəs iyk wið hiz swiyt breθ
 6  inspayrd hæz in evriy holt ænd hiyθ
 7  ðə tendər kraps ænd ðə yəŋ sən
 8  hæz in ðə ræm hiz hæf kɔrs rən
 9  ænd smɔl fawlz meyk melədiy
10  ðæt sliyp ɔl ðə nayt wið owpən ay
11  sow priks ðem neyčər in ðer kərəǰəz
12  ðen lɔŋ fowk tə gow ɔn pilgriməǰəz
```

Comparing the Middle English and the New English texts, we note that the vowels have changed considerably, notably the long vowels. Further, many unstressed syllables have been lost, leading to consonant clusters in New English, as in /pirst beyðd kraps/, and to syllables ending in consonants rather than vowels, as in /swiyt ruwt sən/. Furthermore, the accent of the words that were borrowed from French has generally been moved towards the beginning of words in keeping with the Germanic accent position, as in /líkər mélədiy kə́rəǰ/. In accordance with such accent placement, the vowels of formerly stressed syllables have been shortened, as in the second syllable of *liquor*. These changes brought about great differences between Middle English and New English.

The most notable changes affected the Middle English long vowels, all of which underwent change, as we see from the following examples. ME /iː/, as in /inspiːred/, line 6, and /iːe/, line 10, has changed to NE /ay/. ME /uː/, as in /šuːres/, line 1, and /fluːr/, line 4, has changed to NE /aw/. ME /eː/, as in /eːk/, line 5, has changed to NE /iy/, as has ME /ɛː/, as in /hɛːθ/, line 6. Moreover, ME /aː/, as in /aːpril/, line 1, has changed to NE /ey/. Further, ME /oː/, as in /roːte/, line 2, has changed to NE /uw/, and ME /ɔː/, as in /ɔːpen/, line 10, has changed to NE /ow/. We will examine these changes again below. They are cited here as examples of the kind of sound change with which historical treatments of phonology are especially concerned.

By means of other words in these twelve lines we also note that not every Middle English long vowel is replaced by one of the New English elements given above. For example, *breath*, the modern form of ME /brɛːθ/, line 5, no longer rhymes with *heath*. Its vowel was shortened, as were the vowels of other words ending in dental consonants, such as *dead, red, bread* and *thread*; thus, they did not undergo the change of ME /ɛː/ to NE /iy/. A different type of disruption is found for /swoːte/; like *root* from /roːte/, its modern form should have the element /uw/. Instead, the form found in line 5, /sweːte/ /swiyt/ has been generalized, ousting a potential */swuwt/. As this discussion may indicate, when we write the history of a language, we first determine the regular correspondences of its phonemes, including its major sound changes; and then we account for exceptions. To illustrate this procedure, we will examine the principal correspondences between the sound systems of Middle English and New English.

10.2 THE MIDDLE ENGLISH AND THE NEW ENGLISH PHONOLOGICAL SYSTEMS AS EXAMPLES OF PHONOLOGICAL CHANGE

In dealing with sound change, we require not only that grammars discuss individual changes but also that they present them within the systems of two successive stages of a languge. For, as we have noted above, sound change always involves alterations in a system. Unless we know the systems concerned, we cannot interpret the changes. In studying the changes of Middle English, then, we examine the consonant and vowel systems of New English as well as of Middle English.

Comparing the Middle and the New English consonant systems, we find little difference between them in number of phonemes.

Middle English

p	t		č		k	
b	d		ǰ		g	
	f	θ	s	š	x	h
	v	ð	z			
m	n					
w		l	r	y		

New English

p	t		č		k	
b	d		ǰ		g	
	f	θ	s	š		
	v	ð	z	ž		
m	n				ŋ	
w		l	r	y	h	

One Middle English consonant phoneme /x/ has been lost, as in *light*; compare NHG *Licht* [lixt]. If, however, ME *x* is interpreted as an allophone of *h*, this is merely an allophonic change.

Two new consonant phonemes have been added: /ž/, which developed from the cluster /zy/ as in *vision*, and was carried over in French loanwords such as *rouge*; /ŋ/, which was an allophone of ME /n/ before velars. Italian still has such variation for the phoneme /n/, with the allophone /ŋ/, occurring only before [k] and [g]. Middle English [ŋ] became a separate phoneme when voiced stops after nasals were lost in late Middle English, as in *climb, lawn* (cf. OFr. *launde*) and *long*, cf. *longer*. Through the loss of -*g*, the [ŋ] allophone was split from the phoneme /n/, becoming a separate phoneme as in NE /lɔŋ/ vs. /lɔn/. Apart from the loss of /x/ and the addition of two phonemes, the consonant systems of the two successive stages are similar in structure and number of members.

While the consonant systems differ little, the vowel systems are strikingly different. We give first the Middle English system, using a notation similar to Middle English orthography.

Short vowels		*Long vowels*		*Diphthongs*			
i	u	iː	uː				
e	o	eː	oː	ei	eu	oi	ou
a		ɛː aː ɔː		ai	au		

Apart from rearrangements, the principal allophones of vowels of the Middle English short-vowel system underwent few modifications, as we may illustrate:

ME ship   NE ship   ME busch   NE bush
  ME set   NE set   ME lock   NE (Brit.) lock
       ME bak (OE bæk)   NE back

In the environments given here, the pronunciation of the Middle English short vowels and that of New English short vowels agree, though ME /a/ was probably articulated further back than is NE /æ/. Simply listing these correspondences, however, gives an inadequate view of the relationships between the two systems. For between Middle English and New English, the characterization of vowels and consonants by quantity was abandoned. Moreover, ME [ə] has become a New English phoneme, with additions from ME /u/, which became NE /ə/, as in *cut, tusk, hull*, except after labials, as in *put, bush, full, wolf*.

To illustrate the quantity distinction between long and short consonants in Middle English, we may cite *sunne* 'sun' and *sune* 'son'. Because of the difference in length of *n*, these words did not rhyme in Middle English. With the loss of long consonants, however, they became homophones in New English. Similarly, Middle English vowels that were distinguished by length (somewhat like the vowels in NHG *Stadt* [štat] 'city' and *Staat* [štaːt] 'state') lost the distinction. ME *shamle* 'shamble' had short *a* before two consonants, but ME *sādel* 'saddle' had a long *ā* before consonant plus vowel. When the final syllables of both words came to be pronounced alike, the stem vowels became [æ] as in their New English forms. On the other hand, long vowels maintained until the time of the Great English Vowel Shift, as in *crādel* 'cradle,' underwent the shift described in the following paragraph. In Middle English the vowels were distinguished by quantity as well as by quality, whereas in New English the primary distinction is by quality. The loss of the quantity distinction has resulted in a totally different vowel system.

The change of long vowels between Middle English and the present is known as the Great English Vowel Shift, often abbreviated GVS in historical grammars of English. This change is remarkable. All the Middle English vowels are modified similarly, by raising; /iː uː/, however, were already high vowels and could be raised no further. Their counterparts in Modern English are the diphthongs /ay/ and /aw/. ME /eː/ and /ɛː/ have fallen together to yield NE /iy/; ME /aː/ was fronted and raised to NE /ey/; ME /oː/ was raised to NE /uw/; ME /ɔː/ was raised to NE /ow/. Examples are:

ME	NE	ME	NE	ME	NE
wīf [wiːf]	wife /wáyf/			hous /huːs/	house /háws/
seen [seːn]	seen /síyn/			spon /spoːn/	spoon /spúwn/
see [sæː]	sea /síy/			ham /hɔːm/	home /hówm/
		name / naːme/	name / néym/		

These changes alone would have resulted in a totally different vowel system, but the Middle English symmetrical system of diphthongs (the three low short vowels followed by the two high) was also changed.

Middle English /ei ai/, which had probably fallen together by the time of Chaucer, merged with the reflex of ME /aː/, for example ME *vein*, NE *vein* /véyn/, ME *day, dai* /dai/, NE *day* /déy/. ME /oi/ remained unchanged, for example ME *boi, boy* /boi/, NE *boy* /bóy/.

ME /eu/ merged with /uw/ from ME /oː/, for example ME *fruit* /freut/, NE *fruit* /frúwt/, ME /virteu/, NE *virtue* /vərtʃuw/ (also in New English forms with /yuw/, e.g. *pure*). ME /ou/ merged with /ow/ from ME /aː/, for example ME *boue* /boue/, NE *bow*/bów/. ME /au/ became a low, back vowel, for example ME *cause* /kauze/, NE *cause* /kɔz/.

It is clear from these examples that the Middle English vowel system was modified so greatly that it is difficult to plot the Modern English system beside it, as we have done for the consonants. In accordance with the diphthongal analysis proposed by Sweet, Wyld, Bloomfield, Bloch, Trager and others, the Modern English vowel system characteristic of Midland American English speakers may be presented as follows:

i ship		u bush	iy see			uw spoon
e set	ə some		ey say			ow bow
æ back	a lock	ɔ cause	ay wife	ɔy boy	aw house	

In the vowel system proposed for educated British English, these words are arranged as follows:

Simple	*Complex*	
i ship	iⁱ see	
e set	eⁱ say	
a back	aⁱ wife	aᵘ house
ə some	ɔy boy	əᵘ bow
ɔ not		
u bush		uᵘ spoon

In addition, the six simple vowels of British English, and the vowels of *tie* and *town*, may be followed by [ə], as in *tear, tire, tower*; in the Midland dialect of American English, the corresponding sound is [r]. Except for these combinations with [ə], the British and American systems differ primarily in the low short vowels. In both of these systems, however, the set of Middle English vowels has been completely changed. The conservatism of the consonants, side by side with the innovations in the vowel system and in syllabic structure, may illustrate how languages change in some of their segments while undergoing little change in others.

10.3 THE PROCESSES INVOLVED IN SOUND CHANGE

From the changes between the Middle English and the New English phonological systems, we may illustrate the essentials necessary for a general understanding of sound change. As may be observed from English, sound changes take place by modification of sounds to similarly articulated sounds. For example, ME [eː] became NE [iy] rather than the totally different [uw] or [s]. Moreover, allophones of phonemes often differ in accordance with their environment; when sound changes take place, the direction may be a result of the phonetic surroundings of the sounds concerned. For example, we might expect a rounded vowel like [u] to be maintained in the neighborhood of labial consonants, as was ME [u] in words like *put, bull, full*, when in other environments it became a central vowel, as in *tuck, duck, cut*. A thorough knowledge of articulatory phonetics is thus essential for understanding the processes of change.

Understanding the processes of sound change also involves a knowledge of the kinds of changes that sound systems can undergo. In setting up correspondences between Middle and New English, grammars often list only the most frequent correspondences, as if all Middle English phonemes had merely one reflex in New English, for example, as if all ME /u/ had become NE /u/. Furthermore, accounts of the Great Vowel Shift suggest that all ME /iː/ became NE /ay/. Yet, as we see in the few lines cited from Chaucer above, ME /iː/ also underwent other changes, as in *melodīe*, where it was shortened when the accent was placed on the first syllable. Simple treatments of sound systems are accordingly unrealistic, justifiable only for pedagogical reasons. Sound change of the type we have been considering takes place by subclasses of phonemes, labeled allophones. ME /u/, for example, became NE /u/ only after labials, as noted in the preceding paragraph; elsewhere it became /ə/. The Middle English long vowels underwent the Great Vowel Shift only when they had primary accent. As with the addition of NE /ŋ/, the differing developments correlate with differing allophones in Middle English. The changes we have been discussing, we therefore label **change by allophones**.

10.3.1 Conditioned versus unconditioned change

Allophones are restricted to certain environments in which they are conditioned by their surroundings. For example, ME /n/ was conditioned to velar articulation [ŋ] by a following velar consonant. When such allo-phones undergo a change, we speak of a **conditioned**, or a **combinatory**, **change**. Other examples are PGmc /f θ s χ/ to PGmc /ƀ ð z g/ when not preceded by the primary accent, as in the words accounted for by Verner's law.

Much more rarely, all members of a phoneme change, and we speak of an **unconditioned change**. Examples are: PIE /o/ to PGmc /a/, as in Goth. *asts* "branch" from PIE /ósdos/ [ózdos] (with loss in Germanic of the second vowel); PGmc /z/ to OE /r/, as in OE *wæron* "were." It should be noted, however, that when handbooks speak of unconditioned change, they do not take into account losses of certain members of the earlier phoneme. Thus the change of PIE /o/ to PGmc /a/ is called unconditioned, even though the *o* of unstressed syllables was lost, as in the second syllable of PIE /ósdos/. Moreover, some PGmc /z/ were lost, as in OE *mēd* "meed." Accordingly, it may be true that no change affects all occurrences of a phoneme. Completely unconditioned changes may, then, be impossible to document in languages.

10.3.2 Phonetic processes involved in change

When changes take place, they usually involve modification of one or more distinctive features of a phoneme. NE /t/, for example, is a stop produced by alveolar closure while the velum is raised and the glottis is open. Some of its allophones are also characterized by aspiration, such as its allophone before stressed vowel, as in *top*; that after /s/, as in *stop*, is unaspirated. The allophone of /t/ after stressed vowels and before unstressed, as in *butting, butter, bottom* etc., came to be unaspirated and very short for many speakers of American English; articulated in this way, it became voiced between voiced sounds, so that *butting* and *budding*, *latter* and *ladder* and so on became homophones. For such speakers the short *t* between vowels became voiced, that is, instead of the distinctive feature [−voice], the distinctive feature [+voice] was introduced. In accounts of changes, we accordingly identify the distinctive features of phonemes and allophones, for through their modification sound changes take place.

From the time of Jacob Grimm, historical linguists have indicated sound changes by means of rules. Handbooks of the past state rules of sound change by means of classes of sounds or phonemes, specifying when necessary the environments concerned. Many current analyses state them by means of distinctive features. In the examples given below, rules of both types will be illustrated; the distinctive-feature rules will be provided for only the first few rules, for in general their formulation requires thorough control of the language in question, and these illustrations provide the format that can be followed for any analysed language.

A change may occur in **place of articulation**: labials may become labio-dentals, dentals may become alveolars, velars may become palatals and so on. A change from dental to alveolar occurred when PGmc /t/ became OHG /s/; cf. Eng. hate = Germ. hassen. A change of velar to palatal occurred when PIE /k/ under certain conditions became [ʃ] in some of the dialects; cf. Lat. *centum* = Skt *śatam* "hundred."

This last change is stated as follows in terms of phonemes:

Rule 1a PIE k g gh > PIndic ʃ ž

In terms of distinctive features, it is stated:

Rule 1b [+cns]   [−back]
        [+high] → [+std]
        [−ant]

The distinctive-feature rule indicates that Proto-Indo-European consonants which had the further distinctive features of height and −anterior (that is, no obstruction in the front of the mouth, i.e. back articulation) became strident and palatal.

The rule in both forms indicates that the change is unconditional, that is, that all Proto-Indo-European /k g gh/ became Proto-Indic [ʃ ž]. Yet this change is not found in all words with Proto-Indo-European /k g gh/. For a precise statement of the changes, to the extent they can be determined, one would have to consult a specialized handbook or article; yet even these have been inadequately precise. Complete and accurate descriptions of phonological changes remain to be provided for all languages.

A change may occur in **manner of articulation**: stops may become fricatives or affricates, obstruents may become semivowels or vice versa and so on. A change from stop to fricative occurred when Proto-Indo-European /p/ became PGmc /f/; cf. Lat. *pater* = Goth. *fadar*. A change from stop to affricate occurred when PGmc /p/ became HG /pf/; cf. Eng. *pool* = Germ. *Pfuhl*. A change from semivowel to stop occurred when PGmc *ww* became North and East Gmc *ggw*, as in Goth. *triggws*, ON *tryggr* = OHG *triuwi* "true, faithful"; the two *g*'s indicate that the sound in question was a stop, not a fricative.

The last change is stated as follows in terms of phonemes:

Rule 2a PGmc *ww* > NEGmc *gw* (spelled *ggw*)

In terms of distinctive features, it is stated:

$$
\text{Rule 2b} \quad
\begin{bmatrix} +\text{cns} \\ +\text{back} \\ +\text{vd} \end{bmatrix}
\rightarrow -\text{rd} \Big/ \underline{\quad}
\begin{bmatrix} -\text{cns} \\ +\text{back} \\ +\text{rd} \end{bmatrix}
$$

This rule indicates a conditioned change. The conditioning feature is indicated after the slant line; by the condition PGmc *w* became North and East Germanic [g] only in the environment preceding *w*. For the interpretation of this rule, the omission of the feature [tense] is significant; the change did not take place before PGmc *gʷ*, which was distinguished from

PGmc *w* by tenseness. As the rule may indicate, while indication by means of features provides precision, the result may have a somewhat formidable mathematical flavor.

A change may occur in the **position of the velum**: nasal sounds may become denasalized, non-nasals may become nasals. OIcel. *ellefo* "eleven" corresponds to Goth. *ainlif*; OIcel. *annar* "other," on the other hand, corresponds to Goth. *anþar*. Nasal consonants were lost in Old English with lengthening of the preceding vowel, when they occurred before voiceless fricatives; cf. Eng. *five* = Germ. *fünf*, Eng. *goose* = Germ. *Gans*. Nasal articulation may not be completely lost, but may affect a neighboring vowel, as in Fr. *vin* [vẽ] < Lat. *vinum* "wine."

The change of short vowels to long vowels in pre-Old English, with loss of following nasal, is stated as follows in terms of phonemes:

Rule 3 Pre-OE $\breve{V}$ + m/n + f/θ/s > OE $\bar{V}$ + f/θ/s

A change may take place in **glottal articulation**: voiced sounds may be devoiced, voiceless sounds may be voiced. An example of voiced sounds becoming devoiced is PIE /b d g/ becoming PGmc /p t k/; cf. Lat. *duo* = Eng. *two*. An example of voiceless sounds becoming voiced is PGmc /f θ s χ/, without chief accent on the preceding syllable becoming PGmc /ƀ ð z ǥ/, as in PGmc **tugún* > PGmc *tugun* > OE *tugon* "pulled."

The last change is stated as follows in terms of phonemes:

Rule 4 PGmc f θ s χ χᵂ > ƀ ð z ǥ ǥᵂ when not preceded by the chief accent.

A change may involve **loss**: OE /h/ before /l n r/ was lost, as in *loud* < OE *hlūd*, *nut* < OE *hnutu*, *ring* < OE *hring*. ME /g/ was lost after [ŋ] as in *long*. Final, weakly stressed vowels were lost in early New English, as in /persed/ > /pirst/ *pierced*, *roote* > *root*, and so on. As in these examples, losses may be complete, though they may also have an effect on a neighboring element. When, for example, [x] was lost in *light, thought, fight* (cf. Germ. *Licht, dachte, fechten*) and so on, in early Modern English, the preceding vowel was lengthened. This phenomenon is known as **compensatory lengthening**. Other examples are OE *gōs* < Pre-OE **gans*, cf. Germ. *Gans* 'goose,' OE *ūs* < Pre-OE **uns*, "us," in which nasals were lost before voiceless fricatives, with compensatory lengthening of the preceding vowel, as indicated in Rule 3 above. The same change occurred earlier in OE *brōhte* < PGmc /branχta/ "brought" and OE *þōhte* < PGmc /þanχta/ "thought."

Changes may also take place in the characteristic features of vowels, as in the degree of vowel opening. Open vowels may become more closed; closed vowels, more open. In Middle English /ɛː/, as in *sea*, became more closed, so that we now rhyme its vowel with that of *see*. The closed vowels /iː/ and /uː/ of *wife* and *house*, on the other hand, came to be more open. The change of ME /ɛː/ to NE /iy/ is stated as follows in terms of phonemes:

Rule 5 ME ɛː > NE iy

Changes may take place in the degree of fronting. Back vowels may become front vowels, and vice versa. When umlaut was carried through in Pre-Old English, when for example /uː/ became /yː/, as in /myːs/, the plural of /muːs/ "mouse," back vowels were fronted.

The change of Pre-Old English long and short *o* and *u* to front rounded vowels is stated as follows in terms of phonemes:

Rule 6 Pre-OE ŏ ŭ > early OE ø̆ y̆ before i iː j

Changes may take place in labial articulation. The /yː/ of /myːs/, which was fronted in Pre-Old English times, later lost its lip rounding and coalesced with /iː/, so that in Middle English the vowel of *mice* fell together with that of *wife*. This change is stated as follows:

Rule 7 early OE ø̆ y̆ > late OE ĕ ĭ

The examples given here illustrate changes that have taken place in the Indo-European languages. Examples of the processes illustrated here can also be cited from other languages that have been thoroughly investigated.

10.3.3 Assimilation and other processes

The discussion of processes involved in sound change has examined the effects of change involving one or more distinctive features. Processes also follow general kinds of change. One of the most widely observed of these is **assimilation**, a change in the articulation of a sound to one more like that of neighboring sounds. To illustrate it, we may note changes in the consonant of Lat. *ad* "to" when it was prefixed to morphs beginning with consonants. Lat. *apparātus* "apparatus," from *ad* + *pārāre* "make ready," illustrates assimilation in place of articulation; the dental *d* was changed to a labial. Lat. *assimulātio* "assimilation," from *ad* + *simulāre* "resemble," illustrates assimilation in manner of articulation; the stop *d* was changed to a fricative. Lat. *annexus* "annex," from *ad* + *nectere* "bind," illustrates assimilation in position of the velum; the oral *d* was changed to a nasal. Lat. *attemptō* "attempt," from *ad* + *temptāre* "try," illustrates assimilation in attitude of the glottis; the voiced *d* has become unvoiced.

As in these four examples, the preceding element is commonly assimilated, and the articulation of the second element is anticipated. This type of assimilation is referred to as **regressive**.

The articulation of the prior element may also be maintained, as in the pronunciation [sévm̩] for *seven*; in this pronunciation the labial articulation is maintained for the nasal from the preceding fricative. This type of articulation is referred to as **progressive**.

The articulation of both elements may be modified, by reciprocal assimilation, as in [sébm̩]; in this pronunciation the closure of the second element is anticipated in the *b*, and the position of the *b* is maintained for the nasal.

The assimilated sound may not always be contiguous with the sound to which it is changed. An example is Eng. *orangutang*, which was taken over from Malay *orang* "man" + *ūtan* "forest; wild." The nasal of *ūtan* was modified to the velar position of the nasal in *orang* by **assimilation at a distance**, or **distant assimilation**. Skt *n* is changed to retroflex ṇ if preceded in the same word by a retroflex semivowel or sibilant, as in *rudreṇa* "by Rudra." Umlaut is an example of assimilation at a distance; as in OE *fǣt* < **fōti*, the back vowel *ō* was assimilated to the place of articulation of the following front vowel.

Assimilation may be complete, resulting in two identical sounds, as in *annexus*, or partial, as in [sévm̥].

Assimilation varies greatly from language to language. The Slavic languages have undergone repeated palatalization, that is assimilation of sounds to palatal articulation. English, too, has examples from several periods, as noted in section 10.8.7. But German exhibits little palatalization. We might expect that speakers would find it easier to articulate neighboring sounds alike, and that they would accordingly introduce assimilation. But the structure of individual languages varies so greatly that we cannot propose such a generalization. Before we assume that any one process may have led to specific changes or may be expected to, we must note the characteristic articulation in a given language, as for the following processes.

Changes in word-ending position may lead to development of an additional consonant, as in the pronunciation [sinst] for *since*. In this pronunciation the tongue makes a closure against the alveolar ridge before articulation of the word is completed. The hearer may interpret this hold as a stop [t], and may then imitate the pronunciation, adding the stop, release and all. Such additional consonants are referred to as **excrescent**. Further examples may be taken from English, for example *varmint* < *vermin*, or from German; compare Germ. *Axt*, Eng. *ax*; Germ. *Sekt* "champagne," Eng. *sack* "dry sherry"; Germ. *Habicht*, Eng. *hawk*.

Moreover, final vowels may be lost, a process known as **apocope**. In Old English the first person singular present ended in *-e*, for example *helpe*; in the late Middle English period such final vowels were lost. Apocope, and **syncope**, the loss of medial vowels, are prominent in languages with a strong stress accent on initial syllables. In the Germanic languages many medial and final vowels have been lost, until in present-day English many native words have become monosyllabic. The Old English first singular preterite of *temman* "tame" was *temede*; both weakly stressed vowels have been lost, to yield NE *tamed* [teymd].

Vowels may also be introduced, a process called **epenthesis**. We find epenthetic vowels, for example, in OE *æcer*, cf. OIcel. *akr* "acre," OE *ofen*, cf. OIcel. *ofn* "oven," and in many other words before *r l m n*; we find epenthetic consonants in OE *bræmbel* beside *brēmel* "bramble," OE *gandra* beside *ganra* "gander" and so on. If initial, such elements are called

prothetic. Prothetic vowels were introduced in French before *s* plus consonant, as in Fr. *école* < OFr. *escole* from Lat. *schola, scola* "school." Similar
developments may be noted in Span. *escuela*, Port. *escola*, though in these
languages the development of the prothetic vowel is more narrowly
circumscribed.

10.4 THE PATTERNS OF SOUND CHANGE

In discussing examples and processes of sound change, we have observed
that sound change only occurs when there is a disruption of the phonological system. Such disruption may occur in one of two ways, either by merger
or by split.

Merger occurs when sounds change so completely that they fall together
with the sounds of another phoneme, for example NE *t* as in *bitter* merging
with the /d/ as in *bidder*. It was the pattern by which ME /oː/, as in *roote*,
became established as NE /uw/; for reflexes of ME *ō* merged with those of
ME *eu*, as in *fruit* and *virtue*. Other examples are given below.

By means of split, one or more allophones of a phoneme may move away
from the other allophones of that phoneme: for example, ME [ŋ] split off
from the ME /n/ phoneme upon loss of a following /g/, as in *young*. By
means of split, new phonemes may be introduced, as was NE /ŋ/, or the
diverging allophones may merge with another phoneme as did the reflexes
of PGmc /z/ with Pre-OE /r/, as in *were*.

Merger is the more important of these patterns; for often when a sound
change results from split, the rearrangement has taken place in such a way
that one of the split allophones has merged with allophones from another
source. The [e] which split off from Pre-OE /a/ before *i ī j*, for example,
merged with /e/, as in *men*. Moreover, allophones may become phonemes
when their conditioning entities merge with others; Pre-OE short and long
[ø] and [y] became phonemes when following *i ī j* merged with reflexes of
other weakly stressed vowels or were lost. Merger may therefore be
considered the central mechanism of sound change.

Merger may be conditioned or unconditioned. Unconditioned merger,
when a phoneme merges completely with another phoneme, is relatively
infrequent. An example is PGmc /z/, which merged in Pre-Old English
and other Germanic dialects with PGmc /r/. When such mergers take
place, we cannot determine the earlier forms solely from one language,
unless we have enough linguistic material to use the method of internal
reconstruction. By comparing *was* with *were*, for example, we can distinguish the source of the *r* in *were* (PIE *s*) from that of the *r* in *four* (PIE
r). Examples of other unconditioned mergers are: that of PIE /o/ with PIE
/a/ to PGmc /a/; PIE /bh dh gh/ with /b d g/ in Iranian, Baltic, Slavic and
Celtic.

Much more frequent is conditioned merger, as when NE [t] merged with
/d/ after stressed vowels preceding other vowels plus consonants, but not

/n/; *bitten* did not become a homophone of *bidden*. Numerous instances of such merger can be cited: NE /uː/ in closed syllables merged with earlier ME /u/, as in *blood*, ME *blōd*, cf. Germ. *Blut* [bluːt], and *nut*, ME *nute*, cf. Germ. *Nuss* [nus]. As another example, NE /ž/ from /zy/ merged with /ž/ in borrowings from French, like *rouge*.

Often after such mergers we find alternations that reflect the earlier situation, such as the /ž/ in *vision*, which alternates with the /z/ in *visible*. As noted in chapter 8, these alternating entities are used in applying the method of internal reconstruction.

Since split may be brought about in two different ways, we distinguish two kinds of split. **Primary split** results from a change of some of the members of a phoneme, which then merge with a different phoneme. In this way the fricative reflex of OHG /t/ merged with OHG /s/ from PGmc /s/, as in NHG *hassen*, cf. Eng. *hate*; the phoneme /t/ was maintained as in MHG *treu*, cf. NE *true*. As another example, allophones of ME /uː/ merged with short ME /u/ before consonants, as in late-ME *blud* "blood," but ME /uː/ was maintained, as in *cū* "cow." As these examples indicate, primary split leads to an increase in the number of occurrences of one phoneme; after the merger of late ME /u/ from /uː/ with ME /u/, /u/ occurred more frequently. But primary split does not generally introduce new phonemes.

Secondary split results from a change in the conditioning features of allophones. Such a change may lead to the introduction of new phonemes in a system. In this way the Pre-Old English front rounded allophones [ø: y yː] of /o oː u uː/ became phonemes when the conditioning /i iː j/ were modified. Pre-OE /o oː u uː/ were continued into Old English, but from some of their allophones four new phonemes /ø øː y yː/ were added to the system. Secondary split, however, does not necesarily lead to the introduction of new phonemes. For example, no new phonemes were produced from the fronted allophones of Pre-OE /a aː/ when the conditioning /i iː j/ were modified; for these allophones fell together with earlier /e eː/.

In sum, disruption of phonological systems, that is sound change, is brought about in accordance with two patterns: merger and split. In each of these patterns, the processes that lead to the change may vary, in accordance with the processes described in section 10.3. Moreover, in languages with large numbers of speakers, the results of sound change may only be adopted over a long period of time, as we will note in the following section.

10.5 THE SPREAD OF SOUND CHANGE

After a sound change has taken place, it may be restricted to a given geographical area or it may be extended to other areas in which a language is spoken. In this way the spread of sound change is comparable to the spread of any linguistic innovation. We have observed in chapter 7 that words may be adopted throughout the area influenced by a center of prestige; the French word *lagniappe* was adopted in eastern Texas through influence from Louisiana, while the Spanish word *pilon* was adopted in southern Texas through influence from Mexico. Phonological innovations may be extended similarly, as demonstrated in Kloeke's classical study concerning the change of MDu. *ū* specifically in the words for "house" and "mouse."

MDu. *ū* changed to *ȳ*, apparently in the area around Antwerp. The results of this change were spread to speakers who were influenced by this focal area; in time the change was extended virtually throughout the entire area in which Dutch was spoken. Near Low German territory, however, *ū* was maintained, probably because of the unchanged *ū* in Low German cognates; *ū* was also maintained more widely in *mūs* than in *hūs*, probably because the word for "mouse" is less widely used in communication with members of other communities than is the word for "house, building." The results of the change accordingly reflect both social and geographical influence. A second change of *ȳ* to [øy] took place in the sixteenth and seventeenth centuries in the Antwerp area and was spread over much of the Dutch-speaking area; it became the standard pronunciation of MDu. *huis* and *muis*. These Dutch phenomena provide an excellent illustration of the spread of sound change, of variation from word to word in adoption of new patterns and of the social forces at work in such spread.

Dialect geographers have carried out many studies which demonstrate that the results of sound changes are extended in accordance with communication patterns among geographical and social dialects.

Among the documented examples of sound change and its spread, the High German consonant shift may be the one most thoroughly investigated. Affecting first the High German area proper, as noted in chapter 6, the results of the change have been adopted through more and more of the German-speaking area. With the greater centralization of government in the nineteenth and twentieth centuries, a form of German was adopted that incorporated most of these changes. Today the dialects of north Germany, that is, the dialects of Low German with unchanged obstruents as in English, are being modified or ousted by High German. The results of the changes introduced by the High German consonant shift are accordingly still being spread, though the changes themselves took place approximately 1,500 years ago.

10.5.1 Gradual extension of the Great English Vowel Shift

Our observations based on the spread of the Old High German consonant shift and of the Dutch change of *ū*, may help us to understand other such phenomena in language, such as the spread of the results of the Great Vowel Shift.

When we investigate the adoption of the changes of the shift, we find that they were introduced gradually and over a long period of time. Instances of ME [ɛː], which now rhymes with [eː], were, for example, treated differently in the sixteenth and seventeenth centuries. Dryden rhymed *dream* with *shame*, *sea* with *obey*. Pope rhymed *weak* with *take*, *eat* with *state*; Swift rhymed *seat* with *weight*, *meat* with *say't*, and so on. Much earlier, the pronunciation [iː] for [ɛː] is reported by grammarians, but not favored by them. We assume it was used by Queen Elizabeth I, for she wrote "biquived" for *bequeathed*. Although this pronunciation is known from the sixteenth century, still in 1747 Johnson was troubled about rhyming *great*, whether with *seat* [iː] or with *state* [eː].

We may ascribe Johnson's perplexity in part to the variation of usage among the dialects of Britain, in part to the gradual and slow extension of the shift. As we noted in chapter 6, a sound change may take place in a focal area and be carried to other areas under its cultural influence through many centuries. The change of ME [ɛː] and other long vowels must have been similar to the change of intervocalic *t* in contemporary American English, in which some speakers pronounce *butter* [bə́dər], others [bə́ţər], still others [bə́tər]. As sounds are modified, the new articulation is extended gradually until words containing them reach a stabilized position in the phonological system of the standard language, as have *dream* and *great* today. Yet even today we find variation in English dialects, some of which preserve the pronunciation [diyf] rather than the shortened [def] of standard English. We also find considerable variation in the pronunciation of words like *root, hoof, roof*. This variation illustrates that even after six centuries the effects of the Great Vowel Shift have not become stabilized in English.

10.5.2 Generalization of the results of sound change in small societies

Just how and when sound changes are adopted in any individual speech community is a complicated problem that requires detailed study. Our information about speech communities of the past is less detailed than is our information on contemporary languages and their use. For this reason our interpretations of the spread of sound changes in the past rely largely on studies of interrelationships between geographical dialects; Kloeke's observations of the difference in extent between the spread of the changed pronunciations in *hūs* and *mūs*, however, also involved consideration of social dialects. In this century, important investigations have been made of linguistic communities in which sound changes have been documented; these investigations provide details about the spread of change among various age groups of speakers and various social as well as geographical configurations.

The most comprehensive survey made of a speech community for historical purposes has provided important information on the gradual spread of the results of sound change. In his investigation of the French-speaking village of Charmey, Switzerland, published in 1905, L. Gauchat found differences in the speech of various age groups of the village. For example, where speakers 60–90 years of age used the back vowel *å*, speakers 30–60 years of age used both *å* and *ao* and younger speakers used only *ao*. Moreover, palatalized *l* was in part replaced by *y* among speakers 30–60 years of age, and totally replaced among speakers under 30.

In 1929 E. Hermann published a follow-up study of Charmey, in which he examined the situation regarding some of Gauchat's conclusions at that time. Hermann found that the change of *ō* to *ao* and other diphthongizations had become even more general. Other sound changes noted by Gauchat, however, had not been generally adopted, apparently because of contrary influence from standard French. The studies by Gauchat and Hermann show that sound changes, when adopted, are spread gradually among a community of speakers, as we have noted for the changes of the Great Vowel Shift.

Alf Sommerfelt found similar results concerning differences among speakers of varying age groups in Welsh- and Irish-speaking communities (see 1962: 158–97). Besides supporting the evidence for gradual spread of the results of sound changes, Sommerfelt provided data that illustrate how such gradual shifting takes place. He found that the change was completely carried out in some words, but not yet in others. Sommerfelt's findings remind us of the situation in English after the Great Vowel Shift. A change may not affect all words immediately; but in time it is carried out in all words of similar phonological structure unless social conditions direct the adoption of other patterns.

We may accordingly conclude from the situations in English, in Charmey, and in Wales and Ireland, how sound change takes place and is generalized in relatively small communities. After a sound change has been carried out, it is generalized so that eventually all occurrences of a linguistic element undergo the change, if its environment is the same and if the prestige of the focal area is adequate. If the linguistic community is small and homogeneous, the change may be carried out with complete consistency. This was the situation for the Proto-Germanic consonant shift; we know of no exceptions. If a change were carried out in a small homogeneous commmunity today, we would expect the same results. At the time of the High German consonant shift, however, the linguistic community that spoke High German was so large that the results of the shift were adopted only in a part of the area, presumably the focal area, and those neighboring areas under its influence. A similar situation existed for English in the fifteenth century, so that today "exceptions" to the Great Vowel Shift are found in the language side by side with the reflexes we expect from the shift as indicated in section 10.1.

10.5.3 Generalization of the results of sound changes in the large language communities of today

None of the communities discussed in the previous section approaches in size and complexity the linguistic community speaking English today, or even such a portion of this community as the New York City area. The population of the New York City area is much larger than that of England in the fifteenth century, and the speakers are also far more unlike. Recent immigration of Blacks into New York, and of Puerto Ricans, Haitians, and many other groups, is also far more extensive than were any immigrations in Britain at any time, including the fifteenth century. It is instructive to examine how phonological systems change in such a large and complex community.

William Labov has carried out such studies, concentrating on linguistic variables, that is, items which are not found consistently among all speakers. One such item is [r].

In his study of the status of [r], as in *guard*, in New York City society, Labov found that it has high prestige. When speakers wish to be accepted in certain social contexts, they use the [r]. They also extend [r] and other patterns of high prestige to words in which they do not belong, producing in this way **hyperforms**. From his observations of the spread of variant forms with high prestige, Labov has proposed that such forms may be adopted more widely by speakers outside the focal area.

This observation has also been made for languages of the past, though only for occasional forms. Bloomfield (1933: 479–80) cites an instance of a hyperform in Rhaeto-Romance. Another example is OSax. *tins* "taxes." This word is ultimately from Lat. *census*, through OHG *zins*. When Old Saxon speakers adopted the word from Old High German, they apparently assumed that it belonged to the patterns they observed for the Old High German consonant shift, which differentiated their own word *tolna*, from OHG *zollan* "tax" and the like. Rather than adopt the initial late Latin consonant [ts], they introduced the normal Old Saxon equivalent of OHG [ts], converting OHG *zins* to OSax. *tins*. In *tolna* such a conversion is etymologically justified, for the Latin word is *telōnēum*; in *tins*, however, it is not justified, for the initial Latin consonant was [ts].

For languages of the past, we find such changes only in sporadic forms. In the complex societies of contemporary culture, in which speakers master many varieties and dialects of their own language, such changes may be introduced more widely, as in the speech of New York City. As Weinreich, Labov and Herzog have concluded, "the interpretation of the data in terms of language change depends on the entire sociolinguistic structure" (1968: 177).

In conclusion, the studies of Kloeke, Gauchat, Sommerfelt and the numerous scholars who have concerned themselves with the High German consonant shift and the Great English Vowel Shift, indicate that after sound changes take place, they are spread in accordance with social forces in a given community. If a community is small and compact, they may be adopted throughout it. An example we have cited is the Germanic consonant shift, which spread to all speakers of Proto-Germanic. Larger communities, on the other hand, may show only partial adoption of sound changes, as we may note from the results of the Great English Vowel Shift or from the extension of the High German consonant shift. On the other hand, sound changes may be rejected in favor of competing patterns, as occurred in Charmey. We have noted that the shift of certain PIE *k* to sibilants did not take place in the Baltic, the farthest west of satem dialects. To understand the phenomena involved in sound change, linguists have introduced increasingly precise techniques, such as rules in which the various forces involved can be specified. But there are also changes that affect only a small number of words, or only individual words in a language, as we note in the next section.

10.6 SPORADIC CHANGE, OR CHANGE BY PHONEMES

In section 10.3 of this chapter we dealt with sound changes that arise from the rearrangements of allophones. Some allophones of one phoneme in the course of time come to resemble allophones of another phoneme and may merge with them. Allophones may also be split from the phoneme to which they formerly belonged, or they may be lost. In sound changes of this type, all allophones that are similar in articulation undergo the change. Moreover, when the change has taken place, the new alignment is maintained, until another shift occurs. NE /ŋ/, for example, has remained distinct from /n/ since the loss of a following /g/. Besides such change we find in language sporadic changes which affect sounds only in some of their occurrences. As an example we may cite the change of ME *napron* to NE *apron*; it occurred because of false division of the sequence *a napron*. We call the loss of initial *n* in *napron* a sporadic change because it occurred only in a few Middle English words.

Sporadic changes differ from allophonic changes in that they cannot be ascribed to any one phonological pattern. For example, initial *n* was not lost in phonological patterns similar to that of *napron*; it was maintained in *napkin*, *nape* and so on. By contrast, every *n* was lost before voiceless fricatives in Pre-Old English, as in OE *gōs* "goose" from **gans-*.

Since sporadic changes involve a direct change from one phoneme to another, with no gradual modification of allophones like that in AE *-t-*, we refer to the process as **change by phonemes**. They have also been referred to as **spontaneous**, and **saltatory** – in recognition of the immediate shift from one phoneme to another.

As an example we may cite the pronunciations of NE *seven*. One pronunciation, especially in careful speech is [sévn̩]. But *seven* is often pronounced [sévm̩], or even [sébm̩] When this pronunciation is used, there has been no long gradual development of a final alveolar nasal to a labiodental or bilabial nasal. Speakers use either one of the two phonemes. Moreover, we find many such changes in rapid, informal speech, especially in everyday words. Although a similar change is often observed for NE *eleven* [əlévm̩] rather than [əlévn̩], it would be rare, or nonexistent, in *leaven* [lévn̩], which has the same phonetic environment for *n* but a different status in the social dialects of the language.

Speakers are often conscious of changes by phonemes, though they are unaware of the changes by allophones, as in the gradual voicing of NE *water, bottle* and so on. Changes by allophone are carried through in all morphs in which the allophone occurs, except possibly by self-conscious speakers; the *t* in Modern English forms like *better, bottom*, for example, is consistently modified. On the other hand, a sporadic change like that of [sévn̩] to [sébm̩], or the pronunciation [irévələnt] for [iréləvənt], is often noted and frowned upon. The different attitude of speakers to change by phonemes probably results from an awareness that such phenomena are associated with specific social dialects or styles.

Many of the processes involved in sporadic change are like those involved in more general sound change. In this way many sporadic changes are assimilatory, such as those of *eleven*. Examples may also be found in the frequent palatalization of *ty* to yield *tš*, as in rapid pronunciation of words ending in *-t* before *you*, such as /betšə/ rather than /bet yə/; see also 10.8.3. Moreover, epenthetic vowels may be introduced, as in the pronunciation /éləm/ rather than /élm/. The same process led to the general introduction of epenthetic vowels in Old English, but in Modern English we do not introduce such vowels in all words with /-lm/; for example, *realm* /relm/, *helm* and so on.

One process that is exemplified primarily in sporadic changes is **dissimilation**, the production of sounds so that they will be more unlike one another. With the notable exception of Grassmann's law, dissimilation is generally attested sporadically in languages. We find dissimilation especially among the more complex sounds, which are also those learned last by children; such are *l* and *r*, as in NE *turtle* < Lat. *turtur*, NE *pilgrim* < Lat. *peregrinus*, NE *marble* < Lat. *marmor*. It is less commonly attested for stops, as in Germ. *Kartoffel* "potato," in which the initial *k* was dissimilated from *t* in the seventeenth century; the early form was *Tartuffeln*, which was borrowed from Ital. *tartuffeli*. (When the plant was imported to Italy, from Peru in the sixteenth century, it was named after the truffle.) As in all of these examples, in dissimilation it is usually the sound of the unaccented syllable that is modified.

Dissimilation may also involve the loss of a syllable; this is called **haplology**. As examples we may cite the Modern English adverbs in *-ly* made from adjectives ending in *-le*. In these, one syllables has been lost, as in *gently* rather than **gentlely*, *simply* rather than **simplely*. Another example is *England* < *Engla lond* "land of the Angles." Haplology is relatively infrequent.

Another type of change that is primarily sporadic is **metathesis**, the interchange of phonemes. Although few examples can be cited from Modern English, metathesis was remarkably frequent in late West Saxon, where we find *āxian* [aːksian] "ask," *dox* "dusk," *flaxe* "flask," *waxan* "wash." Metathesis of consonant and vowel (to which some scholars restrict the term metathesis) is also attested in Old English, as in *hors* < *hros*, cf. Germ. *Ross* "horse," *ðirda* < *ðridda* "third," cf. Germ. *dritte* and NE *three*. Reflexes of the nonmetathesized forms are also found in Modern English, as in the dialectal *aks* for *ask*, and in *wal-rus* rather than **whale-horse*. In this way the examples cited here from English illustrate the phenomena of sporadic change, which affects relatively few words of the language, and which often leaves variant forms besides them.

10.7 INTERPRETATIONS OF SOUND CHANGE

In past treatments of phonological change, and in many current treatments, sound change is interpreted as a change of elements in a phonological system, as we have noted in the discussion of the phenomena described under Grimm's law. For example, the first of the changes in the Germanic consonant shift is interpreted as a change of the Proto-Germanic elements *p t k kʷ* to *f θ χ χʷ*. The elements in question are taken to be abstract elements in the phonological system.

As linguistic theory became more explicit, these abstract elements were precisely defined, and labeled phonemes, that is, classes of sounds with specific relationships to other classes of sounds in a given language. Each class was assumed to have one or more allophones, that is, subclasses of **phonemes**. Sound change takes place in such subclasses, except in the rare instances when it is not combinatory; in such instances, the entire phoneme is changed. The process was stated by Grimm in the form of a rule, and has been subsequently stated by the same device, though the shape of rules has been modified.

When interpreting sound changes as changes of abstract elements in a phonological system, linguists also undertook to analyse the components of these elements, as we noted of Trubetzkoy and Jakobson. Such study led to an analysis of phonemes as bundles of distinctive features. When change occurs, one or more of these components is assumed to have been modified. Thus in the Proto-Germanic change of *p t k kʷ* to *f θ χ χʷ*, the manner of articulation was modified from that of a stop to a fricative. Phonological changes could in this way be interpreted as addition, alteration or loss of a feature. Thus the feature [+front] was added to the articulation of Pre-OE *a* by umlaut. In the umlaut of Pre-OE *o* and *u*, the feature [+back] was altered to [+front]. The resulting OE phonemes subsequently lost the feature [+round] to merge with *e* and *i*.

By interpreting sound change as a change in features, we can specify more precisely the components of phonemes that are involved in change than if we simply use symbols for the phonemes. But whether depicted as change of subclasses of phonemes, like *p t k k^w*, or as change of features, sound change is interpreted as a change of elements in the phonological system of a language.

10.7.1 Change as interpreted by change in rules

As we noted in recalling the contributions of Trubetzkoy, he regarded phonological elements and processes as rules. The view was continued by generative linguistics, so that in their treatment change consists of modifications of rules in the competence of speakers. Specific changes, then, have been labeled by the effect on rules.

When sound change involves innovations, the event is described as **rule addition**. The changes described in Grimm's law, in Pre-Old English umlaut and in the Great Vowel Shift are examples of rule addition.

When, on the other hand, the application of a rule is no longer maintained, the event is referred to as **rule loss**. As an example, Gothic regularized the fricatives in most inflected sets; it shows voiceless fricatives where the other Germanic languages maintain voiced fricatives, as in the cognate of *choose*:

Goth.	kiusan	kaus	kusum	kusans
cf. OE	cēosan	cēas	curon	coren

Because other evidence has led us to assume that the Gothic verbs at one time had had such voiced fricatives, the presence of *s* and other voiceless fricatives in the preterite plural and the preterite participle is ascribed to rule loss.

Voiced fricatives as reflexes of Proto-Indo-European voiceless stops are found in Gothic, as in the form *fadar* "father," and in auxiliaries like *aih* : *aigum* "own." Generative grammarians account for such exceptions to rule loss by stating that words like *fadar* and *aigum* have been entered in the lexicon. Lexicalized forms may escape modification when a rule is lost.

A third type of change is ascribed to **rule reordering**. Two languages or dialects may exhibit the same rules, but the rules may differ in order. In this way the area in central Germany that incorporated some changes from the north and others from the south has different surface forms from those of other dialects but is said to incorporate the same rules.

For example, in the twelfth century, *ī > ei* in Austria and south Germany, as in NHG *Seite < MHG sīte*. The change was extended northward, and reached the Mosel area in the sixteenth century. Middle High German also had an *ie* diphthong, pronounced [iə]. This *ie* changed to *ī* in the eleventh and twelfth centuries in central Germany, as in NHG *ließ* "permitted," and the change was extended southward. In the dialect of

Wetterau, the *ī* > *iə* was adopted before the influence of the *ī* > *ei* was transmitted from the south; as a result, the vowel of *ließ* and other words with earlier *iə* also was changed to *ei* when the *ī* > *ei* change reached the Wetterau dialect.

Grammars of the German dialects would therefore have different rule orders. In a grammar of dialects to the south, the *ī* > *ei* rule would be ordered before that of *ie* > *ī*; in a grammar of dialects to the north, the *ie* > *ı* rule would have an earlier order. The relationships between these dialects with regard to these characteristics would therefore be indicated in the order of rules that present the results of previous sound changes.

Besides reinterpeting sound change, and the results of sound change in this way, grammarians with a generative point of view have introduced terms for rules that can be related to other rules. For example, if a rule describes changes that expand the scope of subsequent rules, the earlier rule is labeled a **feeding rule**, and the group of rules is said to stand in a **feeding relationship**. In this way the rules that describe the lengthening of short vowels before the Great Vowel Shift are labeled feeding rules. For, with the addition of more instances of *ī*, a larger number of words underwent the change of *ī* to *ay*. But languages also undergo changes that conflict with the pattern of earlier changes. Such changes are referred to as **bleeding rules**; **bleeding relationship**, then, results in diminution of scope.

In order to understand the publications that deal with sound change as rules change, students must be aware of their basis, and of their difference from earlier descriptions and historical treatments. The use of rules is not new, for, as we noted above, rules have been used since the days of Grimm. Nor is the use of distinctive features in stated sound changes restricted to such treatments, for linguists of the nineteenth century already dealt with changes by means of features. Rather, it is the identification of linguistic phenomena through rules, and the discussion of linguistic changes as rule changes that are characteristic of this approach.

The rules of the past expressed in terms of phonemes and the rules expressed in terms of distinctive features are equivalent, if both types of rules meet the requirements of observational adequacy and descriptive adequacy. Meeting these requirements is still a greater problem in historical linguistics than is the revision of traditional terminology. For example, rules given in distinctive features may be inadequate if they do not observe the forms (rules) that are exceptions.

Other inadequacies in rules result from our lack of information about the distinctive features of phonemes in languages of the past. For example, we do not know the distinctive features of PIE *bh dh gh gʷh*. By one interpretation they were tense voiced stops as opposed to the lenis voiced stops labeled *b d g gʷ*. In attempts to understand the changes of the early Germanic consonant system, we must face such problems. By simply rewriting proposed rules formulated by earlier linguists, no new insights into the phenomena themselves are acquired.

10.8 PROPOSED EXPLANATIONS FOR SOUND CHANGE

Besides studying the processes and patterns by which phonological systems are modified, historical linguists have attempted to determine the causes of modification and to predict its directions.

Some linguists have attempted to account for sound change by proposing that it leads to greater simplicity in language. Such attempts fail when we examine other languages; what is "simple" for speakers of some languages and in specific stages of a language may seem difficult in others, as we noted when we compared sound changes in a given language with the phenomena in other languages. We conclude that assumption of change towards ease of articulation in accordance with the principle of least effort is based on an inadequate view of language. For what seems easy in one language is difficult in another.

For example, German still maintains initial [kn], which has been lost in English and accordingly seems to be a very difficult consonant cluster for English speakers; compare NHG *kneten* "knead," NHG *Knie* "knee," NHG *Knoten* "knot" and so on. As another example we may note that in Latin there was relative freedom of occurrence of final consonants, but in Classical Greek the only final consonants to occur are *r n s*. PIE *-m* in the accusative singular, for example Lat. *lupum* "wolf," shows up as Gk *-n*, *lúkon*. Other final consonants were lost, as illustrated by the vocative singular *paî* of *paîs*, gen. *paidós* "boy"; Gk *tí* "what" corresponds to Lat. *quid*. Moreover, Klaus Wedekind (1990: 1–2, 127–52) has pointed out that glottalics, which seem to be difficult for linguists working in Indo-European languages, are very common in those of Ethiopia. The observation is important for evaluation of the glottalic theory, because one of its supports is based on the absence of roots with initial and final *b d g g^w*; interpreting these as glottalic, glottalicists use the finding as morphological support for the theory. By Wedekind's observation, the support is empty.

It is obvious from differences like these in various languages that only some sound changes tend toward simplicity and that we must look for other explanations (see Jespersen 1922: 319–36).

As we have noted in chapter 1, three major reasons have been proposed for change in language, including change in the phonological system: (1) the effect of one language on another; (2) the effects of modifications introduced when children learn their language; (3) effects of components in the system of a language on other components. We will examine briefly each of these proposed explanations as they apply to sound change.

10.8.1 The proposed explanation of sound change through the effects of one language on another is based on observations of speakers who learn a second language with traces of their first language

This statement is especially true if the speakers have learned the second language after their adolescence. Thus, many speakers of English keep their aspirated stops when they learn French, pronouncing *peau* "skin" as [pʰow] rather than as [poː]. French speakers may do the converse when they learn English. Moreover, many English speakers keep their diphthongized vowels when they learn Spanish, pronouncing the Spanish *si* 'yes' as [siy], *sé* "be" as [sey], *su* "his" as [suw], in accordance with their own pronunciation of *see*, *say*, *sue*. By contrast, many Spanish speakers, who have only five vowels, do not distinguish between such English words as *bit* and *beet*, *let* and *late*, *pull* and *pool*. On the basis of such observations, it has been proposed that sound changes may be introduced by the carry-over of articulatory habits from the native language to a second language, with permanent effect. If, then, a large number of speakers adopt a second language, possibly as a result of conquest or migration, the sound system of the language can be modified.

The underlying language is known as a **substratum**. The proposed explanation for sound change is therefore known as the **substratum theory**. (The terms **adstratum** for an adjacent influencing language, and **superstratum** for a superior influencing language, may also be used.)

Romance historical linguists especially have attempted to account for the separate developments of Spanish, French and other Romance languages by assuming articulatory modifications carried over by speakers who adopted Latin as their second language. The French front rounded vowels are, for example, ascribed to a Celtic substratum. The changes that Latin has undergone in Rumanian are ascribed to a Dacian substratum.

Our primary difficulty with proposing the substratum theory to account for sound change is the lack of evidence. We do not know what the relationships between the Celtic speakers of Gaul and the Latin-speaking settlers were. We know very little about the varieties of Celtic spoken in Gaul. The problems are similar for Spanish, Rumanian and other languages. Until the substratum theory can be supported by large-scale observation of sound changes in contemporary languages, we must be cautious about suggesting it as an explanation for sound changes. On the other hand, speakers in societies that use several languages often have similar syntactic constructions in each. The influences of languages on one another may, then, be more weighty in syntax than in phonology.

The effects of language interaction are determined largely by social conditions. When in some areas non-native speakers acquire a new language, the second generation masters it with general adequacy, if the linguistic tradition is well established. In the United States, grandchildren of Italians, Germans, Spaniards, Africans, Asiatics, Irish, and Danes speak the English used by their associates without notable differences in phonological structure. In other societies, however, different conditions may lead to different results.

When substrata have led to modifications in the pronunciation of a language, as of English in India, the linguistic tradition has been less powerful; native speakers have been outnumbered. In India relatively few native speakers from Britain were available to teach English to speakers who constantly used the indigenous languages.

There is now considerable investigation of multilingual communities such as those in India, Africa and other areas of the world that are predominantly multilingual. The effects of one language on another may become clear after further study and may permit generalizations about sound changes resulting from the interplay of languages. Such study has indicated the effects of other languages in the syntax and in the lexicon, as we note in the following chapters. From our observations, however, we must conclude that sound change has as its major causes other linguistic phenomena.

10.8.2 The hypothesis that sound change is to be attributed to children learning their language is also poorly supported

Under this hypothesis it is assumed that each new generation of speakers must master anew the grammar of their language and that, in the process, phonological change can readily be introduced. It is apparent to anyone observing children learning their language that some of them have difficulty pronouncing certain sounds. An occasional child learning English, for example, may pronounce the *r* as in *rat* with initial rounding, so that the word sounds like *wat*. Although such observations are readily supported, it is also true that these children eventually overcome the difficulties.

Further, even if some young children make idiosyncratic errors in pronunciation, there is no consistency of errors among children. Nor can we determine distinct generations of either young or old speakers who might generalize such mispronunciations. It is difficult, therefore, to conclude that modifications, such as those observed by Gauchat between the speech of different age groups at Charmey, were caused by inadequate learning of the phonemes in question, or of the phonological rules, by children.

Linguists who have studied sound change have observed, however, that when a change has been introduced, it is extended further by young speakers. For example, in 1943 the change of intervocalic AE *t* to *d* was carried through consistently by a group of young speakers (see Lehmann 1953: 271–5). And Sommerfelt observed a sound change in Wales first in a few words, and subsequently in greater numbers, until eventually all sounds in the phonological environment in question were affected (1962: especially 160–3, with reference to Henry Sweet). Apparently, when a sound change is adopted, it is observed by more and more speakers in more and more words, until finally it is carried out in all the pertinent environments among a community of speakers.

We assume that if a sound change is carried out "without exceptions," as was the Proto-Germanic consonant shift, the community of speakers was homogeneous and probably small. When a sound change is carried out only partially throughout a relatively large territory, like the High German consonant shift, the community of speakers is exposed to various influences. As the effects of the High German consonant shift were spread towards Low German territory, influences from the important cultural centers of Low-German-speaking northern Germany interfered with the influences leading to modifications. Similarly, the Great English Vowel Shift was not carried out in Scotland. We may conclude, therefore, that the spread of phonological changes is affected by the learning of language among children. But the initial cause of phonological changes cannot be ascribed to language learning.

10.8.3 Ascribing sound change to attempts to achieve regularity or symmetry in phonological systems seems at first blush most attractive

Examples like NE /ŋ/ can be cited that filled out the set of English nasals corresponding to the stops: /p b m t d n k g –/. While this explanation may apply for English, Italian and other languages with similar gaps in the system have not regularized in this way. Clearly, this explanation, too, has its limits.

Even if we may assume a tendency towards symmetry in phonological systems, we cannot predict sound changes: for example, in Middle High German, which had a long-vowel system similar to that of Middle English, the high vowels were also changed to diphthongs, as in MHG *īs* "ice" : NHG *Eis*, MHG *hūs* "house" : NHG *Haus*. But unlike English, the lower long vowels were not raised. The vowel of NHG *See* "sea" is still pronounced like its Middle High German counterpart, as are the vowels of *Mond* "moon" and *Staat* "state." Thus the Middle High German and Middle English vowel systems are similar in some developments, different in others. If, on the basis of these changes, we should be tempted to speculate that in long-vowel systems like those of the Germanic languages, the high vowels tend to become diphthongized, we would be dismayed by Icelandic, in which the high vowels have remained unchanged but the low vowel has become diphthongized; the *ā* has become [au]. Similarly in Scots English, the *ā*, as in ME *hām*, was modified to *ē*, but the high vowels have not undergone the Great Vowel Shift.

Although we cannot flatly state that changes are caused by the system of a given language, we observe that when changes occur, they are directed by the system. The Germanic reflexes of the Proto-Indo-European stops provide an excellent example of changes that seem to lead to others; after *p t k kʷ* became *f θ χ χʷ*, *bh dh gh gʷh* became *ƀ ð g gʷ*, and finally *b d g gʷ* became *p t k kʷ*. Accordingly, the elements of the system underwent changes, but in the course of these changes the system was largely maintained. Similarly, in Classical Greek the obstruent system was preserved, except for the labiovelars, though PIE *bh dh gh* became the voiceless aspirated stops *ph th kh*. In Latin, however, the symmetry of the Proto-Indo-European system was disrupted when *bh* and *dh* coalesced with *d*, and *gh* became *g* or *h*. Further, in Celtic, Baltic, Slavic and Iranian, the system was reduced by the merger of *bh dh gh* with *b d g*. As these examples may illustrate, the developments in each of these languages were directed in part by the system, although from the earlier system we could not have predicted the changes in question.

After such changes take place, subsequent changes are also directed in part by the later system. Thus we find parallel series of stops and fricatives developing in English, as we have noted earlier. In Sanskrit, on the other hand, we find parallel series of voiceless and voiced stops, unaspirated and aspirated: *p t ṭ c k*　*ph th ṭh ch kh*　*b d ḍ j g*　*bh dh ḍh jh gh*. Just as the development of voiced fricatives seems natural in English, so that of voiceless aspirates seems natural in Sanskrit. Such developments in a specific direction were labeled by Sapir **drift**. Bopp ascribed them to an **"inner principle"** in a language.

Since the language of one family may undergo a variety of changes, it is not meaningful to speak of a development towards simplicity. It is much more appropriate to observe the general articulatory patterns of the speakers of any given language, for these seem to have an effect on its changes.

This conclusion may be supported by phenomena of assimilation and other combinatory changes. For they seem to be determined by the articulatory habits of the speakers of a language and by the possibilities allowed by the structure of that language. In the history of English, we may observe many instances of assimilation of dentals and alveolars, some of which are sporadic; others are allophonic changes leading to modifications of the system. The following assimilatory changes occur sporadically in Modern English:

won't you	did you	miss you	raise you
[wównčə]	[díǰə]	[míšə]	[réžə]

These forms may be used in rapid speech, are considered informal by some speakers, substandard by others, and have by no means replaced the more careful [wównt yùw] and so on.

Similar changes took place in early Modern English, and many of the changed forms have remained in the language. From the eighteenth century [ty] is attested with the pronunciation [š], as in *nation*; similarly [sy], as in *issue*, and especially before [yŭ], as in *sugar, sure, assure*. (This change also took place in such words as *assume, consume, suet*, but subsequently [s] was reintroduced in these words as a **spelling pronunciation**.) Similarly [zy] became [ž], as in *measure, pleasure, treasure*; [dy] became [ǰ], as in *soldier, grandeur, Indian, educate, hideous*; here, too, all words but *soldier* and *grandeur* were remodeled by spelling pronunciation. *Injun* has survived only as a pejorative term, though the British pronunciation of the country also maintains the [j̃]. Similarly, many educators consider the regular pronunciation of the word /éjəkèyt/ undignified and insist on the spelling pronunciation.

In early Old English, allophones of "k" and "g" were palatalized even more generally in the neighborhood of front vowels, so that modifications arose as follows:

cīdan "chide"	*cū* "cow"	*geard* "yard"	*gold* "gold"
[k'iːdan]	[kuː]	[g'ɛard]	[gold]
pic "pitch"	*bōc* "book"	*dæg* "day"	*longra* "longer"
[pik']	[boːk]	[dæg']	[loŋgra]

Gradually the palatalized allophones, as in *chide, pitch, yard, day*, came to be further differentiated from the velar allophones, as in *cow, book, gold, longer*. Eventually the palatalized allophone of /k/ fell together with [tj], as in *feccan* [fetjan] "fetch," and the new phoneme /č/ arose; the palatalized allophone of /g/ fell together with the earlier phoneme /j/ as in OE *gear* "year" and split from the /g/ phoneme.

Palatalization has occurred repeatedly in the Slavic languages. Some phonemes of Slavic can be ascribed to the palatalization that took place in the Indo-European speech community and gave rise to the isogloss separating the satem languages from the remainder of the Indo-European family. The following are examples:

OCS *pĭsati* "write"	cf.	Gk. *poikílos* "variegated"
OCS *zrŭno* "grain"		Goth. *kaurn* "grain"
OCS *zemlja* "earth"		Gk. *khamaí* "on the earth"

At a later time velars were again palatalized in Slavic, for example:

OCS *četyre* "four"	cf.	Lat. *quattuor* "four"
OCS *žena* "woman"		Gk. *gunḗ* "woman"
OCS *četi* "strike"		Hitt. *kuenzi* "strikes"

Later still in Russian virtually all consonants were palatalized before front vowels, so that today consonants are found in two series: palatalized and nonpalatalized. The two branches of Indo-European, Germanic and Slavic, accordingly provide examples of the assimilatory change known as palatalization, as do other Indo-European languages.

In the Germanic languages, assimilation also took place in the articulation of vowels. PIE /e/ before [y] became raised in Germanic, so that PIE /ey/ > PGmc /iː/, as in OE *stīgan* "climb," compare Gk *steíkhō* "come"; Modern English cognates are *sty* and *stile*. PGmc /e/ was also assimilated to an *ī* in the following syllable, as in Goth. *midjis*, OE *midd* "mid" = Lat. *medius*.

The most far-reaching of these assimilations in the Germanic languages took place in the early period of the individual dialects, and is generally known by the term **umlaut**, or **mutation**. As we have noted in the first section of this chapter, Pre-Old English short and long *a o u* standing before *y* or short or long *i* of the following syllable became fronted; *a* > *e*; *o* > *ø*, later *e*; *u* > *y*, later *i*.

Goth. *satjan* = OE *settan* "set"
PGmc *dōmjan* "judge" > OE *døman* > *dēman* > NE *deem*
PGmc *mūsiz* > OE *mӯs* > ME *mīs* > ME *mice*

Back assimilation occurred in Old Norse. Pre-ON *a* before *u* became *o* [ɔ], for example ON *lǫnd* "lands" from **landu*. Before *w* Pre-ON *a* > ɔ, *e* > *ø*, and *i* > *y*, as in ON *søkkua* "sink" < **sekkwa*, ON *lyng* "heather" < **lingwa*. Since the vowels are also rounded, the assimilation in these Old Norse forms involves **labialization**.

The assimilation in the Germanic languages may be related to a prominent accent on words, which made them into a unit so that one pattern of articulation affected the phonemes of an entire word. Besides assimilation, we also find losses of unstressed vowels, as we illustrate below.

By contrast, in Japanese each syllable is pronounced independently. There is no stress accent; all syllables end in a vowel or *ñ*. For as long as Japanese is attested, we find maintenance of vowels; words like *Kojiki*, the name of a literary work completed in AD 712, are pronounced much the same way as they were over a millennium ago. (Syllable-initial consonants were assimilated to following vowels, however, as we shall note in 13.7.) But in Proto-Germanic, which had a syllable structure not unlike that of Japanese before effects of the initial stress accent were brought about, words came to be greatly modified. We may illustrate some of the modifications by means of the Gallehus inscription, dated about AD 325, and subsequent developments of the words it contains:

Ek HlewagastiR HoltijaR   horna tawido

Its syllabic structure, consisting primarily of open syllables, was inherited from Proto-Indo-European, which like Japanese had a pitch accent. But as we know from the effects of Verner's law, Proto-Germanic introduced a strong stress accent on the first syllable of words. This strong stress led to the loss of vowels in weakly stressed syllables. By Old English times the inscription would have read:

*Ic Hleogiest Hylte   horn tēode

Subsequently, other weakly stresed vowels were lost, leading to the monosyllabic structure of native English words. *I*, *guest*, *Holt*, and *horn* may be related directly to the Proto-Germanic words exemplified in the inscription. Moreover, with *hlewa-* "famous" we may compare the adjective *loud*; and *tawido*, the noun *tool*. As these examples illustrate, English has been modified in a specific direction at least in part because of its type of accentuation.

10.9 EFFECTS OF PHONOLOGICAL CHANGES AT OTHER LEVELS OF A LANGUAGE

The phonological changes in English that we have pointed out led to loss of morphological markers, and also affected the syntactic patterns of English. The final syllables of Proto-Germanic indicated syntactic relationships; *horna*, for example, could have been interpreted only as an accusative or nominative singular. Since *HlewagastiR* could only be a nominative, the subject of the inscription was identifiable from the morphological markers, as was the object. After the morphological markers were lost, word order came to distinguish syntactic categories, such as subject and predicate. The phonological changes accordingly led to morphological and syntactic changes.

Moreover, numerous function words have been introduced into English, such as articles and prepositions, leading to a considerably different language from Proto-Germanic. For example, on the loss of the dative ending English indicates the indirect object either with a preposition, or by order, as in *She gave the book to the girl*, *She gave the girl the book*. The differences can be related to phonological changes, many of which in turn we ascribe to one phonological innovation: the introduction of a strong initial stress accent.

While we account for many changes in the Germanic languages by the strong initial stress accent, we do not have adequate information about Germanic in the period before our era to determine the reason for its introduction. That is to say, we cannot account for the sound change by which a stress accent was introduced. Some linguists have proposed that Proto-Germanic adopted the initial stress accent from speakers of adjacent languages whom we cannot identify. In support of this explanation, we can point to a strong stress accent in Celtic as well, which also led to loss of unaccented vowels. Other linguists assume that the accent was developed within the language, without outside influences. We cannot provide an answer to these conflicting views. Possibly a combination of reasons led to the introduction of the change.

In determining the causes of sound change, we will do best to deal with less remote changes than those of Proto-Germanic, such as the change of NE -*t*- to -*d*-. By documenting fully other such changes, as Gauchat and Hermann did in Switzerland, and as Sommerfelt set out to do in Ireland and Wales, we may come to understand how sound change is introduced as well as how changes are extended. Linguists who have concerned themselves with sound change – for example, Sommerfelt, Weinreich, Labov and Herzog – have pointed out the importance of relating linguistic and social phenomena. With our present knowledge of sound change, based largely on that in Indo-European dialects, we can make assured statements about its processes and patterns; about its direction or causes we can only propose hypotheses. Further study is essential to provide information in these spheres comparable to that gathered over the past century and a half on the processes and patterns of sound change.

SELECTED FURTHER READINGS

Sound change is one of the most widely discussed phenomena in historical linguistics. Bloomfield (1933: chs 20–2, pp. 346–403) provides many examples and full discussion; on pp. 329–31 he interprets the data described by Kloeke (1927) concerning the words for "house" and "mouse" in the Dutch–Flemish area, with a map on p. 328. Of the many collections that deal with sound change, we may point to Polomé (1990) and Fisiak (1978).

Specific applications of the findings from work on sound change may be found in standard handbooks such as Schwyzer (1939–53), in which theory is also discussed at some length, or in the various grammars of Antoine Meillet. Further information on sound change may be found in articles, such as Sapir (1938: 248–78). For the history of English, the fullest treatment of historical phonology is given by Luick (1914–40).

Since it is useful to observe as fully as possible the course of a sound change, reports on the voicing of intervocalic *t* in American English are of considerable interest. A phonetician's description of such *t* is provided by Heffner (1949: 129–30).

For additional control over the procedures necessary to understand change in language, and to employ such understanding in historical grammar, students should master Hoenigswald (1960). This also sets out to provide terminology for historical linguistics. The article by Weinreich, Labov and Herzog (1968: 95–195) is important for building on the achievements of nineteenth-century linguistics and for discussing, on the basis of rich data, the problems involved in proposing a theory of language change. Students who wish to deal further with these problems should study the article. For a follow-up see Lehmann and Malkiel (1982), in which Labov supplements the earlier article (pp. 19–91).

PROBLEMS

1 The Proto-Germanic vowel system consisted of four short and four long vowels, generally represented as:

i	u	iː	uː
e	a	æː	oː

Old English examples of the reflexes of these, with a cognate from another Germanic dialect, are as follows:

> *biddan*, Goth. *bidjan* "ask"   *budon*, Goth. *budum* "offered"
> *beran*, ON *bera* "bear"   *fæder*, Goth. *fadar* "father"
> *swīn*, ON *suīn* "swine"   *sūr*, ON *sūrr* "sour"
> *sǣd*, Goth. *-sēþs* "seed"   *blōma*, Goth. *blōma* "flower"

(a) Point out the modifications that have been introduced in Old English.

(b) Proto-Germanic also had the diphthongs *ai au eu* as in:

> *eu cēosan*, Goth. *kiusan* "choose"
> *ai stān*, Goth. *stains* "stone"   *au ēage*, Goth. *augo* "eye"

OE *ēo* and *ēa* are interpreted as having a centralized offglide. Indicate the type of change in the diphthongs. How may the development of Proto-Germanic *ai* have affected that of *a* and *ō* in Old English?

(c) Before *h*, /*n*/[ŋ] was lost in Proto-Germanic, with an effect on the preceding vowel, as in:

> *þōhte*, Goth. *þāhta* "thought"   PIE *aŋh*
> *þūhte*, Goth. *þūhta* "seemed"   PIE *uŋh*
> *þēon*, Goth. *þeihan* "thrive"   PIE *iŋh*

What was the type of the sound change?
How did the change to *ā* affect the long-vowel system?
Suggest a reason for the further change of *ã* to *ō* in Old English. Short *a* before nasal became *o*, as in *lond* "land." Compare the raising of [ɛ] to [i] in southern American speech, as in words like *pen*. *n* was also lost before *s* and *f*, in Frisian as well as English, as in:

> OE *gōs*, OHG *gans* "goose"
> OE *ūs*, Goth. *uns* "us"

(d) In Old English we find the additional vowels given below with cognates in other dialects:

> *fyllan*, OHG *fulljan* "fill"   *brȳd*, Goth. brūþ-*i*- "bride"
> *oksan*, Pre-OE **ohsin* "oxen"   *sǣcan* > *sēcan*, Goth. *sōkjan*
>   "seek"

What is the process involved in the change?
Moreover, *ēa* before *i* and *j* became *īe*, as in *hīeran*, cf. Goth. *hausjan* "hear." Sketch the Old English vowel system after these changes.

2   (a) In German the diphthongs *ai* and *au* were treated differently from their development in Old English, as given in 1(b) above.

> PMmc *ai* > *ei* as in OHG *stein*, cf. Goth. *stains*
> PGmc *au* > *ou* as in OHG *ouga*, cf. Goth. *augo*

Discuss the shift, including its direction and its contrast with that in Old English.

(b) PGmc *eu* became *iu* before *i j* of the following syllable, as in OHG *fliugis* "thou fliest." Discuss the direction of this shift. The shift to *iu* occurred only in the second and third person singular; *iu* later became *eu*, and was maintained in poetic works until the New High German period, as in the line: *was da fleugt und kreucht* "what flies and creeps." Today the vocalic element of the other persons is used, for example *fliegt, kriecht*. Account for the substitution.

(c) The twofold shift led to different development of the same base, such as PIE **teuto-* "people"; this yielded the adjective **þiuðiska-*, NHG *deutsch* [døyč] and *þeoða-(ríks)* "king of the people" > the name *Dietrich*. Indicate the changes of the diphthong from Proto-Indo-European to Modern German. What would be the Modern German equivalent of OE *cēosan* "choose"?

3 (a) In Latin the Proto-Indo-European vowels generally remained unchanged, as illustrated below; but the diphthongs were modified, as illustrated below with a cognate from another dialect.

> *quid* "what," Skt *cid* *iugum*, Goth. *juk* "yoke"
> *est*, Gk. *estí* "is" *domus*, Gk. *dómos* "house"
> *ager*, Gk *akrs* "(acre,) field"
> *vīvus*, Skt *jīvas* "alive" *mūs*, OE *mūs* "mouse"
> *sēmen*, OE *sǣd* "seed" *dōnum*, Gk. *dōron* "gift"
> *māter*, Dor. Gk *mā́ter* "mother"

> *dīcō* "say", Goth. *ga-teihan* "announce" *ūnus*, Gk *oínē* "ace"
> *laevus* [layvus] "left," Gk *laiós*
> *lūx* "light," Gk *leukós*
> *augeō*, Gk *aúksō* "increase"

Discuss the shifts in the diphthongs, including their direction.

(b) In the neighborhood of *w*, PIE *e* was changed as illustrated in the following words:

> *novus*, early Gk. *néwos* "new"
> *somnus*, PIE **swepnos* "sleep"

Discuss the change of *e* with reference to the changes in the diphthongs.

(c) We find an alternation in Latin between *e* and *o*, as in *velim* "I would wish," *volō* "I will." Determine the earlier vowel of the root, and explain its change.

(d) Early Greek *elaíwa* is borrowed into Latin as *olīva* "olive." Account for the change of *e* to *o*.

4 One of the most dramatic set of changes reported is that of PIE **dw-* to Arm. *erk-*, as pointed out by Meillet, for example PIE **dwō* "two," Lat.

duo, Arm. *erku*. In explaining the change, Meillet posits the following steps (1925 (1967):18, 46–7).

(a) Like Germanic, Armenian shifted PIE *b d g* to *p t k*. Greek *twe* "you" corresponds to Arm. *k'o* "of you." Assimilation is also involved here. Discuss the change in place of articulation of the dental in **dwo*. Then account for the shift of the reflex of PIE **d* to Armenian *k*.

(b) *r* was introduced before *k*, reflecting the original voiced stop. Initial *r* does not occur in Armenian (nor in Greek); accordingly, an initial vowel *e-* is prefixed.

   Account similarly for the shift in PIE **dwei-* "fear" to Arm. *erkiwł* "fear" and in PIE **dwāro-* "long" to Arm. *erkar* "long."

5 (a) The past participle of Lat. *scrībō* is *scriptus*. What type of sporadic change has taken place? In Italian it is *scritto*; identify the change of distinctive features in both forms.

(b) The infinitive of Lat. *ferō* "bear" is *ferre* from **ferse*. Identify the type of shift and the distinctive features involved.

(c) Lat. *quīnque* "five" is from PIE **penkwe*. Identify the change. In Vulgar Latin it became *cinque*, thereupon Fr. *cinq*. Identify the type of change.

(d) Lat. *peregrīnus* "pilgrim" became late Lat. *pelegrīnus*, from which *pilgrim* was borrowed. Identify the types of change. (Final *n* was changed to *m* in a number of words, e.g. *vellum*.) A doublet is *peregrine*, as used of falcons, on the grounds that they are foreign; account for the unchanged form.

(e) Lat. *marmor* became Fr. *marbre*, from which ME *marbre* was borrowed, leading to our word *marble*. Describe the changes and identify the processes.

(f) Lat. *formaticum* became Fr. *fromage* "cheese." Describe the changes and identify the processes.

(g) The genitive of Gk *ánēr* "man" is *andrós* from **anros*. Describe the change and identify the process.

(h) OE *þunor* has become NE *thunder*, cf. Germ. *Donner*. Identify the type of change.

(i) Late Lat. *īdōlolatria* "idol-worship" became *īdolatria*, from which our word *idolatry* has come. Identify the type of change.

(j) A common pronunciation of *frustrated* is *flustrated*. Account for the change.

11 Morphological change

11.1 BASES FOR MORPHOLOGICAL CHANGE

Because the elements of the morphological system have meaning as well as form, the system is more tightly structured than is the phonological, in which the elements only have form, not meaning. As a result, the elements within the morphological system, especially those in inflectional paradigms, tend to influence one another. That influence, referred to as **analogy**, is one of the two principal bases for morphological change.

To exemplify the close interrelationships in paradigms, we may examine the first three persons singular of the indicative present of verbs in Indo-European languages. These forms of the Proto-Indo-European root *bher-* are as follows in Sanskrit:

bhárāmi "I bear"
bhárasi "thou bearest"
bhárati "he/she/it bears"

Each form consists of three elements: the Sanskrit root *bhar-*; the thematic vowel; the endings *-mi -si -ti*. The forms are highly symmetrical, except for the long middle vowel in the first person. In other respects they exhibit a close fit between meaning and form. The root *bhar-* with the following vowel conveys the lexical meaning "bear"; the three elements *-m-*, *-s-*, *-t-* convey grammatical meaning of person, and the *-i* serves to indicate present tense.

When we compare the forms of the same root in Greek, we find:

phéro "I bear"
phéreis "thou bearest"
phérei "he/she/it bears"

The endings differ remarkably from those of Sanskrit. For the first person we may also note Lat. *ferō*. On the basis of its equivalence to the Greek form, we reconstruct Proto-Indo-European *bherō*. Skt *bhárāmi* then requires explanation. We account for the *-mi* as an addition by spread from the athematic conjugation, which had this ending; it still survives as a residue in Eng. *am*. The change from the Sanskrit ending in *bhárā* (which is found still in some subjunctive forms) to that in *bhárāmi* is readily accounted for by efforts of the speakers to achieve parallelism between the three singular forms, that is, by analogy.

In the second person, phonological change disrupted the parallelism in Greek. While explanations of the ending differ in detail among specialists, a disruption was caused by the loss of intervocalic *-s-* in Greek, yielding **phérei* from PIE **bhéresi*. This form was then influenced by the second singular secondary ending *-s*, as in the imperfect *épheres*. Accordingly, we account for the Greek second singular through the other major basis of morphological change, that is sound change, followed by analogy. As the neogrammarians indicated, sound change operates regularly; all intervocalic *-s-* were lost in Greek. But the resulting form seemed out of keeping with the paradigm. As a result, final *-s* was added by analogy.

The third-person form in Greek is even more problematic. It cannot be derived from PIE **bhéreti*, for that would have given Dor. Gk **phereti*, Att. **bheresi*. The form is explained as based on the second-singular *phéreis* by analogy with the imperfect endings, second-singular *épheres*, third-singular *éphere*, in which *-s* distinguished the second-singular form from the third.

The Greek paradigm, then, shows evidence of both analogical and phonological change.

When we examine the Gothic forms, we find evidence of only phonological change:

> *baira* "I bear"
> *bairis* "thou bearest"
> *bairiþ* "he/she/it bears"

The Gothic root is pronounced [ber]. Final long *ō* in the first person regularly became *a*; final short vowels were dropped in Germanic, as here in the second- and third-singular; and in Goth. *-e-* shows up as *-i-* except before *r* and *h* (*hʷ*). Of the three sets of forms, only that in Gothic was unmodified analogically. But it is the set that is most affected by sound change. As we noted in chapter 10, vowels of unstressed syllables were weakened or lost in Germanic because of the strong initial stress.

The three sets of forms exemplify the two principal bases for morphological change in their interaction. Means for determining their effects in a given language can best be acquired by examining the bases of morphological change in a number of paradigms that have been accounted for through extensive study. We will review such paradigms in the following sections.

11.2 MORPHOLOGICAL CHANGES IN INFLECTIONALLY DISTINCT SELECTION CLASSES; THE OLD ENGLISH STRONG VERBS

The history of the strong or irregular verbs in English furnishes us with excellent examples of change in selection classes. The Old English strong verbs are generally divided into seven classes in accordance with internal vocalic variation resulting from Proto-Indo-European ablaut. To summarize the possible forms, principal parts are given: (I) the infinitive, (II) the first and third singular preterite indicative, (III) the preterite indicative plural, (IV) the preterite participle. The classes are illustrated with one example for each:

	I		II	III	IV
1	drīfan	"drive"	drāf	drifon	drifen
2	cēosan	"choose"	cēas	curon	coren
3	findan	"find"	fand	fundon	funden
4	beran	"bear"	bær	bǣron	boren
5	sprecan	"speak"	spræc	sprǣcon	sprecen
6	standan	"stand"	stōd	stōdon	standen
7	feallan	"fall"	fēoll	fēollon	feallen

In addition to these strong verbs, there was in Old English a large number of weak or regular verbs, which continued to expand; for almost every new verb was inflected weak. Weak verbs had fewer differing forms than did the strong verbs, as exemplified by three principal parts. Moreover, the only difference between the preterite singular and preterite plural consisted in the endings, as for:

lufian	"love"	lufode	lufodon	lufod

In this situation, with the largest number of verbs having relatively few forms while a small number of verbs had many more, there was reduction of the strong-verb set, especially in the preterite.

The source of the preterite vowel in Modern English strong verbs, whether from the singular or plural, varied from verb to verb. In "drive" the vowel of the preterite singular was generalized throughout the preterite, to NE *drive, drove, driven*. In "bite," however, also of class I, the vowel of the plural was generalized, to NE *bite, bit, bitten*; similarly in "find."

Observing the development of all strong verbs in English, and the basis of selecting either singular or plural vowels in the preterite – or taking over the vowel of the past participle, as in *bear, bore, borne* – would require considerable exposition. Here we are primarily concerned to demonstrate the analogical reduction of forms, on the pattern of weak verbs such as *love, loved, loved*. The general principle of remodeling the strong-verb system is an attempt to distinguish between the stem for the present and that for the preterite, in accordance with the distinction between present and preterite in weak verbs, such as *love*, on the one hand, and *loved*, *loved*, on the other.

In the process some of the verbs were greatly modified. In *choose*, the vowel of the preterite participle was generalized to the preterite, with [č] and [z], the consonants of the present and preterite singular, generalized throughout, so that the *-r-* was replaced. In *speak* the pattern of class IV was adopted. In *stand*, the vowel of the preterite was generalized to the preterite participle. In *fall* we find regular developments of the Old English forms, no new remodeled forms.

The history of the principal parts of the English strong verbs then illustrates thoroughgoing remodeling or regularization. When, as in *drāf*, *drifon*, or *cēas*, *curon*, the differences in a set are regularized, we speak of **leveling**.

11.3 REMODELING IN THE INFLECTED FORMS OF STRONG VERBS

The inflectional endings of the Old English strong verbs also underwent various modifications as a result of sound change and analogy. We may examine these in two of the major dialects, West Saxon and Northumbrian. The present indicative endings in West Saxon with their older forms are as follows:

> *Present indicative*
> 1 sg. *-e*   <   Pre-OE *-a* < *-ū*
> 2 sg. *-(e)st*   <   Pre-OE *-isi* (with addition of *-t*)
> 3 sg. *-(e)ð*   <   Pre-OE *-iþi*
>   pl. *-að*   <   Pre-OE *-anþi*

Since *-i* following *-e-* of the stem syllable occasioned change of *-e-* to *-i-*, the forms of *beran* in West Saxon were as follows; the Northumbrian forms are also given, to illustrate a paradigm with fewer changes.

> | | | | *Northumbrian* |
> |---|-----|------------|----------------|
> | 1 | sg. | *bere* | *bero* |
> | 2 | sg. | *bir(e)st* | *beres* |
> | 3 | sg. | *bir(e)ð* | *bereð, -es* |
> | | pl. | *berað* | *beorað* |

The Pre-Old English sound change of *e* to *i* before *i* had taken place regularly. After the change the stem *bere*, *birest*, etc. contained two vowels, in contrast with other verbs that had no such alternation, such as *findan* and *drīfan*. As we know from the forms today, the *e* was extended throughout the present of *bear*, and the difference in vowels was leveled out.

In other ways as well, the verbs in English have become regularized, so that today they have a maximum of five forms. Similar examples of regularization could be provided from other languages with sets of paradigms.

In the course of leveling, extension may be made from inflected or derived, rather than from base forms. These are known as **back formations**. In Old English the verbs *flēon* "flee" and *flēogan* "fly" were inflected alike in all forms but the infinitive. As in *birest*, *bireð*, the vowels in the second- and third-singular forms underwent modification, and the present indicative was as follows:

1 sg. *flēo*
2 sg. *flīehst*
3 sg. *flīehð*
   pl. *flēoþ*

The first person singular and the plural, with vowels the same as that of *flēon*, developed into NE *flee*. This should have the following alternation: *I flee, thou fliest, he flies*. Instead, a new infinitive, *fly*, was produced. In *flee*, the base allomorph was extended throughout the present; in *fly*, an inflected allomorph was generalized throughout the present, as a back formation.

We may cite further instances of back formations from nouns. When in Middle English, -*s* came to be the general plural marker, the singular : plural contrast was based on presence and absence of *s*, on the pattern:

ME sg. *fader* "father" *fō* "foe"
    pl. *faders* *fōs*

Some nouns that ended in *s* were interpreted as plurals, and a new singular was produced, for example *pes* "pease" from the Lat. sg. *pisum*; the new singular is now commonly used, though the old has survived in the nursery rhyme "Pease porridge hot". Similarly *buriels* < *byrgels* "tomb" was assumed to be plural, and a new singular was produced, which, on the pattern of *funeral*, was spelled with *a*, *burial*. Other such singulars were made as back formations, such as *riddle* from ME *redels* < *rædels*, compare Germ. *Rätsel*, and *cherry* from ME *cheris* < OFr. *cherise*, later again borrowed as *cerise*. In these nouns the new singular forms rather than inflected forms resulted from analogy.

We may illustrate a further complexity of morphological change with WSax. *eom* "am." Like Goth. *im* "am," this form should have had an *i* in the stem, for it developed from PIE *ʔés-mi*, cf. Skt *ás-mi*. In Germanic, however, the copula came to be a composite verb, with forms from the root in *be* and that in *was*, as well as that in *is*. From the northern Old English forms such as *bīom*, *bēom*, we may assume that *eom* is a combination, with the consonant from the root **es-* and the vowel from the root of *be*; such combinations are called **blends** or **contaminations**. Morphological change can in this way lead to forms that have a complex origin, and also to new morphological markers.

11.4 MORPHOLOGICAL CHANGE AS A SOURCE OF NEW INFLECTIONAL MARKERS; GRAMMATICALIZATION

The development of blends, as well as back formations, demonstrates that new, unpredictable forms may be produced in a language by the changes that take place in morphological sets. In this way new suffixes and grammatical markers may result. Examples of new suffixes are English *-dom* and *-hood*. In Old English the words from which these arose were used to form compounds, for example *frēo* "free" + *dōm* "quality" > *frēodom* "freedom," *cynedom* "royalty"; similarly, *camp* "battle" + *hād* "state" > *camphad* "warfare," *werhad* "manhood," and so on. The second elements of the compounds then came to be treated as suffixes and distinguished from the free forms, *doom* and *hood*. In German, the cognates of these two elements also came to be suffixes, *-tum* and *-heit*; their distribution is often different from that of the English suffixes, as in *Freiheit* "freedom," but *Königtum* "kingdom."

Established as independent entities, suffixes come to have a development of their own. From forms like OE *æþeling* "nobleman," made from *æþele* "noble" and the suffix *-ing*, an erroneous division was made to produce a new suffix *-ling*. The process has been called **suffix clipping**. The new suffix was used to form further words, such as *darling*, cf. *dēor* "dear." Similarly, *-able* was taken as suffix in such forms as *habitable*, from Lat. *habitabilis*, and was then used in many new forms, such as *bearable*, *supportable*.

One such element that has enjoyed a wide development is *-burger*. In German, *-er* is commonly used to make adjectives from city names, such as *Berliner* "of Berlin," *Frankfurter* "of Frankfurt," *Wiener* "of Vienna"; these simply meant "of the city," and may have been used as family names, for example *Frankfurter*. Some of them were also used to characterize prepared meats, such as *frankfurter*, *wiener*, *hamburger*, a characteristic meat dish of Hamburg. By chance, the first syllable of *hamburger* coincided with the name of the meat "ham"; it was quite irrelevant that ham was never used in hamburgers. One can now buy *fishburgers*, *cheeseburgers* or even burgers labeled for their producer, such as *Mooreburgers*. Other suffixes produced similarly in recent English are *-teria*, from *cafeteria*, cf. *washeteria*, and *-ware*, from (*computer*) *hardware*, to *software*, and so on.

In the same way of improper clipping, inflectional markers have been produced in the process known as **grammaticalization**. One of the characteristic noun plural markers in German is *-er*, as in *Kind* "child," *Kinder* "children." Historically, it is a derivational suffix, used to form nouns, as in

Skt *ján-as*, Lat. *gen-us* "kind, race," from the root PIE **gen-* "beget." In Pre-Old High German, finals of words were lost in such a way that *-er* survived in the plural, in contrast with its loss in the singular, as in *kalb* "calf," : *kelbir*. It was then taken as a plural marker, and widely extended to many neuter nouns in which the suffix had never been added, such as *Haus* "house" : *Häuser*, and even to masculines, such as *Mann* "man" : *Männer*. We find a similar extension in Middle Dutch, virtually none in English, only *child* : *children*.

Only by chance do we have material to determine the source of the *-er* suffix. For *kalb* is the only *er*-plural in Old High German that can be connected with the Indo-European nouns in *-es-*. Moreover, the great extension of the *er*-plurals occurred in Old High German and Middle High German times, from which we have a fair number of texts. If inflectional markers were produced in this way at an earlier stage of the language, we can merely hypothesize their origin and extension.

Markers of the preterite and perfect in the early Indo-European dialects may have had their origin in this way, although various hypotheses have been proposed for their source. In Germanic we find a *-d-* marker for the preterite, as in Goth. *lagida*, OE *legde* "laid," and with voiceless dental in Goth. *brāhta*, OE *brōhte* "brought." A suffix *-d-* < PIE **-dh-* may have been clipped from stems, and may have come to be used to indicate the preterite tense. Similarly, the *-v-* of the Latin perfect, for example *amāvi* from *amō* "love," the *-k-* of the Greek perfect, for example *pepaídeuka* of *paideúō* "educate," and other preterite markers that we find in other dialects may have their origin in this way. In view of the absence of textual evidence at the time of their origin, our support of such a hypothesis on their development lies in general linguistic theory and the structure of the dialects after the splitting of Proto-Indo-European.

Possibly of greater amusement than significance in the development of languages are new formations that represent fanciful modification, such as Eng. *sirloin*. This is from Fr. *sur-loin*, in which the first element derives from Lat. *super* "upper," so that historically the word refers to the upper part of the loin. In English, however, *sur-*, which was not found in other widespread compounds, seemed aberrant and was modified to the apparently sensible *sirloin*, for the upper part of the loin is a noble piece of meat. Somewhat scornfully, this process has been referred to as **folk etymology**. As a further development, such etymologies may be followed by spurious histories. For example, I have been informed that there is a house in Lancashire which has been identified as the place where a ravenous King James I knighted the humble loin of beef. It does not, however, differ essentially from the process by which a contemporary English suffix *-burger* was formed, or an Old English suffix *-ling*, or an Old High German suffix *-er*. Like these, it illustrates how speakers manipulate language for their own purposes.

In folk etymology the sportive manipulation of language by individuals may be more evident than it is in less fanciful remodeling, as well as the approbation or disapprobation of fellow speakers; but what is essentially involved is the remodeling of less frequent and less favored patterns in the language in accordance with those more highly favored. When the cognate of Lat. *homo* came to be found in English only in the Old English compound *bryd-guma* "espoused man," cf. Germ. *Bräutigam*, it was modified after the more widespread though illogical *groom* to *bridegroom*. When *pentis*, from Fr. *appentis* < Latin *appendix*, was applied to an outgrowth of a large building, it was remodeled to *penthouse*.

Just as folk etymology shows the inventiveness of some language users in making analogical creations, it may illustrate the conservatism of others. The term *Welsh rabbit* for a cheese dish, like *Cape Cod turkey* for the plainest of piscatorial fare, shows an attempt by the ingenious to make simple food more palatable for the credulous. Their stolid fellow speakers may, however, object to this transparent outrage, and insist on *Welsh rarebit*, in much the same way that we today require inventive children to say *men* not *mans*, *better* not *gooder*, *went* not *goes*, and to banish *funner* entirely from their speech.

11.5 REASONS FOR ANALOGICAL CHANGE; INTERNAL INFLUENCES

In accounting for phonological change, we noted that it takes place in accordance with general modifications for which we have been able to provide no specific reasons. The reasons for changes in morphological markers, however, can often be ascribed to regularization of the forms in a morphological, syntactic or lexical set, as we may illustrate by means of NE *father*.

When we trace the history of NE *brother*, by successive steps we can take it back to PIE **bhrātēr*. Between the time of Proto-Indo-European and Modern English, the phonemes of **bhrātēr* have undergone various sound changes; by noting these, we can derive all the phonemes of NE *brother* from those of its Proto-Indo-European etymon. NE *father*, however, cannot be directly related to PIE and Pre-Gmc **patēr* in this way. For the Proto-Indo-European medial *t* became PGmc *þ*, which became *ð*, since the primary accent followed it; this in turn became OE *d*, so that the Old English form was *fæder*; the Middle English, *fader*. Without any further modification, the New English form should also have -*d*-. Yet such a modification did occur. Some time after 1400, [ð] was substituted for -*d*-, giving rise to NE *father*. We assume that the substitution was made partly because the word *father* was associated with the words *brother* and *mother*, and was remodeled after them. The substitution may have also been assisted by the medial, intervocalic position.

Similarly, we would be unable to derive the preterite participle *swelled* from a Proto-Germanic etymon, or even from an Old English form. The earlier preterite participle was *swollen*, which survives primarily as an adjective; *swelled* was made from *swell* on the pattern of such forms as:

fell	=	shell	=	swell
felled	=	shelled	=	x

Swelled, then, replaced the older *swollen*.

Modifications of this type illustrate the chief mode of change introduced in morphological and syntactic systems. By it the members of a morphological, syntactic or lexical set are increased or reduced in number, and the means involved in marking syntactic categories are extended. Since such changes are carried out on the pattern of those already present in the language, they are referred to as **analogical**.

Analogy is a process by which morphs, combinations of morphs, or linguistic patterns are modified, or new ones created, on the pattern of those present in a language.

We can observe analogy most clearly in the learning of language. Most of us have observed children learning forms such as the plural *cups* to *cup* and applying their discovery to other nouns, such as:

cat	=	fork	=	cap
cats	=	forks	=	caps

If then they see a *jet*, and learn the word, they make a plural, *jets*; if they see a specific toy in a toy store, they make a plural, *sputniks*.

We become especially conscious of such extensions if they produce forms that we consider incorrect. Just as children learn to make plurals, they make comparatives, as for:

new	=	old	=	good
newer	=	older	=	gooder

At this point we object, and supply the correct form *better*. If we find a further extension from,

That's new	=	That's fine	=	That's fun
That's newer	=	That's finer	=	That's funner

we may even remark on the child's cleverness after providing the correct form. At some time in the past, however, speakers of English were more tolerant of new comparatives, for the form *older* has replaced *elder* (except in restricted usages); *littler*, *littlest* have generally replaced *lesser* and *least* when adjectives, except in some contexts such as the bird name *least flycatcher*. In this way irregularities may be removed from grammatical sets. But by far the most important use we make of analogy in language learning is in extending forms and patterns that we have mastered.

If we learn a language like German, we do not memorize separately every inflected form. We learn a model such as,

singen	"sing"
ich singe	"I sing"
er singt	"he sings"

and we expect to apply it to *ringen* "wrestle," *bringen* "bring," and so on. We may assume that native speakers learned many forms of their language in much the same way. If on the pattern of the past *ich sang*, *ich rang*, we make a form *ich brang*, we are corrected. We may even be reminded of the cognate of *ich brachte* "I brought" to reinforce our acquisition of the irregular form. In this way we learn one of the limits of such analogical extension.

We acquire other linguistic patterns similarly. If we master the German syntactic patterns:

Wir gehen heute.	"We're going today."
Heute gehen wir.	"Today we're going."

we do not need to learn separately every sentence beginning with *heute* or other adverbs to gain control over this type of subject position. If we have under control the normal word order, *Wir reisen heute*, *Wir lesen morgen*, we have no difficulty saying on the basis of our mastery of the patterns:

Heute reisen wir.	"Today we're traveling."
Morgen lesen wir.	"Tomorrow we'll read."

In this way analogy is constantly applied when we use a language. As in foreign-language learning, there are limits to its application, some of which we may transgress to the consternation of fellow speakers, others to their mild amusement and still others to their admiring imitation. It is difficult to predict when analogical forms will be accepted, when not. We do, however, know some of the conditions under which analogy operates.

11.6 PREREQUISITES FOR THE OPERATION OF ANALOGY

For the operation of analogy, some linguistic set is necessary. The set may be inflectional, like the English verbs, in which the *t/d/əd* suffix has been replacing internal change, as it has done in *swelled*. The set may be derivational, such as the English nouns with *-er* suffix, such as *driver*; this suffix, imported from Lat. *-arius*, has come to be used after virtually any verb. The set may also be syntactic. A number of English verbs that formerly took an object in the genitive case were until quite recently followed by *of*-constructions, for example *miss, desire, remember, forget, hope, thirst, wait*. Sir Walter Scott wrote: *I remember of detesting the man.* By contrast, the common transitive pattern in English consists of a verb followed immediately by an object; this pattern accordingly was generalized and extended to the verbs cited.

Sets may also be semantic, such as the relationship terms, *brother*, *mother, father*. Among such sets are the numerals. In German ordinals, for example, *-te* is used from "two" to "nineteen," for example *der zweite, der neunzehnte*; after that *-ste* is used, for example *der zwanzigste*, until the millionth, where formerly *-te* was used; today *der millionste* is being used widely and promises to replace *millionte*. Numerous examples can be cited from the numerals in the various Indo-European dialects, as we have for English in chapter 1. The spread of Slav. *d-* to "nine," cf. Russ. *d'evyat'*, from "ten," cf. Russ. *d'esyat'*, is among the clearest.

Such sets are very infrequent at the phonological level. An example of analogy at the phonological level is the extension of *-r* before vowels in New England English. Since retroflection was lost before consonants but not before vowels, two forms of such words as *water* exist side by side: *watǝ was* . . ., but *water is* . . .; *watǝ wheels* . . ., but *water always* . . . Nouns with final *ǝ* fell into this pattern, such as *soda, idea*, so that speakers with this variation say: *the idea was* . . ., but *the idea-r is*.

A type of analogy limited to literate cultures is purely graphic. ME *rīm*, for example, came to be written *rhyme* because early Modern English writers thought it was connected with *rhythm*. ME *delite* < OFr. *deliter*, Lat. *dēlectāre* came to be written in Modern English as *delight* because it was considered to be related to *light*, cf. Germ. *Licht*. We are most familiar with this type of analogy from language learners – from errors of students and typesetters, or from our own struggles with English spelling. We may align *proceed* with *precede*, or vice versa; a part of our schooling is spent differentiating among *to, too, two, their, there* and like sets. With our contemporary regard for spelling, a great deal of social prestige is involved in producing the standard spelling; we accordingly resist analogical modifications in our spelling system and maintain the established patterns. Attitudes towards analogical modifications are accordingly of great importance for their acceptance.

11.7 CONDITIONS FOR THE OCCURRENCE AND ACCEPTANCE OF ANALOGICAL CHANGE

Essential problems of analogy that require further study include the conditions (1) under which it takes place and (2) by which new patterns get established. We cannot yet provide satisfactory answers. Some linguists have proposed that analogical change leads to simplification, and that such a development is to be expected when children acquire their language. Otto Jespersen reviewed the evidence for this assumption in his book, *Language* (1922: 161–88), and concluded that the question is complex. His own observations led him to ascribe some linguistic changes to "first learners," whether children or adults. But he did not ascribe a development towards simplicity to children's language, even though he believed that there has been a "tendency . . . [towards] progress, slow and fitful progress, but still progress towards greater and greater clearness, regularity, ease and pliancy" in language (*ibid*.: 441–2). We have mentioned above that children who learn Arabic master the highly complex broken plurals of nouns, and that children who learn Turkish have no difficulty with its intricate rules of vowel harmony.

These and many other examples contradict the view that simplification in language is to be ascribed to children, even though recent scholars have returned to this assumption. By contrast, as Jespersen reported at length, children generally abandon the simplifications they introduced, such as *goed* rather than *went*, *mans* rather than *men* and so on. Rather than unsubstantiated claims about the role of children in language change, further investigations need to be made. Weinreich, Labov and Herzog have attributed the transmission of new patterns to the "community as a whole," rather than to "the generational gap between parent and child" (1968: 187–8). The procedures for change they cite are even more intricate than are those considered by Jespersen.

To ascribe simplification to analogical change and to the influence of children as they acquire language is far too simplistic. This is not to deny the findings of Gauchat and others that the younger speakers in a community extend observed changes further than the older. The findings are to be expected, for changes that are not adopted by younger speakers are lost. But claims about the causes of change are far different from observations of their spread.

Kurylowicz (1960) attempted to suggest reasons for the introduction of analogy in morphological sets. He found these reasons in the relationship of forms in a paradigm. Those forms that are basic tend to influence others. For example, in verbal systems with a present tense category and a passive voice, the present active by his view dominates both the present passive and the perfect active; the perfect passive in turn is dominated by both the present passive and the perfect active. Kurylowicz calls the present the **founding** form; a derived form like the present passive he calls **founded**. A founded form might then be modified in accordance with the founding form, on the pattern of the following chart:

$$\begin{array}{ccc} \text{Present active} & \rightarrow & \text{Perfect active} \\ \downarrow & & \downarrow \\ \text{Present passive} & \rightarrow & \text{Perfect passive} \end{array}$$

If then the perfect active has a segment differing from that of the perfect passive, this segment may be introduced into the perfect passive.

Kurylowicz proposed this relationship in inflectional systems as the cause for a phenomenon in early Latin. There, as Karl Lachmann observed more than a century ago, the past participles of stems ending in -d- and -g- have lengthened vowels, with devoicing of the stop before the participial suffix -*tus*. Thus the past participle of *ăgō* is *āctus*, in contrast with the short vowel in *făctus* from *făciō*; similarly *lēctus* from *legō* "read," *ēsus* from

*ēssus from **ed-t-os*, based on *edō* "eat," and so on. The phenomenon is referred to as Lachmann's law; it had been widely, and ineffectually, discussed before Kurylowicz provided a definitive explanation, explicated further by Calvert Watkins.

The explanation may be illustrated as follows:

Present active *legit* → Perfect active *lēgit*

Present passive *legitur* → Perfect passive **lĕctus* > *lēctus*

By this explanation, original *ĕ* in the perfect passive participle was changed to *ē* by analogy. The change differs from the sound changes discussed in chapter 10 because of its motivation. Kurylowicz has definitely established that some phonological modifications can be brought about by analogy. The reasons for such modifications are the internal patterning in a language.

Kurylowicz finds many more examples of the effects of analogy in the spread of changes in morphological forms rather than in their introduction. For such extension of the results of earlier changes, he has proposed a series of rules. As the counterexamples cited with the rules illustrate, these rules do not permit us to predict when analogy may take place in a given language, nor to determine what its direction has been under poorly known situations in the past. The rules, however, provide explanations for some instances of analogical extension.

Kurylowicz's first rule states that a twofold morphological marker tends to replace one that is single. As example he gives the *-e* plural ending of German nouns, which in some nouns was also associated with umlaut of the stem vowel, for example *Gast* "guest" : *Gäste*. This twofold marking has been extended as in *Baum* "tree" : *Bäume*, replacing earlier *Baume*. Many further instances can be cited in which it does not apply; for example, the German weak verb *trennen, trennte, getrennt* "separate" has maintained a single marker in contrast with *rennen, rannte, gerannt* "run" and similar verbs.

By Kurylowicz's second rule, analogy proceeds from the base form to derived forms. While commonly true, as in *sputnik, sputniks*, changes such as *pease* to *pea* contravene this rule.

By the third rule, any construction consisting of a constant plus a variable is used as a pattern for an isolated entity with the same function. In this way constructions like *wrongly* from *wrong* were used as a pattern for remodeling endingless adverbs such as *slow* to *slowly*.

In the fourth rule, which deals with the results of analogy, Kurylowicz states that a new analogical form takes over the primary function of a contrast, while the replaced form is used for secondary functions. Thus *brothers* is used for the plural of *brother*, while the replaced *brethren* maintains a peripheral function; similarly, *older* versus *elder*, and so on. Yet again, contrary examples can be provided, such as analogical forms in the German article, that is *dessen*, that are used today in the relative pronoun, not in the article itself.

The two other rules proposed by Kurylowicz are of less interest here. A set of such general rules would be highly advantageous if they applied to prehistoric languages, such as Proto-Indo-European or Proto-Afro-Asiatic. Kurylowicz has indeed applied them in this way, especially to problems of Indo-European variation of vowels in ablaut and to accentual problems. Yet if the rules cannot be established in contemporary languages, their application to earlier periods may be unreliable. The problems that we find with the carefully designed rules of Kurylowicz illustrate that modifications of morphological rules are not as consistent as those occurring in sound change.

11.8 INTERPLAY OF CHANGES IN THE MORPHOLOGICAL AND PHONOLOGICAL COMPONENTS OF LANGUAGE, AND IN THE LEXICON

As illustrated above, analogy may be viewed as the central process in modifications introduced in morphological systems. The second process, sound change, may also bring about modifications, as through loss of morphological markers. Moreover, it may introduce irregularities in morphological systems that then are restructured in morphological and lexical sets.

As examples of sound changes leading to change in morphological systems we may cite instances from the Germanic languages, such as the Pre-Old English umlaut changes. When Pre-OE *u* and *o* became *y and ø* before *i i: y*, a new contrastive marker was possible between many singular and plural forms, for *i i:* y were found especially in plural endings. Yet in English this sound change affected the morphological system only to a minor extent, for we have few plurals of the type *man : men, goose : geese, mouse : mice*. In German, on the other hand, this sound change was widely extended to provide one of the prominent plural markers. In this way sound changes may contribute to the possibility of new morphological contrastive devices, which then may be extended by analogy.

Such a contrastive device has recently been made available by the loss of *-t* in some English final clusters. When *-t* is lost in *slept*, a new contrast *sleep : slep* yields new irregular verbs. This phonological change is too recent for its results in the morphological system to be predicted.

As a result of such changes five or more millennia ago, the material was provided for one of the characteristic features of Indo-European languages, ablaut (see section 8.4). It is generally assumed that the ablaut contrast between root structures of the shapes Ce(R)C- (consonant : *e* :

possible resonant : consonant) and C(R)C- resulted from a loss of vowel, which in turn was due to varying accentuation. This assumption is based on contrasts found in forms, such as those of PIE *derk-* "see." The Greek present first-singular form, with accent on the root, is *dérkomai* "I see". The Sanskrit past participle, however, with accent on the suffix, is *dr̥ṣṭás* "seen." The original situation has been obscured by many subsequent changes, so that in most forms it is opaque except to trained Indo-Europeanists. In the participle, the *r* became vocalic on loss of the *e*. The contrast with the Greek present form is, then, in accordance with the shapes given above.

The contrast has been maintained even more clearly in NE *nest* (originally a compound of the adverbial particle **ni-* and the root **sed-* "sit," in which the *e* was lost), as opposed to NE *sit*, a reflex of the Indo-European form with *e* vowel. The contrast has also been maintained between the present stem and the participle of many irregular verbs in English, such as *choose : chosen, bind : bound, steal : stolen*, even though subsequent changes have obscured it.

The original Indo-European sound change, which led to a loss of *e*, may have affected few forms originally. But, like the umlaut change in German, it came to be used as an inflectional marker; and the contrast was widely extended, especially in the Germanic system of irregular or strong verbs. The contrast came to be so well established that it was introduced into words borrowed into the Germanic languages three millennia after the sound change took place, as in the Old English verb borrowed from Latin: *scrīfan* "write (shrive)" : *scrifen* "written (shriven)."

Another major contrast in Indo-European ablaut, that between *e* and *o*, as reflected in Gk *dérkomai* "I see" : *dédorka* "I have seen," has also been explained on the basis of a sound change. While the explanation of this sound change is disputed, the standard reason given is shift of pitch accent from the base, with backing of the *e* vowel to *o*. Russian has a similar change, though with the *o*-vowel under accent, as in the name *Gorbachev* [garbəčóf]. The change to *o* also had a great affect in the morphology of the dialects. It is the basis of the contrast between the present and the past tense in English irregular verbs, for example *sing : sang, sit : sat*, and also for the contrast between simple and causative verbs, such as *sit : set, lie : lay*.

In this way many morphological modifications in languages are spread by analogy, though the innovations may be a result of phonological change, or also of some other process, such as borrowing, that has provided a useful characteristic marker for a set.

11.9 ANALOGY IN THE LEXICON

Similar analogical processes and results are found in the lexicon. In the scientific terminology of today, many entities have been widely spread, with a specific meaning. Thus, *-ide* is used for hundreds of names of chemical compounds, such as *chloride*, *fluoride*; it was apparently taken from the term *oxide*, which was borrowed from Fr. *oxyde*. The suffix *-ate* is found in many names of salts and esters formed from acids with names ending in *-ic*, for example, *nitrate* from *nitric acid* and so on. The suffix *-eme* has come to be used for entities in linguistics, from *phoneme* to *morpheme* to *grapheme* and others. Analogy in this way is useful in expanding and regularizing the derivational system of the greatly expanding vocabularies of contemporary languages as it has served to enlarge and regularize their inflectional and syntactic systems.

The source of the material used in analogy is irrelevant. Any segment of the language may be generalized, whether its origin is in sound change or borrowing, or whether it is simply a segment of the language, like English *-ware* of *hardware*, that has been extended in computer terminology. When new forms are made by analogy in a language, sets of some kind undergo expansion; the process leads to larger sets, and accordingly to greater regularity in the language.

SELECTED FURTHER READINGS

Like sound change, analogy is one of the subjects widely treated in handbooks. Bloomfield (1933: 404–24) and Paul (1920: 106–20) have well-chosen examples. The paper of Kurylowicz referred to, "La Nature des procès dits 'analogiques,' " is reprinted in his *Esquisses linguistiques* (1960). For a full explication of Kurylowicz's views on analogy as they apply to the Indo-European languages, see *The Inflectional Categories of Indo-European* (1964). Another extensive treatment of analogy, with many examples, is given by Mańczak (1958). For a work making extensive use of our understanding of analogy, see Szemerényi (1960).

Essays on morphological change are included in Fisiak (1980), as well as in Polomé (1990). The basic work on the topic is Anttila (1977).

Problems

1 As we have noted, the strong verbs in Germanic have four principal parts, from which all other forms may be made: the infinitive, the preterite singular, the preterite plural, the past participle. The individual forms in the dialects have been modified by sound change and analogy. Selected verbs are given below from Old Norse, with Gothic and Old English as parallels. Comparing the Old Norse forms especially with the Gothic, determine changes and their basis. You may also do so with the Old English forms. The forms given are taken from each of the first five strong-verb classes. (Goth. *q* = [kw]; as in Greek, *g* is written before velars to indicate the velar nasal.)

	Infinitive	Preterite singular	Preterite plural	Past participle	
ON	bīta	beit	bitom	bitenn	"bite"
Goth.	beitan	bait	bitom	bitenn	
OE	bītan	bāt	biton	biten	
ON	giōta	gaut	gutom	gutenn	"pour"
Goth.	giutan	gaut	gutum	gutans	
OE	gēotan	gēat	guton	goten	
ON	drekka	drakk	drukkom	drukkenn	"drink"
Goth.	drigkan	dragk	drugkom	drugkans	
OE	drincan	dranc	druncon	druncen	
ON	koma	kuam, kom	kōmom	komenn	"come"
Goth.	qiman	qam	qēmum	qumans	
OE	cuman	cōm, cwōm	cōmon	cumen	
ON	vesa, vera	vas, var	vǫrom	veret (nt.)	"be"
Goth.	wisan	was	wēsum	*wisans	
OE	wesan	wæs	wǣron	wesen	

2 As we have noted, the final endings in the Germanic dialects were gradually reduced. Examples are given below of singular forms of various stems in Old English and Gothic. Note the reductions in the Old English endings, and account for them. In applying analogical explanations, you may compare inflected forms in the different stem classes.

		Nom.	Acc.	Gen.	Dat.	
"wulf"	OE	wulf	wulf	wulfes	wulfe	o-stem
	Goth.	wulfs	wulf	wulfis	wulfa	
"gift"	OE	giefu	giefe	giefe	giefe	ā-stem
	Goth.	giba	giba	gibōs	gibai	
"son"	OE	sunu	sunu	suna	suna	u-stem
	Goth.	sunus	sunu	sunaus	sunau	
"brother"	OE	brōþor	brōþor	brōþor	brēþer	r-stem
	Goth.	brōþar	brōþar	brōþrs	brōþr	

3 The demonstrative pronoun "that" in Old English is based on the alternating so-/to- of Proto-Indo-European. Singular forms of Old High German as well are given for the masculine and neuter, which differ only

in the nominative and accusative, with Gothic forms included for comparison. Discuss changes in the Old English and the Old High German forms.

	Nom.	*Acc. (m.)*	*Gen.*	*Dat.*
OE	sē/þæt	þone	þæs	þæm
OHG	der/daz	den	des	demu
Goth.	sa/þata	þana	þis	þamma

12 Syntactic change

12.1 LONG DELAYED RECOGNITION OF SYNTACTIC STRUCTURE

The analysis of sentences discloses only with difficulty the structure of syntax. Unlike morphology, syntax cannot be analysed into regular paradigms. Further, syntactic sequences are more open to pragmatic variation than are those of morphology and phonology. For the purpose of phonological variety, we may select unusual forms and also unusual patterns of sound, as in producing rhymes or alliteration; but typically we choose unmarked patterns in both phonology and morphology for general conversation. Syntax, however, we modify readily, placing objects at the beginning of sentences, like this one, for emphasis of the displaced segment. As a result of the multiple possibilities in syntax, linguists long failed to recognize the basic structures of syntax. Instead, they described phrases, clauses and sentences, identifying their components and the categories to which they belong, as well as their uses. Variant patterns were treated in stylistics.

By contrast with such syntactic treatments, in 1844 Henri Weil published a remarkable monograph on the syntax of Latin. Listing its syntactic patterns, he compared them to the patterns of Turkish. That is to say, he recognized that Latin was verb-final, an OV language. This finding has now been firmly supported by the studies of Charles Elerick on the syntax of Cicero, Caesar and Livy. For example, the following sentence in the first book of Livy's history of Rome has OV order, and in addition a preposed relative construction *proelio victum*:

Alii proelio victum   Latinum pacem   cum Aenea, deinde
some battle   conquered L.   peace   with A.   then
affinitatem iunxisse tradunt
relationship made   they-report

"Some report that Latinus, who was conquered in battle, thereupon made peace with Aeneas and then an alliance of marriage."

In providing support for Weil's conclusions, Elerick not only shows that final position of the verb is statistically most frequent in the three authors whose language he analysed; he also provides rules for the alternative patterns.

Weil's monograph was cited, as by Delbrück, but his insight into the patterning of syntax was not recognized. Delbrück in turn determined the patterns of Vedic syntax, especially in his monograph on the *Śatapathabrāhmaṇa*. He recognized that the verb was final in the sentence, and also that Vedic had postpositions rather than prepositions; further, that adjectives preceded nouns. Moreover, he was greatly interested in intonation. He pointed out that verbs of finite clauses were unaccented when they stood finally, but those of non-finite clauses were accented; and he related this situation to the preposed position of non-finite clauses. Since non-finite clauses precede finite clauses in OV languages, Delbrück provided a great deal of evidence that OV was the "traditional order," as he put it, in the Indo-European languages.

We may illustrate the OV patterning of Vedic by some lines of the *Rigveda*.

Rigveda 1.12.7
yáḥ sǘriaṃ, yá uṣásaṃ   jajắna,
who sun   who dawn   created
yó apắṃ netắ – sá janāsa, Indraḥ.
who waters' guide   he men   Indra
"Indra, oh men, is the one who created the sun and the dawn, and who is guide of the waters."

This short Rigvedic passage exemplifies the following OV characteristics. The verb *jajắna* stands at the end of its clause. The relative clauses introduced by *ya-* precede their antecedent *sa*. The genitive *apắm* precedes its noun. Moreover, the first line exhibits gapping of the type expected in OV languages; the verb is deleted from the first clause, and is found only in the second. Like early Latin and Hittite, Vedic, then, provides a great deal of evidence for OV structure.

12.2 PROTO-INDO-EUROPEAN AS AN OV LANGUAGE, AS DEMONSTRATED BY THE COMPARATIVE METHOD

If we apply the principles of the comparative method to the syntactic patterns, identified in the early dialects, we conclude that Proto-Indo-European was an OV language. As we have observed in chapter 7, the comparative method is applied to abstract features, not to surface manifestations. In the phonological component it is applied to phonemes and to subclasses of phonemes, not to phones. Similarly, in syntax, the comparative method must be applied to abstract structures like the order of genitives with regard to their head nouns (GN), or the order of relative constructions to their antecedents (RelCl + Ant). Indo-Europeanists in the nineteenth century applied the method only to phonological and morphological patterns, and accordingly they did not reconstruct the syntactic patterns of the proto-language.

The findings of Weil and Delbrück did not lead to recognition of the structure of syntax, nor did the patterning of early texts like the *Rigveda*. When Brugmann wrote his work of 1925 on the simple sentence of Indo-European, he proceeded in his systematic fashion, describing sentences, clauses and phrases and the relationships between their elements. That is to say, his work dealt largely with morphological features that signal syntactic relationships

Numerous monographs on specific constructions were produced by other historical linguists, but the results were not co-ordinated. George Small, for example, published two monographs on comparative constructions in the early Germanic dialects; in these he showed that the texts included many examples like the following Old English one in *Elene* 565:

Hēo wǽron stearce   stāne heardran
"They were immovable, stronger than stone"

In this line the comparative follows the standard *stāne*; an Old Icelandic example shows the same construction with *konu* preceding the comparative:

Hón var hverri konu fríðari
"She was more beautiful than any other woman"

While Small's monographs were and remain important for their data, linguists did not recognize the interrelationships between specific syntactic patterns, and accordingly the findings were received as uncoordinated contributions.

12.3 GREENBERG'S SYNTACTIC UNIVERSALS

The structure of syntax became clear through an important article published by Joseph Greenberg in 1963. The article made two significant points. As one, it established relationships among syntactic patterns like the relationship between verbs and objects, adpositions and objects, comparatives and standards, labeling them **universals**. These three constructions, and more, some of which will be examined below, are characterized by **government**; if verbs precede objects, as in a VO language, so adpositions (prepositions) will precede nouns, and in comparison adjectives will precede standards when we are dealing with consistent languages. Moreover, if verbs follow the objects that they govern, as in OV languages, the other two constructions will be parallel.

Similarly, elements that modify nouns, like relative clauses, genitives and adjectives stand on the side of objects and other nouns, that is, opposite the verb. Examples have been given in section 5.4.

As a second significant point, Greenberg proposed **implicational univer-sals**. A consistent language with object–verb order would also have object–adposition order and so on. That is to say, if in texts examined for historical purposes postpositions rather than prepositions were found, the language concerned could be recognized as OV rather than VO.

Both points are significant for historical linguistics. Syntactic patterning is based on abstract rules made up of categories, much like the rules for the formation of cases or the sequence of phonological elements. As we noted in section 5.9, such syntactic rules can be treated by the comparative method or by the method of internal reconstruction, and the prior pattern can then be reconstructed. That is to say, a comparative pattern like *stāne heardran* "stone-from harder" = "harder than a stone" in Germanic, Vedic and Latin, provides the data for reconstructing earlier syntactic patterns much as do morphological patterns like the formation of the third-singular indicative active.

Moreover, if we find only characteristic OV patterns, like postpositions or comparatives with standards before adjectives, in a language for which we have few texts, we have grounds enough to conclude that the language is OV.

The universals identified by Greenberg then are highly important for historical linguistic purposes. They enable linguists to interpret the findings of earlier scholars, like Delbrück. They also provide means for reconstruction of syntax comparable to the phonological and morphological reconstruction that had long been carried out.

12.4 RE-EXAMINATION OF FINDINGS BY DELBRÜCK AND EARLY SYNTACTICIANS

As we noted in section 5.6, we now deal with syntax through the structures made up of syntactic universals. As in phonology, we propose a frame-work. The syntactic framework is not as tightly interrelated as is the paradigm of a noun or verb; but we assume that if a characteristic element of the framework, such as use of postpositions, is represented in a given language, that language can be identified as OV.

Yet we must also remember that languages are constantly changing. Changes are slower in syntax than in phonology and morphology. As a result, we commonly find residues of past constructions side by side with the current patterns. We find those residues in literature, and especially in poetry, which tends to follow traditional norms. If, as in Old English, the OV comparative constructions are maintained only in the older language, with gradual replacement by VO constructions, we assume that the language is shifting from OV to VO order. We have more evidence for such a shift in English, as we will see below. Here we may simply note that the other Germanic dialects also contain OV comparative constructions; accordingly, we reconstruct Proto-Germanic as an OV language. We find assurance for our reconstruction in the OV patterning of Vedic Sanskrit and Latin.

We also note the segments of the language that maintain older constructions. As in the lexicon, these are generally the common segments, such as the pronouns; for example, in Latin we find postpositional use of *cum* with pronouns, such as *mēcum* "with me," *sēcum* "with (him)self." Frozen forms like these in syntax are as important for historical reconstruction as are aberrant forms in morphology, for example the English strong verbs, or residues testifying to Verner's law like *was : were, lose : forlorn*.

We must also be aware of the ready modification of some characteristic patterns, such as descriptive adjectives. While literary writers would not modify the comparative pattern, and probably not the order of adpositions, they readily place adjectives after nouns, as in Longfellow's "This is the forest primeval." Because of the ready manipulation of adjectives, and other patterns, we determine basic word order by more fixed patterns, such as comparison, adpositions and the position of the relative clause.

Following such guidelines, we interpret the findings of Weil, Delbrück and others. In one of the many monographs based on a dissertation, Wende (1915) located the postpositions in Old English texts. His findings are in keeping with the statements above. The postpositions occur largely in traditional texts, *ac ðis . . . we willa her æfter areccean* (*Cura Pastoralis* 75.17) "but this we will relate hereafter." They become less and less frequent in the course of Old English writings. We interpret such findings as we have those of Small, as residues of OV patterning. Moreover, we find residues in English today in such adverbs as *herein*, *hereafter*, and the like. It is also useful to note that such residues are more common in archaic style, as in legal language. Even without the Old English texts, we could conclude from the current English forms that English was at one time an OV language.

In the same way, we examine the characteristic constructions in texts of the other dialects, such as the Homeric poems. In them we find comparatives of the OV pattern, as in the first book of the *Iliad*, line 249:

toû kaĩ apò glóssēs mélitos   glukíōn hréen audé
his ptc. from tongue honey-than sweeter flowed sound
"Speech sweeter than honey flowed from his tongue."

While the Homeric poems contain such OV comparative constructions, they also have VO constructions with particles such as "than." In interpreting these constructions, we must note that, like other epic verse, the Homeric poems contain much traditional material. Such passages may be identified by the OV patterns; but we must always be aware that poets may create pseudo-archaic expressions. None the less, the variety of comparative constructions indicates to us that Greek was shifting from OV to VO structure in the early part of the first millennium BC.

Residues of OV patterning in many of the Indo-European languages remain to be interpreted. Similar studies must now be done for other language families. It is clear, for example, that the books of the Old Testament show a progression of change. Unlike the Indo-European languages, however, the progression is from VSO structure to SVO. The change may be illustrated by citing relative constructions. VSO languages may have no relative particle, but may simply place finite verbs after their head. This is the construction in Genesis 1.1:

> bərésith   bārā? ?elohim . . .
> in (the) beginning created God
> "In the beginning when God created . . ."

Only the new translations, as well as the earlier Hebrew grammarians, recognize that the second and third words make up a relative clause modifying the first word. Accordingly, the older translations, like the King James version, are wrong. The translators were ignorant of VSO patterning, and treated the initial prepositional construction as an adverb with the following principal verb.

Proper interpretation of the type of language, and the types of universals found in it, as well as the other features as illustrated above, are then important for greater understanding of the historical background of individual languages. The constructions have often been described. But since the patterns of syntactic structure were unknown, the interpretation of the constructions is often erroneous, just as the syntactic patterns were unexplained.

12.5 PROCESSES IN THE SHIFT OF THE RELATIVE CLAUSE CONSTRUCTION

We may illustrate the change of some characteristic constructions for fuller understanding of the processes involved in syntactic change.

Hittite texts from the eighteenth to the twelfth centuries BC provide materials for understanding the shift from OV relative constructions towards the VO construction. Those materials are supplemented by early Latin texts, which still contain OV relative constructions. Before examining passages, we may note that many relative constructions serve to identify specifically, or to topicalize, the nouns they modify, as in *the girl who left is his sister*, or *that girl who left is his sister*.

It is also useful to mention that OV languages are more asyndetic than are SVO languages; clauses often seem strung together, without conjunctions. In this way, the earliest Hittite texts contain such parallel clauses, some of which we would treat as relative clauses if we produced them in English.

In Old Hittite, a particle was attached to nouns, topicalizing them much as relative clauses do, as in the following example taken from Justus (1975: 213–35):

kuis   sagais kisari   ta LUGALi . . . tarueni
which sign   appears it to-king   we report

We may translate the sentence: "We report to the king whichever sign appears." But in approximating the meaning of the sentence in English, the translation would be "We report the sign that appears to the king."

In a fuller version of the Old Hittite construction, the relative noun is given in both clauses:

gud-puhugarin ma kuedani UDti nu-za UTUSI   apedani UDti
ox-substitute   ptc on-which day ptc-ptc my-sungod on-that day
warapta
bathed
"The king (< sungod) bathed on the day on which they adorned the substitute-ox."

In both of these examples, the relative noun is topicalized by an element that later came to be used for a relative pronoun.

We may cite a similar example from the Latin Agrarian Laws of about 111 BC:

Quei ager publicus populi Rom. in terra Italia . . . fuit, de eo agro loco quem agrum locum populus ex publico in privatum commutavit, is ager locus . . . domneis privatus ita. . .
"Whatever public land of the Roman people there was in the country of Italy, from that land and place whatever land and place the people changed from public to private, that land and place shall be private for the owners."

The two initial early clauses beginning with *quei* and *quem* seem, on the one hand, to be preposed relative clauses, on the other hand, to be topicalized statements. The resumption of the relative noun by means of *de eo agro* recalls the Hittite example, indicating that the previous clause is taken as relative in this stage and style of Latin. At a later stage, and in the subsequent language, the sentence would be given as "the land that belonged to the people . . . shall be private for the owners."

As languages become VO in structure, relative clauses generally come to be placed after principal clauses. Moreover, the relative noun is not included in the relative clause, but only in the principal clause, as in the translation of the examples given above. The topicalizing pronominal element then becomes a relative marker, generally placed directly after the relative noun, as in "the land that." In this way the relative clause pattern may shift completely from an original OV structure to VO structure such as that we know in English.

We may still note that the relative marker may be omitted at this stage, much as it was in the earliest Hittite. Its omission in English is possible when the relative noun is object of the verb in the relative clause, as in *This is the book she brought*. In medieval German, the relative pronoun could also be omitted when the relative noun was subject of the relative clause, as in the Old High German sentence:

er sār   in   thō gisagēta thia sālida in   thō gaganta
he at-once them then told   the fortune them then had-befallen
"He at once told them the fortune that had then befallen them."

The construction is known as *apò koinoũ*, common to both clauses. It is found also in Middle High German, where the common element may be object to the verbs of the two clauses, as in:

Gâwân an den zīten
Gawain at   the   time
sach in der siule rīten
saw in the hall   ride
ein rīter   und ein frouwen
a   knight and a   lady
moht er dâ   beidiu schouwen
could he there both   see
"Then Gawain saw riding in the hall, a knight and a lady, (whom) he then could see both."

In the long period of shifting from the OV relative construction to the VO there are many further matters of interest. The data may be consulted in handbooks; they are not explained, however, and accordingly many syntactic problems remain to be more fully accounted for. Here we have only provided a few examples to illustrate how relative constructions of OV patterning were shifted to the relative construction we find in English and other Indo-European languages of today.

12.6 THE GRADUAL SHIFT OF OTHER CONSTRUCTIONS

If English were an OV language, genitives would be placed before the nouns they modify. This construction is found today only for animate nouns, unless we set out to provide playful examples. We say *Joe's legs were tired after the game*, but we hesitate to say *The table's legs are scratched* rather than *The legs of the table are scratched*. Finding the preposed genitive more frequent in the older period of the language, Fries (1940) investigated the construction as well as others.

In Old English texts of AD 900 52 per cent of genitives stood before nouns, as in the following phrase (*Ben. Rule* 95.14):

on ænium oþerum mynstres þingum
in any   other   minster's things
"in any other affairs of the minster"

But periphrastic genitives, that is, those made with prepositions, are found in only 0.5 per cent of the uses. By AD 1300 84.5 per cent of all genitives are periphrastic, as in the translation above and in current use. Fries concluded in his article that "in present-day standard English the pressure of position is such that all word groups tend to modify the word immediately preceding" (*ibid*. 206). But he did not relate his finding to general conclusions about language, as that the shift in position of the genitive is expected when a language changes from OV to VO structure. None the less, the essay is of great interest, also for indicating the length of time required for introduction of the VO pattern of the genitive into English.

It is also instructive to examine the development of the comparative pattern in English and the other Germanic languages. As we noted above, in the early period of these languages, the comparative could be simply placed after the dative, as in *stāne heardran*. VO languages, in contrast with OV, require particles between the adjective and its standard, as in our construction: *older than Jack*. As English was moving to VO structure, a number of particles were applied, some of which are still found in dialects. Among these is *as*, which corresponds to the comparative particle *als* of German; another is *nor*; another is *be*, a reflex of an old instrumental *by*. The VO structure required a particle, but allowed a number of possibilities. Only after some time was the particle *than* fixed in standard English; in German, on the other hand, the particle *dann* is dialectal in contrast with *als*.

12.7 THE SHIFT IN ORDER OF COMPLEMENTS

In OV languages complements, also known as object clauses, are preposed. In Japanese, for example, object clauses precede main clauses. These commonly end in nouns, such as *koto* "fact," which are objects of the principal verb, as in:

> fune no deta koto o   shiranai
> boat ptc. left fact ptc. not-know
> "He does not know that the boat has left."

Hittite preserves similar examples, though with participles, as in:

> ammuk-war-an akkantan *IQ.BI*
> me   ptc him dead   he stated
> "He stated to me that he was dead."

This construction is similar to that in Turkish: for example:

> onun gideceğini biliyorum
> his coming   I know
> "I know that he will come."

If a language comes to be VO in structure, such object clauses must stand after the verb. When placed there, they are generally introduced by a marker that indicates complementation.

The various Indo-European languages are highly interesting for the devices that were introduced to mark complements. In Sanskrit, *yád* "what" is a common initial marker; it corresponds to Homeric *hó*. In the course of time other markers were introduced, such as *hóte* in Greek. Moreover, the construction of the accusative with infinitive is also common, in Latin as well as Greek, for example *keleúō se apeltheîn* "I command you to go," Lat. *iter patefierī volēbat* "he wished the road to be opened."

These are the two major patterns for complementation in the Indo-European languages of VO structure. In examining their development in any language, details, like the verbs with which they are used, provide topics for further studies. Grammars of the past list the patterns and the complementizers; but they do not relate them to the structural changes in syntax.

The Germanic languages developed their own constructions, by some views with influence from Latin; yet the independent patterns in each of the languages suggest that the constructions are native. In Old English one of the common patterns is a clause introduced by *þæt*, as in:

bæd þæt he wære Cristen   gedon
bade that he were Christian made
"He asked that he be made a Christian."

Like the principal verb here, verbs meaning "request," "make known," "say," "promise" and "intend," are followed by *þæt* complements in Old English. On the other hand, verbs meaning "command," "wish," "begin," and "dare" are followed by infinitival complements, as in:

het   hine gan to þam cininge
commanded him go to the king
"He commanded him to go to the king."

Only later was the "*-ing*" construction introduced, by some assumptions on the basis of Celtic, as in *she intended driving the children to school, They began going slowly to the door*. Since this third complementation pattern is not found in the other Germanic languages, the proposed origin in Celtic, which has verbal nouns, is highly likely.

Old Icelandic developed a construction introduced by the particle *at*, comparable to OE *þæt*, and also used the infinitive with accusative construction. In Old High German the particle *huueo*, Germ. *wie* "how," was used as well as the *that*-construction and the accusative with infinitive construction. These two constructions are also found in Old Saxon. Except for the English *-ing* construction, the dialects are parallel in complementation types, suggesting that the patterns were being introduced into Proto-Germanic, to be fixed only in the individual dialects.

The dialects and even individual authors of the early period differ in their uses of the possible constructions, indicating that the patterns were still fluid. Moreover, the verbs with which either the *that*-construction or the accusative with infinitive were used often differ from those of Latin. We conclude, then, that complement structures were being devised for each of the Germanic languages, much as were comparative constructions with their particles.

The development is of primary interest here in indicating how complement clauses following verbs arose in one of the Indo-European languages. There were similar needs for the other types of clauses, such as conditional, result, purpose and so on. We find different markers for many such types of clauses, even between English and German, as in Eng. *if* versus Germ. *wenn*. Investigating the origin and development of these provides fascinating syntactic studies, for the Romance languages and the other branches of the Indo-European family as well as for Germanic.

12.8 SYNTACTIC CHANGE FROM ACTIVE TO ACCUSATIVE LANGUAGES

While the differences between the OV patterning of Hittite or Vedic Sanskrit and the VO patterning of later dialects may seem considerable, the syntactic changes between active and accusative structure are far more comprehensive. Such a shift took place between Pre-Indo-European and Proto-Indo-European. In examining the evidence for the change, we may recall some of the characteristics of active languages.

As we have noted in chapter 5, active languages differ from accusative and ergative languages in having clauses bound together by agreement rather than by government. Verbs and nouns fall into one of two classes, stative/inanimate or active/animate. Moreover, verbs are the central elements of sentences. In constructing sentences, an active noun is matched with an active verb, and a stative noun with a stative verb. Active languages have other pertinent characteristics; for example, the stative subsystem of the verb has relatively few forms. Nouns have few inflections. Interrelationships in clauses are indicated by a large number of particles.

Before relating these characteristics with those of Proto-Indo-European, we may recall some of the long-standing problems in its verb system. The present system contrasts with the perfect system in tense–aspect. The present system indicates ongoing action; the perfect system indicates a completed action, that is, a state. Moreover, in Sanskrit, Hittite and early Greek, there is a primary contrast in voice between the active and the middle; the middle often indicates a state, and is also used with reflexive meaning. The perfect and the middle have long been aligned with each other by Indo-Europeanists, though the basis for the alignment has been disputed.

Moreover, when we examine the forms in the early dialects, we find that there are few characteristic forms for the perfect and the middle; in building the paradigm, the remaining forms have been built on those of the present. In accounting for this situation, we remember that the stative inflection of active languages has few forms. In view of the correspondence in meaning of the stative with that of the Indo-European perfect and the middle, coupled with the morphological correspondences, we conclude that Pre-Indo-European was an active language.

The conclusion can be supported by additional data. Among these are sets of roots that are inflected only as actives or as middles. Among roots inflected only as actives are those meaning "bite," "blow," "eat," "give," "go"; among those inflected only as middles are "lie (be lying down)," "smile," "fear," "turn," "wish for." These meanings coincide with the meanings of active and stative verbs in active languages. Accordingly, the contrast between such roots may be interpreted as a residue from the earlier Pre-Indo-European active structure.

Moreover, we cannot reconstruct a verb "have" for Proto-Indo-European, let alone Pre-Indo-European. The Germanic verb "have" cannot be securely explained; it may be based on the verb found in Latin, *capiō* "seize, take"; if so, the *-p-* should have become *-f-* by Grimm's law. Because of the phonological and semantic difficulties, some Germanic scholars derive "have" from the same root as they do Lat. *habēō*, with influence from the root in *capiō*. Morover, a totally different root is used for the verb "have" in Gk *ékhein*. Further, a phrase made up of the verb "be" accompanied by a dative is used in Latin to indicate possession, as in *mihi est liber* "to me is book" = "I have a book." Since active languages lack a verb for "have," we account for the diversity of expression in the Indo-European dialects by the assumption that there was no verb for "have" in Pre-Indo-European; the individual dialects developed their own.

The early dialects include other residues of active inflection. We may also recall the lexical evidence provided by the presence of two words for "water" and "fire," as well as for verbs like "lie," "sit"; we have noted that one of these refers to the substance or action as active and animate, that is, the word for "water" attested in Sanskrit as *āp-* and that for "fire" in Latin as *ignis*, while the other refers to the substance or action as inactive or inanimate, that is, the words *water* and *fire* are reflexes of the inactive, inanimate nouns in Pre-Indo-European.

The presentation here may illustrate how, on the one hand, we can account for problems in Proto-Indo-European and the early dialects that have long been unexplained. They may also indicate the great changes that take place when an active language shifts to accusative or ergative structure.

12.9 EXPLANATIONS FOR SYNTACTIC CHANGES AND PROBLEMS IN RECONSTRUCTING EARLIER SYNTACTIC PATTERNS

In attempting to account for syntactic changes, we take our evidence from modifications that have been attested and from syntactic patterning. There is little question that syntactic change proceeds in accordance with the drift of a language. We have noted that when the Indo-European languages become VO in structure, the various constructions were modified to VO patterning, some like the English genitive construction over a long period of time. As objects were placed after verbs, so were object clauses, in our terminology, complements. Moreover, markers were developed to introduce complements. Some of these were taken from particles, such as forms of Proto-Indo-European *yo-*, or as in the Germanic languages, forms of *to-*.

Similarly, prepositions were introduced, many of them from previous postpositions. And comparative constructions in the VO pattern were developed, with particles selected to function as pivots between the adjective and the standard.

In addition, VO modifier constructions were introduced, as we have seen in reviewing the evidence in Hittite and Latin for relative clauses, and in English for genitive constructions.

In short, the characteristic VO patterns were gradually incorporated in the syntactic structure of the changing languages. Residues survived, as they do in morphology and the lexicon. But the shift is straightforward, so that we may assume similar shifts in other languages that undergo syntactic change. The change may be from other initial types; Hebrew shifted from a VSO language to one of SVO structure. The processes, however, are comparable.

Such observations do not provide us with information on the original cause of the change. Two such causes may be briefly sketched.

The first has to do with adoption of a language by non-native speakers. When large numbers of non-native speakers adopt a language, the language tends to be shifted to SVO structure. Apparently, the basis for the shift is ease in understanding. In both VSO and SOV languages the two frequent nominal constituents of sentences, subject and object, stand side by side. In SVO languages, by contrast, they are clearly separated by the verb. We may note that all widely used languages with more than 100 million speakers today have become SVO. A number of these are Indo-European: English, French, German, Italian, Portuguese, Russian, Spanish. Another example is Chinese, which apparently in an early stage was verb final. The last major language to change towards SVO structure is Arabic, which is increasingly assuming SVO characteristics. An apparent counterexample is Japanese; but it has not been adopted by large numbers of speakers outside Japan. The evidence of widely spoken languages, then, supports the hypothesis that they tend towards SVO structure. If the basic sentence pattern is changed, the remaining constructions gradually change as well, as we have observed above.

A second cause of syntactic change is comparable. Speakers of two or more languages tend to use the same syntax for the language or languages over which they have least control or which they use least. In a personal observation, I found that an individual speaker, a third-generation Fijian of Indian descent, claimed to know Tamil, Fijian and Hindi. When he produced Tamil sentences, however, they were halting and in VO, rather than OV, order. His Fijian was correctly VO. But of the three languages he spoke Hindi most accurately, with consistent OV order. When questioned about Tamil, he replied with some embarrassment that it had been his grandfather's language and that he now used it rarely. Yet it is quite remarkable that he spoke it with the VO order of Fijian rather than the OV order of Hindi, in which he was most at home. Such an example permits no general conclusions, inasmuch as too many variables may be involved; but it does suggest that the basic syntactic patterns of a language may be modified on the basis of patterns in other languages.

Such modifications have been proposed for a number of languages. Akkadian, for example, is OV, in contrast with the basic VO structure of Semitic languages. It was brought into an area occupied by speakers of the OV language Sumerian, and presumably was adopted by many speakers of Sumerian. In time, Sumerian became extinct. The influence it may have exerted on Akkadian, however, is our best explanation of the change in order of Akkadian. Similarly, the Semitic languages of Ethiopia have become OV, presumably also by influence of languages spoken in the area before the Semitic languages were introduced.

Such examples provide further support for the hypothesis that the Indo-European languages became VO in structure when they were introduced into the various regions in which we find them. By the time of Classical Greek, Classical Latin, and the earliest other western dialects, these languages were adopting VO order. The recently found Celtic inscriptions in Spain indicate that early Celtic, like Proto-Indo-European, had OV order; but in Britain the Celtic languages went on to develop VSO order, a change that has been attributed to indigenous speakers of VSO languages. Such explanations find support in the Indo-Aryan languages of today; for like the Dravidian languages, which are spoken by many bilingual speakers of Indo-Aryan languages, these are now consistently OV. Yet Classical Sanskrit was ambivalent in structure. The patterns of syntax are apparently less strongly regulated than are those in phonology and morphology, so that they are more likely to be modified under the influence of other languages.

SELECTED FURTHER READINGS

For essays on change in syntax see Polomé (1990) and Fisiak (1984). The 1844 monograph of Henri Weil has been reprinted in translation in the series Amsterdam Classics in Linguistics. Delbrück (1871–88), is still an important source of information.

PROBLEMS

1 In examining syntactic change, the study of texts from successive periods is illuminating. Translations of the Bible provide such texts, as in the following versions of Mark 1.13:

> *The King James version:* "And he was there in the wilderness forty days, tempted of Satan; and was with the wild beasts; and the angels ministered unto him."

> *Wyclif's translation, made about AD 1380:* "And he was in desert fourty days and fourty niȝtes, and was temptid of Sathanas, and was with beestis, and angelis mynstriden to him."

> *Old English:* "And hē on wēstenne wæs fēowertig daga and fēowertig nihta and hē wæs from Satane gecostnod, and hē mid wilddēorum wæs, and hym englas þēnodan."

Discuss differences between these texts in order, use of articles and other features.

One of our oldest Germanic texts is the Gallehus runic inscription on a horn of about AD 325: *Ek HlewagastiR HoltijaR   horna tawido* "I H. of Holt horn made" = "I HlewagastiR of Holt made the horn." Note the position of the verb, contrasting it with those in the previous texts.

2 (a) The longest early runic inscription is that found on the Tune stone in Norway; it is dated about AD 400, somewhat later than the Gallehus inscription. It is given below (spaces between words have been added here; the two letters in brackets have been supplied). Examine the syntax, noting any changes in syntax from that of the Gallehus inscription. Commentary on the inscription is voluminous. You may note that the compound in the first line recalls the etymology of "Lord" < *hlāf-weard* "loaf-warden." As a participial form of the root **weyd-* "see," the first element is comparable to that of the synthetic compounds discussed above. A capital *R* is the traditional transcription of the rune in question, but recent texts may substitute *z*.

> ek wiwaR after woduride witadahalaiban worahto
> I W.   for W   warden-of-bread worked
> meR woduride staina þrijoR dohtriR dalidun
> me   W.   stone three daughters prepared
> arbija   arjosteR arbijano
> inheritance most-noble of-heirs
> "I WiwaR for Wodurid, the lord, did the work.
> For me, Wodurid, three daughters prepared the stone,
> the most legitimate of heirs for the inheritance."

(b) The earliest Old Icelandic history was written by Ari, some 700 years after the Tune inscription. The excerpt here reports on the discovery of America (Vinland). Acute accents are used to indicate long vowels. Compare the syntax with that of the runic inscriptions, and that of current English.

Um várit	bjoggu		þeir	Hjalti	ok	Gizurr	skip	sítt	til	Íslandz;
in spring	prepared		they	H.	and	G.	ship	their	for	Island

margir menn löttu   þess Hjalta, en hann gaf sér ekki um   þat.
many men dissuaded this H.,   but he gave self not about that.

þat sumar fór Óláfr konungr ór   landi   suðr til Vindlandz.
That summer went O.   king   out-of country south to Wendland

þá sendi hann ok Leif Eríksson til Grœnlandz at boða
then sent he also L. E.   to Greenland to announce

þar trú; þá fann Leifr Vínland it góða; hann fann ok men
there faith then found L. V.   the good he   found also men

á skip-flaki í hafi, því   var hann kallaðr Leifr inn heppni
at shipwreck in harbor therefore was he   called   L.   the lucky

"In the spring Hjalti and Gizurr prepared their ship [to go] to Iceland; many men tried to dissuade Hjalti from this, but he disregarded it. That summer King Olaf went out of the country south to Wendland. Then he also sent Leif Eiriksson to Greenland to proclaim the faith there; then Leif discovered Vinland the good; he also found men on a shipwreck in the harbor; for that reason he was called Leif the lucky."

(c) Charms have been preserved in the Germanic dialects, and in other dialects as well. The following is an example from Old High German. You may recall from Wagner's operas that Wotan had Valkyries to assist his favored warriors in battle. They are here referred to as *idisi*. Examine the syntax, comparing it with that of the runic period and with the Old Norse text, but also noting that word order may have been modified to achieve alliteration.

Eiris sazun idisi,   sazun hera duoder.
once sat Idisi   sat   here (and) there.
suma hapt heptidun,   suma heri lezidun.
some bonds prepared,   some armies harassed.
suma clubodun   umbi cuoniouuidi
some clubbed   around restraining-bonds
insprinc   haptbandun, invar vigandun.
spring-from bonds   escape enemies

3 The following are lines from an archaic Vedic hymn to Rudra, *Rigveda* 2.33. Identify OV characteristics.

Stanza 1
á   té, pitar Marutām, sumnám etu
ptc you father of-M. good-will may-it-come
mā́ naḥ sū́ryasya saṃdṛ́ṣo yuyothāḥ.
not us of-sun sight separate
"Father of Maruts, let your good will come to us;
Do not separate us from the sight of the sun."

While the following are not directly pertinent to the task, you may wish to note how, at this stage of the language, adverbial particles that go with the final verb are placed initially in the sentence. Then, in accordance with Wackernagel's law (see 14.6.1), they are followed by enclitics. Note also that vocatives, such as *pitar Marutām*, and verbs at the ends of clauses do not have accents, that is, they are pronounced with low pitch.

Stanza 5
hávīmabhir   hávate yó   havírbhir
with-invocations is-called who/that-one with-oblations
áva stómebhī   Rudarám diṣīya
ptc. songs-of-praise R.   I-would appease
"Rudra, who is called on with invocations,
I would like to appease with songs of praise."

13 Semantic change and changes in the lexicon

13.1 FRAMEWORKS FOR UNDERSTANDING SEMANTIC CHANGE

In the preceding chapters we have seen that an understanding and explanation of linguistic change depends on an adequate framework. Such a framework for sound change was provided in phonological study during the nineteenth century. The well-known rules describing sound change – Grimm's law, Verner's law and many others – were proposed when linguists increased their insights into the sound system of language and worked out a universal treatment of phonology. As information on speech sounds and the principles underlying the sound systems of various languages increased, improved formulations of phonological rules were provided. Subsequently, the formulations for specific changes have been improved and are still being improved. These improvements are based on an increasingly adequate framework for dealing with changes in the phonological component of language, the groundwork for which was provided in the nineteenth century and used subsequently in interpreting sound change.

Treatment of the syntactic component of language has undergone a similar development though more recently. Eduard Sievers and other linguists of the nineteenth and early twentieth centuries dealt with an underlying phonological structure. But only recently have linguists begun to deal with underlying structures in the syntactic component. The advances have been made possible by the framework of syntax that was initially proposed by Greenberg, as we have noted in the previous chapter.

In order to deal with semantic change, we need a similar framework. As in the study of phonology, morphology and syntax, we need to determine characteristic entities of semantic structures and the characteristic relationships among such entities. In the past many individual changes have been described in semantic study. For example, the Latin word for "maternal uncle" *avunculus* is a form derived from the Latin word for "maternal grandfather" *avus*. The derivation is quite clear, as is the development of Lat. *avunculus* to Fr. *oncle*; NE *uncle* has the same source, through borrowing from French. Although the external development of the Latin terms causes no problems, no explanation could be given for a semantic development that would lead to calling an "uncle" something like "little grandfather." An explanation has recently been provided from study of the systems in language referring to kinship. A variety of distinct systems has been determined. The system in which the mother's brother is associated with the grandfather is known as the Omaha kinship system. In a group of speakers with an Omaha kinship system one can expect to find the same or similar terms for mother's brother and for maternal grandfather. This expectation is parallel to the expectation we have observed in syntactic study of finding postpositions in a language of OV order, or of finding noun–adjective order in VO languages.

The expectation may not be fulfilled, as we have observed for English, with adjective-noun order in a VO language. If it is not, the language is in flux and we look for an explanation. Thus, the system of kinship terms in late Latin was changing to the system of terms we find in the Romance languages today, such as French, Italian, Portuguese and Spanish. Changes in the kinship system led to changes in the kinship terms. French *oncle* is not restricted to "maternal uncle," nor are the further terms Ital. *zio*, Span. *tío*, or Port. *tío*. The kinship system has changed, and with this change the kinship terms have a different meaning from the corresponding term in Latin. But during a period in the development of the Romance languages, the meanings of these terms must have been in flux, just as in late Old English. At that time the distinctive terms for "paternal uncle" OE *fædera*, and "maternal uncle," OE *ēam*, were yielding to a single term *uncle*.

This example of the change in meaning for the term *avunculus* may illustrate the procedures we follow in dealing with semantic change. We determine coherent sets of terms in language corresponding to conceptual sets; we then examine the position of individual items like *avunculus* in such a set. The term **field** was introduced for such sets by the German scholar Jost Trier, who carried out a widely influential semantic study by investigating the terms referring to the intellect in early German. As yet, no subclassifications of the "intellectual field" comparable to the subclassifications for kinship terms have been determined. None the less, it is useful in dealing with semantic change to focus one's study on a restricted set of terms, like those for the intellectual field, for colors, for kinship, for numerals and so on.

The observation of semantic changes in kinship systems points to a difference between the study of semantic change, on the one hand, and phonological and syntactic change, on the other. Semantic change may be intimately related to change in other social structures. For example, the shift in meaning of Lat. *penna* "feather" to "writing implement" is related to a change in cultural activities by which feathers came to be used as writing implements. As far as we have been able to determine, there is no such relationship between cultural changes and syntactic, morphological or phonological changes, even though some scholars have proposed such relationships. We may also note that not all semantic changes are related to cultural changes: for example, the restriction in meaning of the word *wife* from "woman," as still in Germ. *Weib*, to "female spouse" is unrelatable to any shift in the cultural status of women in English-speaking areas.

Nevertheless, many semantic features that are prominent in a language, and accordingly many semantic changes, are related to the physical situations of the speakers of a given language. This observation may be supported by semantic changes that are introduced when speakers move to different locations. Edward Sapir provided an excellent example when he demonstrated that the Navaho of the American southwest migrated to their present home from the Athapaskan territory in northern Canada (see Sapir 1963: 213–24). One of these examples is the Navaho verb for "seed lies": *-sàs*, from "underlying *zàs* or *yàs*," (*ibid.*: 216). For this word Sapir provided the etymology: Ath. **yàxs* "snow lying on the ground." The word maintained its meaning in the Athapaskan languages of the north but changed its meaning remarkably when Athapaskan speakers moved into a region with no snow. In somewhat the same way the words *robin*, (*mountain*) *lion*, and so on changed in meaning when English speakers brought these terms to America. The relationship between semantic change and other cultural change adds a complexity to the study of change in meaning that is not found in the study of change in phonological, morphological and syntactic systems.

It is hardly surprising, therefore, that general principles have not been determined for semantic change. Modifications in the means of indicating meaning are associated with modifications in the lexicon, and for these we can propose some general patterns, as will be apparent later in the chapter. But rules have only recently been proposed; they are restricted to small sets like kinship terms. Further such rules may be expected as the study of semantic change is pursued with the rigor applied to phonological, morphological and syntactic change.

To deal with the complexity of semantic change, three terms are used: (1) the **word**, or linguistic **symbol**; (2) the **referent** denoted by a word, whether concrete like "pen" or abstract like "thought"; (3) the **reference**, or notion symbolized. Each of these may change, as examples given below will illustrate. A word like OE *ēam* "uncle" may be lost; a referent like a feather may be replaced by a plastic cylinder with a point; a notion associated with an object, like a bear, may come to convey dread, and changes in the designation may result. In dealing with semantic changes, the meanings of words have come to be expressed increasingly by means of features.

13.2 CHANGE IN SEMANTIC FEATURES

In proposing a framework for semantic analysis, fields have been analysed for their distinctive features. If we analyse the kinship system for Modern English in this way, we would propose the features: gender, generation, lineality, The basic set of kinship terms may be presented in a matrix as follows:

	Father	*Mother*	*Brother*	*Sister*	*Son*	*Daughter*	*Uncle*	*Aunt*	*Cousin*	*Nephew*	*Niece*
Sex	0	1	0	1	0	1	0	1	–	0	1
Generation	0	0	1	1	2	2	0	0	1	2	2
Lineality	0	0	0	0	0	0	1	1	1	1	1

Such a matrix permits ready understanding of semantic change. For example, the system of kinship terms in Modern English is not completely symmetrical; it does not have a distinction for gender manifested in the "cousin" relationship. If this feature were extended to the term "cousin," a semantic change would be brought about. As in German, a further kinship term might introduced; a male cousin in German is called *Vetter*, a female cousin *Kusine*. In Classical Greek the term *métrōs* was used for "maternal uncle," *pátrōs* for paternal uncle. Thereupon the feature of consanguinity came to be more important than that for gender, and the word *theíos* "uncle" was introduced for either "father's brother" or "mother's brother." Apparently, cultural changes had led to disregarding distinctions between paternal and maternal relationships. The change in meaning in the new system can be indicated precisely if we analyse the set of kinship terms in Classical Greek into distinctive features.

Moreover, the use of distinctive features in a semantic field may be specified by rules that indicate the relationships among them. For example, in Latin the word *gener* was used for "man's sister's husband" and for "son-in-law." Both designations involve no more meanings than those found in the English set of kinship terms. But English does not have the same rules as Latin. This situation may illustrate the need for proposing rules depicting the use of features in a given language, as well as the need for analysing semantic entities into features. For the Latin word *gener*, Floyd Lounsbury proposed the following rule: "Let any woman's brother, as linking relative, be regarded as equivalent to that woman's son, as linking relative." (1964: 1089). Formalized, in symbolism used for kinship terminology, the rule reads +B . . . → +s. This rule, which Lounsbury labels an asymmetrical skewing rule characteristic of an Omaha kinship system, was replaced by bilaterally symmetrical skewing rules in Italian, French, Spanish and Portuguese. These languages, like English, distinguish between lineal and collateral relatives, containing separate words for "brother-in-law" and "son-in-law."

This example may illustrate that semantic change may be represented much as is phonological, morphological or syntactic change. Features may be added or lost; or rules expressing the relationships between features may be modified or lost.

Other semantic modifications may be understood by means of feature analysis. For example, NE *mother* is used not only as a kinship term, but also in such expressions as *mother-of-pearl*, *mother-of-vinegar*, *mother of battles*. In these expressions the semantic feature <+Human> has been eliminated and the feature <+Relationship> has been aligned in a different way with other features.

Extensions of use for other words may illustrate the discussion of meaning change in this way. The term *clothes' horse* also involves the loss of a feature: <+Animate>. The use of the term *house* for a body of representatives, on the other hand, involves the addition of the features <+Animate> and <+Human>. Few studies have been carried out that exemplify such rules and their role in change of meaning. The examples included in the rest of this chapter may, however, be examined in this way. By analysis of the words into features and by examination of the specific modification involved, the semantic change in question may be more precisely understood.

13.3 ON DETERMINING CHANGE IN MEANING

Change of meaning is readily apparent in any language for which we have a series of texts. As example we may cite *persona*, for which a considerable change of meaning can be substantiated in the several millennia over which it and its reflexes are found in Latin and English texts. When we first encounter *persona*, it means "mask." In Roman drama, masks were used on the stage, and varied in accordance with roles. Soon *persona* came to mean a "character indicated by a mask," thereupon a "character" as such or a "role in a play." From this developed the meaning "representative of a character," then a "representative in general." For us its central meaning is "representative of the human race." A peripheral meaning, "representative of the church," has survived in the form *parson*, which has retained the pronunciation found in such words as *Derby* (British), and is spelled accordingly. The word *persona* has accordingly undergone a considerable change, from referring to an article of stage costume through designation for human roles to a general designation for human being, all of which can be attested in Latin and subsequent English texts.

Even if we lacked these texts, we could make conjectures about its development of meaning by comparing Modern English usages like *ten persons were at the meeting, the three persons of the trinity* and *He is a parson.* Peripheral meanings, as well as the central meaning, may be found in texts produced at one time, and may be used to infer the change of meaning a word has undergone. In the Old English *Beowulf*, for example, the etymon of *thank* is attested in a compound with the meaning "thought," line 1060 *fore-þanc* "forethought." In *Beowulf*, line 359, it means "satisfaction, pleasure." On the basis of further examples, we can infer a change of meaning for *thank* from "thought" to "recognition" to "acknowledgment." Numerous examples are available for conjecturing change of meaning from texts for which we have no long succession of predecessors.

As with *thank*, conjectures on meaning change may be supported by a third procedure, comparison with elements similar in form, that is, through etymology. It is scarcely hazardous to assume that *thank* is related to *think*. Internal vowel change is a common device for deriving words in the Germanic languages, as in *drink : drench, wind : wend one's way* and so on. One may therefore suggest for *thank* on the basis of etymology, the earlier meaning we find attested in Old English.

Inferences about meaning from etymology, however, require caution, for, as we have observed in the previous chapters, forms may be modified in accordance with phonological, morphological and syntactic sets. If, for example, we had only the form Germ. *Sündflut* for the flood that Noah survived, we would relate the first element to *Sünde* "sin" and assume *Sündflut* to be a compound describing the long flood caused by man's sinfulness. Actually, from older forms we find the analysis wrong; the first component was modified by folk etymology from MHG *sin-*, a cognate of Lat. *senex* "old person," so that it originally meant the "long-lasting" flood. Suggesting change of meaning on the basis of etymology or similarity of form may thus be erroneous.

The same caution applies when we attempt to reconstruct change of meaning from forms in related languages. We would have to know considerably more than the fact of their relationship to decide that of the pair Eng. *silly* : Germ. *selig* "blessed," the German form preserves the earlier meaning, while of the pair Eng. *cup* : Germ. *Kopf* "head," the English form does. We can conclude from comparisons of related forms which differ in meaning that change of meaning has indeed taken place. For its exact course we speak with certainty only when we have texts in which the earlier, as well as the later, meanings can be established.

In discussing the changes in semantic systems, for convenience we deal with words. Actually, any morphological element may undergo semantic change. We can observe it in affixes: *super-* in *superman* differs in meaning from *super-* in *superstition* or *superstructure*. In section 11.4 we saw how the segment *-burger* has changed considerably in meaning. We must make the same assumption for morphemes consisting of suprasegmental material, such as intonation patterns; but with our ignorance of suprasegmental morphemes of the past, we cannot provide sure examples. In this brief introduction to change of meaning, we will deal only with well-established examples, such as the words used for illustration so far in this chapter. Interpreting such examples, we will discuss semantic change in relation to the processes and to the causes that have been proposed for it.

13.4 PROCESSES BY WHICH SEMANTIC CHANGE AND CHANGE IN THE LEXICON ARE CARRIED OUT

In a celebrated article (1926–8: 230–71), Meillet proposes three processes by which semantic change takes place.

The first of these is change in the contexts in which given words are used. An example is the restriction of meaning of Fr. *pas, personne, rien, jamais*. These words were used with *ne* "not" to strengthen the negation; *pas*, for example, originally meant "step." When *ne* was omitted, they came to have a negative meaning.

The second process results from a change in the object referred to, or in the speakers' view of such an object. An example of a change in the object referred to is *pen* from Lat. *penna* "feather, quill." Used for a writing implement dispensing some kind of fluid ink, *pen* no longer means "feather." Among such changes Meillet classes those resulting from taboo. One can readily cite circumlocutions for nonfavored objects, such as Gk *aristerós* "better" for "left (hand)," *left*, itself from an Old English word for "weak," Lat. *sinister* "more useful," itself replaced by *gauche* in French, which now also has an unfavorable connotation. The Slavs and Welsh substituted so commonly for "bear" the circumlocution "honey-eater, honey-pig," that the original was lost from their languages. Through enforced disuse of the tetragrammaton JHWH, the Hebrews lost knowledge of its pronunciation. Many tabooed words are restricted in usage only in certain social situations, so that the word is not totally lost from the language. The attempts to bar *Lady Chatterley's Lover* were determined in part by Lawrence's used of a term tabooed in print, even though it is widely used in the spoken language.

Such words under only a partial taboo do not undergo a change in meaning because of the taboo, as can be demonstrated from the long history of the often cited Anglo-Saxon four-letter words, many of which can be traced back to Proto-Indo-European. If, however, a word is under complete taboo, such as the reflex of the Proto-Indo-European word for "bear" in Germanic-speaking areas, it may be lost; the word has reflexes in dialects spoken where the bear was not a present danger, for example Gk *árktos*, Lat. *ursus*, Skt. *ŕkṣas*.

The third basis for semantic change, and change in the lexical component of language, Meillet found in the influence of other languages and dialects, including social dialects. The process by which words are imported into a language is known as **borrowing**. It has by far the greatest effect on the lexicon of the three processes discussed by Meillet, as will be illustrated below for English. A large number of words in English have been borrowed from French, though their earlier source is Latin or Greek. An example is priest. Originally a specialized use of the Greek adjective for "older," *presbúteros* became a part of the technical language of the early Christians. The English form *presbyter*, as well as the related *priest*, has retained the specialized meaning, besides leading to a modification of *elder*. Such borrowings and lexical changes result from complex historical, social and linguistic processes. We will discuss some of these, using primarily examples from the history of English.

13.5 SEMANTIC CHANGE RESULTING FROM CHANGE IN LINGUISTIC CONTEXTS

As we have noted, the omission of a word may lead to a change in meaning of other words. Modifiers may be omitted, as was French *ne* in expressions with *pas*, so that *pas* alone now means "not." An example from English is the word *undertaker*, which once meant "one who undertakes, an energetic promoter." One translation of the Twenty-third Psalm began: "The Lord is my undertaker." A common context in which the word was used was that of *funeral undertaker*; *funeral* then was omitted, and until morticians thought they could sweeten their trade with a new name, the chief context for *undertaker* was for people who assist in the obsequies for the dead. The head noun itself may be omitted, as with *main*, which came to be used for "main ocean," as in the *Spanish Main*; *mainland*, on the other hand, was retained as a compound. As other examples we may cite *fall* "autumn," from "fall of leaves," and *private* "lowest-ranking soldier," from *private soldier*.

Semantic changes brought about by such linguistic modifications are rare. Similarly infrequent are changes resulting from similarities between forms. As examples we may cite NE *demean* and *presently*. NE *demean* "behave" was associated with *mean* "inferior" and today is generally used as a synonym for "debase." NE *presently* "soon" was associated with *present* "now" and has come to be used as an adverb meaning "at present" rather than "in the future." While semantic changes resulting from linguistic influences may be cited, they are far less frequent than changes resulting from modifications in the reference or referent.

13.6 SEMANTIC CHANGE RESULTING FROM CHANGE OF REFERENCE OR REFERENT

Scientific advances, or social changes, bring about extensions of words to new uses. Examples may be given from almost any field of scientific or social change. As the scale of living has improved, for example, the term *pool* has undergone a change in meaning. Earlier, *garage* came to replace *stable*. In some regions *landing strip* is equally favored. Other words referring to transportation by air have undergone striking modifications in meaning. The term *plane* was formerly found chiefly in modest scientific contexts, as in the term *plane geometry*. Unless restricted in use by the knowledgeable younger generation, who scorn it in favor of *B-747, DC-10* and the like, it has great frequency. Other items used in its linguistic environment, *pilot, jet,* and so on, have a considerably different meaning from that associated with these words before the age of flight.

We can also cite examples from the past. A *picture* formerly was something painted; now we can have our picture taken with a camera, itself formerly a term for a room. For the Romans a *street, strāta via*, was a "paved way." In the course of time it came to represent any passageway for vehicles.

Other examples may be observed today in the expansion of comfortable living. With the increased shift to suburbia came increased prestige for linguistic items suggesting life in the hills outside the city. Lots on "trails" and "lanes" sell rapidly. While "avenues" were formerly the grand entrances for cities, they may now be the ways along which commercial firms are located, with the former favorable meaning maintained only where some modicum of urban elegance is retained, as in *Fifth Avenue* or *Pennsylvania Avenue*. In many areas the formerly humble *trail* and *lane* have in this way outdistanced *avenue*. What entrepreneurs will do in the future, when all the haves live on trails and the have-mores are in search of elegant housing, will provide students of semantic change with further examples of changes in meaning resulting from nonlinguistic influences. It is instructive, as well as amusing, to examine the designations for new developments around a city, with their designations including words like *hill, brook, wood*.

Among the greatest sources of such influences are technical changes, with resultant changes in technical dialects and consequent influences on the language in general. Intellectual historians may look to meteorology, and speak of a *climate of opinion*. The intellectual climate may undergo a *renaissance*, with *nerves* of communication strengthened, especially for those who are *off center*. The technical dialects of sports have been widely exploited in English. In building a strong group, one tries to avoid *bush leaguers* (baseball) or those with a *bias* (bowling); otherwise one may find oneself *out in left field* as far as the competition is concerned. More recently, the dialect of computer technicians has been extended, as in the words ending in *-ware*: *hardware, software, courseware* and so on, even *wetware* for the brain. When the former meaning is still the more prominent, we may call such transfers of context **metaphors**. In the course of time, the new meanings may prevail and cause the metaphor to fade. Today we scarcely think of the former meaning of *decide* "cut off" or *detail* "cut in pieces" as we *bat around* a topic.

Often the shift in reference is from a serene to an emotionally active connotation, which corresponds to the hyperbole of literary analysis. *Astonish*, somewhat like *stun*, once meant "strike by thunder." In Shakespeare's *King Henry the Fifth* 5.1, Gower points out to Fluellen that he astonished Pistol when he struck him a second time. Such shifts seem to lead to a less vivid meaning, as may be illustrated by words of strong assent, such as *certainly, sure, indeed* – which today have less force than does *yes*; similarly, words that indicate degree, especially of behavior or appearance, such as *fine*, which now is scarcely more satisfactory than are *superb, grand, perfect, magnificent, great.*

Shifts in reference are readily attested for terms of address, as in Span. *don, donna* from spoken Lat. *domnus, domna* "lord, mistress." In French, *domina* gave rise to *dame, madame*. The similar German *Herr*, like Eng. *Mister*, scarcely carries the connotation of mastery today. Lofty terms, when generalized, come to take on meanings resembling their everyday contexts. Some terms, in shifting from an indication of social to moral inferiority, have undergone even less favorable change. A *villain* was once a worker at a *villa*; other terms for rural work that have developed similarly are *churl* <OE *ceorl* "common man, farmer" and *boor* – compare the stolid Dutch farmers who settled South Africa. A *knave*, as in the *Knave of Hearts*, was a boy; see Germ. *Knabe*. Terms for government officials may also suffer, for example *publican* "a public servant" or *cheater*, earlier *escheater*, an officer whose duty it was to assure the return of property to the state if the owner died without heirs or without leaving a will.

Some shifts result from cultural or geographical changes rather than from modifications introduced by imaginative speakers. When people from Britain settled in America, they gave a red-breasted thrush the name of their robin, a much smaller bird with similar coloring. *Holiday*, which once referred to a sacred festival day, has lost much of its religious connotation.

Other shifts follow attitudes of the speakers. When members of a society consider it essential to use a circumlocution for a tabooed term, it may change entirely to the new meaning. *Bear* is scarcely "the brown one" for any speaker of English today. Various words were changed in meaning as they were introduced for the tabooed names for *hand, left, right* in Indo-European languages, as we may illustrate from the panoply of Indo-European words for hand – OE *folm*, Skt *hástas*, Gk *kheír*, Lat. *manus*, Lith. *ranká*, Goth. *handus*. The tabooed words may then be totally lost, as was the cognate of Gk *árktos* "bear" in Germanic and Slavic.

It should be noted that *taboo*, or avoidance of the unspeakable, varies from culture to culture, and accordingly from language to language. It is applied to clothing in Japanese; to animal names by hunters; and to names of excretory functions, death and divinity for many of us. It also varies with generations; younger speakers today may abandon the taboo on excretory functions. Terms for races, such as *Negro, Black, African–American* or *Mexican, Chicano*, and the like are also candidates for taboo, with considerable variation in attitude and consequent use.

In cultures that absolutely forbid the use of certain words, such as any homophone of the name of a deceased person, taboo may have an effect on the lexical stock of a language. In this way the attitudes towards objects, that is, the **reference** of individual words, may be influential in bringing about semantic change.

13.7 SEMANTIC CHANGE RESULTING FROM BORROWING

By far the most important effect on the semantic component of language is brought about by the influence of other languages or dialects, a process referred to by linguists as **borrowing**. Borrowing may be viewed as cultural diffusion. In accounting for it, we set out to determine the conditions under which borrowing takes place.

We also note that there are borrowings of various types. Some borrowings, known as **loanwords**, mirror the phonemes of the foreign language. In Eng. *poet*, for example, the French phonemes were reproduced almost exactly in English. Most recent borrowings in English are of this type; words like *oxygen*, *hydrogen*, *telephone* are made up of entities borrowed from Greek, with English sounds substituted for those assumed to be pronounced in the original.

Other borrowings reproduce the morphemes of a foreign language, using native material. Examples are academic terms like *handbook*, a translation of Lat. *manuālis liber*, which itself has survived in the abbreviated form *manual*. Words similarly reproduced by translation are the names for the days of the week: *Monday = diēs Lunae*, "the day of the Moon goddess," *Tuesday = diēs Martis*, "the day of Mars" and so on. These are known as **loan-shifts**, **loan translations** or **calques**. In German, loan-shifts are especially prominent; instead of taking over the Greek components for "acid" and "material," as did English in *oxygen*, German translated them to form the loan-shift *Sauerstoff*; similarly, *Wasserstoff* for "hydrogen," *Fernsprecher* for "telephone," and so on.

In a further type of borrowing, only the meaning of a linguistic entity may be changed. OE *eorl* "earl" meant "brave warrior"; the present meaning was taken over from Old Norse, where the word indicated a rank of nobility. Similarly, OE *dwellan* meant "lead astray" but was modified in meaning by ON *dvelja* "abide" to present-day "dwell." Changes in meaning under the influence of a foreign language are known as **extensions**.

To understand borrowings of various types, we must know the degree of command that speakers have of the languages in question; for the extent of reproduction is often determined by the extent of control that speakers have acquired of a second language, especially before conventions of borrowing have been established.

We may illustrate possible modifications by noting how English words are treated in Japanese. The English word *violin* is reproduced variously, depending on the speaker's command over English. Sophisticated speakers may use a very similar form when they speak Japanese, that is *vaiorin*, even though their own language does not contain a /v/. Most speakers, however, substitute /b/ for English v, and say *baiorin*. Both sets of speakers reproduce *l* as *r*. But especially among naive speakers, borrowings show substitution of phonemic, not phonetic, entities, as the examples given below indicate.

The role of phonemic structure in borrowings may be illustrated through the treatment of English *t* in Japanese. The stop [t] occurs in Japanese only before [e a o]; before [u] we find the affricate [ts]; before [i y], the affricate [tš]. If a work like *tank* is borrowed into Japanese, the result is *tanku*, different largely in the mandatory final vowel. For *touring*, the Japanese form is *tsuringu*; for *team* and *tube*, *tšiimu* and *tšyuubu*. In Japanese, [t ts tš] are in complementary distribution; they are members of the same phoneme. Naive speakers automatically substitute any of the allophones of /t/ in accordance with their distribution before following vowels in Japanese.

To illustrate a different treatment, we may note the forms of *jet* in Japanese. Like [tš], [dž] may occur in Japanese only before [i] and [y]; *jib* is then taken over with the similar pronunciation [džibu]. Before [e a o], on the other hand, [z] is found, in complementary distribution with [dž]. With these limitations of Japanese phonological structure, the word *jet* has been borrowed in two forms: [džietto] and [zetto] In the first the initial consonant is similar to that of English, with vowel modification; in the second the vowel is unchanged, but the initial consonant has been altered.

For the examples cited, knowledge of the phonological structure of Japanese and English is necessary to explain the Japanese forms. One must know the allophones of the English phonemes and their possible Japanese counterparts. (Details are given in the workbook which accompanies this volume.) To illustrate the Japanese treatment of English *s*, the following examples may be cited; Jap. *sanmā-sōruto* corresponds to Eng. *sommersault*; *setto-požišon* to Eng. *set position* (of a pitcher); *šinema*, to Eng. *cinema*; *šōradu-rain*, to *shoulder line*; *sūpu* to *soup*. As comparison with the statement of correspondences given in the workbook will illustrate, the English words have undergone modifications determined largely by the possibilities in Japanese.

The borrowing language also brings about morphological modifications, for borrowings generally take on the patterns of native elements. When, for example, *bask* was borrowed into Old English from ON *báða sik* "bathe oneself" and *busk* from ON *búask* < *búa sik* "ready oneself," they were treated like simple verbs in English. Reflexives were not combined with verbs in English, and accordingly the speakers failed to recognize the final pronouns. To be sure, foreign inflections may occasionally be maintained, especially by sophisticated speakers. Many nouns were imported into English with their Latin or Greek plural inflections, such as *datum* : *data*, *colon* : *cola*, *skeleton* : *skeleta*, *maximum* : *maxima*, and so on. Except in learned contexts, these now make their plurals in *-s*, with the exception of the first, *data*, which is increasingly treated as a singular, as in *the data is*.

Similarly, in Japanese, borrowings are equipped with the Japanese morphological markers. Words borrowed into Japanese from Chinese, such as *kenkyuu* "study" were treated as verbs with the addition of *suru* "do," *shita* "did," for example *kenkyuu shita* "studied." When English words were borrowed into Japanese, they too followed this pattern. The loanword *taipu*, from Eng. *type*, as well as others, may be accompanied by forms of *suru*. The large number of borrowings into Japanese from Chinese and English could be inflected in this way, though without introducing any new morphological markers.

Further, syntactic expressions borrowed from another language are difficult to maintain. Eng. *marriage of convenience* <Fr. *mariage de convenance* "marriage for advantage" may be misinterpreted today. To be sure, the phrase *it goes without saying* <Fr. *cela va sans dire* has currently become established among many speakers. Yet neither of these expressions has affected the language deeply. A more widespread example of syntactic borrowing may be the German favoring of highly complicated sentence patterns, as a result of the influence of Latin syntax. As with other proposed borrowings of syntactic patterns, such as the introduction of numeral classifiers into Japanese from Chinese, the evidence is not conclusive. For the clearest instances of borrowing are in the lexical and semantic sphere. Below, however, we examine evidence that general syntactic patterns may be affected by borrowing.

13.8 RESULTS OF BORROWING UNDER DIFFERENT SOCIAL AND LINGUISTIC CONDITIONS

Various situations in the history of English provide us with good examples of different results of borrowing. These results may be ascribed to different types of language contact, with differing effects on the language.

13.8.1 Borrowing when a language of prestige is adopted

The first major contact of English speakers was with Celtic speakers. When English was brought to the British Isles in the fifth century AD, presumably there were more Celtic speakers than Germanic invaders. Yet English survived and ousted Celtic. Moreover, it adopted very few words from Celtic, a few common nouns like *bannock* "cake" and *brock* "badger," and numerous place names, such as *London, Thames, Dover*. The resulting linguistic situation is much like that of American English and the American Indian languages. A few nouns from American Indian languages were borrowed: *tomahawk, skunk*, and many place names, such as *Chicago, Mississippi, Kentucky*. The two linguistic situations had much in common; from them, with the support of other parallels, we can suggest the typical situation in which few lexical borrowings are made.

When speakers learn a prestige language, they are under social pressure to acquire it without flaws. They speak the acquired language as well as possible and avoid carrying over into it items from their native language. Examples may be taken from America in the nineteenth century. Immigrants who came to this country attempted to learn accurate English. Their own language, however, was grossly modified, often with importations from English. In the German area of Chicago, a mixed German was referred to as *die schönste lengevitsch* "the most beautiful language." It consisted in great part of German structures filled with borrowings from English. On the basis of this situation, and those just cited, we may conclude that speakers modify the language they are certain of much more readily than they do a language that they know imperfectly.

As a further well-documented example, we may cite Germany in the eighteenth century. At the courts French was the language of prestige; German, that of everyday communication. Frederick the Great of Prussia considered German a language fit only for peasants. He often wrote in French; when he did, he avoided German borrowings. His German letters, on the other hand, abound with French loanwords.

From these and other examples, we may view the English–Celtic relationship as a typical situation in the contact of languages. Old English was regarded as the language of cultural prestige. Although they may have been preponderant numerically, native Celtic speakers set out to learn English, gradually abandoning their native language. In the course of time an English resulted with few lexical importations. Apart from place names, only those items were borrowed from the receding into the dominant language for which the dominant language had no readily available terms.

Although we can provide no evidence for this type of language inter-relationship in prehistoric situations, from the results we may assume it for many areas. It is especially relevant in the spread of Indo-European languages: of Hittite into Anatolia, of Greek into the Hellenic peninsula, of Italic into Italy, even of Indic into India, although in India there was considerable phonological modification resulting from the borrowing of retroflex consonants. This situation applied also for the spread of Arabic, which was adopted from Iraq to Morocco with little change in grammatical structure. Except for special situations discussed below, it also applied for the spread in recent centuries of three of the most widely spoken languages, today: French, Russian and English.

13.8.2 Borrowing when a language of prestige is used simultaneously with a surviving indigenous language

A second typical situation, English in the eleventh century, at first glance parallels that of the fifth century. A relatively small group of invaders took over political control of an established population and continued as the ruling class. Yet the results were quite different. In the centuries after 1066, Norman French was used by a small segment of the population, but eventually it was ousted by English.

We explain the different result by noting that the type of contact was completely different from that in the fifth century. During the eleventh and subsequent centuries, the indigenous speakers adopted words for only those cultural spheres in which they maintained contact with the ruling classes. For everyday communication they used their own language. We may illustrate this restriction of contact by noting the spheres of borrowing.

One notable sphere of borrowing was government and administration. A great number of English words in these areas was borrowed from French, for example *council, country, crown, government, minister, nation, parliament, people, state*. For titles, *prince, duke, marquis, viscount, baron* were borrowed; only the native *earl* was kept, but the earl's wife is a *countess*, and *count* is the equivalent rank for foreign nobles. In the related area of heraldry, many French terms were taken over, including those for colors such as *sable, gules, vert*. Moreover, military words were borrowed: *armor, army, banner, navy, siege, war*; similarly, such legal terms as *court, crime, defendant, judge, jury, justice, plaintiff*. In the sphere of legal terminology, some French idioms were introduced and maintained, presumably because of the extended period of French influence. Although English became the official language in 1362, legal French was not given up in courts of justice until 1731. The phrase *puis né* "later born, lower" was borrowed as an adjective, surviving in *puisne judge*, and more widely as *puny*. Moreover, some syntactic phrases, with adjective following noun, have been maintained: *attorney general, malice aforethought*.

The difference in social status of the two languages may be illustrated in contrasting words: for a small crime, the English *theft* is used; for a serious one, the French *larceny*.

Today still, words for food reflect the social relation between the Norman French and their English subjects. English terms are used for animals in the field: *cow, calf, ox, sheep, boar, swine*; French, for animals on the table: *beef, veal, mutton, bacon, pork*. Moreover, the humble meal *breakfast* has an English name; the more elegant *dinner* and *supper*, at which *jelly* and *pastry* may be served, have French names. The social relationship is further reflected in words for *sport* < *desport*, the *chase, falconry, cards*, and *dice*, where even words for numbers were taken over: *ace, deuce, tray*. As with foods, names for artisans in the lower groups are English: *baker, fisherman, miller, shepherd, shoemaker, smith*; those in contact with upper classes are Norman French in origin: *carpenter, mason, painter, tailor*.

The general situation is clear. Upper-class invaders, though in the minority, occupied positions of prestige in Britain for three centuries. They were gradually replaced, however, by bilingual natives of Britain; and descendants of the invaders learned English. The French terms introduced into English reflect a feudal system, with various class distinctions. We conclude that the language of lesser prestige maintained itself because of the numerical, and eventually political, preponderance of its speakers. Yet the language of greater prestige has left a great effect on certain segments of the vocabulary.

We find this situation in other areas as well. The Dravidian languages of India have been maintained, though with numerous borrowings from Indic languages. In early Mesopotamia, Akkadian ousted Sumerian, though it took over many words from the earlier language of prestige. When the Japanese became aware of the higher culture of China in the second half of the first millennium after Christ, they sent emissaries to China, who imported with the higher culture a large number of borrowings; but Japanese was maintained as the national language.

To a certain extent this type of contact exists today wherever western civilization and science are being imitated or adopted. Words like *electricity*, *telephone*, *airplane* are being introduced as loanwords or loan-shifts. We find a variety of parallels to the English–French contact, in which the invading language leaves a marked effect in the native language without replacing it.

13.8.3 Borrowing when the languages concerned are on an equal plane

A third typical situation is the contact between English and Scandinavian, in the ninth to eleventh centuries. Both languages existed side by side for some time, until eventually Scandinavian was lost; but, unlike Celtic several centuries earlier, it left a considerable imprint on English. This imprint, on the other hand, was not in higher segments of culture, as was the later Norman French influence, but extended through much of the everyday vocabulary. To be sure, there were various martial and legal terms of Scandinavian origin in early English, but few of these have persisted; one that has remained, *bylaw* (*by* = "village"), has merely a vestige of its original sense.

The Scandinavian borrowings show no specific areas of cultural superiority. The term for a possible architectural improvement, window ("wind-eye"), merely replaced an older *eagþyrel* ("eye-hole," cf. ME *nosethirl*, OE *nosþyrl* (nose-hole), *nostril*); it did not accompany a cultural innovation. Little more can be claimed for the borrowed *steak* and *knife*. Unlike French, Scandinavian furnished many elements of the common vocabulary: *gift*, *husband*, *root*, *skill*, *skin*, *sky*, *wing*; *happy*, *loose*, *low*, *same*, *wrong*; *addle*, *call*, *die*, *drown*, *gape*, *get*, *give*, *hit*, *screech*, *take*, *want*. Still others may have been borrowed, but cannot be identified, for many words were alike in tenth-century Old English and Old Norse.

Most interesting are grammatical elements: *they*, *them*, *their* have taken the place of older *hīe*, *heom*, *heora*. In these borrowings the central core of the vocabulary was affected. The inflections of English nouns and verbs may even have been simplified by the contact between the two linguistic groups. We can also suggest that the type of contact existing between English and Scandinavian may have been one force in the morphological simplification of English.

This was a contrast between two languages of equal prestige. We are not certain to what extent the two were mutually intelligible; this question may also lack pertinence. For the significant point may be that the two languages were used for communication on an everyday level. The language with the larger number of speakers was maintained, though with simplification of structure.

Still further simplification is evident when speakers communicate only on simple cultural levels. A readily attested example may be found in baby-talk. Speakers, in using it, may avoid lexical items that border on the grammatical, such as pronouns: *Baby like candy?* In even more unabashed utterances, such as *baby go seepee*, we find phonological as well as morphological simplification. Such simplification, used not only to infants when attempting to convey affection, is very similar to that found in the so-called pidgin languages and creolized languages.

Pidgins (apparently a simplification of *business*: Chin. p = Eng. b, ž = z, yielding [pižins] < [biznis]) have arisen in areas where people communicated on a very simple level. On the Chinese coast, intercommunication was carried on in English for commerce; in the Pacific islands, it was carried on for the direction of work. In South America, descendants of slaves evolved a simple common language called *Taki-taki*. When such simplified languages are the sole languages of a community, as in Haiti, they are referred to as **creolized languages** or **creoles**. To illustrate the changes that may take place when speakers are in contact on a low cultural level, examples may be cited from Hall (1943).

For a long time Melanesian Pidgin was not learned as a first language by any speaker except possibly by children of parents who could not understand each other's language. It was spoken by speakers with a Melanesian or Papuan background, and by Europeans. Remarkably, when Papua came to have its own government, Pidgin was the only widely used language, and it was adopted as an official language.

When spoken, it is not uniform. Speakers carry over their native speech habits. Melanesians, for example, may pronounce voiced stops with pre-nasalization; *nəbawt* "about" may be [nə^{m}bawt]. Germans may use *tæsɔl* "but" like Germ. *aber*, which corresponds to Eng. *but* and *however*.

In Melanesian Pidgin, the sound system of English was considerably simplified. There are no /θ ð z ž/; for example, *this* is [dis], *nose* is [nos]. Further, in speaking Melanesian Pidgin English, Melanesians generally substitute the following:

[p]   for   [f v]: [pinis]   =   [finis] "already"
              [æp]   =   [hæf] "piece"

[s] for [š č] [masin] = [mašin]
[š] or [tš] for [dž] as in [pičin]

[h] is omitted, as in [bi ayn] "later." Moreover, consonant clusters may be simplified by intercalating vowels, as in [gəris] for [gris] "pig."

In morphology none of the bound forms of English are attested. There are, however, characteristic bound forms. The suffix *-felə* is used as an adjective suffix for monosyllables, and also for numerals, for example:

disfelə haws i-bigfelə	"this house is large"
tufelə pikinini	"two children"
nədəfelə səmtiŋ	"another thing"

It is also added to first- and second-person pronouns to indicate plurals:

mi "I, me"	*mifelə* "we, us"
ju "you"	*jufelə* "you"

Characteristic affixes are also used with verbs; *-im* is used as objective suffix for most verbs when transitive, as in:

ju faytim pig "you strike the pig"

A predicate marker is used as prefix, unless the subject is *mi, mifelə, ju, jufelə, jumi*, for example:

mašin i-bəgərəp finiš "the machine is broken"

The syntax too is simple, with sequences of co-ordinated clauses.

In Melanesian and other pidgins, then, we see an extreme effect of language contact. A language is stripped down for the essentials of communication, with resulting phonological and morphological simplification. How often such processes of simplification took place in the past, we do not know; whether the Assyrian merchants in Asia Minor used simplified forms of communication during the second millennium BC, or the Romans in Gaul, the Hittites in Asia Minor, the Phoenicians in their wanderings. Observing the simplification of structure in contemporary pidgin languages, we may wonder whether a somewhat similar situation may not have led to the form of English that we find spoken after the tenth century, with its progressive loss of inflections, and to other similar reductions of complexity in language structure. This is not to suggest that English is, or ever was, a pidgin.

13.8.4 Borrowing between dialects

In discussing these three types of contact, we have dealt only with the relations of languages among one another. We must assume, however, similar types of contact between all different forms of speech: geographical dialects, social dialects, technical dialects and even idiolects. Borrowings are made from any such dialect to any other, from all of them into the general language. Illustrations could be given in abundance. For "edible corn on the cob," the northern American *sweet corn* seems to be becoming the standard term rather than the southern *roasting ears*. With the interest in jazz and rock music, many terms have been adopted into the standard language from uneducated speech, such as *the blues*. Technical dialects of the present have introduced so many new terms that we may forget the strong influence of those in the past. We are quite aware of the time of introduction of *x-ray, radium, irradiate, isotope*. Other sources in earlier times were from the technical terms of the ecclesiastical vocabulary. Our *noon* is from OE *nōn*, Lat. *nōna hōra* "ninth hour," the time of the nones, a service held originally at 3 p.m. but later shifted to noon.

The extent to which these have been modified may be illustrated by our use of legal terms. For us, *subpoena*, originally a phrase meaning "under penalty" can be used as a verb. *Affidavit*, on the other hand, a Latin verb form meaning "he has pledged his faith" is a noun today, as is *alibi* "elsewhere," in origin a Latin adverb. Such borrowings then are inflected, as Lat. *caveat* "let him beware" has been, especially by the military with forms like *It was caveated all over the place*.

Although genetics has changed our views on biological inheritance, we still maintain the technical language of medieval science. We may excuse a failing by saying *It's in my blood*. Our disposition we still refer to as our *liquid*, Lat. *humor*, for according to medieval science there were four important liquids in people: blood, phlegm, bile, black bile. Those who were assumed to have too much blood were *sanguine*; too much phlegm, *phlegmatic*; too much bile, *bilious*; too much black bile or melancholy, *melancholic*. Those whose liquids were in balance were *good-humored*. Their *temperament* was evident in the "weaving together" of the humors, and indicated by their *complection*, now *complexion*.

From words like these in the vocabulary we could reconstruct medieval scientific ideas. As we will see in chapter 15, such reconstruction is of great interest for early languages.

Like the borrowings in medieval and Modern English, borrowings adopted in technical dialects are generally based on a learned language. In Arabic-speaking countries, Classical Arabic is used as a source; in India, Sanskrit. In the languages of western Europe, Latin and Greek are the sources for technical terms. Since European technology and science have been spread throughout the world, the influence of Latin and Greek has not been confined to Indo-European languages. Names of chemical elements provide examples. The word for "hydrogen" in Japanese is *suiso* "water-substance"; the word for "nitrogen," *chisso* "suffocating substance" and so on.

Often the translation or adaptation is not literal. In Chinese and Japanese, the morph for "electricity" is extended from the meaning "lightning"; "electricity" in Japanese is *denki* "lightning spirit"; "telephone," *denwa* "lightning speech"; "telegraph," *denpō* "lightning report," and so on.

Moreover, the adaptations may fail to follow forms of the model. In linguistic terminology, for example, the proper Greek suffix for terms ending in *-eme* would be *-ematic*; *phonematic* would then be the adjective for *phoneme* rather than *phonemic* and so on. Yet the adjectival suffix *-ic* is so common, for example *base*, *basic*, that it is applied to terms ending in *-eme*, contrary to classical practice. The complexities of such formations and the attitudes of speakers towards these formations are topics that students may find highly interesting to explore.

In contemporary languages we may find results of borrowings made at different times from the same ultimate source. In this way *frail*, ME *freyl*, was borrowed from OFr. *fraile*, which is from Lat. *fragilis*, the source of our *fragile*; *male* is from Fr. *mâle*, OFr. *mascle*, which is from Lat. *masculus*; a derivative, *masculīnus*, is the source of *masculine* and so on. Such related words are known as doublets.

13.8.5 Borrowings from the written language

Another contemporary source for adaptations is the written language. Abbreviations, such as *Prof.* may be used as full words. With the expansion of government agencies, many such terms have been incorporated into everyday speech; /yənéskòw/, *UNESCO*, from *United Nations Economic, Social and Cultural Organization*, may be as widely used today as /nəbískòw/, *Nabisco*, from *National Biscuit company*. We also refer to states in this way, for example /yûw ès ès ès ár/, *USSR*, or in the former Soviet Union, /és ès ès ér/. The written language has become such an important source for borrowings of this kind that new names for organizations are generally contrived so that they will provide suitable abbreviations.

Written languages have furnished other modifications for spoken languages. A slight novelty is the odd form of *ye* for the English definite article, as in the name *Ye olde gifte shoppe*; this arose from the use of *y* for *þ* when printing was introduced into England in the fifteenth century. If the form /yíy/ is only jocular and hardly more general than this context, the pronunciations /əšúwm/ or /əšyuwm/ for *assume*, /šuwət/ or /syúwət/ for *suet*, exemplify deeper modifications from the written langurge. The historically modified /š/ from /sy/ has been maintained only in *sure*, *assure*, *sugar*, and among some speakers in *sumac*, while imitation of the written form has brought about change in pronunciation in *assume*, *consume*, *ensue*, *suet*, and others.

Influences from the written language indicate a socially favorable attitude of speakers towards it. Spelling pronunciations, such as /índiyən ɪndyən/ for *Indian* (compare Injun Joe in *Huckleberry Finn* and the British pronunciation of /injə/) have completely replaced the former pronunciation.

When such influences are exerted, the effect of individual speakers may be as significant as is that of varying dialects. With the development of widespread education, the idiolects of school teachers, for example, have exerted a considerable effect on languages during the last few centuries. Modifications such as those in *assume* may serve as one illustration. Virtually anyone can supply examples from their schooldays. A favorite target in some American schools was *aunt*. Some teachers considered it undignified to label a close relative with a homonym for an insect. The spelling contributes a possible distinctive pronunciation, /ánt/, /ɔ́nt/, or the like. Another is *buoy*; it apparently would not do to suggest that a youth was floating in the water directing traffic. The spelling provided a way out of the difficulty.

Teachers and the bureaucracies supporting them may be responsible for even greater modifications in the language. Since the high front offglide used in parts of New York City instead of retroflection in words like *bird* and *earl* has come to seem substandard, the weight of the New York City school system has been thrown behind an effort to restore retroflection. School teachers are also undoubtedly responsible for depriving American English speakers of a negative in the first person of the auxiliary *be* that is parallel to *isn't, aren't, wasn't, weren't*; for some reason /éynt/ seemed undignified for the graduates of a forward-looking educational system.

Such exertions have given rise to **hyperforms** in contemporary languages. This term is used for attempted corrections that are extended erroneously. Brooklyn children taught to modify /bəyd/ to /bərd/ for *bird* may extend their new learning to /bɔyd/ in *Boyd* or to /ɔyl/ in *oil*, and pronounce these something like *bird* and *earl*. German children speaking dialects without rounded front vowels may round vowels in which rounding is not present in the standard language; taught to change from [fílə] to [fýlə] in *Fülle* "abundance," they may also change the vowel in *bilden* "cultivate" and similar words; the use of such hyperforms is referred to as "gebüldetes Deutsch." Such modifications may be introduced without aid from a teacher or a school system, merely in an attempt to speak like the folks in the city; they are therefore also known as **hyperurbanisms**.

Besides illustrating conflicting influences that result from differing dialects, hyperforms are examples of the effects of analogy. If one is taught to substitute *I* for *me* in contexts like *It wasn't me*, one may also be led to say *with Mary and I*. The hypercorrection *I* has been taught as the prestige pattern, and as illustrated, extended in use. Weinreich, Labov and Herzog consider hypercorrection "an important mechanism in the transmission of prestige patterns" (1968: 181). As we have seen in this section, it is only one of the processes by which borrowings are carried out in language.

13.9 THE IMPORTANCE OF BORROWING IN LANGUAGE CHANGE

Whether spontaneous or induced, borrowing is one of the important influences on language. In using speech, one of our aims is adequate communication. To achieve the readiest communication, we constantly modify our phonological, morphological and syntactic systems as well as our vocabulary to the speech of our associates. If we wish to impress fellow speakers, we may borrow words they use, or imitate their grammatical patterns. If they prefer a plural verb form with *data*, we may use *the data are*. If they prefer the spelling pronunciations /lítəratyùwr néytyùwr/, we may adopt these. We may also be considered out of date unless we adopt new extensions of meaning.

In their 1968 article Weinreich, Labov and Herzog have re-emphasized the effects on language change of the various subsystems found in any language. They have also attempted to determine precisely how language changes; in this attempt they have assumed a model of language which consists of "discrete layers" that coexist within one speech community and that contain "intrinsic variables." Among the variables they have studied are phonological characteristics, such as the position of *r* in New York City speech, and syntactic characteristics, such as the use of the copula *be* in the speech of young Blacks in northern cities of America.

One of the important processes they identify in linguistic change is the "embedding" of the change, both in the structure of a given language and in the social structure of the society using that language. For example, statements have been made about the lack of the copula *be* in the speech of Black children. Labov has demonstrated that it is not lacking in their grammar (1969: 715–62). For example, *is*, the most frequently deleted form of the copula, is found in their emphatic sentences, such as *He is an expert*. In order to improve our understanding of language change, precise information such as that presented by Labov is essential. Thereupon the social significance of the variable in question, such as use or absence of *be*, must be determined. After the type of embedding in the language structure and the social structure is understood, the change may be discussed with authority.

Yet such information does not provide the answer to the question on the origin of language change. Weinreich, Labov and Herzog ascribe it to spread of a varying feature. For example, if in a subgroup of speakers a voiced form of intervocalic -*t*- were to spread, and if it were then widely adopted, we would acknowledge a language change. As further groups adopt such a variable, that is, intervocalic [d] rather than [t], it would shift in status to a constant. The change would be considered a completed linguistic change. And the origin of the change would have been in the varying dialects of a contemporary speech community.

Such an explanation for the "actuation" of linguistic changes applies to complex societies of today, which are made up of heterogeneous speakers like those in a large composite community such as New York City. But sound changes or other linguistic changes in the past may not have been actuated in this way. The much smaller communities of the past, like the Proto-Germanic speech community, undoubtedly were far more homogeneous than are today's large urban communities. They may better be compared with the Charmey community, studied by Gauchat and Hermann. Even in these compact communities, we may better understand language by acknowledging a variety of possible causes for linguistic change.

In addition to changes actuated by variation in language, we may assume that changes are brought about by the structure of a given language. Aberrant sound systems or syntactic systems may be modified, as we have noted in chapter 14. Yakov Malkiel ascribed some sound changes to morphological sets (see Lehmann and Malkiel 1968: 21–64).

Another possible cause for change may lie in human imagination. Speakers tire of expressions handed down from generation to generation, as the practice of poets indicates. In everyday speech the desire for change is especially apparent in terms of endearment or evaluation. The inventiveness of individual speakers must, however, be generally accepted, and their new patterns must be adopted to bring about a significant change in a linguistic community.

Van Helmont indeed added the word *gas* to his and other languages, yet his proposed *blas* "emanation from stars" was a failure. George Eastman introduced *Kodak* as a deliberate creation, after he noted the restrictions on the letter *k* in the English writing system; other merchants have followed him in introducing names such as *Kix* for breakfast cereals, *Krax* for crackers, *Klenso* for soaps, yet these have had an effect primarily on external features of the language. Similarly, when Murray Gell-Mann used the word *quark* in Joyce's *Finnegans Wake* for naming elementary particles, the effect was restricted to this one word. For major linguistic changes to be carried out, social factors as well as linguistic factors are involved.

Explanations for changes must draw on both factors. Fortunately, considerable attention is again being given to language change. The resultant study will lead to our understanding of the development of languages in the past, and of language as a phenomenon.

SELECTED FURTHER READINGS

Ullmann (1957: esp. 171–257) provides a good introduction to change of meaning; the book includes a thorough discussion of previous work, and a lengthy bibliography. Sommerfelt (1962: 87–136) deals broadly with meaning changes in their social settings. Stern (1931) is a full and excellent work on meaning change, especially in English.

Greenough and Kittredge (1902) provide an interesting discussion of various types of meaning change in English; its prime source of interest today is its examples, some of which were used here, rather than their analysis.

Weinreich, Labov and Herzog give a searching examination of the causes of linguistic change in their 1968 article. The other articles in Lehmann and Malkiel (1968), such as Yakov Malkiel's, are also worth note.

For an extensive statement on borrowing, see Bloomfield (1933: 444–95). Otto Jespersen, who was much interested in the influence of one language on another, deals at some length with borrowings in English in his widely read book, *The Growth and Structure of the English Language* (1946). It, like many introductory histories of languages, treats the external history of the language. Jespersen's theoretical views are expressed in *Mankind, nation, and individual from a linguistic point of view*.

A full treatment of a Pidgin language is available in Hall (1943). Haugen (1953) deals with theory while describing the situation.

General study of the intereffects of languages can start best from Weinreich (1953), which discusses the synchronic problems and gives an extensive bibliography.

Any student interested in linguistics has probably made thorough use of the data available in dictionaries, including desk dictionaries. Historical linguists should also acquire the standard etymological dictionaries for their fields of specialty, Skeat (1879–82) or Onions (1966) for English, Kluge (1989) or Pfeifer (1989) for German and so on. Because of its price, the *Oxford English Dictionary* may be best used in libraries, although a compact version with reading glass has been published. Buck (1949) now available in paperback, is a copious source for the study of semantic change, as well as a good portion of the Indo-European vocabulary, with sober comments on the conclusions that may be drawn about Indo-European culture.

PROBLEMS

1 The Greek word *páthos* "disease" came to have great currency in Stoic philosophy of the fifth century BC and later. A chief aim of the Stoics was to achieve composure and serenity. Emotions that disturbed serenity, for example love, hate, desire, fear, were referred to as *páthē* "diseases." Achievement of serenity was known as *apátheia* "freedom from disease."

When Stoic philosophy developed its Latin terminology, the term *passio* "suffering" was used for Gk *páthos*.

In the course of time these technical terms were adopted in the general vocabulary, with shifts of connotation and meaning. Account for the meaning of the following.

(a) apathy
(b) passion, as in "the passion of our Lord," "the passion of love"
(c) patient, as in "a patient scholar," "a hospital patient"
(d) impassive
(e) passive (from the point of view of word formation, this should be the opposite of impassive)
(f) pathetic and pathos itself.

2 *Diamond* is from ME *diama(u)nt*, which was borrowed from OFr. *diamant*, that was based on medieval Lat. *diamant-*, *diamas*, from Lat. *adamas* "steel, hard ore." Final *d* is comparable to that in *card*, from OFr. *carte*, Lat. *charta* "paper."

For *adamant* "hard rock," cf. Ezekiel 3.9; it is from OFr. *adamaunt*, Lat. *adamat*, Gk *adamant-*, *adámās* "hardest iron" > "invincible."

The Proto-Indo-European root is **dem-* "tame, subdue," as in Lat. *domāre*, Gk *damáō*, *tame*, from OE *tam*.

Comment on the history of *diamond*, *adamant* and *tame*, pointing out the phonological and semantic changes.

3 *Ransom* is from ME *ransoun* (with change of final *n* to *m* as in *random*), which is from MFr. *rançon*, and this from Lat. *redemptiōnem*, (acc. sg).

Redemption is found in Wyclif's translation of the Bible as *redempcion*; it too is based on *redemptiōnem*.

Comment on the history of the two words, noting the difference in meaning and area of application.

4 *Entire* is from ME *entyre*, and this from OFr. *entier*, which is from Lat. *integrum*, acc. sg. of *integer* "whole."

Integer was taken over from Lat. *integer*, and is attested in 1715 as an arithmetical term.

Comment on the history of the two words, especially their semantic differences; discuss also the relationships of the verb *integrate* and the noun *integrity* to the other related words.

5 *Elf* is from ME *elf*, and this is from OE *ælf*, cf. OIcel. *ālfr*.

Oaf is from a dialect form *auph*, which developed from *aulf*, and this from *elf*, or possibly from the Scand. *ālfr*. Noting words like *calf*, *half*, comment on the phonological relationship of the two words. Comment also on the pejorative meaning of *oaf*.

6 *Posse* is based on the medieval Lat. *posse* "to be able," and came to be used for a body of men that a sheriff may call to arms – in fuller form *posse comitātus* "force of the county."

Power is from ME *pouer*, Anglo-Norman *po(u)air*, OFr. *poeir*, late Lat. *potēre*, an infinitive that replaced *posse*.

Comment on the relationship between the two forms, and also the use of an infinitive as a noun. Note also the pejorative meaning of *posse* today.

14 Interrelationships among changes

14.1 INTERRELATIONSHIPS IN THE PHONOLOGICAL COMPONENT

Changes in the phonological component differ considerably according to the kind of accent. Languages, like Japanese, with pitch rather than stress accent, tend to maintain all the elements of words, including final vowels. Languages, like the Germanic, on the other hand, have undergone many changes, as we have noted above. Some of these changes have resulted from the strong initial stress accent that was introduced into Proto-Germanic before our era. We can determine the Germanic changes by comparing cognates in Sanskrit, Greek and early Latin from the period when they had a pitch accent. Baltic and Slavic languages also maintained a pitch accent for a long period, as Lithuanian does today, and accordingly they maintain many final syllables. By noting forms in these languages we determine losses that the Germanic cognates have undergone. We find support for our conclusions in Finnish borrowings taken from Proto-Germanic or one of the early dialects, such as *kuningas*, cf. ON *konungr* "king." We also have evidence in forms recorded in the runic inscriptions, as in the form *stainaR*, cf. Goth. *stains*, and in forms cited by classical authors.

If we examine nouns, we find that the *-os* ending of the most frequent class of masculine nouns lost its vowel between Proto-Germanic and the dialects. Goth. *wulfs*, ON *ulfr*, OE *wulf* "wulf" correspond to Gk *lúkos*, Lat. *lupus*, Lith. *vīlkas* and so on; PIE *-o-* was lost in the second syllable in Germanic. Moreover, Goth. *gasts* "guest" corresponds to Lat. *hostis*; here PIE *-i-* was lost. We place the loss relatively late in Proto-Germanic because the *-i-* was still written in the Gallehus inscription, *-gastiR*; similarly *-o-* is maintained in the forms we have in Greek and Roman writers, usually in names, like *Marco-manni*. As these examples may indicate, short vowels were lost in final syllables.

Long vowels, on the other hand, were reduced. The dative singular ending of the Indo-European *o*-stems is posited as *-ōi*. In the Germanic dialects this is reflected as *-a* in Gothic, *-e* in the other dialects, as in Goth. *wulfa*, ON *ulfe*, OE *wulfe*. The specific reductions of the various vowels are highly complex; details may be checked in handbooks. Our interest here is simply the observation that segments of the phonological system can bring about changes in other segments of the system. The most evident such process is the one we have exemplified: loss of final or medial syllables as a result of strong stress on the initial syllable.

Losses may vary with the difference in intensity of the stress. When we examine the Romance languages we find that Spanish has preserved final endings while French generally has not, for example Lat. *lupus* "wulf," Fr. *loup*, Spanish *lobo*. We ascribe the difference to difference in strength of the stress in each.

Not only final vowels of final syllables may be affected. In Irish, vowels of alternate syllables, such as the second in trisyllabic words, were lost, as in the borrowing OIr. *apstal*, cf. Lat. *apostolus*.

The results in any language depend on its phonological system. With adequate information on loss in general, we attempt to reconstruct such systems. We can reconstruct the earlier items only if we have related forms in other dialects of the family.

14.2 INTERRELATIONSHIPS BETWEEN THE PHONOLOGICAL AND THE MORPHOLOGICAL COMPONENTS

When final syllables are lost, morphological paradigms are disrupted. Thus, the Pre-Germanic *o*-stem inflection was relatively parallel in forms in late Indo-European, with stem vowel varying between *o* and *e*, as in nom. *-os*, acc. *-om*, gen. *-eso*. Upon loss of the vowels of final syllables the three forms in Gothic were nom. *dags*, acc. *dag*, Gen. *dagis*, in OE *dæg*, *dæg*, *dæges*. Thus, by Old English times there was no morphological distinction between the nominative and the accusative.

The effects in the verb system were similar, as may be illustrated by comparing the present indicative endings of thematic verbs in Proto-Indo-European and Sanskrit with those in selected Germanic languages. Since the Sanskrit root *bandh-* 'bind' is not inflected as is its cognate in Germanic, we give forms of the root *bhū-* here:

	PIE	Sanskrit	Gothic	Old Norse	Old English
1 sg.	*-ō	bhavāmi	binda	bind	binde
2 sg.	*-esi	bhávasi	bindis	bindr	bindes
3 sg.	*-eti	bhávati	bindiþ	bindr	bindeð
1 pl.	*-omos	bhávāmas	bindam	bindom	bindað
2 pl.	*-ete	bhávatha	bindiþ	bindeð	bindað
3 pl.	*-onti	bhávanti	bindand	binda	bindað

In Gothic the endings are still relatively distinctive, though the third singular and the second plural have fallen together. In Old Norse the second- and third-singular forms have fallen together; in Old English all three persons of the plural have fallen together. The losses of vowels have obscured differences, and forms that were distinctive, like the third plural in Old English, may be taken over in the other persons. Since the strong stress was maintained in the Germanic dialects, the losses also continued. Today all forms of the present are alike in Norwegian; in English a distinction is made only for the third singular.

Losses in the phonological system accordingly have considerable effect on the morphological system. The Sanskrit noun inflection consisted of eight cases. Of these, Lithuanian has maintained the most, lacking only the ablative; on the other hand, by suffixing postpositions it has added three. But most of the dialects have reduced the set of cases greatly. With those reductions other means have been introduced to represent nominal relationships, which is done chiefly through prepositions.

In a similar way, the losses in the verbal system required the use of pronouns to indicate the subject, unless a noun was the subject with third person verb forms. Phonological changes, then, ultimately affect the syntactic system as well as the morphological system.

It should be noted that such changes typically result from modifications in both systems. For example, the shift to SVO structure in the Indo-European languages fostered use of prepositions rather than case endings. Similarly, the requirement of subjects in SVO languages mandates use of first- and second-person pronouns in subject position, reducing the importance of verb endings. When, in addition, the endings were weakly articulated, they tended to be indistinct and were often lost, as in English and French.

14.3 CHANGES RESULTING FROM INTERRELATIONSHIPS BETWEEN MORPHOLOGICAL SUBSYSTEMS

Before examining the effects of morphological losses on the syntactic system we may briefly note changes resulting from lack of symmetry in the morphological system. Indo-European nominal inflection provides examples.

In Proto-Indo-European, declensional endings were added either directly to noun bases or to bases followed by a stem vowel or affix. The so-called root nouns were followed directly by endings, which themselves might be modified, for example Skt *pā́t*, Gk *poús*, Lat. *pēs* "foot," from underlying **pods*. But by far the majority of nouns had affixes added to the root before the inflectional endings, for example PIE *-o-* as in Skt *jánas* "creature," Gk. *génos* "family," cf. Lat. *genus* "kind"; other nouns added *-i-*, with or without a consonant, as *-ti-*, for example Skt *dā́tis* "gift," Gk *dósis*, Lat. *dōs* "gift"; still others added *-u-*, or *-tu-*, *-en-* or *-on-* and so on.

When the pitch accent was maintained, the syllables with these vowels were fully pronounced, and the endings as well as the vowels of the root were maintained. When, however, a stress accent was introduced, the vowels of the ending were either reduced, as in Lat. *genus*, cf. Eng. *kin*, or lost, as in Lat. *dōs* and Eng. *kin*. The separate stems then interacted with one another, leading to reduction of inflections through leveling.

The third declension in Latin provides many examples. Root nouns like *pēs*, Gen. *pedis* "foot" belong to it, but also *-ter* stems, like *pater*, *patris* "father," *-en* stems like *nōmen*, *nōminis* "name," *-s*-stems, like *flōs*, *flōris*. Parallelism between such diverse stems led to further reduction and conflation of the various forms.

We find the same conflation in verbs. In Sanskrit there were ten different present classes; in Latin there were only four. Today there is no distinction of present classes in Germanic languages. The different Indo-European classes interacted, and in the course of time the distinctive markers were lost, in part through loss of final syllables but also through loss of different markers by means of analogical leveling.

The loss of such inflectional classes requires the introduction of other devices to convey certain meanings. Thus, Sanskrit had a distinctive method of deriving causatives from simple verbs inherited from Proto-Indo-European *-eyo-*. In Germanic this class was being lost, partly through merger of the distinctive marker with markers indicating other values. In English the class has been reduced to a few forms, for example *set* beside *sit*, *lay* beside *lie*. Current English conveys causative force with the use of auxiliaries, such as *have*, as in *she had her car repaired*, *get* in *she got the work done* or *cause* as in *that caused the pump to break*. Similarly, the loss of the subjunctive and the optative required the use of auxiliaries to convey the former meaning. The modal auxiliaries were introduced for this purpose, for example *may*, *must*, *might*, *can*, *could*, etc.

Internal changes in the morphological system may in this way have a great effect on the syntactic system. It is instructive to compare the situation in Japanese, where morphological elements were not lost by phonological erosion. Roots of verbs end in consonants, for example *yom-u* "read," or in vowels, for example *tabe-ru* "eat." Causatives may be made from these in a long-established inflection based on forms of the verb *suru* "make," for example *yomaseru* "cause to read," *tabesaseru* "cause to eat"; these forms can be found in Japanese of a millennium ago. Other verbal inflections in Japanese are similarly conservative. With a pitch accent and a simple inflectional system, Japanese reduced its conjugation only in details in contrast with the massive reduction in the Indo-European languages. The syntax also has remained constant.

14.4 EFFECTS OF MORPHOLOGICAL REDUCTION ON THE SYNTACTIC COMPONENT

We have noted above that the loss of morphological markers leads to the introduction of syntactic replacements. Chief among these are function words: adpositions take the place of declensional endings; auxiliaries take the place of conjugational endings or internal markers. We may illustrate the effects by citing several syntactic patterns.

A pattern common for nouns is that of comparison of inequality. For example, the sequence *She is bigger than you* compares unequals, whereas *She is as big as you* indicates similarity or equality. We have noted above that the comparison of inequality involves, besides the adjective, a standard and a pivot. The standard with pivot was inflected in the ablative case in early Sanskrit, as in the Vedic phrase: *ghṛtā́t svā́dīyaḥ* "ghee-from sweeter" = "sweeter than ghee." As the language was moving towards VO structure, the standard could be placed after the adjective, as in *pā́pīyān áśvād gardabháḥ* "poorer horse-from donkey" = "a donkey is less useful than a horse." Even with the shift in location, the standard with its pivot was indicated by inflection.

In Greek the ablative was not maintained, but the genitive replaced it in some uses. As we have noted above, early Greek attests OV comparative constructions like the Vedic above; so does early Germanic, where the dative has replaced the ablative in this use. But as the dative lost its distinctiveness, a particle was introduced, in English of today *than*, in German *als*. Syntactic constructions involving inflections in this way introduce purely syntactic devices when morphological markers are eroded.

In much the same way auxiliaries and other devices, such as derivational constructions, have been introduced as verbal inflections came to be indistinct or not available for extension. The process had already begun in the early Indo-European dialects. Germanic verbs like Goth. *bindan* : *band*, Eng. *bind* : *bound* reflect the basic Indo-European contrast that today indicates tense difference. The phonological distinction, as we noted above, is based on sound changes in Pre-Indo-European and Proto-Indo-European that are referred to as ablaut. These did not fit the structure of derived verbs, such as Goth. *nasjan* "save," *salbon* "anoint," *haban* "have," *fullnan* "fill." Yet pattern congruity required a past-tense form parallel to that of the strong verbs.

A new form was introduced with a *-d-* marker, as illustrated in *nasida* "saved," *salboda* "anointed," *habaida* "had," *fullnoda* "filled." The source of the marker has been strenuously disputed; while its origin is not of primary concern here, in my view it is derivational, like the *-k-* of the Greek perfect, as in *lúō* "I loose" : *léluka* "I have loosed," and like the *-v-* of the Latin perfect, as in *amō* "I love" : *amāvī* "I have loved," as well as other such derivational affixes in the early dialects. This source for morphological categories, however, did not fit the structure of the languages as they became increasingly VO. For VO languages make heavy use of auxiliaries placed before the basic verb to indicate tense, mood and other verbal categories like the causative.

In the historically attested periods of the Indo-European languages such auxiliaries were introduced from a variety of sources. To indicate the perfect forms Germanic made use of the auxiliaries "have" and "be." The auxiliary "have" was used with transitive and many intransitive verbs; the auxiliary "be" was used with intransitive verbs indicating change of place, for example *he is come*, and change of condition, such as *he is become*. In German these rules have been maintained.

In English, on the other hand, *be* is also used to indicate the passive, as in the sentence *Since he is still swimming, the steaks were barbecued by his uncle*. As a result, a form like *he is gone* was ambiguous. Today *have* is the sole auxiliary for the English perfect.

The introduction of auxiliaries, among them *will* for the future, German *werden* for the future and the passive, *esse* "be" for the perfect passive in Latin and others in other languages, has been thoroughly studied. The handbooks, like Jespersen's grammar of English, provide details. These have been reformulated in accordance with the views of individual scholars. The facts are clear; students may wish to examine them in accordance with their own views of language structure.

14.5 GREATER FIXING OF SYNTACTIC ORDER WITH LOSS OF MORPHOLOGICAL MARKERS

When morphological markers or particles are ample in a language, the word order may be relatively free. Latin is notoriously presented as a language with variable word order. Virtually any sentence of Cicero or the classical authors might be cited as an example, for example one of Cicero's orations:

> sī hoc optimum factū iūdicārem, ūnīus ūsūram hōrae
> if this best for-doing I-had-thought of-one use of-hour
> gladiātōrī istī ad vīvendum nōn dedissem
> to-gladiator this for living not I-had-given
> "If I had thought this the best thing to do, I would not have given this scoundrel the leisure of one hour for living."

Modifiers, like *ūnīus* of *hōrae* "of one hour" can be separated as here, because their inflections leave no ambiguity about interpretation. If, however, Cicero's sentence were repeated literally in English, it would be difficult to understand.

As inflections were lost in the Romance languages, their word order became relatively fixed. Similarly in the Germanic languages. We cannot place a noun between the modifier of a genitive and the genitive, as in the Latin above *ūnīus ūsōrem hōrae*; nor can we vary the order of sentence components as did Latin writers. English has a relatively fixed word order, with the subject first, followed by the verb, that in turn followed by the object. And if a sentence includes an indirect object, it must precede the direct object unless it is introduced by a preposition, for example *He brought her the lunch/He brought the lunch to her*.

In general, when languages lose their morphological markers, syntactic patterns are fixed, so that by their position they indicate interrelationships in the sentence that languages with many inflections indicate morphologically.

14.6 SYNTACTIC TENDENCIES AND RULES, WITH EFFECTS ON PATTERNS OF SYNTAX

In the course of syntactic studies various general rules have been determined. These not only regulate syntactic sequences; they may also lead to disruption of syntactic patterning in a given language.

14.6.1 Wackernagel's law

One of the most commonly discussed rules states that enclitics tend to be placed after the first accented word in sentences. Formulated for Indo-European in an impressive article by the great syntactician, Jacob Wackernagel, the rule places weakly accented words like particles and pronouns in second position; the rule is often referred to as Wackernagel's law. For example, the *Odyssey* begins as follows with the weakly accented pronoun *moi* in second position:

ándra moi énnepe . . .
man   me tell
"Tell me of a man . . ."

A number of enclitics may be placed in this position, as in the following clause from Thucydides 4.47:

eí poú   tís tina ídoi   ekhthrón . . .
if anywhere one one   may-see enemy
"If anyone ever saw an enemy anywhere . . ."

Here three clitics are placed after the initial conjunction; in such a sequence each but the last receives an accent, as in this clause.

Since verbs are unaccented in principal clauses in Proto-Indo-European, they are treated as clitics. Consequently, they frequently stand in second place. For example, line 33 of the *Odyssey* begins with the clause:

eks hēméōn gár phasi   kák' émmenai
from us   ptc they-say evils are
"(Humans) say that evil comes from us."

Here the verb *phasi* stands after the initial phrase *eks hēméōn* and a particle; *phasi* shares second position with *gár* rather than standing in final position. The first sentence of Caesar's account of the war in Gaul also has a form of "be" in second position: *Gallia est omnis . . .* "Gaul as a whole is . . ."

Since verbs provide one of the two constituents of the OV/VO nucleus of the clause, any modification of their sequence weakens the standard position. For this reason Wackernagel's law may have been one of the forces that led to the shift from OV order to VO order in the early dialects.

14.6.2 Negative movement, strengthening and attraction

Further syntactic rules have to do with expression of the negative. Patterns of negation received a great deal of attention in the nineteenth century. A short monograph by Otto Jespersen of 1917 summarizes the history of negative expression in English. Jespersen, however, did not relate its position to English typology.

In OV languages, negation is expressed by a suffix after the verb, as in Jap. *tabenai* "does not eat." In VO languages, by contrast, a particle is placed before the verb. This was the situation in Old English, given by Jespersen as the first stage. In that stage negation was expressed by *ne*, as in the example given by Jespersen:

1 *ic ne secge* "I do not say."

The negative marker in this position is weakly stressed. By the process known as **negative strengthening** a noun or particle is added as support later in the sentence, as in more recent examples like *He was not impressed a bit*. In Old English the element *wiht* "thing" was used for this purpose; in this use it is similar to OF. *pas*, and to Lat. *oenum = unum* "one thing," which with Lat. *ne* gave rise to the Latin particle *non*.

By the further process known as **negative attraction** the negative marker was prefixed to *wiht*, giving *nawiht, noht, not*. The second stage of negative expression in English, then, may be illustrated by the Middle English sequence:

2 *ic ne seye not.*

The negation is now doubly expressed, producing redundancy that is not favored in language. Moreover, the weakly stressed *ne* before the verb is open to loss. Accordingly, in a third stage the expression is:

3 *I say not.*

These three stages are paralleled by the development from Lat. *ne dicō* to OFr. *je ne dis pas*, later *je dis pas*. German has remained at this third stage, as in *ich gehe nicht* "I'm not going."

English, on the other hand, came to use auxiliaries extensively in the verb system, among them *do*. Moreover, in a VO language, negation is typically expressed before the principal verb. Accordingly, in a fourth stage the basic pattern is as follows:

4 *I do not say.*

This stage was followed by a fifth, representing current usage:

5 *I don't say.*

English has a large stock of such negative auxiliaries, *aren't, isn't, wasn't, can't, couldn't,* etc.; the English linguist John Rupert Firth suggested regarding them as making up a distinct paradigm. However they are treated in grammars, the history of negative expression in English illustrates how syntactic rules bring about changes in the language.

14.6.3 Afterthoughts

A tendency of OV languages places certain elements after the final verb. Delbrück referred to such elements as a *Schleppe* ("train – as of a dress") (1878: 51–6); a modern term is *afterthought.* In a simple example, the subject is added after the verb, for example Vedic *sá hovāca gā́rgyaḥ* "he now said . . . Gargyas" = "Gargyas then said."

The afterthough may be prompted by the following sentence, as a discourse effect, as in Delbrück's example: *té 'anyám evá pratiprá jighur áṅgirasó'cha* "they another now thither sent . . . to the Angirasas" = "they sent another one . . . to the Angirasas."

If the construction is commonly used, it may lead to a shift from OV structure to VO. Like enclisis of verbs, the use of afterthoughts may have contributed to the shift towards VO order in the early Indo-European dialects.

14.7 INFLUENCE OF BASIC CLAUSE STRUCTURE ON OTHER SYNTACTIC PATTERNS

In chapter 5 we have observed that languages tend to have characteristic VO or OV patterns, as of adpositions, relative clauses and so on. Few documented instances of changing word order have been carefully investigated, and consequently the evidence for the effects of changing clause order is tentative. Two examples may be cited.

The first example deals with constructions in New High German. At the time of humanism in the fifteenth century and later, writers introduced rules for word order that they viewed as based on that of Latin. The prime targets were dependent clauses; in humanistic style they were to conclude with the finite verb. Such a verbal position was not characteristic of medieval German; but it came to be followed carefully in the written language, and is the rule today.

When we examine the subsequent written language, we find two constructions arising. One is the preposed adjectival or participial modifier of nouns, notorious in scientific German, as in the following sentence of Hermann Hirt:

die ursprünglich zugrunde liegende Bildung   ist nicht mehr
the originally   at-basis   lying   formation is no   longer
erkennbar
recognizable
"The formation that originally was underlying is no longer recognizable."

As the translation indicates, the modifier construction is comparable to a relative clause. German, however, as a VO language places relative clauses after their heads. If we analyse the modifier construction rigorously, we find that it is comparable to the relative construction in such OV languages as Turkish. Since its gradual development during the centuries after OV order was introduced in German dependent clauses can be traced in written texts, we may suggest that that order led to the introduction of the OV nominal modifier construction in the written language.

The texts document another OV construction, the use of postpositions. These also arose gradually, such as *entgegen* "opposed to," *entlang* "along," *gegenüber* "opposite," *nach* "after," and so on. Used often, though not exclusively, in the written language, these postpositions can be dated in the large German dictionaries; the postposition *entlang*, for example, is first attested as a postposition in 1741. We may suggest that the postposed position was prompted by the OV order of dependent clauses. English cognates, like *along*, have not been moved in this way.

It would be useful if the hypothesis that change in basic verb order can result in change of parallel constructions would be examined in many further languages.

One such shift has been explained in this way for Sinhalese. Like other Indo-Aryan languages of the south of India, Sinhalese has been strongly influenced towards OV word order by the neighboring Dravidian languages. When we examine Sanskrit, we find that, like the other Indo-European languages, it is shifting from OV to VO word order. We may assume that the modern Indo-Aryan languages would have VO order if they had not been influenced by many speakers of OV languages in the subcontinent. Middle Sinhalese, for example, was strongly VO in order.

The construction of interest in Modern Sinhalese is found in the additive numerals. These, typically "eleven" to "nineteen" are arranged like comparative constructions, with the teen as standard, for example Eng. *seventeen* versus Turkish *onyedi* "ten + seven" = "seventeen." When we examine the Sinhalese teens we find evidence that in Middle Sinhalese they observed VO word order, but then shifted to OV order, as in *daha-hatə* "ten + seven" = "seventeen," presumably due to the strong effect of the OV syntax of Tamil.

These examples may indicate that syntactic patterning and processes may bring about changes within the syntactic component. Syntactic structure is then parallel to phonological and to morphological structure in tending towards pattern congruity, with aberrant constructions modified in accordance with the basic structure.

14.8 SYNTACTIC EFFECTS ON DERIVATIONAL CONSTRUCTIONS

Syntactic patterning affects derivational constructions, notably compounds. It has also long been noted that OV languages favor suffixes over affixes. We will discuss only compounding rules so affected.

Compounds may be regarded as abbreviated clauses. As such, they might be expected to reflect the order of elements in clauses. Yet, once fixed, they tend to be conservative. In English, for example, the bulk of compounds follow modifier + noun patterning, as in *greenpeace, doghouse* etc. While this is the OV pattern, and might not be expected to be so prominent in a VO language, it may owe some of its predominance to the typical adjective–noun sequence as well as to conservatism in language.

In early Greek and Sanskrit, two different types of compounds were most prominent. Synthetic compounds consist of roots in object–verb order, as in Skt *go-sǻ* "acquiring cattle." Possessive compounds consist of a modifier followed by a head, as in Skt *gó-magha* "having an abundance of cattle"; cf. *Bluebeard* "one who possesses a blue beard" beside *bluebird*.

The compounds are exhaustively described by the Sanskrit grammarians, and subsequently by modern grammarians though without explanations for them except for Jacobi's interpretation of synthetics as reduced relative clauses. We explain both synthetics and possessives as abbreviations of clauses. The synthetics are comparable in meaning to relative clauses. Examples with reflexes of PIE *bher-* "bear, bring" are: Skt *vṛṣabharán* "providing virility," Gk *boulēphóros* "providing counsel," Lat. *fructifer* "bearing fruit." As the Sanskrit and Greek forms illustrate, synthetics have the accent on the second component. In this way they correspond to dependent clauses of Proto-Indo-European, which have the verbal element accented.

The possessive compounds are abbreviations of the Pre-Indo-European clause type used for "have"-constructions. That stage of the language expressed possession by means of a dative construction comparable to Lat. *mihi est . . . .* At an earlier stage of the language, the form of "be" would not have been essential. Assuming "have"-clauses of this stage as the pattern for possessive compounds, we propose that in the abbreviated form the pronoun was omitted. Of the numerous possessive compounds in the early dialects we may cite from Sanskrit: *bṛhádratha* "having great chariots," *agnítejas* "having the brightness of fire," *jīváputra* "having living sons." It may be noted that these have the accent on the first component as if they were independent clauses, with meanings like "he has great chariots."

In this way we account for the early compounds in the Indo-European dialects. As the languages came to be VO in structure, the basis for the patterning was lost. In English the *Bluebeard* type of compound survives for pejorative use, for example *redneck* "uneducated rustic," etc. When new compounds are created, like *greenpeace*, the modifier + noun sequence is observed.

These examples may illustrate that both in early Indo-European and in Modern English the prevailing types of compounds reflect a predominant syntactic pattern when the compound structure came to be fixed. In this way syntactic structure may affect morphological patterns as well as other syntactic constructions.

14.9 CHANGES THAT MAY RESULT FROM DISCOURSE PATTERNING

In recent years linguists have concerned themselves at some length with discourse, that is, complete accounts rather than sentences, whether conversations, paragraphs or longer written texts. Among reasons for the concern is the finding that some languages structure sentences differently in paragraphs. The Fore language of New Guinea has the final verb only at the end of a paragraph, using medial verbs to end sentences within the paragraph (see Longacre 1983: 295). The western languages include no such distinction, but they have various devices like anaphoric constructions, or repeated words like *concerned* and *concern* in the first two sentences above, which bind sentences together within paragraphs. When discourse is studied, it is regarded as a higher level than that of syntax.

Western scholars have long dealt with patterning in larger structures under the label stylistics. The standard grammars of Greek by Schwyzer (1939–53) and of Latin by Leumann, Hofmann and Szantyr (1963–79) include extensive treatments of stylistics. Discourse specialists have not yet correlated their efforts with the massive work in stylistics. Nor have they studied effects of discourse structure on syntactic change. Accordingly, we can only provide examples that may suggest how discourse rules may contribute to change of syntax.

We may use the first paragraph of Caesar's report on the Gallic War as illustration. Caesar is acknowledged to be an excellent stylist; like contemporaries in the period of Classical Latin, he went to great pains to provide an elegant report. It begins:

Gallia est omnis divisa   in   partes tres, quarum unam incolunt Belgae,
Gaul is   entire divided into parts three of which one   inhabit Belgae
aliam   Aquitani, tertiam qui ipsorum lingua Celtae, nostra Galli
another Aquitani third   who of-their tongue Celts   in ours Galli

appellantur. Hi   omnes lingua,   institutis, legibus inter   se differunt.
are-called These all   in-tongue institutions laws   among self differ
Horum omnium fortissimi sunt Belgae, . . . proximi sunt Germanis. . . .
of-them of-all   bravest   are Belgae   next   are Germans

> "Gaul as a whole is divided into three parts, one of which is inhabited
> by the Belgae, another by the Aquitani, a third by those who in their
> own language are called Celts, in ours Gauls. All of them differ
> among themselves in language, institutions, laws. Of all of them the
> bravest are the Belgae, . . . they are next to the Germans. . . ."

A thorough analysis of the discourse markers would be lengthy, and
should be based on the entire passage. Since we are concerned with the
effect of discourse on possible syntactic change we may confine ourselves
to observing the position of *est* in the first sentence, of *sunt* in the third. As
we have noted above, Latin has chiefly OV order in sentences, as in the
second here. But these verbs are in second position. That position in the
first sentence is all the more remarkable because the form *divisa est* is
equivalent to the perfect passive. Apparently, the tendency to place unaccented verbs in second position outweighed any other with reference to its
position. Caesar clearly wanted to end the first clause with the phrase *in
partes tres* because of the three following qualifiers. As a result, that clause
is comparable to the English expression.

With such forces in the language, it is almost inevitable that the OV
order would have been modified, as it was in the various areas that adopted
Latin. Since we have noted that languages in general change to VO order
when they are learned by many non-native speakers, the change from OV
order in Latin to VO in late Latin and the dialects may be attributable to
that observation. Yet Caesar's rhetorical device of placing the subject
Belgae after *incolunt* provides support for the proposal that discourse
patterning may have been a contributing reason for syntactic change.
Interrelationships between the levels of discourse and syntax may in this
way lead to changes much as do those between syntax and morphology and
still other levels.

SELECTED FURTHER READING

Examples of changes resulting from interrelationship between various
components may be found in historical grammars. Benveniste (1971) deals
with the changes in various constructions. For an explanation of compounds, see Lehmann (1969: 1–20). For a handbook on discourse see
Longacre (1983).

PROBLEMS

1 In Greek the only final consonants permitted were *n, r, s.* As a result, other final consonants were lost, such as *d* of *tí*, cf. Lat. *quid* "what," Gk *állo*, Lat. *aliud* "other."

 (a) Vocative forms of nouns in some declensions have no ending. The earlier form of such words, as well as the stem, must be determined from other case forms, such as the genitive. Reconstruct the earlier vocative of the following:

   paĩ "oh child," gen. *paidós* _____

   gúnai "oh woman," gen. *gunaikós* _____

   ána "oh ruler," gen. *ánaktos* _____

 (b) Final clusters were also restricted, so that some consonants in nominative singular form were simplified; reconstruct their earlier form:

   paĩs "child" _____

   poús "foot," gen. *podós* _____

   hẽpar "liver," gen. *hḗpatos*, cf. Skt *yakṛt* _____

2 Phonological changes may lead to complex inflections, as in many Greek nouns with earlier *-w-*; for *w* was lost in the language. In examining the forms below, note that pre-Greek /w/ in accordance with Sievers's law varied between [u] and [w]; [u] would not be lost, but often combined with a neighboring vowel to form a diphthong.

 (a) Reconstruct the earlier forms of the genitive and dative of *boũs* "cow":

   Nom. *boũs*   cf. Lat. *bōs*

   Acc. *boũn*

   Gen. *boós* _____

   Dat. *boí* _____

 Reconstruct the earlier forms of *Zeús*; note that Gk *dy* > *z* [dz].

   Nom. *Zeús* _____ cf. Skt *dyaus* "sky"

   Acc. *Día* _____ cf. Lat. *Iovem*

   Gen. *Diós* _____ cf. Lat. *Iovis*, early Lat. *Diovis*

   Dat. *Dií* _____ cf. Lat. *Iovi*

 (c) A form *Zẽn* occurs in *Iliad* 8.206, parallel to the Sanskrit accusative *dyām*. Homer also has the forms: acc. *Zẽna*, gen. *Zēnós*, dat. *Zēní*. how do you account for these three forms?

3 (a) The Old English poem, "The Wanderer," begins as follows. Point out morphological and syntactic differences from patterns in the language today; further, analyse the compounds, indicating current means of expressing their meaning.

   Oft him ānhaga   āre gebīdeð
   often him lone-dweller   mercy experiences
   Metudes miltse,   þēahþē hē mōdcearig
   measurer's grace   although he mind-troubled
   geond lagulāde   longe sceolde
   about sea-ways   long should

hrēran mid hondom   hrīmcealde sǣ
stir with hands   frost-cold sea,
wadan wræclāstas;   wyrd bið ful ārǣd.
travel exile-paths   fate is fully settled

"The lone individual often finds mercy,
grace of the Lord, though, troubled in spirit,
in the paths of the sea he must long
stir with his hands the ice-cold sea,
travel paths of exile; a man's fate is completely determined."

(b) The syntax of *Piers Plowman*, from the fifteenth century, is much more like that of current English than that of Old English; note patterns similar to ours, as well as differences, in morphology as well (the raised dots indicate the metrical division of the line into half-lines.)

In A somer Sesun · whon softe was þe sonne,
I schop me in-to a schroud · A scheep as I were;   (*schop* "put")
In Habite of an Hermite · vn-holy of werkes,
Wende I wydene in þis world · wondres to here,
Bote in a Mayes Morwnynge · on Maluerne hulles
Me bi-fel a ferly · A Feyrie, me þoughte;   (*ferly* "portent")
I was weori of wandringe · and wente me to reste
Vndur a brod banke · by a Bourne syde,   (*bourne* "creek")
And as I lay and leonede · and lokede on þe watres,
I slumberde in A slepyng · hit sownede so murie.

4 English noun compounds have the first element modifying the second except for a small number like the *Bluebeard* or *forget-me-not* patterns. The semantic relationships between the two components may, however, differ, in reflecting patterns of the compounding. Examine the following, determine the interrelationships between the two components and suggest the earlier relationship between them.
(a) rainbow, bedtime, birthday
(b) highway, holiday, sweetheart
(c) frontiersman, salesman, statesman
(d) blowtorch, crybaby, rattlesnake
(e) sunrise, fleabite, dogfight
(f) shoemaker, shopkeeper, stockholder
(g) *Mac* in names is based on the Irish word "son," as *Fitz* is on the Anglo-Norman spelling of OFr. *fils* "son." Discuss the relationships in the compounds: *Macdonald*, *Fitzsimmons*, and account for them with reference to English compounds like *Johnson* as well as to the structure of English. You may note that the relationship in Hebrew compound names like *Ben-Gurion* "son of G." is similar.

15 Linguistic and cultural change

15.1 EARLY ATTENTION TO LANGUAGE AND CULTURE

From the beginnings of historical linguistic study scholars concerned them-selves with culture as well as with language. Jones's celebrated paragraph (cf. Lehmann, ed., 1967 : 15) makes up a very small part of his third anniversary discourse, which is devoted to the culture of the Indians. Schlegel's monograph of 1808 indicates by its title that it deals with culture and the wisdom it may convey as well as with the language. And Bopp's initial work of 1816 gives almost as many pages to his translation of Sanskrit literary works as to the verb system. Many other publications on the two areas appeared in the early part of the century. They include accurate data accompanied by errors, so that today they have been super-seded. Yet they inform us of the established aim of dealing with the early languages in conjunction with the cultures of their speakers.

To illustrate the early attempts we may recall two of the publications. Friedrich Schlegel's older brother, August, wrote on the names of animals and metals. He recognized accurately that Skt *áyas*, Lat. *aes* and Germ. *Eisen* "iron" are cognates. But he also related Lat. *ursus* "bear" with OHG *ors* "horse." As these examples may illustrate, much remained to be done in determining the actual interrelationships, as well as to avoid error. Celtic was scarcely known at the time, so that the source of *Eisen* as a borrowing from Celtic remained for future scholars to determine. And it soon became clear that the word "horse" is not cognate with the Latin word for "bear."

The publication that raised study of language and culture to a higher level of accuracy is Adalbert Kuhn's essay of 1845 "On the history of the Indo-Germanic peoples in the most ancient times." While cautious in its procedures, the essay proposes the aim of determining the conditions of these peoples at the time before their dispersal, that is, of determining the culture of the Indo-Europeans. From his analysis of kinship terms and words like Skt *rājan*, Lat. *rex* "king," Kuhn concluded that the Indo-Europeans had already progressed beyond a patriarchal society. The terms for domesticated animals led him to propose that the Indo-Europeans already possessed the same animals as those of his day; and words for "to plough," Gk *aróō*, Lat. *arāre* indicated to him that they practiced agriculture. They were therefore "a settled people," as terms for habitations substantiate. Kuhn's conclusions, which are remarkably similar to those held today, if not as extensive, indicate that greater control of the early languages, as assembled by Pott and others, brought about improved understanding of the early culture.

In their efforts to determine the culture of the Indo-European peoples, scholars generally maintained the view that Asia was the original home. The phrase *ex oriente lux* was irresistible; it is applied once again by Gamkrelidze and Ivanov (1984), not to the approval of all their critics. Indian literature and philosophy were very impressive. The time of the national archaeologists had not yet come. The general assumptions concerning the Indo-Europeans had them moving from a homeland in India to their later sites in Europe and elsewhere. Whatever the proposals for the Indo-Europeans, procedures were being worked out to determine the origins and the development of early peoples.

Yet similar studies of other language families and their speakers did not appear until later. In 1875 Kremer proposed central Asia as homeland for the Semitic peoples, adding that their oldest center of civilization was in Mesopotamia. Using techniques similar to those applied by Pott and Kuhn, he credited the Semites with use of the camel and the donkey in their expansion. Moreover, he assumed that when they were established in their center, they had goats and sheep, and knew barley, beans, lentils, onions and wheat. In the same year Ahlqvist published his views on the Finnish peoples. He depicted them as making great use of hunting and fishing, though they also possessed horses and cows; but they did not practice agriculture. And unlike the Indo-Europeans, they had no hereditary chiefs and no state organization.

As in linguistic study, the study of cultural conditions of language families other than the Indo-European did not attract so early nor so wide a group of specialists. Yet when it did, the aims were similar in attempting to determine the culture as well as the language of the early speakers. None the less, the attention to the Indo-Europeans remained much greater than that to speakers of other early languages; as a result the information that has been proposed about their culture is also much fuller. Today Afro-Asiatic specialists would be much more likely to locate the homeland of the family in the Sahara than in central Asia. But they have not provided the extensive handbooks on the early period of the family that we find for the Indo-European family of speakers. As a result, we will deal largely with the procedures taken and methods applied to determine their culture and their homeland.

15.2 WORDS AND THINGS – *WÖRTER UND SACHEN*

Interest in the early culture, as well as methods for determining it, were greatly advanced by Jacob Grimm (1848). As in the title of his German grammar, the adjective corresponds to Germanic of today, so that his *History* encompasses the entire subgroup. His methods were announced in a celebrated phrase of the preface, amplified by a metaphor: "I have never been satisfied by words [*Wörter*] without proceeding to things [*Sachen*]. My aim has been not only to build houses, but also to live in them" (1848: xiii).

On the basis of his extensive concern with cultural areas, such as law, Grimm presents an account of the Germanic peoples based on their texts, their traditions, and on the evidence in their language. The chapter titles are quite unlike any we would find in a history of a language today: 1 "Age (era) and language," 2 "Shepherds and farmers," 3 "Cattle," 4 "Hawking," 5 "Farming," 6 "Feasts and months," 7 "Faith, law, customs." Glancing through the thousand and more pages one is almost surprised to find chapters on linguistic matters like the vowels or the consonants.

Grimm's standing at the close of his career would have brought great attention to any work of his. His *History* was very influential; it is still highly readable and informative on the basis of his extensive control of early texts. The approach attracted numerous scholars. Their journal, *Wörter und Sachen*, was one of the important avenues of publication until its end at the beginning of the Second World War. In its pages language was not investigated for its own sake but rather for the information it provides on its speakers.

15.3 THE BEGINNINGS OF SPECIALIZATION;
CONCENTRATION ON LANGUAGE

By the middle of the nineteenth century so much information was available and so many problems had to be solved that younger scholars could not deal with as broad a scope as that controlled by Grimm. Moreover, notable advances were being made in solving linguistic problems, so that attention was drawn to the study of the language. While Grimm threw up his hands at the prospect of dealing with ablaut in 1822, phonologists were beginning to understand the relationships among the Indo-European vowels. In addition, the first group of exceptions to Grimm's law had been solved, and the second as well by Rudolph von Raumer in 1837, but in a brief note that lacked impact. None the less the techniques were being developed that led to Grassmann's important essay of 1862 and Verner's of 1875. (For translations of the cited articles of von Raumer, Grassmann and Verner see Lehmann, ed., 1967 : 67–86, 109–31, 152–63.) Pure linguistic study accordingly was highly attractive.

On the other hand, archaeology was virtually nonexistent. Grimm despaired about getting information from the "old graves." The secure sources were texts and language. Use of language for determining culture came to have its own designation: **linguistic palaeontology**. Since the texts were obviously designed for literary rather than for scientific purposes, more information might be determined about the culture of the Indo-Europeans from words in the Vedas and the Homeric poems than from their fanciful story, much of it concerned with religion rather than with the Indo-European individual. The use of language to determine cultural conditions increased the growing concentration on it.

The leading Indo-Europeanist in the middle of the nineteenth century, August Schleicher (1821–68), published a purely linguistic work four years after Grimm's *History* appeared. That work, a morphology of Old Church Slavonic, was followed by a grammar of Lithuanian (1856–7), based chiefly on fieldwork, not literary texts. And in 1861 he published his *Compendium*. (The author has used the 3rd edn, published in 1871.) The difference between his grammar and Grimm's is apparent from Schleicher's opening sentences (trans. by W.P. Lehmann):

> Grammar forms one part of the science of language; this science is itself a part of the natural history of human beings. Its method is in substance that of natural science generally; it consists in accurate investigation of our object and in conclusions founded upon that investigation. . . . By grammar we mean the scientific comprehension and explanation of the sounds, the forms, the function of words and their parts, and the constructions of sentences.

There is no mention of culture nor of the speaker. Language is to be treated clinically, in line with procedures that had been developed by the natural sciences. While the languages had been spread by the wanderings of its speakers, those wanderings and the peoples were left to the attention of others.

In chapter 2 we have sketched a selection of linguistic problems that occupied linguists in the second half of the century. Many more problems might have been cited. The history of each of the languages and each of the subgroups had to be clarified. A glance at the journals of the time provides information on the many attempts at solutions as well as the advances. The increasing publication made it difficult for specialists to deal with the entire family, let alone culture as well as language; instead, individual scholars devoted themselves chiefly to one branch, like Germanic, or to one period, like Classical Latin or to Proto-Indo-European. Brugmann in the manifesto could warn that the speaker was being neglected in favor of the language. Attracted by linguistic problems, linguists disregarded the warning.

15.4 ATTENTION TO CULTURE

Much as many of the linguists concentrated on the study of languages, others devoted themselves to study of the early cultures. The most influential of these was Max Müller, whose lectures at Oxford University established him as one of the pre-eminent popularizers of language and culture. Opinions on the culture of the Indo-Europeans were still disputed, for example as to whether they knew iron. Regardless of the uncertainties, Müller presented his views so charmingly that he attracted a large audience. To take one example, he assumed that the word for "daughter" was based on the root *dheugh* "extract, milk." The daughter was therefore the milkmaid in the "poetical and pastoral life of the early Aryans . . . It discloses a kind of delicacy and humor even in the rudest state of society, if we imagine a father calling his daughter his little milkmaid" (1891: I, 324). Especially in Germany, novels on early history were very popular.

A comprehensive presentation of the achievements in determining the early culture was given by Otto Schrader (1883 (1890)). Using elegant argumentation, Schrader based his conclusions about Indo-European culture on "the three sisters, linguistic research, prehistoric research, and history" (*ibid.*: 149). He indicates the shortcomings of each, and assigns to linguistics the role of taking over when "historical evidence or ambiguous myths and sagas" no longer give "clues." "Archaeological palaeontology . . . takes us a step further, and then only where it is possible, with some probability, to assign the monuments recovered by archaeology to a definite people" (*ibid.*: 148). That is to say, Schrader recognized the same problems in dealing with archaeological data that subsequent archaeologists characterize by statements like "stones do not speak" or "pots do not equal people." He also provides a full picture of the early culture, devoting a great deal of space to the use of metals (150–239) before describing the "primeval period" (240–425). In view of Schrader's summary of nineteenth-century findings, we may note the twelve topics in his description of the society and culture of the Indo-Europeans. They are: the animal kingdom, cattle, plant-world, agriculture, computation of time, food and drink, clothing, dwellings, traffic and trade, family and state, religion, the original home.

Schrader places the home in the south Russian steppe, about half-way up the Volga. As we note below, this is approximately the site proposed by Gimbutas and also by Childe. Schrader's argumentation is comparable to that we use. The Indo-Europeans were acquainted with the horse, but not with the camel and ass. The proposed location provides the simplest explanation of the early contacts with the Finns. In addition, Schrader makes use of the Finnic Mordwin name for the Volga, *Rau*, which he relates to the Indo-European root *sreu* "flow," by argumentation that we find less compelling. But, given the restriction to information from the language and texts, it may be clear that his work on Indo-European culture provides a definitive statement on the achievements of nineteenth-century scholars, much like that of Brugmann on the early languages and the proto-language. Brugmann wrote approvingly of Schrader's work.

Its recognized shortcoming consisted in the lack of archaeological support. The last edition of the book appeared at a time when archaeology was beginning to use strict methods. Flinders Petrie introduced the practice of determining strata. Yet for some time the major contributions of archaeology to historical linguistics came from discoveries of materials, the Hittite texts in Turkey, the Tocharian manuscripts in Chinese Turkestan, the Linear B texts in Crete. These contributions have continued. But today the greatest interest comes from precise identification of artifacts and the time of their deposit.

Works on the early culture continued to be published, for example by Hirt. These came to be affected increasingly by nationalism, and worse, by racism. Many scholars in Germany now proposed a homeland in northern or in central Europe. A crucial argument for them was provided by the Indo-European etymon of *lox* and the presence of salmon in its rivers. They also relied heavily on the name *beech*, and its habitat only west of a line extending approximately from Danzig to the Crimea. Both arguments ruled out Asia, and also southern Russia, as home. Subsequently, both arguments were nullified; the presence elsewhere of salmon in the third millennium was established, and linguistic evidence for the beech in the eastern dialects was disproved, so that the word may have originated in the western subgroup rather than in the proto-language. But many scholars still place the homeland in areas of Europe.

Articles with racist bias mar an elaborate publication on the state of the art of Indo-European studies that commemorated Hirt's seventieth birthday (Arntz 1936). The 436 pages of the first volume deal with the results of cultural history and anthropology, the 602 pages of the second with the results of linguistics. Many of the essays are still pertinent, especially in the second volume; but we are taken aback by others with titles like "Origin of the Nordic race and the Indo-European question" (I 287–316). The disruption of the Second World War was equally devastating to the study of Indo-European culture. The continuity extending from Kuhn to Hirt was broken. It has taken some time for resumption of concentrated work, and that is to be credited to archaeologists.

15.5 TWO FURTHER CONTRIBUTIONS ON INDO-EUROPEAN CULTURE

While publications on the culture of the Indo-Europeans after the appearance of Schrader's work dealt primarily with details, two further works provided notable advances. One was Franz Specht's book of 1944, reprinted in 1947 to make up for the loss of the first printing. In its major contribution Specht demonstrated the importance of determining chronological strata in the lexicon. That had long been achieved in phonology and grammar. The vowel changes leading to the ablaut relationships clearly took place at various times. And after the discovery of laryngeals, it was also clear that these were being lost in certain environments while the ablaut changes were taking place. Consonant changes also were viewed by strata, though chiefly in the dialects, as by the first Germanic shift and the second, or Old High German, consonant shift.

Specht made use of conclusions that had been reached regarding morphological sets. It was generally held that root noun inflection represented an earlier stage than did the thematic *o*-stems and *ā*-stems. Accepting that finding, Specht pointed out that many of the words for nature and everyday culture were inflected as root nouns. A notable group that is inflected thematically has to do with transportation. The nouns for the wagon and its parts, such as the wheel, Gk *kúklos*, and for the horse, Gk *híppos*, are *o*-stems. On the basis of their formation, Specht proposed that transportation by means of wagons and horses was introduced late in the Indo-European community, shortly before the time of dispersion.

In this way Specht made use of the technique of identifying strata in the proto-language, much as Flinders Petrie had in archaeology. Oddly, archaeologists have failed to use Specht's contributions. Linguists have expanded them, proposing successive strata with data co-ordinated from phonology, morphology and syntax as well as the lexicon.

More recently the eminent Indo-Europeanist, Emile Benveniste, published an impresssive work on selected social and cultural topics, *Indo-European Language and Society* (1973). Its omissions may be almost as significant as the topics discussed; for, by disregarding the data on everyday life, Benveniste virtually suggests that Schrader's are valid. He concentrates on six topics: economy, the vocabulary of kinship, social status, royalty and its privileges, law, religion. In spite of archaeological advances that provided information on daily life, which was lacking to Schrader, Benveniste confines his study to social practices. As we have noted above, Szemerényi subsequently published a monograph on the Indo-European kinship terms. In directing their attention to specific social practices, Benveniste and Szemerényi have amplified our understanding of Indo-European culture. But the restricted scope of their efforts may also illustrate the expanding body of knowledge about the proto-language and its speakers.

15.6 THE KURGAN HYPOTHESIS

Marija Gimbutas begins a paper given in 1966 and published in 1970 with the bold statement:

Post-World War II developments in archaeology in general and the breath-taking pace of excavations in the Soviet Union and the satellite countries have changed many of the old views on "die indogermanische Urheimat." Chronological and geographical gaps gradually are being filled and archaeologists can present some facts with some certainty. The existence of Indo-European homelands advocated by linguists for more than 100 years is no longer an abstraction; results achieved by archaeological research make it possible to visualize the homelands, at a certain time and place, as a historical reality. (1970: 155).

Ten years earlier Gimbutas had introduced the term **kurgan** ("round mound") as a designation for a culture with various earlier names, among them the Russian Sredniy Stog II and Yamna, as well as Corded, Battle-Axe, Ochre-Grave and so on. Taking the practice of burial under barrows as a significant marker of Indo-European culture, she located their home-land in southern Russia and then identified their extension by numerous barrows found throughout Europe. The practice of burying heroes under mounds is indeed characteristic of Indo-European culture, as demon-strated by the final book of the *Iliad* and the conclusion of the *Beowulf*. And archaeological finds, such as the horse bones dated 4400 BC at Dereivka, an archaeological site on the Dnieper, agree well with assump-tions about the Indo-Europeans and their culture that had been deter-mined on the basis of linguistic evidence. Further support was given by the "remains of two- and four-wheeled wooden vehicles with solid wheels of oak and their models in clay [that] have been found in the lower Dnieper and Volga region" (*ibid.*: 161). The kurgan culture, as presented by Gimbutas (1970), and by others in numerous subsequent publications, agrees with the conclusions of Schrader and the other scholars who based their conclusions on the texts and inferences from the lexicon. Everything seemed to fall in place.

In her article of 1970 Gimbutas speaks of infiltration by kurgan elements and waves of expansion (*ibid.*: 180, 181). But in subsequent years the kurgan hypothesis came to be associated with spread by migrations similar to those of the Germanic peoples from the first century BC. Moreover, the kurgan peoples came to be regarded as warriors who disrupted the peace-ful agricultural peoples living in Europe. The contrast was intensified by the proposal that these agricultural peoples had kindly matrilineal rulers, in contrast with the warlike patriarchal control of the Indo-Europeans.

Whoever proposed these views, they were unrealistic for the period concerned; the sparse population of the time would not have provided large groups comparable to those of the Cimbri and Teutons who invaded southern France around 110 BC. The kurgan hypothesis aroused strong opposition. None the less, it attracted devoted followers, especially in the United States, who published vigorously in its support. Decisive archaeolo-gical data in its favor were not assembled. While it remained the hypothesis to disprove, it did not establish itself generally.

15.7 EXTENSION OF LANGUAGES IN CONJUNCTION WITH ECONOMIC ADVANCES

While Gimbutas assembled archaeological data that agreed with conclusions determined by linguists, in 1987 the archaeologist Colin Renfrew proposed a solution to "the puzzle of Indo-European origins" purely on archaeological grounds. He associated the spread of the Indo-Europeans and their languages with that of agriculture. Archaeologists had determined that domesticated plants and animals had been introduced to Europe from Anatolia around 6000 BC. Correlating the two innovations, Renfrew identified the carriers of the new agricultural procedures with speakers of the Indo-European languages.

Renfrew's proposal received a great deal of publicity and elicited vigorous comment. It seemed very attractive to have economic advances associated with the spread of new speakers. And diffusion was much more likely around 6000 BC than even small-scale migrations. But the proposal lacked linguistic and cultural bases.

There is no evidence for Indo-European languages in Anatolia until the entry of the Hittites in the last part of the third millennium. And the iconography of central Anatolia gives evidence for a totally different type of religion and other cultural practices from that of the Indo-Europeans. The Indo-Europeans recognized a sungod, whose name is reflected in Zeus and Jupiter, accompanied by few other divines, notably two horsemen, reflected as Castor and Pollux. There were no goddesses, even in Vedic times, with the minor exception of dawn. By contrast, the Mediterranean world recognized many goddesses, as is clear from those added to the Greek and Latin pantheons. Accordingly, the proposed basis for solving the puzzle came to be seen as weak.

Many further counterarguments have been advanced to Renfrew's hypothesis, such as the introduction of new terms for domesticated plants in the northern European languages. If Indo-European speakers had introduced the plants, they would have had names for them. But that argumentation is outside our basic concern. What interests us here is the methodology by which the "puzzle" may be solved.

Renfrew's book has shown definitively that economic developments may have nothing to do with the spread of languages. Like linguistics, archaeology must determine its methods through examination of comparable phenomena. Archaeologists studying the spread of corn in North America have found that it was brought out of Mexico to the north without spread of languages (Smith, 1989). By making such prominent use of a failed comparison between economic and linguistic change, Renfrew has made clear that we will be able to determine the early location of the Indo-European peoples only through ever finer analysis of linguistic and textual as well as archaeological data.

15.8 INCREASE IN PRECISION OF ARCHAEOLOGICAL AS WELL AS LINGUISTIC DATA

While Renfrew's book was being reviewed, David W. Anthony was carrying on precise research that reaffirmed the homeland in southern Russia while illustrating the methods that must now be used to draw conclusions from archaeological as well as linguistic data. Through painstaking analysis of horses' teeth, Anthony determined how one might detect the wear caused by rope bridles. After such determination he analysed large quantities of horses' teeth from various sites. Using elaborate techniques currently available, he found the earliest evidence in teeth excavated at Dereivka and dated around 4000 BC. There is, of course, no direct correlation between that finding and the Indo-Europeans or their language. But we have long known that Indo-Europeans were among the earliest to ride horses. It is, then, a simple matter to relate the horse buried at Dereivka with the homeland of the Indo-Europeans.

The evidence fits with Specht's based on his analysis of the inflectional system. Moreover, it is in accord with the proposals of Gimbutas on the Sredniy Stog culture. Linguists and prehistorians will no doubt continue to examine the evidence. Whatever the outcome, it is clear that any further statements must be based on precise linguistic analysis, like that of Specht, and equally precise archaeological analysis, like that of Anthony.

A similarly minute topic has been elegantly treated by Watkins (1990). Taking a phrase from Varro, *tarentum Accas*, Watkins subjects it and its cognates to meticulous analysis. In addition, he examines associated cultural practices, the *ludi Saeculares*, secular games performed at Rome once a century. On the basis of meanings of the root *$*terh_2$-* "overcome" in Hittite and *tīrat-* "crossing" in the *Rigveda*, he concludes that "the Roman ritual for the dead at the Tarentum, the 'crossing place,' is at the same time a ritual to assure the long life and orderly succession of the generations; it is a reaffirmation of the crossing of the *saecula* of a hundred years" (1990: 143). In this way he reconstructs Indo-European ritual, largely from a passage that had to be restored to provide its meaning.

These illustrations may indicate procedures that are now necessary to make further advances in correlating data provided from archaeological finds and linguistic analysis. The advances are built on information that has been assembled since the days of Bopp and Grimm. As in other scientific fields, the methodology is meticulous. The two illustrations may also suggest that careful work based on thorough knowledge of previous contributions will result in additional understanding of the Indo-European family of speakers as well as those of other languages.

15.9 LINGUISTIC INFERENCES IN PREHISTORIC PERIODS

Although our earliest texts date from around 3000 BC, archaeological finds give us evidence about much earlier cultures. Relating those finds to residues in the languages provides important opportunities for fuller understanding of the speakers of the proto-languages in their background. Conclusions may be based on tenuous evidence. Yet new procedures in applying technologies in the sciences, such as molecular biology and genetics, make available data that were totally unavailable to our predecessors. Further, as Watkins has demonstrated, residual data in the texts may be interpreted to illuminate those data. We may note briefly two examples, the first based chiefly on archaeological finds.

In an elegant book, Barber (1991) treats "the development of cloth in the neolithic and bronze ages," with special reference to the Aegean. Of the 471 pages, only one chapter, 12 (260–82), deals with language. The remainder presents in great detail the evidence for producing cloth from 20,000 BC. By limiting its treatment to such a restricted set the chapter clarifies terms for the technology that had previously been obscure or misinterpreted. Distinct subsets within the set are recognized, one from the proto-language; others are borrowings, probably from two different languages. One of these is located in the Balkans, suggesting that the Greeks came to the Hellenic peninsula by that route, in contrast with Renfrew's notion of spread from Asia Minor.

Moreover, for many of the items there are two terms, one derived from the proto-language, the other borrowed. Such arrays of synonyms leave little doubt that the Greeks adopted the technology, as well as technical terms, from indigenous speakers.

The concentrated attention to the set of words enables Barber to correct previous lexicographers, who glossed *ēlakátē* as "distaff" rather than "spindle," as Barber has determined it to be. In this way she has improved our understanding of the Greek as well as the Indo-European lexicon.

A prime interest here is an inference made by Barber in an appendix to the first chapter (36–8), about the borrowing Lat. *cannabis*, Gk *kánnabis*, Eng. *hemp*. It has long been assumed that the word was borrowed into these languages, probably from Thracian. Further, since the word underwent the Germanic consonant shift [k > h, b > p], the borrowing is placed early in the first millennium BC. Pointing out that the Indo-Europeans "knew and were using hemp since 5000 BC," Barber suggests that the word was taken over because it referred to a narcotic-bearing hemp, adding that there is evidence for such use of narcotics from this time. The inference is of great interest, for it assumes that "enough people were travelling *back and forth* between Iran (where [the THC-bearing hemp] grew) and eastern Europe that they could spread a *habit*" (*ibid.*: 36). We leave further support for the hypothesis to specialists. Our prime interest here has to do with an inference based on extensive study of a restricted sphere and on an assumption about a change in culture of the speakers. Before Barber's hypothesis, the terms for "hemp" were cited largely to date the time of the Germanic consonant shift.

In connection with a second such hypothesis we recall Schmandt-Besserat's determination of the origins of writing. Moreover, we note again that the tokens referred to quantities of specific substances, rather than to abstract numerals as in our system today. That is to say, the tokens were comparable to number systems with mandatory classifiers, like those in languages of southeast Asia, including Chinese, and of Central America. In those languages any listing of quantities must be accompanied by a classifier, as in our expression "a hundred head of cattle." While the pre-Sumerian languages using the system of tokens are unknown, we may assume that they had number systems like those with classifiers. As testimony for that inference we may note that the Sumerian word for "one," *as*, means "man," and that for "two," *min*, means "woman"; at this point such references stop, for *eš* "three" means "many," and *geš* "the great unit" comes to stand beside *aš* for "one." Moreover, Joran Friberg has determined numerical references that correspond to measures (1984: 110–18). Presumably, a number system resembling use of tokens was first developed, and then superseded by one with a word for each numeral.

When by contrast, we examine the Indo-European set of numbers we find that **oinos*, the primary word for "one" is based on the root **ʔey-* "this," that for "two" on the root **dew-* "distant," that for three on the root **ter* "beyond." That is to say, the words are based on pointing to objects, rather than on specific references like Jap. *ichi-nin* "one man," etc.

While tokens have been found throughout the Middle East, none have been discovered in southern Russia, the presumed homeland of the Indo-Europeans. Accordingly, I have proposed that the Indo-Europeans used a totally different basis for their number system from one based on classifiers (1990: 38–42). The inference may be supported by further numbers that can be identified. The term for "five", **penkwe*, has been determined to refer to a total set; that is, in a pointing system, use of the whole hand provided the number. And Hittite has given us the presumable Indo-European word for "four," *mi-ia-u-e-es*, which Neu has related to the root **mey-* "lessen," that is, the "lesser hand, the hand without counting the thumb." The remaining numbers, including the etymon of our word "four," are obscure in origin, and may well have been borrowed.

These two illustrations may suggest further opportunities in use of linguistic and archaeological data for determining in greater detail the linguistic as well as the cultural situation of social groups in prehistoric times. Barber concludes her chapter on "word excavation" as follows:

> We have shown that languages, like habitation sites, can contain "excavatable" strata that turn out to correlate with tangible cultures. And we have demonstrated that as linguistics and archaeology pass their

information back and forth and build on each other's findings, both fields stand to gain enormously from this process of word excavation.

(1991: 282)

Many opportunities, then, are open for better understanding of the early periods of language families. But they can be exploited only on the basis of minute control of the linguistic and the archaeological data.

SELECTED FURTHER READING

Schrader (1883 (1890)) is still worth consulting for its sober evaluation of evidence and its collections of data, even though it lacks archaeological evidence. Cardona *et al.*, (1970) contains articles that deal with theoretical approaches applicable also outside the Indo-European sphere. Skomal and Polomé (1987) also includes articles of general reference while focussed on Indo-European, and Renfrew (1987) also deals with the Indo-Europeans, but exemplifies an approach based on a specific archaeological theory.

PROBLEMS

1 Earlier treatments that set out to depict the culture of speakers of proto-languages, especially Proto-Indo-European, are criticized for relying too heavily on linguistic palaeontology. But after pointing out the extent of recorded historical data, Schrader states:

> that at the very most language can only give us a skeleton, and that to cover the dry bones with flesh and blood is the prerogative of the Comparative History of culture. That the Indo-Europeans did possess the notion of a house the philologists show us, for the Sans. *damá*, Lat. *domus*, G. *dómos*, Slav. *domŭ*, correspond; but how these houses were constituted the historian of primitive culture alone can ascertain.

(1883 (1890): 149)

(a) Interpreting "historian of primitive culture" as archaeologist, discuss Schrader's views on the data to be expected from historians, linguists and archaeologists.
(b) Recalling Mallory's statement that "pots do not equal people," what are the difficulties faced by archaeologists? How can archaeologists identify specific peoples, whether recorded by historians or posited by linguists, with data obtained from language?

2 In cautioning linguists to be wary of overinterpreting possible data, Schrader points out that even exact lexical correspondences must be carefully scrutinized. As an example he points out that "an equation such as Sans. *paktár* "cook": rt. *pac* = Lat. *coctor* : *coquo* – might lead to the conclusion that chefs de cuisine formed a professional class in

primeval times" (1883 (1890): 136). He even urges caution about assuming a class of carpenters on the basis of "Sans. *tákshan* = Greek *téktōn* 'carpenter,' " pointing out that individuals might fill such roles only occasionally. Discuss some of the problems that may arise from ascribing activities of today to speakers of early languages on the basis of words with apparently the same meanings.

3 Renfrew associated the spread of the Indo-European languages with the extension of agriculture to Europe, treating that as a technological advance. But D. Mackenzie Wallace, quoted by Schrader (1883 (1890): 285–6), has a somewhat different opinion of the advantages provided by agriculture. Wallace goes to great length to present a different view. In his opinion

> pastoral life is so incomparably more agreeable than the hard lot of the agriculturist, and so much more in accordance with the natural indolence of human nature, that no great legislator . . . could possibly induce his fellow-countrymen to pass voluntarily from the one to the other. Of the ordinary means of gaining a livelihood – with the exception perhaps of mining – agriculture is the most laborious, and is never voluntarily adopted by men who have not been accustomed to it from their childhood.

Wallace holds that only "the prospect of starvation could induce men who live by their flocks and herds to make the transition to agricultural life."

Discuss Renfrew's theory with reference to Wallace's views. Can Renfrew have drawn his conclusions without taking into consideration the difficulty of practicing agriculture, especially in early times when in "dense primeval forests . . . the impatient nomad [would be forced] to take in hand . . . the plough which the man and master by preference left to women, children, grey-beards," as reported by Tacitus? Or are Wallace's views on the life of the agriculturist overly pessimistic? Compare the settling of the west in the United States, including motives of the settlers.

16 Conclusion

16.1 THE IMPORTANCE OF DEALING WITH LANGUAGE AS A WHOLE IN STUDYING CHANGE

When we deal with individual changes in language – changes in sound, form or meaning – we may give the impression that entities in a language are undergoing change of only one type at one time. We may fail to observe that as phonological changes are taking place, morphological, syntactic or semantic changes may be going on at the same time, and also that importations may be introduced; moreover, that none of these changes may be related to one another. Yet, as indicated below, such changes interact, and in time affect the language as a whole, not merely one segment of it.

Further, when we deal with any problem, we generally use a single method among those established in historical linguistics. To secure our data for Old English strong verbs, we simply master the writing system of Old English and compile the essential material. If we wish to deal with Proto-Germanic strong verbs, we use the comparative method. In attempting to find an explanation for the vowel variation in Germanic strong verbs and related forms in other languages, which is already present in the reconstructed Proto-Indo-European, we use the method of internal reconstruction. Again, however, we cannot isolate one method from another. Especially if we are dealing with the history of a language rather than with an isolated problem, we must be prepared to use at one time all the methods developed in historical linguistics. Even when we deal with an isolated problem, our explanation may be inadequate if we rely solely on one method. The interlocking of the various changes and our use of all possible methods may be illustrated with virtually any linguistic material. We may use as examples some of the developments that the English verbs *write* and *shrive* have undergone.

16.2 CHANGES IN THE PHONOLOGICAL SYSTEM

OE *wrītan* and *scrīfan* belong in the class with *bītan* and *drīfan,* having the principal parts:

wrītan	wrāt	writon	writen
scrīfan	scrāf	scrifon	scrifen

Between Old English and contemporary English, the *ī* of the first principal part underwent the same sound change to NE /ay/ as did accented *ī* in words of whatever class, nouns such as *life*, pronouns, such as *I*, adjectives such as *blind*, and so on. Still other sound changes affected the forms of these verbs, such as the loss of *w* before *r*, the raising of *ā* to *ō*, compare NE *home* <OE *hām*, and others. Through sound changes that modified their forms but did not affect their morphological contrasts, the Old English forms of *write* and *shrive* developed to the forms we know today: *write, wrote, written*; *shrive, shrove, shriven*.

16.3 CHANGES IN THE MORPHOLOGICAL SYSTEM

At the same time changes were taking place that affected the morphological system in which the two verbs belong. If the Old English forms had been continued with the intervening sound changes, we today would say *I wrote* but *we writ*. The complication of distinguishing the preterite plural from the singular through internal vowel differentiation was absent in the numerous weak verbs, and in classes 6 and 7 of the strong verbs; in classes 4 and 5 of strong verbs, it was essentially a contrast of quantity, and this was eliminated in Middle English as in OE *bær* "I carried" : *bǣron* "we carried." Accordingly, only the first three classes of strong verbs indicated the distinction; they were regularized in keeping with the predominant pattern. The morphological change, by analogical regularization, was wholly unconnected with sound changes of the time. We have noted that in the morphological rearrangement the plural vowel was generalized in *bite, bit*, whereas in *write, wrote* like *drive, drove*, the singular vowel came to be used through the past.

Other morphological changes are directly connected with sound change. The Old English first-singular present *wrīte* became a monosyllable as final vowels were lost, falling together with the imperative. Moreover, the infinitive ending, OE *-an*, became *-en*, *-e* and was eventually lost.

The plural of the present underwent further changes, which we cannot account for without drawing information from study of the English dialects. The Old English plural ending *-þ*, as in *wrītaþ* "we, you, they write," should have been maintained as some sort of final dental today. But, as noted in chapter 6, contemporary standard English is not a direct continuation of the Old English in which most texts survived, rather a reflex of the Midland dialects. In Middle English the Midland dialects generalized the subjunctive plural ending *-en* to the indicative. Chaucer, for example, who used the Midland dialect of London, says in the Prologue to the *Canterbury Tales*, line 12: *thanne longen folk to goon on pilgrimages*. Like the infinitive ending, the plural -*en* was gradually lost, though -*en* survives in the infinitive to the time of Shakespeare.

16.4 CHANGES IN THE SYNTACTIC SYSTEM

Through the sound changes affecting endings like the -*e* and -*an/-en* of verbs, the syntactic system was greatly modified. These sound changes are partially responsible for the reduction of the contemporary English verb system to a small number of forms, and consequent requirement of overt subjects for verbs as well as fixed word order. When the first person singular was distinguished from the second and third persons singular, and from the plural by endings, pronouns were not essential. In *Beowulf*, verbs may be used, as in Latin and Greek, with no pronoun specifying the subject. Today a telegraphic statement like *wrote* is quite ambiguous, for the subject could be singular or plural, first or third person, possibly even second.

Among other syntactic changes, the final verb position in the clause was being modified. *Beowulf* still is predominantly OV, as in the initial lines:

Hwæt, wē Gār-dena   in gēardagum
þēodcyninga   þrym gefrūnon,
hū ðā æþelingas   ellen fremedon!

"Now we have heard stories   of high valor
in times long past   of the tribal monarchs
lords of Denmark,   how those leaders strove."

In both lines 2 and 3, the verbs are final, and in line 2 the genitive precedes its noun *þrym*; but even in late Old English this order of verbs with regard to their objects, and of genitive constructions, is being modified to the VO order found in English today.

16.5 CHANGES IN THE SEMANTIC SYSTEM

As these and other shifts were taking place in the phonological and syntactic systems, entities in the semantic system were being modified. When the Germanic peoples came into contact with the Romans, they learned new activities, such as writing. With the process they took over the name, borrowing Lat. *scrībere*. Their early writing was done on wood, bone, even stone. Accordingly, a native term, the etymon of *write*, meaning "scratch," was modified and extended as a synonym for the borrowed form of *scrībere*. In New High German its cognate *reissen* still means "tear," earlier "scratch," though compounds like *Reissbrett* "drawing board" exemplify the meaning "write." In English, however, *shrive* came to be restricted more and more to the technical dialect of ecclesiastics, with the meaning of "hear confessions and give absolution." The related *Shrove* was used primarily for the Sunday, Monday and Tuesday preceding Ash

Wednesday, when one confessed in preparation for Lent. With growing abandonment of confession, *shrive* and *Shrove* have virtually passed out of use; but nonecclesiastics may still give offenders *short shrift.*

16.6 CHANGES RESULTING FROM BORROWING

Shrive as loanword and *write* as extension illustrate changes that may result from contact with a foreign language. In their development both illustrate the interplay of technical dialects. One such dialect was that associated with the production of runes, which were commonly inscribed on beech tablets, as we know today from the modification of meaning in *book* <*bōk* "book, beech tree." The technical dialect subsequently involved was that of the church. At the same time forms of *shrive* and *write* were changed by the contacts between northern and southern English geographical dialects. Without a readiness to admit variables introduced in the development of a set of forms by borrowing, which (noted in the analysis of *shrive* and *write*) may be superimposed on changes in the phonological, syntactic, and semantic systems, we would be unable to account for many phenomena in language.

16.7 THE IMPORTANCE OF DEALING WITH CHANGES IN RELATION TO SPECIFIC LINGUISTIC STRUCTURES

Although for simplicity we are restricting our discussion here primarily to two words, we cannot account for their development if we isolate them from the structural sets to which they belong. Both *write* and *shrive* belonged in Old English to a phonological set in which the initial consonantal segment was a cluster composed of consonant plus *r*. Morphologically, their roots fell into a set with roots like *bītan*, in which the initial consonantal element was followed by *ī* plus consonant. This structure characterizes strong verbs of the first class; as a result of its coinciding with this structure, the borrowed Lat. *scrībere* was taken over as a strong verb. To understand phonological, morphological, syntactic and semantic changes we must deal with entities in the context of their structures.

Historical linguistics, to be adequate, must be structural, as the founders of the field noted on the basis of conclusions reached by Cuvier as well as the practices of the Schlegels, Bopp and Grimm among others. Recent linguistic study has extended the emphasis of structure to the syntactic and the semantic components, as we have seen in examining the developments in typological study.

In semantic study we must deal with words in their semantic fields. Unless we dealt with OE *wrītan* and *scrīfan* as members of a semantic set that were used for writing and related activities, explaining their shifts of meaning would be difficult. It may be an oversimplification to ascribe the shift of meaning found in *shrive* to its presence in a semantic set with *write*;

we find this shift, however, in the Germanic area in which the term used especially for production of runes was generalized for all kinds of writing.

16.8 THE IMPORTANCE OF DEALING WITH CHANGES IN RELATION TO SPECIFIC SOCIAL CONDITIONS

Besides coming to know the changes that elements of a language may undergo, each in its several components, we must master the techniques that give us our information. Through knowledge of the Old English writing system as it was developed from the Roman, with modifications because of strong Irish influence, we learn to know our basic Old English material. Unless we bring to the study of Old English a mastery of the lessons taught by the study of dialect geography, our understanding of it and its changes to the Middle English and the Modern English periods will be poor.

We have noted complexities in the develement of the English verb paradigm. More such complexities are involved in the development of the third-singular present ending -*s*. Its etymon is found in northern texts in Old English times, but the reflex of OE -*eþ* persists in southern dialects; Chaucer still uses it, for example *hath*. In the fifteenth and sixteenth centuries there is increasing evidence for -*s* in the speech of London, but literary texts use -*th* even later, as in the Authorized Version of the Bible. In the course of time, -*s* replaced -*th*, through influences about which scholars are not yet agreed. An influence besides the northern -*s* forms may be the third-singular ending in the frequent verb form *is*.

16.9 THE USE OF THE COMPARATIVE METHOD AND THE METHOD OF INTERNAL RECONSTRUCTION

Since English is well attested, for information on its development we rely almost entirely on written texts. When, however, we wish to deal with the grammar of Proto-Germanic, in the absence of texts we must use the comparative method to determine our materials. Comparing OE *wrītan*, OSax. *wrītan*, OHG *riẓan*, the runic ON *wrait* "wrote" and Goth. *writs* "stroke," as well as other forms, we reconstruct the Proto-Germanic verb forms. With the help of the comparative method we can assume for Proto-Germanic a strong verb system in which the roots show a variation which for the etymon of *write* would be:

*wreyt- *wrayt- < *wroyt- *writ- *writ-

We apply the comparative method also to our reconstructed Proto-Germanic forms and cognates in other dialects, such as Gk *rhī́nē* "file," reconstructing Proto-Indo-European in the same way as we reconstruct Proto-Germanic.

Our understanding of Proto-Indo-European and its dialects is deepened

in various ways, by study of texts that are available, by applying the comparative method and the method of internal reconstruction, and testing the results by contributions provided by typological studies. Since Proto-Indo-European has no demonstrated cognates, the comparative method does not permit us to carry our investigations of language further back in time.

The method of internal reconstruction enables us to analyse Proto-Indo-European itself and to make inferences about segments of it at an earlier time. In section 8.4 we noted the application we may make of the method for reconstructing the vowel alternations found in Germanic strong verbs. This method has led us to conclude that the various forms of the vocalic nucleus can ultimately be related, through sound changes that we may indicate in a simplified manner as:

e > *o* (in the form we know as preterite singular and in other derived forms)
e > ∅ [zero] (in the forms we know as preterite plural, in the preterite participle and in other derived forms)

Although these sound changes took place so early that very little evidence remains by which we might reconstruct the linguistic conditions for them, we assume the following environments. PIE *e* became *o* when the pitch accent was shifted to another syllable. The shift was carried out when derived forms were made with the Indo-European suffix *-eyo-*, as in Gk *phoréō* "bear constantly, wear" from the root **bher-* "carry," or Lat. *monēo* "advise" < "cause to think," from the root **men-* "think." This form of the root has been maintained in the borrowing from Latin, *admonish*.

At a later time PIE *e* was lost when a stress accent fell on another syllable of a word. An example is Gk *díphros* from PIE **-bhr-*, based on the root **bher-* "bear"; the term refers to that part of a chariot that bears the driver and the warrior. Many other examples are available, although subsequent changes have obscured the original Indo-European situation. We have also observed in section 8.5 how with the method of internal reconstruction Saussure posited for Pre-Indo-European laryngeal consonants for which distinct reflexes were later discovered in Hittite. The comparative method accordingly permits us to reconstruct the Proto-Indo-European language of approximately 5,000 years ago; the method of internal reconstruction enables us to posit even earlier segments of the language.

16.10 CONCLUSIONS OBTAINED BY HISTORICAL LINGUISTIC STUDY REGARDING HUMAN HISTORY

The methods developed in historical linguistics have in this way enabled us to push our knowledge of one language family back to 3000 BC and earlier.

The same methods can be applied to other language families, the Finno-Ugric, Afro-Asiatic, Sino-Tibetan, even to families in which we have only contemporary materials and must rely heavily on the method of internal reconstruction. After we have in this way reconstructed proto-languages for each of the language families from which materials are available, we may find relations between some of them. Yet even after we reconstruct proto-languages other than Proto-Indo-European, we may find the differences between them so great that they cannot be interrelated. It is possible that the near relatives of Proto-Indo-European were all lost and that it alone was widely carried into areas where it displaced other quite unrelated languages, such as the Hattic language superseded by Hittite.

Historical linguistics in this way takes us back along a route we know to be much longer, the development of human language, from its ultimate origin. Although the question of the origin of language has encouraged historical linguists to continue reconstruction from proto-languages, the origin of human speech has been demonstrated to be so remote that it is now considered quite outside the sphere of historical linguistics, and instead, included as a part of the study of early human beings. As we have seen from examples in this book, we can determine the origins of much of the English grammatical system and vocabulary; but such study takes us back only about 5,000 years, a long time after the origin of speech. Here it is sufficient to warn of naive theories which have gained wide circulation, such as the bow-wow theory that language is in origin like animal cries, the ding-dong theory that imitation of natural noises sparked the first speech, and so on. The essence of language is its use by a social group as a system with a definite structure. We may speculate how such a system was first evolved. Recently, proposals have been made concerning adequate phonological control to achieve speech, on the one hand, adequate syntactic mastery, on the other. On the basis of examination of early skulls, Philip Lieberman (1991) has proposed the approximate period when human beings could produce speech. And after long study of pidgins and creoles Derek Bickerton (1991) has suggested how human beings came to control syntax. Both hypotheses are based on tenuous evidence.

It has also been suggested that a well-established language had its origin as a hybrid language. Katsue Akiba-Reynolds has supported the view that Japanese is a mixed language based on Altaic and Austronesian, similar in origin to a pidgin (in Fisiak 1984: 1–23). When we consider how Old Irish, Armenian and Tocharian, the languages that have undergone the greatest change from the proto-language, maintain characteristics of it, we might expect clearer evidence for even such a dual source.

While historical linguists may contemplate such problems, and many consider the problem of the origin of language beyond the techniques they control, there is no shortage of activities. Problems still remain in the most widely studied language family, the Indo-European. Indo-Europeanists are working to incorporate the contributions resulting from the availability of the Anatolian languages and of Mycenaean Greek, for which additional texts are found almost annually. The new perspectives produced by the discovery that Greek was the language of a brilliant civilization from 1450 BC have brought about a revision in our view of the Indo-European languages in the second millennium. These revised views must be applied in a re-evaluation of the ancient inscriptions found elsewhere, especially those in Asia Minor, where archaeological work promises further clarification of the language interrelationships through the second and first millennia BC.

Even without new data, our study of Proto-Indo-European must deal with suprasegmental phenomena and with syntactic patterns; it must also bring previous analyses into accord with a structural approach and with typological findings that promise a more complete description of Proto-Indo-European and its dialects than that available in many past works on historical linguistics. Evidence that such optimism may be realized can be found in recent articles and works like Gamkrelidze and Ivanov (1984). But we still need new comprehensive dictionaries and compendia for the early dialects and for Proto-Indo-European.

Outside the Indo-European family, historical linguistics has many opportunities and obligations. Historical grammars of individual languages, of language families and of their branches are almost universally needed, as are studies in the dialect geography and sociolinguistics of such families, and in their vocabulary and its etymology. Even in a set of languages so well known as the Arabic, historical grammars must be produced on the basis of the descriptive grammars that are becoming available for its various dialects. When we have an adequate historical grammar of Arabic, we hope that the other South Semitic branches will be similarly equipped. Then a historical grammar of South Semitic will be possible, followed by comparison between North Semitic and South Semitic to yield a Proto-Semitic grammar. With this a historical grammar for earlier stages of the language will be possible, if in the meantime Egyptian, Berber, Chad and Cushitic have been equally well studied.

The Afro-Asiatic languages represent only one of the families that need such a series of studies on which syntheses will be based. As they are being produced, new insights and techniques may be developed or discoveries made, by which some of the further problems of historical linguistics may be solved, such as the decipherment of Linear A, or of the Mohenjo-Daro inscriptions, the discovery of cognate languages for Sumerian, demonstration of relationship between American Indian languages and those of Asia – all of which would permit us to expand our hypotheses of linguistic conditions in the third and fourth millennia BC and even earlier, in much the same way as work in the first half of this century has expanded our knowledge of the second millennium. The increasingly detailed information provided by archaeology provides optimism for the assumption that we will indeed increase our knowledge of early civilizations and their languages.

As we work to extend our knowledge of early languages, careful control of linguistic techniques is increasingly important. This can be derived only from mastery of the techniques applied to well-known languages. Initial mastery of the principles of historical linguistics can best be obtained through control of the historical analysis of one's native language. For this reason it is essential that historical grammars of one's own and other languages be available that incorporate the current techniques of historical linguistics. On their pattern grammars will be produced when adequate data and interest are available regarding any language.

SELECTED FURTHER READINGS

Gamkrelidze and Ivanov (1984) includes material on method as well as data on the Indo-European languages so that it is useful for consultation by specialists in any language family. Reports on linguistic and archaeological discoveries are to be found in journals and reports of conferences, as well as in newsletters and computer communications. For example, the newsletter *Nestor* provides current information on Mycenaean. Compendia, like those of Renfrew and Mallory on the Indo-Europeans are welcome, but reviews should also be examined. Publication is now so copious that access to current information is easy, if time is available to consult it.

Recent works on the origin of language are Bickerton (1991) and Lieberman (1991).

PROBLEMS

1 (a) Among words for wild animals that can be securely reconstructed for Proto-Indo-European are those for the bear and the wolf. The word for dog can also be reconstructed.

The evidence for *bear* is as follows: Hitt. *hartagga-*, Skt. *r̥kṣas*, Av. *arəšō*, Gk *árktos*, Arm. *arǰ*, OI. *art*.

Reconstructions of the Proto-Indo-European etymon have varied. Before Hittite was known a series *þ þh ð ðh* was proposed for the phonological system; in the word for "bear" and others these were assumed to have formed a cluster with a velar stop, yielding reflexes like those above. The reconstruction was supported by similar reflexes among common words, such as that for earth: Skt *kṣam*, Gk *khthṓn*, Lat. *hūmus*, OCS *zemlja*, for which an aspirated *þ* was posited.

Benveniste (1955) by contrast, assumed a single phoneme, with affrication, for example *kθ*, *gð*.

After the Hittite word was known, a cluster *tk dhgh*, etc. was proposed.

Vennemann (1989: 110), applying the glottalic theory, assumes that PIE *k* > -*g*- as in *hartagga*- was glottalic, and that the cluster developed in two ways:

(i) *hr̥kt'os > *hr̥ktos > (arktos, art)

(ii) *hr̥kt'os > *hr̥kc'os > *hr̥ksos (r̥kṣas, arǰ)

Discuss the varying reconstructions, assessing the evidence for each.

(b) The evidence for "dog" is as follows. Hieroglyphic Luw. *sù-wa-nà-i*, Skt *śvā́*, gen. *śúnas*, Av. *span*-, Arm. *šun*, Gk *kúōn*, gen. *kunós*, Lat. *canis*, OIr. *cú*, Goth. *hunds*, Lith. *šuo*, Toch. A *ku*. The word has been reconstructed as *k'won*-, *k'un*.

(i) Like the word for "bear," the reconstructed form has consonantal inflection. In Latin, however, the word is an *i*-stem. In Germanic it is inflected thematically. Account for the morphological change.

(ii) The forms listed above demonstrate that the Indo-European designation for "dog" was maintained much more widely in the dialects than was that for "bear." As we have noted, the Germanic word, such as OE *bera*, meant "brown one," the Slavic, such as OCS *medvědǐ*, meant "honey-eater," the Welsh "honey-pig." These have been explained as taboo replacements. Discuss the reasons for taboo for the designation for the bear but not for the dog.

(iii) The Ancient Chinese word for dog, *k'iuèn* has been identified as a borrowing from Indo-European. Discuss the plausibility of this claim, including the phonological and areal possibilities.

(c) The designations for "wolf" are as follows: Skt *vr̥kas*, Av. *vəhrka*-, Gk *lúkos*, OCS *vlǐkǔ*, Alb. *ulk*; Hitt. *ulippana*, Lat. *lupus*, Goth. *wulfs*. Dictionaries provide the reconstructed etyma **wl̥k*-, **wl̥p*-. Szemerényi, on the other hand, derives the Germanic forms from *wulhwas (1989: 66).

(i) Discuss the different reconstructions, including the two stems in the dictionaries, assessing their plausibility. The Armenian word is *gayl*, with no final obstruent.

(ii) In contrast with the words for "bear" and "dog," these are thematic stems. What explanation might be given for the difference?

(iii) A different term is attested as follows: Hitt. *wetna*-, OIcel. *vitnir*, cf. Ukr. *viščun* "werewolf." What may be the reason for multiple terms for the wolf though not for the bear?

2 Generic terms have been reconstructed in Proto-Indo-European for "animal," "bird," and "fish."

(a) The evidence for animal is as follows: Gk *θέr*, *φέr*, Lith. *žverǐs*, OCS *zvěrǐ*, on the basis of which PIE **g'wer*- has been reconstructed.

In Latin the base has yielded the adjective *ferus* "wild," and the designation for "animal" is *animal*, derived from the root *an-

"breathe." In Old English the word is *dēor*, also assumed to be based on a root meaning breathe. Why might replacements have been introduced? Note that in English the word "deer" has been specialized for application to only one animal.

(b) The evidence for "bird" is as follows: Skt *víḥ*, *véḥ*, Av. *vayo* (nom. pl.), Lat. *avis*; Gk *aetós* < **avi-etos*.

The word for "egg" is as follows: Gk. *ōión*, OCS *ajǐce*, OIcel. *egg*, Crim. Goth. *ada*, on the basis of which a root **ōw-* is constructed, with the suffix *-yo-*. The Latin form is a thematic stem *ōvum*.

The word for bird is assumed to have weak ablaut grade.

(i) Discuss the plausibility of relating the two words.

(ii) As illustrated, the word for bird is attested in only a few dialects. In others, such as Germanic and Slavic it would have been a homophone of the reflex of PIE **owis* "sheep." Recalling Gilliéron's findings, how might this development have led to the loss of the word for "bird"? In Old English the word for "bird" was *fugol* > NE *fowl*; it was replaced by *bird*, which is from OE *brid* "young bird." Do these replacements help account for the loss of the reflexes of the Proto-Indo-European word?

(c) The evidence for "fish" is as follows: Gk. *ikhthûs*, Lith. *žuvìs*, Arm. *jukn*. Other dialects have reflexes of PIE **peiskos*, for example Lat. *piscis*, Goth. *fisks*, OIr. *íasc*; Pol. *piskorz*, a kind of fish; because of the presence of ablaut in these forms, they are also considered to be old. In addition, Slavic has *ryba*; Skt *mátsya-*, Av. *masya-*, apparently from a root **mad-* "wet." How would you account for the several words?

3 The word for horse is found in all the early dialects: Hieroglyphic Luw. *á-sù-wa*, Skt *áśva-*, Av. *aspa-*, Myc. Gk *i-qo*, Gk. *híppos*, Lat. *equus*, OIr. *ech*, OE *eoh*, Toch. A *yuk*, Toch. B. *yakwe* "horse," Lith. *ešvà* "mare." The Indo-European term is reconstructed **ek'wos*.

(a) In contrast with the words for bear and other animals, that for horse is thematic. What inferences can be drawn about its relative age from this inflection?

(b) The Greek word has long been puzzling. It has initial *h*; the medial consonant is doubled; the *i-* requires explanation.

In addition, the presence of palatal *k* before *w* is unusual.

Recalling the various hypotheses on the homeland of the Indo-Europeans, what explanations might be given for the phonological development in Greek and the reconstructed form?

4 Gamkrelidze and Ivanov (1984) support the assumption of words for some of the animals in the Proto-Indo-European lexicon by pointing to cults devoted to specific animals. For example, King Hattusilis I of the seventeenth century BC called on his warriors to unite like a wolfpack; Germanic traditions refer to warriors as wolves. Moreover, dressing in wolf skins provides a magical power. And similar rituals are attested

in the Indic, Greek, Slavic and Germanic areas.

On the other hand, in Germanic custom someone outlawed from society is to be treated as a wolf, and in the Old English term wears a *wulfes heáfod* "wolf's head."

How do you account for the contrast in regard of the wolf? To what extent can one reconstruct cultural practices from such textual references? If the early records suggest the presence of wolf cults, how may we account for the use in Old English?

In Icelandic lore, wizards were said to change their shape to wolves at night. Tradition then speaks of the *kveld-úlfr* "evening wolf," or werewolf who torments people. Would you relate these views with the supposed earlier cultic veneration for the wolf?

5 We have noted that Proto-Indo-European had a word for "metal," based on the following: Skt *áyas*, Av. *ayah-* "metal," Lat. *aes*, Goth. *aiz* "copper, ore." Yet Greek attests the term *khalkós*, Lat. *cuprum*, based on *aes Cyprium* "ore of Cyprus," which is the basis of our term.

When we examine other names of metals, we find a variety of designations. For gold, Latin has *aurum*, OPruss. *ausis*, Toch. *wäs*, Arm. *(v)aski*; Sanskrit has *híranya-*, which is related to *yellow*; OE *gold*, OCS *zlato*, Latv. *zèlts* are also derived from a root meaning "yellow"; Gk *khrusós* is assumed to be borrowed from Semitic, cf. Akk. *hurāsu*.

The word for iron in Greek is *síderos*, in Latin *ferrum*, in Irish *iarn*, the origin of our designation.

How do these terms support the position that the speakers of Proto-Indo-European had a neolithic technology?

References

Adelung, Johann Christoph (1860–16) *Mithridates, oder allgemeine Sprachen-kunde*, 3 vols, completed by J. S. Vater, Berlin: Voss.

Algeo, John (1972) *Problems in the Origin and Development of the English Language*, 2nd edn, New York: Harcourt Brace Jovanovich.

Allen, W. Sidney (1973) *Accent and Rhythm. Prosodic Features of Latin and Greek: a Study in Theory and Reconstruction*, Cambridge: Cambridge University Press.

Anthony, David W. and Dorcas R. Brown (1991) "The origins of horseback riding," *Antiquity*, 65: 22–38.

Anttila, Raimo (1977) *Analogy*, The Hague: Mouton.

—— (1989) *Historical and Comparative Linguistics*, 2nd edn, Amsterdam: Benjamins.

Arens, Hans (1969) *Sprachwissenschaft: der Gang ihrer Entwicklung von der Antike bis zur Gegenwart*, 2nd edn, Freiburg: Alber.

Arntz, Helmuth, ed. (1936) *Germanen und Indogermanen: Volkstum, Sprache, Heimat, Kultur* (Festschrift for Herman Hirt), 2 vols, Heidelberg: Winter.

Atwood, Elmer B. (1953) *A Survey of Verb Forms in the Eastern United States*, Ann Arbor: University of Michigan Press.

—— (1962) *The Regional Vocabulary of Texas*, Austin: University of Texas Press.

Bach, Adolf (1950) *Deutsche Mundartforschung*, 2nd edn, Heidelberg: Winter.

Baldi, Philip, ed. (1990) *Linguistic Change and Reconstruction Methodology*, Berlin: Mouton de Gruyter.

Bammesberger, Alfred, ed. (1988) *Die Laryngaltheorie und die Rekonstruktion des indogermanischen Laut- und Formensystems*, Heidelberg: Winter.

Barber, E.J.W. (1991) *Prehistoric Textiles*, Princeton, Princeton University Press.

Benveniste, Emile (1955) "Etudes hittites et indo-européennes," *BSL* 50: 29–43.

—— (1971) *Problems in General Linguistics*, trans. by Mary Elizabeth Meek, Coral Gables, FL: University of Miami Press.

—— (1973) *Indo-European Language and Society*, trans. by Elizabeth Palmer, Coral Gables, FL: University of Miami Press.

Beowulf (1988) trans. by Ruth P. M. Lehmann, Austin: University of Texas Press.

Bergsland, Knut and Hans Vogt (1962) "On the validity of glottochronology," *Current Anthropology* 3: 115–53.

Bickerton, Derek (1991) *Language and Species*, Chicago: University of Chicago Press.

Bloomfield, Leonard (1923) "Review of Saussure, *Cours de linguistique générale*," *Modern Language Journal* 8: 317–19.

—— (1933) *Language*, New York: Holt; repr. Chicago: University of Chicago Press, 1984.

Bopp, Franz (1816) *Über das Conjugationssystem der Sanskritsprache in Vergleichung mit jenem der griechischen, lateinischen, persischen und germanischen Sprache*, Frankfurt-am-Main: Andreä.

—— (1868–71) *Vergleichende Grammatik des Sanskrit, Send, Griechischen, Lateinischen, Litauischen, Gotischen und Deutschen*, 3 vols, 3rd edn (1st 1833, 2nd 1857–61), Berlin: Dümmler.

Braune, Wilhelm and Ernst A. Ebbinghaus (1981) *Gotische Grammatik*, 19th edn, Tübingen: Niemeyer.

Brugmann, Karl (1878) Preface to *Morphologische Untersuchungen auf dem Gebiete der indogermanischen Sprachen*, I: iii–xx, Leipzig: Hirzel. Transl. in Lehmann 1967: 197–209.

—— (1897–1916) *Grundriss der vergleichenden Grammatik der indogermanischen Sprachen*, 2nd edn, Strasburg: Trübner.

—— and Berthold Delbrück *Grundriss der vergleichenden Grammatik der indogermanischen Sprachen*, I. Einleitung und Lautlehre, II. Lehre von den Wortformen und ihrem Gebrauch (K.B. 1886–90), III–V. Syntax (B.D. 1893–1900), Strasburg: Trübner.

—— (1904) *Die Demonstrativpronomina der indogermanischen Sprachen*, Leipzig: Teubner.

—— (1925) *Die Syntax des einfachen Satzes im Indogermanischen*, Berlin and Leipzig: de Gruyter.

Buck, Carl Darling (1949) *A Dictionary of Selected Synonyms in the Principal Indo-European Languages*, Chicago: University of Chicago Press.

Bynon, Theodora (1977) *Historical Linguistics*, Cambridge: Cambridge University Press.

Cardona, George, Henry M. Hoenigswald and Alfred Senn, eds (1970) *Indo-European and Indo-Europeans*, Philadelphia: University of Pennsylvania Press.

Cassidy, Frederic G. (1985–) *The Dictionary of American Regional English*, vols 1 and 2, Cambridge, MA: Harvard University Press.

Chafe, Wallace L. (1959) "International reconstruction of Seneca," *Language* 35: 477–95.

Comrie, Bernard, ed. (1987) *The World's Major Languages*, London: Croom Helm; repr. Oxford: Oxford University Press, 1990.

Cuvier, Georges (1812) *Recherches sur les ossemens fossiles de quadrupèdes* (5th edn 1828), Paris: Dufour & Ocagne.

Dauzat, A. (1922) *La Geographie linguistique*, Paris: Flammarion.

Delbrück, Berthold (1871–88) *Syntaktische Forschungen*, 5 vols, Halle: Waisenhaus.

—— (1893–1900) *Vergleichende Syntax der indogermanischen Sprachen*, Strasburg: Trübner.

Diringer, D. (1968) *The Alphabet*, 3rd edn, completely revised with the collaboration of R. Regensburger, New York: Funk & Wagnalls.

Dolgopolsky, Aaron B. (1986) "A probabalistic hypothesis concerning the oldest relationship among the language families of northern Eurasia," in V. J. Shevoroshkin and T. L. Markey (eds) *Typology Relationships and Time*, Ann Arbor: Karoma, 27–50.

Edgerton, Franklin (1943) "The Indo-European semi-vowels," *Language* 19: 83–124.

Emeneau, Murray B. (1956) "India as a linguistic area," *Language* 32: 3–16.

Ernout, Alfred and Antoine Meillet (1967) *Dictionnaire étymologique de la langue latine. Histoire des mots*, Paris: Klinksieck.

Finck, F. N. (1909) *Die Haupttypen des Sprachbaus*, Berlin and Leipzig: Teubner.

Fisiak, Jacek, ed. (1978) *Recent Developments in Historical Phonology*, The Hague: Mouton.

— ed. (1980) *Historical Morphology*, The Hague: Mouton.
— (1984) *Historical Syntax*, Berlin: Mouton.
— (1988) *Historical Dialectology*, Berlin: Mouton de Gruyter.
— (1990) *Historical Linguistics and Philology*, Berlin: Mouton de Gruyter.
Francis, W. Nelson (1958) *The Structure of American English*, New York: Norton.
Friberg, Joran (1984) "Numbers and measures in the earliest written records," *Scientific American* 250: 110–18.
Fries, Charles (1940) "On the development of the structural use of word-order in modern English," *Language* 16: 199–208.
Gamkrelidze, Thomas and V. V. Ivanov (1973) "Sprachtypologie und die Rekonstruktion der gemeinindogermanischen Verschlüsse," *Phonetica* 27: 150–6.
— (1984) *Indo-European and the Indo-Europeans*, Tbilisi: Publishing House of the Tbilisi State University.
Gauchat, L. (1905) "L'Unité phonétique dans le patois d'une commune," in *Aus romanischen Sprachen und Literaturen: Festschrift Heinrich Morf*, Halle: Niemeyer, 175–232.
Gelb, I. J. (1963) *A Study of Writing: the Foundations of Grammatology*, 2nd edn, Chicago: Phoenix.
Gimbutas, Marija (1970) "Proto-Indo-European culture: the Kurgan culture during the fifth, fourth and third millennia BC," in George Cardona, Henry M. Hoenigswald and Alfred Senn (eds) *Indo-European and Indo-Europeans*, Philadelphia: University of Pennsylvania Press, 155–97.
— ed. (1980–1) "The transformation of European and Anatolian culture, 4500–2500 BC and its legacy," *Journal of Indo-European Studies* 8: 1 and 2, 3 and 4, 9: 1 and 2.
Grassmann, Hermann (1862) "Über die Aspiraten und ihr gleichzeitiger Vorhandensein im An. und Auslaute der Wurzeln," *Zeitschrift für Vergleichende Sprachforschung* 12: 81–110. Transl. in Lehmann 1967: 109–31.
Greenberg, Joseph H. (1963) "Some universals of grammar with particular reference to the order of meaningful elements," in Joseph H. Greenberg, *Universals of Language*, Cambridge, MA: MIT Press, 73–113.
Greenberg, Joseph H., Charles A. Ferguson and E. A. Moravczik, eds (1978) *Universals of Human Language*, 4 vols, Stanford: Stanford University Press.
Greenough, James B. and George L. Kittredge (1902) *Words and their Ways in English Speech*, New York: Macmillan; publ. as paperback 1961.
Grimm, Jacob (1819/1822–37) *Deutsche Grammatik*, Göttingen: Dietrich; Berlin: Dümmler; repr. and ed. by W. Scherer and G. Roethe, Gütersloh: Bertelsmann, 1870–98.
— (1848) *Geschichte der deutschen Sprache* (3rd edn 1868), Leipzig: Hirzel.
— and Wilhelm Grimm, *Deutsches Wörterbuch*, Leipzig: Hirzel, 1854–1954.
Gudschinsky, Sarah C. (1956) "The ABC's of lexicostatistics (glottochronology)," *Word* 12: 175–220.
Hall, Robert A. Jr (1943) *Melanesian Pidgin English: Grammar, Texts, Vocabulary*, Baltimore: Linguistic Society of America.
Harris, Roy and Talbot J. Taylor (1989) *Landmarks in Linguistic Thought: the Western Tradition from Socrates to Saussure*, London: Routledge.
Haugen, Einar (1953) *The Norwegian Language in America: a Study in Bilingual Behavior*, Philadelphia: University of Pennsylvania Press.
Heffner, Roe-Merrill S. (1949) *General Phonetics*, Madison: University of Wisconsin Press.
Hermann, E. (1929) "Lautveränderung in der Individualsprache einer Mundart," *Nachrichten der Gesellschaft der Wissenschaften zu Göttingen* 9: 195–214.

Hock, Hans Henrich (1986) *Principles of Historical Linguistics*, Berlin: Mouton de Gruyter.

Hoenigswald, Henry M. (1960) *Language Change and Linguistic Reconstruction*, Chicago: University of Chicago Press; Phoenix.

Hoijer, Harry (1956) "Lexicostatistics: a critique," *Language* 32: 49–60.

Hopper, Paul J. (1973) "Glottalized and murmured occlusives in Indo-European," *Glossa* 7: 141–66.

Humboldt, Wilhelm von (1836) *Über die Verschiedenheit des menschlichen Sprachbaus und ihren Einfluss auf die geistige Entwicklung des Menschengeschlechts*, Berlin: Dümmler. For the passage cited see Lehmann 1967: 61–6, specifically p. 63.

Jakobson, Roman (1968) *Child Language, Aphasia and Phonological Universals*, trans. A. R. Keiler, The Hague: Mouton.

Jakobson, R., C. Gunnar, M. Fant and Morris Halle (1969) *Preliminaries to Speech Analysis*, Cambridge, MA: MIT Press.

Jeffers, Robert J. and Ilse Lehiste (1979) *Principles and Methods for Historical Linguistics*, Cambridge, MA: MIT Press.

Jellinek, Max H. (1913–14) *Geschichte der neuhochdeutschen Grammatik*, Heidelberg: Winter.

Jensen, Hans (1970) *Sign, Symbol, and Script*, trans. by George Unwin, 3rd edn (revised and enlarged), London: Allen & Unwin.

Jespersen, Otto (1909–49) *A Modern English Grammar on Historical Principles*, 7 vols, Copenhagen: Munksgaard.

— (1922) *Language, its Nature, Development and Origin*, London: Allen & Unwin; reissued as a paperback, New York: Norton, 1964.

— (1946) *The Growth and Structure of the English Language*, 9th edn, Oxford: Oxford University Press; Anchor.

— (n.d.) *Selected Writings of Otto Jespersen*, London: Allen & Unwin.

Justus, Carol (1975) "Relativization and topicalization in Hittite," in Charles N. Li (ed.) *Subject and Topic*, New York.

Klimov, Georgij A. (1977) *Tipologija Jazykov Aktivnogo Stroja*, Moscow: Nauka.

— (1983) *Principy Kontensivnoj Tipologii*, Moscow: Nauka.

Kloeke, G. G. (1927) *De Hollandsche expansie in de zestinde en zeventiende eeuw*, The Hague: Nijhoff.

Kluge, Friedrich (1895) *Deutsche Studentensprache*, Strasburg.

— (1989) *Etymologisches Wörterbuch der deutschen Sprache*, 22nd edn, ed. Elmar Seebold, Berlin: de Gruyter.

Koerner, E. F. Konrad, ed. (1977–) *Amsterdam Classics in Linguistics*, Amsterdam: Benjamins.

Kuhn, Adalbert (1845) *Zur ältesten Geschichte der indogermanischen Völker*, Berlin: Nauck.

Kurath, Hans, Marcus L. Hansen, Julia Bloch and Bernard Bloch (1939) *Handbook of the Linguistic Geography of New England*, Providence: Brown University.

Kurath, Hans and Raven I. McDavid (1961) *The Pronunciation of English in the Atlantic States*, Ann Arbor: University of Michigan Press.

Kurylowicz, Jerzy (1927) "ə indoeuropéen et ḫ hittite," *Symbolae grammaticae in honorem J. Roswadowski* I: 95–104, Krakow: Gebethner & Wolff.

— (1960) "La nature des procès dits 'analogiques,'" in his *Esquisses linguistiques*, Wroclaw and Krakow.

— (1964) *The Inflectional Categories of Indo-European*, Heidelberg: Winter.

Labov, William (1966) *The Social Stratification of English in New York City*, Washington, DC: Center for Applied Linguistics.

— (1969) "Contraction, deletion, and inherent variability of the English copula," *Language* 45: 715–62.

— (1972) *Sociolinguistic Patterns*, Philadelphia: University of Pennsylvania Press.

Lees, Robert B. (1953) "The basis of glottochronology," *Language* 29: 113–27.
Lehmann, Ruth P.M. (1988) *Beowulf. An Imitative Translation*, Austin: University of Texas Press.
Lehmann, Winfred P. (1953) "A note on the change of American English /t/," *American Speech* 28: 271–5.
— ed. (1967) *A Reader in Nineteenth Century Historical Indo-European Linguistics*, Bloomington: University of Indiana Press.
— (1969) "Proto-Indo-European compounds in relation to other Proto-Indo-European syntactic patterns," *Acta Linguistica Hafniensia* 12: 1–20.
— ed. (1978) *Syntactic Typology*, Austin: University of Texas Press.
— (1990) "The current thrust of Indo-European studies," *General Linguistics* 30: 1–52.
Lehmann, Winfred P. and Helen-Jo Jakusz Hewitt, eds (1991) *Language Typology 1988: Typological Models in Reconstruction*, Amsterdam: Benjamins.
Lehmann, Winfred P. and Yakov Malkiel, eds (1968) *Directions for Historical Linguistics*, Austin: University of Texas Press.
— (1982) *Perspectives on Historical Linguistics*, Amsterdam: Benjamins.
Lehmann, Winfred P. and Ladislav Zgusta (1979) "Schleicher's tale after a century," in Bela Brogyanyi (ed.) *Festschrift für Oswald Szemerényi*, vol. 1, Amsterdam: Benjamins, 455–66.
Leumann, Manu, Johann B. Hofmann, Anton Szantyr (1963–79) *Lateinische Grammatik*, 3 vols, Munich: Beck.
Lieberman, Philip (1991) *Uniquely Human*, Cambridge, MA: Harvard University Press.
Lightfoot, David (1979) *Principles of Diachronic Syntax*, Cambridge: Cambridge University Press.
Longacre, Robert E. (1983) *The Grammar of Discourse*, New York: Plenum.
Lounsbury, Floyd G. (1964) "The structural analysis of kinship semantics," in Horace G. Lunt (ed.) *Proceedings of the Ninth International Congress of Linguistics*, The Hague: Mouton, 1073–93.
Luick, Karl (1914–40) *Historische Grammatik der englischen Sprache*, Leipzig: Tauchnitz; repr. Stuttgart: Tauchnitz, 1964.
Malkiel, Yakov (1990) *Diachronic Problems in Phonosymbolism*, vol. 1, Amsterdam: Benjamins.
Mallory, J. P. (1989) *In Search of the Indo-Europeans: Language, Archaeology and Myth*, London: Thames & Hudson.
Mańczak, Witold (1958) "Tendances générales des changements analogiques," *Lingua* 7: 198–325, 387–420.
Meillet, Antoine (1925) *La Méthode comparative en linguistique historique*, Oslo: Klincksieck; trans. by G. B. Ford Jr as *The Comparative Method in Historical Linguistics*, Paris: Champion, 1967.
— (1926–8) *Linguistique historique et linguistique générale*, Paris: Champion.
— (1937) *Introduction à l'étude comparative des langues indo-européennes*, 8th edn, Paris: Hachette; repr. Alabama: University of Alabama Press, 1964.
Meillet, Antoine and Marcel Cohen (1952) *Les Langues du monde*, 2nd edn, Paris: Champion.
Mitzka, Walther (1952) *Handbuch zur deutschen Sprachatlas*, Marburg: Elwert.
Müller, Max (1871–2) *Lectures on the Science of Language*, New York: Scribner.
— (1891) *Selected Essays* I, London: Longmans Green.
Nichols, Johanna (1986) "Head-marking and dependent-marking grammars," *Language* 62: 56–119.
Norman, Jerry (1988) *Chinese*, Cambridge: Cambridge University Press.
Nottebohm, Fernando (1970) "Ontogeny of bird song," *Science* 167: 950–60.

Onions, C. T. (1966) *The Oxford Dictionary of English Etymology*, Oxford: Clarendon Press.

Orton, Harold and Eugen Dieth (1962–8) *Survey of English Dialects*, Leeds: Arnold.

Paul, Hermann (1920) *Prinzipien der Sprachgeschichte*, 5th edn, Halle: Niemeyer. Subsequently repr. as further editions.

Pedersen, Holger (1931) *Linguistic Science in the Nineteenth Century*, trans. by John Spargo, Cambridge, MA: Harvard University Press; reissued under the title *The Discovery of Language*, Bloomington: Indiana University Press, 1962.

Pfeifer, Wolfgang (1989) *Etymologisches Wörterbuch des Deutschen*, 3 vols, Berlin: Akademie-Verlag.

Polomé, Edgar G., ed. (1990) *Research Guide on Language Change*, Berlin: Mouton de Gruyter.

Pop, Sever (1950) *La Dialectologie: aperçu historique et méthodes d'enquêtes linguistiques*, vol. I: *Dialectologie romane*, vol. II: *Dialectologie non romane*, Louvain: Bibliothèque de l'Université.

Porzig, Walter (1954) *Die Gliederung des indogermanischen Sprachgebiets*, Heidelberg: Winter.

Pott, August F. (1833–6) *Etymologische Forschungen auf dem Gebiete der indogermanischen Sprachen* (2nd edn 1958–76), Lemgo: Meyer.

Prokosch, E. (1939) *Comparative Germanic Grammar*, Philadelphia: University of Pennsylvania, Linguistic Society of America.

Rask, Rasmus (1818) *Undersögelse om det gamle norske eller Islandske Sprogs Oprindelse*, Copenhagen: Gyldendal.

Renfrew, Colin (1987) *Archaeology and Language: The Puzzle of Indo-European Origins*, London: Cape.

Robb, John (1991) "Random cases with directed effects, the Indo-European language spread and the stochastic loss of lineages," *Antiquity* 65: 287–91.

Sadock, Jerrold M. (1991) *Autolexical Syntax: a Theory of Parallel Grammatical Representations*, Chicago: University of Chicago Press.

Sandfeld, Kristian (1930) *Linguistique balkanique: problèmes et résultats*, Paris: Klincksieck.

Sapir, Edward (1917) Review of C.C. Uhlenbeck, *Het Passieve Karakter van het Verbum Transitivum of van het Verbum Actionis in Talen van Noord-America*, *International Journal of American Linguistics* 1: 76–81.

—— (1921) *Language*, New York: Harvest.

—— (1938) "Glottalized continuants in Navaho, Nootka, and Kwakiutl," *Language* 14: 248–78.

—— (1963) "Internal linguistic evidence suggestive of the northern origin of Navaho," in David G. Mandelbaum (ed.) *Selected Writings of Edward Sapir*, Berkeley: University of California Press, 213–23.

Saussure, Ferdinand de (1879) *Mémoire sur le système primitif des voyelles dans les langues indo-européennes*, Leipzig: Teubner.

—— (1916) *Cours de linguistique générale*, eds Charles Bally and Albert Sechehaye, Paris: Payot; repr. 1949; trans. and annotated by Roy Harris, as *Course in General Linguistics*, London: Duckworth, 1983.

Schlegel, Friedrich (1808) *Über die Sprache und Weisheit der Indier*, Heidelberg: Mohn and Zimmer; repr. (Amsterdam Classics in Linguistics), Amsterdam: Benjamins, 1977.

Schleicher, August (1871) *Compendium der vergleichenden Grammatik der indogermanischen Sprachen*, 3rd edn (4th edn 1876), Weimar: Böhlau.

Schmandt-Besserat, Denise (1992) *Before Writing*, Austin: University of Texas Press.

Schmidt, Pater Wilhelm (1926) *Die Sprachfamilien und Sprachenkreise der Erde* (with atlas), Heidelberg: Winter.

Schrader, Otto (1883) *Sprachvergleichung und Urgeschichte*, 1st edn (2nd edn

1890, 3rd edn 1906–7), Jena: Costenobel; trans. by Frank H. Jevons as *Prehistoric Antiquities of the Aryan Peoples: a Manual of Comparative Philology and the Earliest Cultures*, London: Griffin, 1890.

Schwyzer, Eduard (1939–53) *Griechische Grammatik*, 3 vols, Munich: Beck.

Sebeok, Thomas A., ed. (1966) *Portraits of Linguists: a Biographical Sourcebook for the History of Western Linguists, 1746–1962*, Bloomington: University of Indiana Press.

—— gen. ed. *Current Trends in Linguistics*, The Hague: Mouton.

Senner, Wayne M., ed. (1989) *The Origins of Writing*, Lincoln: University of Nebraska Press.

Shevoroshkin, V. J. and Thomas L. Markey, eds (1986) *Typology Relationship and Time*, Ann Arbor: Karoma.

Sievers, Eduard and Karl Brunner (1951) *Altenglische Grammatik*, 2nd edn, Halle: Niemeyer.

Sjoberg, Andrée and Gideon Sjoberg (1956) "Problems in glottochronology. Culture as a significant variable in lexical change," *American Anthropologist* 58: 296–300.

Skeat, Walter (1879–82) *An Etymological Dictionary of the English Language*, Oxford: Clarendon Press.

Skomal, Susan Nacev and Edgar C. Polomé (1987) *Proto-Indo-European: the Archaeology of a Linguistic Problem*, Washington, DC: Institute for the Study of Man.

Smith, Bruce D. (1989) "Origins of agriculture in Eastern North America," *Science* 246: 1566–71.

Sommerfelt, Alf (1962) *Diachronic and Synchronic Aspects of Language*, The Hague: Mouton.

Specht, Franz (1947) *Der Ursprung der indogermanischen Deklination*, Göttingen: Vandenhoeck & Ruprecht.

Stern, Gustav (1931) *Meaning and Change of Meaning, with Special Reference to the English Language*, Göteborg: Elander; repr. Bloomington: Indiana University Press, 1955.

Swadesh, Morris (1951) "Diffusional cumulation and archaic residue as historical explanations," *Southwest Journal of Anthropology* 7: 1–21. Since revised and reprinted.

—— (1971) *The Origin and Diversification of Language*, ed. Joel Sherzer, Chicago: University of Chicago Press.

Szemerényi, Oswald (1960) *Studies in the Indo-European System of Numerals*, Heidelberg: Winter.

—— (1989) *Einführung in die vergleichende Sprachwissenschaft*, 3rd edn, Darmstadt: Wissenschaftliche Buchgesellschaft.

Thomason, Sarah Gray and Terence Kaufmann (1988) *Language Contact, Creolization, and Genetic Linguistics*, Berkeley: University of California Press.

Trier, Jost (1931) *Der deutsche Wortschatz im Sinnbezirk des Verstandes: die Geschichte eines sprachlichen Feldes*, vol. 1, Heidelberg: Winter.

Troike, Rudolph C. (1969) "The glottochronology of six Turkic languages," *International Journal of American Linguistics* 35: 183–91.

Trubetzkoy, Nikolai S. (1939) *Grundzüge der Phonologie*, Prague: Travaux de Cercle Linguistique de Prague 7; trans. by C. A. M. Baltaxe as *Principles of Phonology*, Berkeley: University of California Press, 1969.

—— (1939b) "Gedanken über das Indogermanenproblem," *Acta linguistica* 1.

—— (1939c) "Wie soll das Lautsystem einer künstlichen internationalen Hilfssprache beschaffen sein?," *Travaux du cercle linguistique de Prague* 8: 5–21.

Ullmann, Stephen (1957) *The Principles of Semantics*, 2nd edn, Glasgow: Jackson.

Vennemann, Theo (1975) "An explanation of drift," in Charles N. Li (ed.) *Word*

Order and Word Order Change, Austin: University of Texas Press, 269–305.

—— ed. (1989) *The New Sound of Indo-European: Essays in Phonological Reconstruction*, Berlin: Mouton de Gruyter.

Ventris, Michael and John Chadwick (1973) *Documents in Mycenaean Greek*, 2nd edn, Cambridge: Cambridge University Press.

Voegelin, Carl F. and Florence V. Voegelin (1977) *Classification and Index of the World's Languages*, New York: Elsevier.

Wackernagel, Jacob (1892) "Über ein Gesetz der indogermanischen Wortstellung," *Indogermanische Forschungen* 1: 333–436.

Watkins, Calvert (1985) *The American Heritage Dictionary of Indo-European Roots*, Boston: Houghton Mifflin.

—— (1991) "Latin *tarentum Accas*, the *ludi saeculares*, and Indo-European eschatology," in Winfred P. Lehmann and Helen-Jo Jakusz Hewitt (eds) *Language Typology 1988: Typological Models in Reconstruction*, Amsterdam: Benjamins, 135–47.

Weil, Henri (1844) *The Order of Words in the Ancient Languages compared with that of the Modern Languages*, trans. by Charles W. Super, ed. Aldo Scaglione, Amsterdam: Benjamins, 1978.

Weinreich, Uriel (1953) *Languages in Contact: Findings and Problems*, New York: Linguistic Circle of New York; repr. The Hague: Mouton.

Weinreich, Uriel, William Labov and Marvin I. Herzog (1968) "Empirical foundations for a theory of language change," in Winfred P. Lehmann and Yakov Malkiel (eds) *Directions for Historical Linguistics*, Austin: University of Texas Press, 95–195.

Wende, Fritz (1915) *Über die nachgestellten Präpositionen im Angelsächsischen*, Berlin: Mayer & Müller.

Whitney, William Dwight (1892) *Language and the Study of Language*, New York: Scribner.

Whorf, Benjamin Lee (1956) *Language, Thought and Reality*, ed. John B. Carroll, Cambridge MA: MIT Press.

Index

A Workbook for Historical Linguistics is being published concurrently with this textbook and is available at the address below. The chapter topics of the workbook correspond to those of this volume but the exercises are independent of it. The exercises were selected to acquaint students with classical problems in the development of historical linguistics, notably those of the Indo-European family. Along with the exercises are study guides and terms to note. The workbook may be ordered from:

International Academic Bookstore
7500 W. Camp Wisdom Road
Dallas
TX 75236
United States of America